The Second Letter to the Corinthians

RUDOLF BULTMANN

Original German Edition
Edited by Erich Dinkler
.
Translated by Roy A. Harrisville

Augsburg Publishing House
Minneapolis

THE SECOND LETTER TO THE CORINTHIANS

Originally published in German as *Der zweite Brief an die Korinther,* copyright © 1976. Translated from the German edition with the approval of Verlag Vandenhoeck & Ruprecht, Göttingen. © Vandenhoeck & Ruprecht in Göttingen.

First English language edition © 1985 Augsburg Publishing House

Scripture quotations unless otherwise noted are from the Revised Standard Version of the Bible, copyright 1946, 1952, and 1971 by the Division of Christian Education of the National Council of Churches.

Library of Congress Cataloging in Publication Data

Bultmann, Rudolf Karl, 1884-1976.
  THE SECOND LETTER TO THE CORINTHIANS.

  Translation of: Der zweite Brief an die Korinther.
  Bibliography: p. 263.
  Includes indexes.
  1. Bible. N.T. Corinthians. 2nd — Commentaries.
I. Dinkler, Erich, 1909-   II. Title.
BS2675.3.B8413 1985   227'.3077   83-70517
ISBN 0-8066-2023-4

Manufactured in the U.S.A.   APH 10-5633

1 2 3 4 5 6 7 8 9 0 1 2 3 4 5 6 7 8 9

Contents

Editor's Foreword 5
Author's Preface 9
Translator's Introduction 10
Preliminary Remarks 16

Prescript and Thanksgiving [Letter D]: 1:1-11 19

PRESCRIPT: 1:1-2 19
INTRODUCTION TO THE LETTER (THANKSGIVING): 1:3-11 20

Paul's καύχησις (or πεποίθησις) [Letter D]: 1:12—2:13; 7:5-16 ... 32
1. The theme of καύχησις and εἰλικρίνεια: 1:12-14 33
2. Apostolic πεποίθησις and εἰλικρίνεια in
   Paul's behavior: 1:15—2:4 37
3. Elimination of the quarrel: 2:5-11 47
4. Paul's yearning for the community: 2:12-13; 7:5 51
5. Justification for the πεποίθησις: 7:6-16 53

The apostolic office [Letter C]: 2:14—7:4 61
1. Paul's παρρησία 2:14—4:6 61
   a. The apostle's ἱκανότης: 2:14—3:6
   b. From this διακονία results παρρησία: 3:7-18

EXCURSUS: κύριος and πνεῦμα 96

   c. Actualizing παρρησία in apostolic activity: 4:1-6
2. δόξα or ζωή as hidden and revealed: 4:7—6:10 109
   a. The hiddenness of ζωή under cover of the
      old aeon: 4:7—5:10
   b. The revelation of ζωή in proclamation: 5:11—6:10

3. The plea for trust [6:14—7:1 is an interpolation]: 6:11—7:4 ... 175

Chapters 10–13 [Letter C] 181
1. Paul's ταπεινότης and πεποίθησις: 10:1-11 181
   a. The appeal not to provoke him: 10:1-2
   b. Proof and purpose of the πεποίθησις: 10:3-6
   c. The threat accompanying his personal appearance: 10:7-11
2. Paul's τόλμα: 10:12—12:18 191
   a. The first introduction: The criterion for boasting: 10:12-18
   b. The second introduction: The plea to endure
      his καυχᾶσθαι: 11:1-21
   c. Boasting: 11:22—12:18
3. The threat of δοκιμή at the third visit: 12:19—13:10 236
   a. The threat: 12:19—13:4
   b. Admonition: 13:5-9
   c. The threat: 13:10
4. Conclusion of the Letter: 13:11-14 249

Chapters 8 and 9 253
[Letter D] The gift as χάρις: 8:1-7 253
   The voluntary nature of the gift: 8:8-12 254
   The gift as a concretizing of fellowship: 8:13-15 255
   Formal correctness in giving the gift: 8:16-24 255
[Letter C] Exhortation to complete the promised
   ingathering: 9:1-5 256
   Trust in God as presupposition for the gift: 9:6-10 257
   Praise of God as the meaning of the gift: 9:11-15 258

Abbreviations 259
List of Sources 260
Bibliography 263

Indexes
1. Greek terms 268
2. Literary and historical-critical concepts and questions 270
3. Theological themes 271
4. History of religions concepts and references 272

Editor's Foreword

The text published here is without exception Rudolf Bultmann's hand-written commentary, written down somewhere between 1940 and 1952, which served as basis for his course of lectures. Only the German translations of the Greek text which are prefixed to the various sections derive from the editor, and attempt, often at the expense of a literal rendering, to lift out what the author gave more detailed foundation in his exegesis. The notes reproduce Rudolf Bultmann's own marginal glosses.

All references to sources and literature were researched. At the same time, the newest editions were used, cited in the given instance in the list of sources. To give one example, what was quoted in Rudolf Bultmann's manuscript according to the Hermetica edition of W. Scott of 1924, is now quoted according to Festugière-Nock's edition of 1945/54. Ancient sources are also cited according to the method of abbreviation in Kittel-Friedrich, *Theologisches Wörterbuch zum Neuen Testament*. The secondary literature, together with all periodicals, is cited according to *Die Religion in Geschichte und Gegenwart,* the third edition. My research collaborator, Dr. Oda Wischmeyer-Schüttpelz, shouldered the task of unifying the method of quotation and researching as well as correcting quotations from the sources. The indexes are also her work.

The ancient sources used by Rudolf Bultmann and the literature cited are listed at the end of the commentary. A selection of the literature on Second Corinthians appearing since 1952 is grouped by the editor at the end [cf. the remarks in the translator's preface]. In the exegesis following the citing of the verse, the Greek clauses or portions thereof which are due for exposition are set in cursive type, in contrast to Greek words and clauses which are resumed in the context of the exegesis or are cited from the literature to be compared.

The reader and user of the text which follows should consider that in essence what is at issue here are the philological-historical materials for exegesis, then their initial evaluation for the interpretation of the text. The lines of theological exposition are drawn by the exegetical decisions made, and finally also by the distance from or agreement with Hans Windisch's commentary on the one hand, and Hans Lietzmann's and W. G. Kümmel's commentaries on the other. The interpretation as hermeneutical process, however, was not concluded. In the given instance, this only occurred orally, in the context of Bultmann's lecture and address to his hearers, and thus in the *actu docendi* led to unfolding the insight gained. The handwritten text gradually grew from course to course, not in one breath, and was worked out and written down in concentration on the one theme, just as occurred, for example, with the commentary on the Gospel of John. From the author's point of view the manuscript published here was not yet "ready" — even apart from the merely preliminary expositions on Chapters 8 and 9. Still, publishing the manuscript in this form requires an explanation.

In 1954, Prof. Bultmann had given the editor free use of his manuscript, so that at his discretion he could produce a complete commentary with it. According to an agreement concluded in 1955 between the author and editor with the publisher, Mr. Günther Ruprecht, this was supposed to appear in the *Kritisch-exegetischer Kommentar über das Neue Testament* founded by H. A. Meyer. For various reasons, this work was delayed for years. After the editor, as early as 1955/56, had transcribed Prof. Bultmann's handwritten manuscript into a typewritten working copy, hindrances of a personal nature stood in the way of further uninterrupted work. In the years 1956/62, these involved the coediting of *Religion in Geschichte und Gegenwart*. In the years following, hindrances included the direction and publication of German excavations in the Sudanese Nile Valley, together with the double burden attached to representing two disciplines — New Testament and Christian Archaeology — and membership in two faculties. Next, the difficulty attaching to the subject itself became more and more evident; that is, the obligation constantly felt — despite the freedom generously given by Professor Bultmann for personal disposal of the handwritten leaves — to author the commentary in an adequate fashion as a work of Bultmann, to do justice to his methodological and theological intention, and not to endanger uniformity through one's own insights.

When in the winter of 1973/74 the editor's work had nevertheless proceeded to Chapter 7 and the publisher was pressing for completion. after consultation with Professor Bultmann, the proposal of the publishing house was adopted (deferring the editor's elaboration), that is, to prepare for publication only the original Bultmann text together with the above-named additions of translation, bibliography, and indexes.

The fact that this decision could actually be realized within one year the editor owes to his co-worker, Frau Dr. Wischmeyer-Schüttpelz, and to the Deutsche Forschungsgemeinschaft which generously donated 'Sachbeihilfe' (grant) for a year. The edition of the text of Professor Bultmann's lectures on Second Corinthians should not only assist the one interested in theology and exegesis as such, but also contribute to the understanding of Bultmann's total work. The reader can certainly gain insight into his scholar's workshop, trace the basis for some portions of his *Theology of the New Testament,* and also recognize how in the last analysis for Bultmann the exegetical-interpretative work is basic to his theological statement.

The theology of Bultmann is more strongly influenced by the theology inherent in Paul's Second Letter to the Corinthians than by any other letter or Gospel of the New Testament canon — to the extent the theme at issue here is "the word of proclamation," a theme which coincides with that of the "apostolic office." After all, what is involved is the office of proclamation, of the revelation of the "fragrance of the knowledge of [God]" (2:14), "the light of the knowledge of the glory of God in the face of Christ" (4:6). The enlightenment which this brings is paralleled by the shining of the light at creation, and interpreted in its significance (4:6). In the event of proclamation occurs the new creation (5:17), for which reason this accosting event of proclamation — as Bultmann repeatedly underscores — is an eschatological event. According to Paul, it proves to be eschatological by the fact that it brings death and life, that it is the great crisis — "to one a fragrance from death to death, to the other a fragrance from life to life" (2:16). Therefore, in the proclamation of the Christ event there occurs a judgment, *hic et nunc* in the church's proclamation of the Word.

That the apostle's — and thus the church's — proclamation has this character lies in the fact that it proclaims the saving event taken place in Christ, not, of course, as a historical report to be researched, but as the event of God's reconciliation with the world, an event effective for its hearers in the actual proclamation. Since the proclamation proclaims the Christ event, it also summons: "Be reconciled to God;" "we are ambassadors for Christ, God making his appeal through us;" "we beseech you on behalf of Christ" (5:20f.). For Paul, therefore, the proclamation itself belongs to the saving occurrence, the eschatological event. Together with the Christ event, God has initiated the office, the word of reconciliation (5:18f.).

In the proclamation Christ, indeed God himself, is encountered (5:20), so that the eschatological "day of salvation" is present in the "now" of preaching (6:2): "Behold, now is the acceptable time; behold, now is the day of salvation." In this theology of the Word, which also makes clear the dual efficacy of the preaching of Christ, Bultmann recognizes the genuine theological and homiletical task debated by Luther and Zwingli; that is, the task of making clear the paradox that an historical fact — the crucifixion of Christ — is at the same time an eschatological event, namely, the event of God's reconciliation with the world. This event becomes contemporaneous in an address which proclaims, or better, in a proclamation which addresses.

From the observation that in Chapters 3–5 of Second Corinthians statements about the apostle continually change into statements about the community, Bultmann concludes that apostolic existence serves as example for Christian existence. But to exist as Christian means to understand oneself as standing beneath the cross and thus beneath the resurrection; it means to surrender all "boasting according to the flesh" and "external things"; it means to boast of one's weakness in the knowledge that "power is made perfect in weakness . . . for when I am weak, then I am strong" (12:9f.).

Naturally, it is also significant for Bultmann's theological anthropology that the apostle, as example of the Christian and especially of the preacher, is liable to the misunderstanding that his summons to obedience (2:9; 7:15) is a bid for authority, in order to tyrannize the community (1:24). The apostle is an authority only as bearer of the word, and over against the community cannot legitimize himself in any other way than as such. But in addition we encounter in Paul, in the proclaimer of the word, the paradox of the crucified and risen One who is strong only in weakness (13:4). The proclaimer himself becomes the word which addresses, inquires, and calls to decision. What is visible in him is merely "weakness" — death at work. That the "power of Christ," the resurrection life, is at work in it (4:7ff.; 6:9) he can only witness to, or as outwardly seen, can only assert. After all, only those can believe him who understand themselves beneath the proclaimed word, who decide for the cross of Christ.

This brief survey of the content of Second Corinthians, drawn up at a few typical points, may trace not only the arc toward Bultmann's theology, but also indicate the relevance of this epistle and commentary for our time in theology and church. It is precisely what is "out of season" in this letter which is kerygmatic and relevant. Our desire for Rudolf Bultmann is that this characteristic of his commentary will be understood by many and bear fruit in the proclamation of the word. For the trust shown me I must heartily thank Professor Bultman.

ERICH DINKLER

Heidelberg, the 30th of April, 1975

Postscript: For essential assistance in the reading of galleys and page-proof corrections, I have my wife to thank as well as my assistant, Dr. Holger Kaiser. E.D.

Author's Preface

The lecture on Second Corinthians was particularly dear to me, and it was also my last lecture upon leaving my post in the summer semester of 1951. Since I was often asked for the text, I put the manuscript at the disposal of Mr. Dinkler in the opinion that publication would soon follow. Because this was delayed for various reasons, only now can I publish the text as a farewell gift for my earlier and later hearers. I must heartily thank Mr. Dinkler for undertaking to edit the text and for prefacing it with an introduction which thoroughly expresses the intention of my text.

RUDOLF BULTMANN

Marburg, the fifth of July, 1975

Translator's Introduction

When Paul Tillich returned from a visit to his native Germany following the collapse of Hitler's Reich, he was asked what was occurring in German theology and answered "Bultmann and demythologizing," adding that such would be the case for a long time to come. Tillich's words proved truer than he spoke. Even after his ninetieth year, Bultmann was still topic for discussion. He is yet. There is scarcely a commentary on a Pauline epistle or the gospel of John, a volume on the biblical theology of the New Testament, or a treatment of the hermeneutical question which does not take its point of origin or reference from Bultmann, whether in opposition or in continuation of his views.

Reference to Bultmann now is no longer freighted with the passion aroused when his publications first appeared in print. The mood is quieter, the criticism more measured, the attacks blunted, the consent or agreement muted. At the sound of his name or program, there are no drum rolls, trumpets, raising of flags, choosing of sides, and rushing into battle. And what a battle it was! Those volumes prepared by Hans-Werner Bartsch, beginning with Bultmann's essays on the New Testament and mythology, their spines broken and covers torn from once constant use (to say nothing of the innumerable books, monographs, essays, and tracts in every language of the West, even a few of the East) mirror the clash between protagonist and opponent. Universities rendered *Gutachten,* "opinions"; the press interpreted for the uninitiated; broadcasting studios sponsored dialogs, and bishops enjoined their flocks against "doctrines new and strange":

> Resist the attempt to interpret the Gospel with the notion of myth and its corresponding abridgement by transference into an interpretation of existence allegedly free of myth; no one will be able to justify your desire to offer your congregation Christ's truth in such an abridgement. . . . You have no timeless doctrine, no morality, no religion and no interpretation of existence to offer the world as salvation but the living Lord himself who is Savior of the world, Jesus of Nazareth. . . . The Church honors theological scholarship, so long and to the extent it honors God's Word and its blessed mysteries, and does not become the

10

slave of an immanent notion of science. The Church is heartily open and grateful to its theological teachers who instruct it toward blessedness, but it can and dare not submit to a theology which tears down rather than builds up . . . (Episcopal statements contained in Fritz Rienecker's *Stellungnahme zu Bultmanns 'Entmythologisierung,' Biblische Studien und Zeitfragen,* p. 83).

Those days are gone, and in a period when there is less to stir the blood over the themes of theology than over the affairs of ecclesiastical function, or in which the questions of theology have taken on radically different shape, a period in which Bultmann's "old Marburgers" have inched toward retirement or gone the way of all flesh, those who still remember huddle together and reminisce about the old days of battle. There is a certain clannishness about them, perhaps, akin to that of old Civil War veterans, and, it may be, for the same reason:

> They stuck together as much as they could because they shared an understanding other folk did not have. Like Adam, they had been cast out of the enchanted garden, leaving innocence behind. . . . They had more innocence to lose, they had farther to fall, and if the actual shock was not really greater, they were less well prepared to adjust to its effects. . . . [They] lived happily in [the great garden] up to the moment when the flaming sword was swung, and . . . came out into the workaday world all unprepared (Bruce Catton, *Reflections on the Civil War,* p. 159).

And yet, Bultmann never founded a "school." The name "Bultmannian" never carried the same weight as did, for example, that of "Barthian." He never received the adulation of a Bonhoeffer, whose friends, interpreters, and biographers meet yearly to recall the heroic past. Bultmann's wife, unlike Bonhoeffer's fiancee, was never an honored guest at great anniversaries. After the *Kairos* had passed and the smell of cordite had been dissipated by the wind, after the question of the relation between the concerns of faith and reason or history or science or the "modern man" had assumed another shape or been replaced with other questions, there was no tatterdemalioned band waiting to rally to some last charge. With the exception of a few epigones, Bultmann's "pupils" bore slight resemblance to the master. Ernst Käsemann, for example, began his career with a volume on the concept of the body which was virtually captive to that wing of comparative religions represented by his teacher, and which accented Hellenistic religion as the primary nexus of the New Testament message. He continued with a study in Hebrews which allowed for the use of Hellenistic language and conceptuality, but insisted upon the author's greater sympathy for a Judaism unmarked by religiosity sprung from anxiety in face of death. Now, at the close of his working life, he writes that he has unlearned not only Bultmann's historical-critical conclusions, but more significantly, his penchant for beginning exegesis and theology from the perspective of anthropology:

> The Word of Christian preaching, and thus in fact of the Church, replaces
> [Jesus], just as does the Paraclete of the Johannine farewell speeches.
> Actually, the Incarnation is symbol of the Word's taking on flesh ever
> new. But are we not then obliged to ask whether or not ecclesiology
> sets Christology in the shadows — modified in Protestant fashion, of
> course — that is, in that central emphasis upon anthropology? . . . Not
> the self-understanding of the believer as a call to one's becoming flesh,
> but the worldwide lordship of the Crucified became for me the scopus
> of preaching . . . (*Kirchliche Konflikte,* Bd. 1, pp. 239f.).

Perhaps, for the readers of this book too young to remember, a word
or two concerning what that ancient battle was about is in order here.
Bultmann was convinced that the problem confronting the theological
world was the breakdown in the communication of the New Testament
message to the "aggravatedly modern person." This breakdown, Bultmann
continued, was due to the irreconcilability of the New Testament thought-
forms with the thought-world furnished by modern science. Bultmann's
goal was thus to reconcile these irreconcilables, and by way of that program which has since been attached to his name. First, Bultmann contended that the thought-forms of the New Testament are "mythical."
That is, the Bible conceives the universe as divided into three parts —
heaven above, hell beneath, and earth in the middle, the theater of the
activity of celestial and demonic forces. To this worldview, Bultmann
insisted, corresponds the biblical description of the events of salvation.
And to this worldview, modern thought is irreconcilably opposed, since
moderns understand themselves as self-contained entities which are not
open to the seizure of supernatural powers. To insist on the retention of
the myth, Bultmann asserted, was impossible. It would be tantamount
to returning to some primitive era in human history and would make of
faith a sacrifice of the intellect, an equal impossibility, since faith involves
answerability in the area of thought and judgment. Further, Bultmann
argued, the New Testament itself does not intend to provide us with myth.
To the question concerning the primary intention of the New Testament —
an intention which its mythology allegedly does not serve — Bultmann
responded that it seeks to provide people with an understanding of themselves. He thus set to work to expose that primary intention by "demythologizing," or by reinterpreting the mythology of the New Testament in
terms of the categories of a philosophy of existence, in particular, in
terms of the phenomenology of the Black Forest philosopher, Martin
Heidegger. Justification for the use of such categories, Bultmann insisted,
lay in the fact that the inquiry into *being* on the part of the New Testament
and of Heidegger's phenomenology were identical. To the question concerning the legitimacy of such reinterpretation, Bultmann replied that the
New Testament itself, principally Paul and John, had already begun the
process. In this fashion, then Bultmann believed he could effect the reconciliation between the gospel message and modern man.

The conclusions to which Bultmann's program led him were often extreme, and moved one critic to paraphrase the Apostles' Creed at Bultmann's hands in these words.

> He was *not* conceived by the Holy Ghost, *not* Born of the Virgin Mary: Suffered, to be sure, under Pontius Pilate, Was crucified, dead and buried, but did *not* descend into hell; The third day He did *not* rise again from the dead; did *not* ascend into heaven, did *not* sit on the right hand of God the Father Almighty; From thence He shall *not* come again to judge the quick and the dead.

It was Bultmann's "evangelistic" program, his concern to reconcile the concerns of faith and reason or science which drove him to such radical criticism as the theological world had not seen since the days of Ferdinand Christian Baur. The fire of criticism, Bultmann contended, could only burn away false securities, while what was decisive for Jesus, for the primitive church, as well as for us, the Word of God summoning to a decision of faith, remained untouched by it all. Indeed, that Word actually cooperated in the destruction of all false supports for faith. What linked Bultmann to his Reformation heritage was that unremitting emphasis upon faith in the proclamation of the fate and destiny of Jesus of Nazareth, unsupported by proofs or probabilities, as the means to righteousness or authentic existence. It was, after all, Luther who wrote:

> But the word "ears" is emphatic and forceful to an extraordinary degree; for in the new law all those countless burdens of the ceremonies, that is, dangers of sins, have been taken away. God no longer requires the feet or the hands or any other member; he requires only the ears. To such an extent has everything been reduced to an easy way of life. For if you ask a Christian what the work is by which he becomes worthy of the name "Christian," he will be able to give absolutely no other answer than that it is the hearing of the Word of God, that is, faith. Therefore the ears alone are the organs of a Christian man, for he is justified and declared to be a Christian, not because of the works of any member, but because of faith (*Lectures on Titus, Philemon and Hebrews, Luther's Works,* Vol. 29, p. 224).

But Bultmann was more than an heir of the Reformation. He was also heir of that 19th century, idealistic notion according to which transcendence made its home in the human self-consciousness, that therefore religious self-consciousness was the point at which to begin speaking of God. Bultmann had written that there is not talk about God which is not at the same talk about humankind. That concession to the idealistic notion of anthropology as key to the understanding of God, a concession which he believed necessary for the sake of reconciling the irreconcilables, put the God for us as he is in himself, the miraculous, and finally history itself, to the blade, and left Bultmann a divided man. It brought on him the curse of the theologian, who regarded him as traitor to the Reformation which asserted that God was present before ever faith appeared, and the curse of the philosopher, who regarded him as traitor to that description of existence which asserted that authentic life did not require the aid of revelation or of faith. Which commitment was the greater — that to the Reformation, as Bultmann's noblest opponent, Julius Schniewind, contended, or that to the idealistic understanding of existence, as a majority of his critics assume? Bultmann himself argued that the former, not the latter, was true.

Aside from the question whether or not Bultmann was able properly to judge his own work, if this last piece from his pen had been the only thing he ever wrote, he would have ranked among the great biblical interpreters of his age, but would never have earned the notoriety sprung from his attempts at evangelizing his generation. The text is lean, even sparse, singularly free of the advocacy of this or that philosophical vehicle for its communication, of summonses to attempts at translating the text in the modern idiom. Words and phrases are examined within their original, historical contexts, then the degree of their transformation at the hands of Paul is marked and noted, in order from that point to demonstrate the apostle's uniqueness. All throughout, sholarship, science, presuppositions, everything is bent, warped to the service of the message and apostolate of that giant for the Gentiles. The result is Paul, as pure a Paul as has emerged in contemporary exposition. The book reflects a man at the end of his work, done with jousting or debate for debate's sake which marks youth or middle years, intent on summing up without apology or extenuation, seeking after the heart of things without equivocation, a man resolved to write one clean, hard, clear thing — a last testament incapable of mininterpretation. And if Dinkler is correct that Bultmann's theology was more profoundly influenced by what lay in Paul's Second Letter to the Corinthians than by any other part of the New Testament canon, then perhaps those who agree with the man's own judgment of his work are, after all, in the right.

Here, at least, or here, at last, is the message of the cross of Christ as the signal event of human history and the one, pure object of faith. And it is here, I choose to believe, that a modest, slight, balding, mustached man with a raised shoe (who spent recess at his gymnasium in the classroom, while a later, much-advertised popular thinker, Karl Jaspers, for whom that quiet boy was a nonentity, romped with his friends) furnished in his own body the analogy to that weakness which the apostle claimed as the mark of the appearance of the crucified and risen one in his own poor flesh — "always carrying in the body the death of Jesus." And in that Word of the cross the fidelity of a professor who rarely missed worship or the Sacrament of the Altar in all the years of his tenure, who for more than twenty years took up Sunday collection in his home parish, derived its sense and meaning — "as servants of God we commend ourselves in every way."

Now to the text of the commentary itself. Since Bultmann gave considerable attention to the definition of terms in the Greek, the translation of each term in the order of its occurrence — a frequent practice in the translation of modern commentaries — seemed unnecessary. It also appeared unnecessary to reproduce Bultmann's index of selected publications on 2 Corinthians since 1952, for the reason that the list is now no longer complete and that such indexes are readily available to the student elsewhere.

At the commencement of each section, the text translation is from the Revised Standard Version of the New Testament. For the Greek text and apparatus on which Bultmann depended, the reader may consult any edition of Nestle's *Novum Testamentum Graecum* prior to the 26th. With the exception of English translations of classical works in *The Loeb Classical Library,* and of Christian sources in *The New Oxford Annotated Bible With The Apocrypha,* quotations from classical and Christian sources appear as indicated in Butlmann's lists of sources and literature employed, the references to which appear as indicated in Dinkler's Foreword (cf. p. 5).

Lastly, thanks are due my son, the Rev. Roy A. Harrisville III, for assistance in the preparation of this translation.

ROY A. HARRISVILLE
LUTHER NORTHWESTERN THEOLOGICAL SEMINARY
ST. PAUL, MINNESOTA

Preliminary Remarks

According to Jülicher (*Einleitung,* 87), 2 Corinthians is "the most personal of the extant letters of Paul," containing "self-defence and polemic throughout." Correct! But exegesis dare not allow itself to be misled into explaining the letter as an essentially biographical document or making its goal a portrait of Paul's personality, for Paul conceives his writing throughout as an apostolic writing. This feature is no more eliminated by the tone of personal relationship and pugnacity which dominates certain sections, than by the utterances of a confessional nature in other sections. Paul's person is at issue only insofar as he is bearer of the apostolic office, and the theme of the epistle is the apostolic office. The establishment of Paul's apostolic authority has to do with his suit for the community's trust and obedience (2:9; 7:12; 10:6, 11; 13:2f.). The apostolic office is the express theme of 2:17—6:10, and the dispute in Chapters 10–13 concerns Paul's apostolic character. He does not intend to be understood as a man and as friend of the Corinthians, or as such only in order to be understood as the apostle in whom the Lord is speaking (13:3). He does not preach himself, but Christ Jesus as Lord (4:5). And if his letter is more than a sermon or theoretical exposition, that is, a friendly suit for the community's love and trust, an apologetic, or a polemic, then it is so only because he has become as it were Christ's slave, not only in the proclaiming word, but in his entire existence (2:14), since Christ is revealed in his entire life, in working and suffering (4:10f.).

An exegesis which intends to pursue the peculiar intention of the letter thus has its real object of understanding in the apostolic office or, since it is primarily the office of proclamation, in the word of proclamation. What is Christian proclamation, both as to content and execution?

For an introduction to 2 Corinthians it is not necessary to sketch a picture of Corinth and the Christian community there — in contrast to 1 Corinthians, in which concrete questions of community life are discussed. The conditions of the Hellenistic metropolis of Corinth with its social, moral, and religious problems do not play a role, nor is there any echo of the actual questions which agitate the community — the factions in

16

1 Corinthians 1–4, the questions regarding the order of worship, meat offered to idols, marriage and celibacy, etc. The sole concern is the question of the relation between the community and its apostle.

The only question of introduction which needs mentioning concerns the situation from which 2 Corinthians was written, and that means also the events between 1 and 2 Corinthians (in saying which we assume here that 2 Corinthians was written after 1 Corinthians).

According to 1 Corinthians, Paul was in Corinth only once, that is, when he founded the community. According to 2 Corinthians he had already been there twice; cf. 12:14: ἰδοὺ τρίτον τοῦτο ἑτοίμως ἔχω ἐλθεῖν πρὸς ὑμᾶς, and 13:1: τρίτον τοῦτο ἔρχομαι πρὸς ὑμᾶς. A visit of Paul to Corinth, therefore, must lie between 1 and 2 Corinthians. To this visit 2:1 obviously refers: ἔκρινα δὲ ἐμαυτῷ τοῦτο, τὸ μὴ πάλιν ἐν λύπῃ πρὸς ὑμᾶς ἐλθεῖν (cf. 12:21: μὴ πάλιν ἐλθόντος μου ταπεινώσῃ με ὁ θεός μου πρὸς ὑμᾶς).

The sorrow (λύπη) evidently consisted in a member of the community's having insulted Paul (2:5-11; 7:11f.).

Naturally, this visit is not the first. But it is also not the one planned in 1 Corinthians 16:5-9, according to which Paul, coming from Ephesus to Corinth by way of Macedonia, intends to stay there longer (perhaps to spend winter), in order from there to travel to Jerusalem with the collection. For 2 Corinthians is written from Macedonia, to which Paul travelled from Ephesus (2:12f.; 7:5f.). There is thus an interim visit not yet forseen in 1 Corinthians.

Further, between 1 and 2 Corinthians there is a letter of Paul to Corinth, cf. 2:3f.: καὶ ἔγραψα τοῦτο αὐτὸ ἵνα μὴ ἐλθὼν λύπην σχῶ . . . etc.; verse 4: ἐκ γὰρ πολλῆς θλίψεως καὶ συνοχῆς καρδίας ἔγραψα ὑμῖν διὰ πολλῶν δακρύων . . . and 2:9: εἰς τοῦτο γὰρ καὶ ἔγραψα ἵνα γνῶ τὴν δοκιμὴν ὑμῶν, εἰ εἰς πάντα ὑπήκοοί ἐστε.

Naturally, this "tearful letter" cannot be 1 Corinthians, but rather a letter following that interim visit, connected with the insult to Paul on that occasion; cf. 7:12: ἄρα εἰ καὶ ἔγραψα ὑμῖν, οὐχ ἕνεκεν τοῦ ἀδικήσαντος οὐδὲ ἕνεκεν τοῦ ἀδικηθέντος, ἀλλ᾽ ἕνεκεν τοῦ φανερωθῆναι τὴν σπουδὴν ὑμῶν τὴν ὑπὲρ ἡμῶν πρὸς ὑμᾶς. . . .

Evidently, Paul sent this letter to Corinth through Titus, whose return — first of all ardently awaited, 2:13; 7:5 — is then the occasion for 2 Corinthians (7:6ff.), and of course Titus reported the success of the interim epistle. The community submitted (2:5f.; 7:11).

Apart from this, the occasion of the epistle is the behavior of Paul's rivals in Corinth, "false apostles" according to this characterization in chapters 10–13.

In addition, a few literary-critical questions must be considered be- forehand. Since, as 1 and 2 Corinthians indicate, Paul wrote at least four letters to the Corinthian community,[1] it may be assumed that the community which published only two letters inserted into these letters portions from the other two. And, as 1 Corinthians proves to be a combination of A and B, so 2 Corinthians a combination of C and D. It has long been recognized (Hausrath, *Vier-Capital-Brief*) that 2 Corinthians 10–13 does not comprise a unity with 1–9. But it is not sufficient to assign Chapters 10–13 to interim letter C.

Chapters 2:14—7:4 stand out from Chapters 1—7; 7:5 is connected with 2:13, and of course it is clear that 1:1—2:13 and 7:5-16 are the last letter of the correspondence, thus letter D, while 2:14—7:4 and Chapters 10–13 comprise the interim letter C. Further, Chapters 8 and 9 cannot possibly have belonged together originally, and of course Chapter 8 originally — as now — came after 7:16, and thus belonged to D, while Chapter 9 is presumably to be attached to letter C.[2]

---

[1] Cf. 1 Cor. 5:9.
[2] On the material question, cf. Bultmann, *Exegetica*, 307, n. 17, and Dinkler, *RGG*[3], IV, 18.

Prescript and Thanksgiving
[Letter D]: 1:1-11

PRESCRIPT: 1:1-2

Paul, an apostle of Christ Jesus by the will of God, and Timothy our brother. To the church of God which is at Corinth, with all the saints who are in the whole of Achaia: Grace to you and peace from God our Father and the Lord Jesus Christ.

Verse 1: The writer of the letter is **Παῦλος ἀπόστολος Χριστοῦ Ἰησοῦ διὰ θελήματος θεοῦ,** just as in 1 Corinthians 1:1 (where κλητός is added to ἀπόστολος) — thus the emphasis on apostolic authority as in almost all the epistles, with the exception of 1 (2) Thessalonians, Philippians and Philemon.

The co-writer is **καὶ Τιμόθεος ὁ ἀδελφός,** that is, Timothy, Paul's companion and co-worker since the so-called second missionary journey (Acts 16:1). He is also named as coauthor of 1 Thessalonians, and in addition is Paul's companion on the mission at Corinth, and thus regarded in 2 Cor. 1:19 as founder of the community together with Paul and Silvanus. According to 1 Cor. 4:17 and 16:10, Paul had sent Timothy to Corinth from Ephesus during his sojourn there on the third missionary journey, and from Corinth he has now again returned to Paul. To what extent he is responsible as coauthor, is, of course, a question.

The addressee is the Corinthian community — **τῇ ἐκκλησίᾳ τοῦ θεοῦ τῇ οὔσῃ ἐν Κορίνθῳ.** As ἐκκλησία τοῦ θεοῦ it is the eschatological community of God to the extent it exists at Corinth or is represented in the congregation there. The letter is not intended for Corinth alone, however, but **σὺν τοῖς ἁγίοις πᾶσιν τοῖς οὖσιν ἐν ὅλῃ τῇ Ἀχαΐᾳ,** thus also for all the ἅγιοι (an eschatological designation for Christians) in Achaia, that is, the Roman province spanning all of Greece. Corinth, capital and seat of the proconsul,

19

is thus also the center of the Christian communities. "Here lie the roots for the later formation of the metropolis" (Lietzmann, 99).

Verse 2: χάρις ὑμῖν καὶ εἰρήνη ἀπὸ θεοῦ πατρὸς ἡμῶν καὶ κυρίου Ἰησοῦ Χριστοῦ.

INTRODUCTION TO THE LETTER (THANKSGIVING): 1:3-11

Blessed be the God and Father of our Lord Jesus Christ, the Father of mercies and God of all comfort, who comforts us in all our affliction, so that we may be able to comfort those who are in any affliction, with the comfort with which we ourselves are comforted by God. For as we share abundantly in Christ's sufferings, so through Christ we share abundantly in comfort too. If we are afflicted, it is for your comfort and salvation; and if we are comforted, it is for your comfort, which you experience when you patiently endure the same sufferings that we suffer. Our hope for you is unshaken; for we know that as you share in our sufferings, you will also share in our comfort. For we do not want you to be ignorant, brethren, of the affliction we experienced in Asia; for we were so utterly, unbearably crushed that we despaired of life itself. Why, we felt that we had received the sentence of death; but that was to make us rely not on ourselves but on God who raises the dead; he delivered us from so deadly a peril, and he will deliver us; on him we have set our hope that he will deliver us again. You also must help us by prayer, so that many will give thanks on our behalf for the blessing granted us in answer to many prayers.

1. Praise of God who comforts Paul and enables him to give comfort: 1:3-4.
2. Support for the latter statement: 1:5-7.
   Verse 5: For Paul sufferings are the παθήματα Χριστοῦ, for which reason he also takes comfort.
   Verses 6-7: Paul's θλῖψις and παράκλησις must then also be of benefit to the community.
3. Information regarding Paul's θλῖψις and its effect: 1:8-11.
   Verse 8: θλῖψις led to mortal danger.
   Verse 9: It thus led to Paul's own death sentence.
   Verse 10: Therefore, trust in God could spring from rescue,
   Verse 11: As could the community's intercession. This leads to abundant thanks toward God.

1. Praise of God, who comforts Paul and enables him to give comfort

Verse 3 is written in liturgical style, cf. Windisch, 36ff.; Str.-B. III, 494 and Knopf, *Briefe Petri und Judä,* 40ff. on 1 Peter 1:3ff.; cf. also Harder, *Gebet,* 88f.

In the introduction to a letter, **εὐλογητός** is used instead of the usual εὐχαριστῶ or εὐχαριστοῦμεν.

Paul thus neither speaks in the first person nor gives thanks for the condition of the community. The motif of remembrance or of intercession is lacking; v. 11 is a variation on the latter. The formula appears as in Ephesians 1:3 and 1 Peter 1:3. It is a Jewish formula such as the בָּרוּךְ אֱלֹהִים, the concluding formula in Psalms 40:14; 65:20; 71:18; 105:48 (LXX), the introduction to the Song of the Three Children in Dan. 3:26, in the formula of blessing in Gen. 9:26, or as the refrain in the Eighteen Benedictions. Naturally, εἴη or ἐστίν is used imperatively.

ὁ θεὸς καὶ πατὴρ τοῦ κυρίου ἡμῶν Ἰησοῦ Χριστοῦ (does the genitive belong only with πατήρ, or also with ὁ θεός? Ὁ θεὸς τοῦ κυρίου ἡμῶν Ἰησοῦ Χριστοῦ appears in Eph. 1:17) is a formula as in 11:31; Rom. 15:6; Eph. 1:3; and 1 Peter 1:3. "The formula emerged in such fashion that the Jewish formula, 'God is praised,' was Christianized by καὶ πατήρ, etc." (Kümmel, 196).

Regarding the phrase **ὁ πατὴρ τῶν οἰκτιρμῶν καὶ θεὸς πάσης παρακλήσεως,** cf. the Jewish formulas in Marmorstein, *Doctrine of God,* I. Marmorstein notes that God is referred to as אָב הָרַחֲמִים: Father of mercy (p. 56), and as בַּעַל הַנֶּחָמוֹת: Lord of comforts (p. 80). Cf. also the phrase in K^eth 8b, 27 (Str.-B. III, 494): "the Lord of comfort comfort you!"

Characterizations of God in the genitive

2 Cor. 13:11: καὶ ὁ θεὸς τῆς ἀγάπης καὶ εἰρήνης ἔσται μεθ᾿ ὑμῶν.

Rom. 15:5: ὁ δὲ θεὸς τῆς ὑπομονῆς καὶ τῆς παρακλήσεως δῴη ὑμῖν τὸ αὐτὸ φρονεῖν ἐν ἀλλήοις . . . 15:13: ὁ δὲ θεὸς τῆς ἐλπίδος πληρώσαι ὑμᾶς πάσης χαρᾶς καὶ εἰρήνης . . . 15:33: ὁ δὲ θεὸς τῆς εἰρήνης μετὰ πάντων ὑμῶν (cf. Phil. 4:9); 16:20: ὁ δὲ θεὸς τῆς εἰρήνης συντρίψει τὸν σατανᾶν ὑπὸ τοὺς πόδας ὑμῶν ἐν τάχει.

1 Thess. 5:23: αὐτὸς δὲ ὁ θεὸς τῆς εἰρήνης ἁγιάσαι ὑμᾶς ὁλοτελεῖς . . .

2 Thess. 3:16: αὐτὸς δὲ ὁ κύριος τῆς εἰρήνης δῴη ὑμῖν τὴν εἰρήνην . . .

1 Peter 5:10: ὁ δὲ θεὸς πάσης χάριτος, ὁ καλέσας ὑμᾶς . . . αὐτὸς καταρτίσει, στηρίξει, σθενώσει, θεμελιώσει.

Heb. 13:20f.: ὁ δὲ θεὸς τῆς εἰρήνης, ὁ ἀναγαγὼν ἐκ νεκρῶν . . . καταρτίσαι ὑμᾶς.

The fact that this letter, just as Galatians, does not begin with εὐχαριστῶ or εὐχαριστοῦμεν may be explained in part by Paul's relation to the community, but certainly also at least by Paul's situation.

πάσης as well as the twice-used πάσῃ in verse 4 belongs to liturgical style. This style raises the personal to the universal, the profane to the "sacred." Thus the thanksgiving motif is used in a peculiar way. The thanks for Paul's deliverance (v. 10) becomes a praise of God and with that a thanks for the community which benefits from Paul's deliverance —

not for its external situation, but for its Christian position, which is enriched by what was given to Paul.

Verse 4: Why God is characterized in precisely this way is indicated in verse 4. If God is described as Father and God of mercies and comfort, that of course does not mean primarily that he is merciful and gives comfort, but that all mercy and comfort have their origin in him (Windisch, 38), that he is the one "from whom come mercy and comfort." Naturally, it also means that God is merciful and gives comfort, as is continued in verse 4 — ὁ **παρακαλῶν ἡμᾶς** — but with the addition, εἰς τὸ δύνασθαι ἡμᾶς παρακαλεῖν.

ὁ παρακαλῶν ἡμᾶς continues in liturgical style; cf. Gunkel, *Psalmen*, 43, and Norden, *Agnostos Theos*, 201ff. (The participle with the article is Semitic in style, in contrast to the Greek predicative use of the participles; cf. Norden, 166ff. who draws questionable religious-historical conclusions, 220ff.).

Supplement on liturgical style

Ps. 135:3f.: ἐξομολογεῖσθε τῷ κυρίῳ τῶν κυρίων . . . τῷ ποιοῦντι θαυμάσια μεγάλα μόνῳ.

Ps. 143:1: εὐλογητὸς κύριος ὁ θεός μου ὁ διδάσκων τὰς χεῖράς μου εἰς παράταξιν.

Ps. 102:1ff.: εὐλόγει, ἡ ψυχή μου, τὸν κύριον . . . τὸν εὐιλατεύοντα πάσαις ταῖς ἀνομίαις σου . . . τὸν στεφανοῦντά σε ἐν ἐλέει καὶ οἰκτιρμοῖς.

Ps. 146:7ff.: ἐξάρξατε τῷ κυρίῳ ἐν ἐξομολογήσει, ψάλατε τῶ θεῷ ἡμῶν ἐν κιθάρᾳ, τῶ περιβάλλοντι τὸν οὐρανὸν ἐν νεφέλαις, τῷ ἑτοιμάζοντι τῇ γῇ ὑετόν, τῷ ἐξανατέλλοντι ἐν ὄρεσι χόρτον . . . διδόντι τοῖς κτήνεσι τροφὴν αὐτῶν. . . .

The liturgical style is continued also in the **ἐπὶ πάσῃ τῇ θλίψει ἡμῶν**, for what is actually involved is rescue from a specific θλῖψις.[1] (Deissmann, *Licht von Osten*, 145ff.; BGU, 423: Ἀπίων Ἐπιμάχω τῶι πατρὶ καὶ κυρίῳ πλεῖστα χαίρειν. πρὸ μὲν πάντων εὔχομαί σε ὑγιαίνειν καὶ διὰ παντὸς ἐρωμένον εὐτυχεῖν μετὰ τῆς ἀδελφῆς μου καὶ τῆς θυγατρὸς αὐτῆς καὶ τοῦ ἀδελφοῦ μου. Εὐχαριστῶ τῷ κυρίῳ Σεράπιδι, ὅτι μου κινδυνεύσαντος εἰς θάλασσαν ἔσωσε εὐθέως. "Apion to Epimachus his father and lord, many greetings. Before all things I pray that thou art in health, and that thou dost prosper and fare well continually together with my sister and her daughter and my brother. I thank the lord Serapis that, when I was in peril in the sea, he saved me immediately.")

---

[1] But the article means, in the affliction which has actually taken place in its totality, in contrast to what might happen later. τοὺς ἐν πάσῃ θλίψει means, in any kind of affliction which may occur, cf. Bl.-D. para. 275, 3.

εἰς τὸ δύνασθαι ἡμᾶς παρακαλεῖν τοὺς ἐν πάσῃ θλίψει[2] keeps to the universal as does also verse 5. The ἡμεῖς appears first in verse 6; cf. above. Paul's experience of παράκλησις from God furnishes the reason why he can comfort others. This is something totally different from "the universal human experience that only he can aid another in his distress who has himself experienced something similar" (Windisch, 39, for which he then gives examples from Epictetus and Seneca).

διὰ τῆς παρακλήσεως ἧς παρακαλούμεθα αὐτοὶ ὑπὸ τοῦ θεοῦ.[3] But wherein does the παράκλησις which Paul has experienced consist? In the fact that he was delivered? According to verse 5 he has experienced his God-given παράκλησις διὰ τοῦ Χριστοῦ, and, to be sure, because he has experienced his affliction as participation in the παθήματα τοῦ Χριστοῦ. Only in this way could he express it, that is to say, not as an affliction experienced by anyone, but experienced by faith, as it is characterized in verse 9, that is, in surrender to the creator God by which one knows oneself to be nothing before God. In this way Paul understands himself in light of the σταυρός. He experiences his θλίψεις as παθήματα Χριστοῦ in a believing understanding. In that case, παράκλησις is not mere deliverance as such, but the understanding of deliverance which is given with it as participation in the life of Christ, which as such is not limited to him, the one delivered, but through him benefits others. This is stated in verses 5-7.

2. The basis for the statement that Paul can give comfort: 1:5-7

Verse 5: From the standpoint of content (not grammar), verses 5 through 7 are enclosed by the ὅτι of verse 5, and as a whole give the reason for the δύνασθαι in verse 4.

Paul writes, ὅτι καθὼς περισσεύει τὰ παθήματα τοῦ Χριστοῦ εἰς ἡμᾶς, οὕτως διὰ τοῦ Χριστοῦ περισσεύει καὶ ἡ παράκλησις ἡμῶν[4] instead of the more exact parallel, "thus also the comfort which Christ experienced streams toward us" — a thought merely alluded to in the διὰ τοῦ Χριστοῦ. Everything Christ has encountered, he has encountered not as a historical individual. Rather, it all has cosmic significance (cf. the Gnostic idea of the Christ-Aion), though Paul does not conceive the connection between Christ and his own in a natural way, but through faith, and thus as historically mediated. The συσταυρωθῆναι (Rom. 6:6) is effected in a conscious conduct of life, in a "crucifixion" of the σάρξ with its παθήματα and ἐπιθυμίαι

---

[2] εἰς τὸ with the infinitive to denote purpose or result; cf. Bl.-D. para. 402, 2.

[3] ἧς by attraction of the dative, cf. Bl.-D. para. 294, 2; to be resolved in an ᾗ (cf. Eph. 4:1) or ἥν (cf. Eph. 1:6). The present tense ὁ παρακαλῶν and ἧς παρακαλούμεθα indicate that Paul alters the actual experience to a principle.

[4] περισσεύει is intransitive as in 9:8a and Rom. 5:15 (transitive use in 1 Thess. 3:12; Eph. 1:8); ἡ παράκλησις ἡμῶν denotes the comfort which we experience.

(Gal. 5:24), in allowing the κόσμος to be crucified (Gal. 6:14). For believers, Christ's suffering and death are not pure facts of the past, nor is the Baptism, in which the believer entered into fellowship with Christ (Rom. 6:1ff.).

But it is precisely in suffering that the possibility of perceiving fellowship with Christ is given. Thus, the περισσεύειν of the παθήματα τοῦ Χριστοῦ (v. 5), or the κοινωνοὶ εἶναι τῶν παθημάτων (v. 7) does not simply denote a suffering as Christ endured it, nor necessarily a suffering for Christ's sake (though naturally it can be that). It does not mean only the apostle's suffering, because the community also suffers (v. 7). It certainly does not denote the suffering of an *imitatio,* but rather sufferings which as such can affect anyone. They become παθήματα Χριστοῦ only by virtue of the sufferer's union with Christ, that is, through the new understanding of one's own existence (a new existence is not theoretical, but existential, since self-understanding is a structural element of existence). United with Christ, life with joy and suffering has gained a new sense for the believer, cf. Rom. 14:7-9 and Phil. 1:21. In the surrender of all πεποιθέναι ἐν σαρκί (Phil. 3:3), of all one's own δικαιοσύνη (Phil. 3:9), there occurs that συμμορφίζεσθαι τῷ θανάτῳ αὐτοῦ, which results in a γνῶναι αὐτὸν καὶ τὴν δύναμιν τῆς ἀναστάσεως αὐτοῦ καὶ κοινωνίαν παθημάτων αὐτοῦ (Phil. 3:10). Thus nothing new and different from what happens to other persons need happen to the one united with Christ. But this one experiences and understands everything new and thus exists as καινὴ κτίσις (5:17). Indeed, before all others, being a Christian or an apostle brings the Christian, and especially the apostle (cf. 4:7-18), into situations of suffering. But for him this merely corroborates the fact that he is bound to Christ in life as in death (cf. 12:9f.).

Just as Christ's sufferings are not his individual sufferings,[5] but embrace the sufferings of those who are his, so the sufferings of his own followers are παθήματα Χριστοῦ, not merely sufferings which they undergo in their individual relation to Christ and in which they become certain of that relationship. Rather, in those sufferings they are at the same time united with the others. For insofar as these others suffer, their sufferings too — when understood in faith — are παθήματα Χριστοῦ. To take care that they are understood as such is the duty of one who understands his sufferings as παθήματα Χριστοῦ. And by taking care for it, his παράκλησις passes over to others. He can really comfort others, so that they become κοινωνοὶ τῶν παθημάτων, thus also κοινωνοὶ τῆς παρακλήσεως. This is stated in verses 6f.

Verse 6: εἴτε δὲ θλιβόμεθα, ὑπὲρ τῆς ὑμῶν παρακλήσεως καὶ σωτηρίας· εἴτε παρακαλούμεθα, ὑπὲρ τῆς ὑμῶν παρακλήσεως. The ὑπέρ means

---

[5] Cf. Col. 1:24: νῦν χαίρω ἐν τοῖς παθήμασιν ὑπὲρ ὑμῶν, καὶ ἀνταναπληρῶ τὰ ὑστερήματα τῶν θλίψεων τοῦ Χριστοῦ ἐν τῇ σαρκί μου ὑπὲρ τοῦ σώματος αὐτοῦ, ὅ ἐστιν ἡ ἐκκλησία.

"in the interest of," equal to "for" as in classical Greek, cf. Bl.-D, para. 231, 2. Τῆς ὑμῶν παρακλήσεως is an objective genitive, cf. Bl.-D, para. 284, 2. In general, σωτηρία denotes salvation, "for your best."

Supplement on the text of 1:6f.

𝔥 (א AC) bo sa vg syᵖ and P⁴⁶ read: εἴτε δὲ θλιβόμεθα, ὑπὲρ τῆς ὑμῶν παρακλήσεως καὶ σωτηρίας· εἴτε παρακαλούμεθα, ὑπὲρ τῆς ὑμῶν παρακλήσεως τῆς ἐνεργουμένης ἐν ὑπομονῇ τῶν αὐτῶν παθημάτων ὧν καὶ ἡμεῖς πάσχομεν, καὶ ἡ ἐλπὶς ἡμῶν βεβαία ὑπὲρ ὑμῶν εἰδότες ὅτι . . .

B and pc read: εἴτε δὲ θλιβόμεθα, ὑπὲρ τῆς ὑμῶν παρακλήσεως, τῆς ἐνεργουμένης ἐν ὑπομονῇ τῶν αὐτῶν παθημάτων ὧν καὶ ἡμεῖς πάσχομεν καὶ ἡ ἐλπὶς ἡμῶν βεβαία ὑπὲρ ὑμῶν· εἴτε παρακαλούμεθα, ὑπὲρ τῆς ὑμῶν παρακλήσεως καὶ σωτηρίας.

𝔐 D G al it got and Chr read: εἴτε δὲ θλιβόμεθα, ὑπὲρ τῆς ὑμῶν παρακλήσεως καὶ σωτηρίας, τῆς ἐνεργουμένης ἐν ὑπομονῇ τῶν αὐτῶν παθημάτων ὧν καὶ ἡμεῖς πάσχομεν καὶ ἡ ἐλπὶς βεβαία ὑπὲρ ὑμῶν· εἴτε παρακαλούμεθα, ὑπὲρ τῆς ὑμῶν παρακλήσεως καὶ σωτηρίας.

The text of 𝔥 etc. must be the original, for in B, 𝔐 etc. the καὶ ἡ ἐλπὶς ἡμῶν βεβαία ὑπὲρ ὑμῶν is isolated. But it may not be separated from εἰδότες κτλ. Evidently, the reading in B arose through straying from the first παρακλήσεως to the second, and the omitted middle portion was then added after καὶ ἡ ἐλπὶς κτλ., "but, in order to yield some sense by putting καὶ σωτηρίας at the end" (Lietzmann, 100). This text was taken over by 𝔐 etc. in which only the καὶ σωτηρίας is added after the first παρακλήσεως.

The contrast εἴτε θλιβόμεθα — εἴτε παρακαλούμεθα does not result in a further contrast in the definition of ὑπέρ, as if the meaning were εἴτε θλιβόμεθα ὑπὲρ τῆς ὑμῶν θλίψεως. Rather, Paul's θλίβεσθαι has the same purpose as his παρακαλεῖσθαι — ὑπὲρ τῆς ὑμῶν παρακλήσεως (καὶ σωτηρίας). Both, of course, do not work in isolation, but as a unity. His θλίβεσθαι can only effect an ὑπὲρ τῆς παρακλήσεως, because the παρακαλεῖσθαι is bound up with it, and only to the extent this is true does his θλίβεσθαι have any consequence at all for others. For it is naturally only his παρακαλεῖσθαι, not his θλίβεσθαι, which draws the others into κοινωνία. He does not give them a share in his suffering, but in his comfort (cf. 4:12: ὥστε ὁ θάνατος ἐν ἡμῖν ἐνεργεῖται, ἡ δὲ ζωὴ ἐν ὑμῖν). In sufferings they are in any event one with him; he need not be concerned with that; they have them without him. Rather, his παράκλησις is effective for them — **τῆς ἐνεργουμένης ἐν ὑπομονῇ τῶν αὐτῶν παθημάτων ὧν καὶ ἡμεῖς πάσχομεν.** Naturally it could also be said that just as Paul thoroughly shares the παθήματα Χριστοῦ so also do the Corinthians, and, naturally, this too can be a suffering for Christ's sake. But they become παθήματα Χριστοῦ only when the Corinthians understand them by faith — and they are understood by faith when the παράκλησις is experienced along with them. In this sense we could say that Paul does not give the Corinthians a share in παθήματα (as such), but indeed in the παθήματα Χριστοῦ. But he does so precisely when he gives them a share in the παράκλησις. (For the rest, whether or not the Corinthians' and Paul's sufferings are simultaneous, is not at issue [Lietzmann, 100], which of course they are, according to the formulation in vv. 6 and 7).

Since Paul gives the Corinthians a share in the παράκλησις by virtue of his share in the παθήματα Χριστοῦ, it may indeed be said that he plays the role of "mediator" and "(stands) before the others in Christ's stead" (Windisch, 39). Indeed, it is not that as "apostolic, pneumatic leader of the community" he speaks "out of the consciousness of a superior experience of God and a superabundant possession of the Spirit." He does so simply as one comforted by God through Christ.

Now how does Paul give the community a share in his παράκλησις? Nowhere in 2 Corinthians is there a direct promise of comfort to the suffering Christians, nowhere direct instruction as to the meaning of their suffering.

Of course, this comfort does not stream forth magically, and there is no idea here of a mystical union between Paul and the Corinthians which renders his παράκλησις automatically effective. And Paul, of course, is not at all aware that his παράκλησις is actually effective, but he hopes it is.

Verse 7: καὶ ἡ ἐλπὶς ἡμῶν βεβαία ὑπὲρ ὑμῶν εἰδότες ὅτι ὡς κοινωνοί ἐστε τῶν παθημάτων, οὕτως καὶ τῆς παρακλήσεως. The knowledge is naturally (as in 1 Cor. 15:58) a knowledge of faith (not based on information, say, through Titus! Windisch, 43).

Paul's comfort thus does not consist in directly comforting words. In what then? Simply in the fact that he allows himself to be seen as one who is comforted and united with the Corinthians. This makes him take the κοινωνία seriously. By giving himself to them as he is (cf. 6:11!), he draws them into fellowship with him. If they will understand him, then they will also understand their παθήματα as παθήματα Χριστοῦ and be comforted in that. Comfort, therefore, does not mean to talk suffering away, say, in the conveying of a theodicy, but it is the understanding of suffering as suffering with Christ. And its effect is to be ὑπομονή, patience in suffering.

The understanding of suffering is thus more than (pp. 23f.) abandoning its deciphering and assuming the enigma in submission to the Creator God. Rather, it is clear that such understanding frees from the solitariness of suffering and sets one in community, in which the suffering of each becomes fruitful for others. In suffering, believers understand themselves as members of the Body of Christ — καὶ εἴτε πάσχει ἓν μέλος, συμπάσχει πάντα τὰ μέλη; εἴτε δοξάζεται μέλος, συγχαίρει πάντα τὰ μέλη (1 Cor. 12:26). And in this fellowship the imperative has meaning: χαίρειν μετὰ χαιρόντων, κλαίειν μετὰ κλαιόντων (Rom. 12:15).

For a reverse example, cf. the complaint of the Egyptians after the slaughter of the firstborn in Philo Vit Mos I, 137 (Windisch, 39). When each sees that the other is also affected, διπλοῦν πένθος πρὸς τῷ ἰδίῳ καὶ τὸ κοινὸν εὐθὺς ἐλάμβανεν . . . ἅτε καὶ τὴν ἐλπίδα τῆς παραμυθίας ἀφῃρημένος· τὶς γὰρ ἔμελλε παρηγορεῖν ἕτερον αὐτὸς ὢν τοῦδε χρεῖος;

3. Information concerning Paul's θλῖψις and its effect: 1:8-11

The news of Paul's personal fate is attached by the γάρ. It does not really serve to inform his readers, but to confirm verses 3(5)-7, since in giving such information Paul allows himself to be seen as the suffering and comforted one, and precisely by this means mediates his παράκλησις.

Because of the new beginning in verse 8 (note the address ἀδελφοί, and the introductory formula: οὐ γὰρ θέλομεν ὑμᾶς ἀγνοεῖν, cf. Phil. 1:12), and because of the stylistic difference between verses 8ff. and verses 3-7 (here every liturgical stylizing or rhetoric is lacking), Bachmann, 35, and others want to let the first main part begin with verse 8, so that 1:8-7:16 are a survey of events of the last period.

But 1:8-7:16 is not a continuous report, and verse 11 which concludes the proem is a variation on the motif of intercession, thus on the traditional proem-conclusion. (And the connection is supplied precisely by a γάρ and not by a δέ as in Phil. 1:12!) It is also clear that verses 8-11 belong to verses 3-7, for something concrete still needed to be said of the παθήματα and παράκλησις experienced by Paul.

Verse 8: οὐ γὰρ θέλομεν ὑμᾶς ἀγνοεῖν, ἀδελφοί, ὑπὲρ τῆς θλίψεως ἡμῶν τῆς γενομένης ἐν τῇ Ἀσίᾳ, ὅτι καθ᾽ ὑπερβολὴν ὑπὲρ δύναμιν ἐβαρήθημεν.[6] Of course, something concrete about the θλῖψις[7] is stated only to the extent it is reported that Paul endured it in Asia and that it imperiled his life.[8a] Anything of greater detail is unimportant to him beyond the one fact that he grasped the meaning of this distress. If the ὥστε **ἐξαπορηθῆναι ἡμᾶς καὶ τοῦ ζῆν** (cf. Jos Ant X, 201: τοὺς μὲν ἀπεγνωκότας ἤδη τοῦ ζῆν; "though they were already in despair of their lives.")[8b] first of all expresses the objective fact that Paul envisioned no deliverance from death, then verse 9 adds that he found meaning in it.

Verse 9: ἀλλὰ αὐτοὶ ἐν ἑαυτοῖς τὸ ἀπόκριμα τοῦ θανάτου ἐσχήκαμεν.[9]

---

[6] The formula appears as in 1 Cor. 10:1; 1 Thess. 4:13, etc.

[7] The affliction must have occurred at the end of the Ephesian sojourn. Because it recently occurred, it cannot be identical with the peril of 1 Cor. 15:32. Is it perhaps the event reported in Acts 19:23-40? And because of the ἐν τῇ Ἀσίᾳ it can scarcely have been a shipwreck. Asia is the Roman province with its chief city at Ephesus; cf. PW II/2, 1538ff.

[8a] In Paul, καθ᾽ ὑπερβολήν is a favorite expression; cf. Rom. 7:13; 1 Cor. 12:31; 2 Cor. 4:17; Gal. 1:13. On ὑπὲρ δύναμιν, cf. 8:3; 1 Cor. 10:13.

[8b] Unless otherwise noted, English translations of quotations from nonbiblical sources are from The Loeb Classical Library. Translations furnished by the translator of this work are indicated by "R.A.H."

[9] ἀπόκριμα is a technical term denoting an official answer or decision; cf. Deissmann, *Neue Bibelstudien*, 85; Nägeli, *Wortschatz*, 30, and Lietzmann, 101.

The clause means, "but we ourselves had already uttered our death sentence." (The ἐσχήκαμεν is hardly a genuine perfect; "we have once for all. . . ." It is rather to be construed as aorist, just as in 2:13, where one would expect an ἔσχεν; cf. Bl.-D, para. 343, and Windisch, 46).

The ἐξαπορηθῆναι was thus not only an external constraint (v. 8). Paul rather said "yes!" to it — αὐτοί — that is, he voluntarily affirmed death. And because of the αὐτοὶ ἐν ἑαυτοῖς, the ἐσχήκαμεν cannot mean, "we had received the death sentence" (as an objective confirmation), but "we had accepted it" — "for ourselves we had already uttered the sentence of death" (Lietzmann, 100). The ἀλλά is thus not a comparative of "yes," "actually," or "rather" (Lietzmann, 100; Windisch, 46), but an adversative.[10] And the contrast is expressed by the fact that the new thought is detached from the ὥστε-construction in verse 8, and made independent (why does Luther let it depend on the ὥστε?).

The meaning of this voluntary renunciation of life, however, only becomes clear through the ἵνα μὴ πεποιθότες ὦμεν ἐφ᾿ ἑαυτοῖς ἀλλ᾿ ἐπὶ τῷ θεῷ τῷ ἐγείροντι τοὺς νεκρούς. The ἵνα is hardly consecutive (Lietzmann, 101). It is better to construe it as final (cf. Bousset, *Schriften N.T.*, 174: "For we should learn . . ." and Windisch, 46), indeed not from human resolve, but from the divine intention.

Because the ἵνα-clause is not attached to the ἐξαπορηθῆναι τοῦ ζῆν in verse 8, but to the ἀλλὰ αὐτοὶ κτλ, the translation of Bachmann, 40, cannot be correct: "But of course it is not so much the magnitude of the trouble itself as the rescue experienced which leads to this height of trust." Rather, it was precisely in his distress that the meaning of distress dawned on Paul. The death sentence which he uttered over himself is absolute surrender to God.

God is thus characterized as τῷ ἐγείροντι τοὺς νεκρούς, a universally oriental Jewish predicate (cf. Windisch, 47), which also occurs in the Eighteen Benedictions: "Praised be thou, Yahweh, who maketh the dead alive!" Cf. the characterization of Abraham's πίστις in Rom. 4:17: κατέναντι οὗ ἐπίστευσεν θεοῦ τοῦ ζωοποιοῦντος τοὺς νεκροὺς καὶ καλοῦντος τὰ μὴ ὄντα ὡς ὄντα. The formula is "not Christianized," as Windisch, 47, correctly states. "Every reference to Jesus Christ is lacking." But for Paul it is obvious that radical faith in God arises by faith in the cross of Christ. In the σταυρός God has revealed that he wakens the dead, for the crucified is the Risen One.

The alternative of trust in the future resurrection or in God's help in present distress (cf. Windisch, 48, who prefers the latter) is to be rejected. A voluntary renunciation of life just leaves it to God how he wakens life out of death.

---

[10] Later, a question mark was set in the margin of the manuscript.

Paul soon experienced the truth of such trust.

Verse 10: ὃς ἐκ τηλικούτου θανάτου ἐρρύσατο ἡμᾶς καὶ ῥύσεται.[11] Circumstances of the deliverance are of no interest; and it is basically a matter of indifference to what degree caution, shrewdness, or happy accident played a part. For the one who has taken suffering upon himself and surrendered his life to God, God's deliverance is a gift.

Thus the experience can establish new hope — καὶ ῥύσεται (ῥύεται appears in ℵ, G pm vg^cl; it is omitted in A D* sy ᵖ and Chr — a correction?).[12] Is the εἰς ὃν ἠλπίκαμεν [ὅτι] καὶ ἔτι ῥύσεται a periphrastic dictation doublet? (Cf. Lietzmann, 101). The ὅτι is omitted in P⁴⁶ B 1739 D* and Or.

Verse 11: The future protection hoped for seems to be attached to a condition — συνυπουργούντων καὶ ὑμῶν ὑπὲρ ἡμῶν τῇ δεήσει. Yet the expression is basically an indirect summons to intercession, as in 4:8, or Rom. 15:30: παρακαλῶ δὲ ὑμᾶς [, ἀδελφοί,] . . . συναγωνίσασθαί μοι ἐν ταῖς προσευχαῖς ὑπὲρ ἐμοῦ πρὸς τὸν θεόν. The συνυπουργεῖν here corresponds to the συναγωνίσασθαι there; the συν- thus means, together with me.

In this direct summons lies the admonition to the community to actualize its union with Paul. And by the fact that when the one suffers, the others pray for him, the suffering is made fruitful — and precisely for them, since they are bound in intercession with him to God. Thus in just such an admonition Paul allows the community to share the παράκλησις.

Paul's hope and the community's intercession always assume that both leave everything to God. This is finally expressed where the praise of God is spoken of as the meaning of Paul's deliverance brought about by the community's intercession — ἵνα ἐκ πολλῶν προσώπων τὸ εἰς ἡμᾶς χάρισμα διὰ πολλῶν εὐχαριστηθῇ ὑπὲρ ἡμῶν. The general sense is clear: "A manifold prayer of thanksgiving should be the goal." The ἵνα is final, not consecutive.

The ἐκ πολλῶν προσώπων means "from many persons" (customarily, πρόσωπον denotes person; cf. Lietzmann, 101, and Windisch, 50; thus πολλῶν is not a subjective genitive, *ex multorum personis* as in the Vulgate, but rather an attributive adjective — *ex multis personis*). The community's cultic prayer of thanksgiving is to be kept in mind (Windisch, 50).[13]

The διὰ πολλῶν hardly takes up the ἐκ πολλῶν προσώπων again, but is rather to be construed as neutral, such as διὰ βραχέων (Heb. 13:22),

---

[11] P⁴⁶, 1739, latt, syᵖ and Or read ἐκ τηλικούτων θανάτων (cf. 11:23: dangers of death). ὅς is the equivalent of "who then also." θάνατος is used here instead of peril of death, since according to v. 9 Paul had already regarded himself as νεκρός; cf. the style of the Psalms.

[12] Are these corrections due to rivalry with the subsequent ὅτι καὶ ῥύσεται?

[13] Cf. Ign. Eph. 5:2, and Sifre Deut. 9:14, para. 27 (p. 41f., ed. Horowitz-Finkelstein): "If the prayer of one for the many is heard in such a way, then how much more the prayer of the many for the one."

or δι' ὀλίγων (1 Peter 5:12), and could thus denote a long prayer of thanksgiving. It is perhaps better to construe it as a musical term such as διὰ τεσσάρων, διὰ πολλῶν, thus "many-voiced." In any event, it is not to be translated "in order that the proof of grace, which has become ours through the intercession of many, may also be gratefully praised by many" (Bousset, *Schriften N.T.* 174), according to which ἐν πολλῶν προσώπων, contrary to its position in the sentence, would be connected to the τὸ εἰς ἡμᾶς χάρισμα.

The τὸ εἰς ἡμᾶς χάρισμα is the object of the thanksgiving — Paul's deliverance. For in the context, χάρισμα cannot be the bestowal of grace or Paul's equipping by the Spirit (Windisch, 51), only the deliverance. But it is characteristic that Paul calls this a χάρισμα (cf. χάρις in v. 12). (The construction εὐχαριστεῖν τι, "to give thanks for something," appears seldom, cf. Lietzmann, 101).[14]

The object of thanks is stated once more in the ὑπὲρ ἡμῶν. For this certainly does not state the purpose of the thanksgiving, so that the reading would be, "for our salvation" (Windisch, 51), as though it were motivated by the ancient cultic faith, according to which the thanks which the deity receives moves it to be gracious again. Rather, the object (or occasion) of the thanksgiving is stated as "for us" (cf. εὐχαριστεῖν ὑπὲρ in 1 Cor. 10:30; Eph. 1:16; 5:20 in which περί is used; Rom. 1:8; 1 Cor. 1:4; 1 Thess. 1:2; 2 Thess. 1:3 and 2:13).

But what deliverance of Paul should the object of thanks be? According to Windisch, 49, the aorist εὐχαριστηθῇ (rather than the present) requires reference to a deliverance just experienced. But the thanks is supposed to be the result of an intercession yet to follow.

Therefore, a future deliverance must be in mind — "so that eventually the prayer of thanks resounds." Of course, Paul may be thinking more concretely of a present distress, if we may construe the present ὧν καὶ ἡμεῖς πάσχομεν as a genuine present.[15]

Thanks to God should thus be the goal on which human hope is finally set, just as elsewhere for Paul God's δόξα is the ultimate goal of all happening and striving. Cf. 1:20; 1 Cor. 10:31; Rom. 15:6f.; Phil. 1:11; 2:11; and especially 2 Cor. 4:15: τὰ γὰρ πάντα δι' ὑμᾶς, ἵνα ἡ χάρις πλεονάσασα διὰ τῶν πλειόνων τὴν εὐχαριστίαν περισσεύσῃ εἰς τὴν δόξαν τοῦ θεοῦ, and also 9:12 (on the duty of εὐχαριστεῖν, cf. 1 Thess. 3:9; 5:18; Col. 1:12; 2:7; 3:16f.; 4:2; and Eph. 5:20).

Stylistically, the proem concludes with the writer's intercession on behalf

---

[14] εὐχαριστεῖν in the passive with an impersonal subject, cf. Bl.-D. para. 312, 2. Cf. also Schubert, *Thanksgivings*.

[15] "This concept of glorifying God through thanksgiving, by which God's gift to men returns to God, appears in Hellenism as well as in Judaism," Kümmel, 197, with reference to Boobyer, *Thanksgiving*.

of his readers. Just as Paul has varied the epistle's beginning, since the thanksgiving does not apply to the community's condition but rather to his own deliverance and is thus only indirectly a thanksgiving for what has been given the community, so the theme of the conclusion is not Paul's intercession for the community, but that of the community for Paul — thus by indirection it is an intercession for the community, insofar as Paul's summons to intercession mutually strengthens the community in its Christian existence.

Chapter 1

Paul's καύχησις (or πεποίθησις)
[Letter D] 1:12—2:13; 7:5-16

Its Retention in the Relations between Paul and the Community
(The Justification of Paul before the Community)

1. The theme of καύχησις and εἰλικρίνεια. (The reproach of boasting and untruthfulness): 1:12-14.
2. Apostolic πεποίθησις and εἰλικρίνεια in Paul's behavior. (The reproach of the unreliability of his promise): 1:15—2:4.
   a. In principle: The altering of travel plans does not spell unreliability: 1:15-22.
   b. In fact: The apostle's relation to the community was determinative: 1:23—2:4.
3. Πεποίθησις and εἰλικρίνεια are determinative also in the present relation to the community: 2:5-11. (The ending of the quarrel.)
4. Paul's yearning for the community: 2:12-13; 7:5.
5. Justification for the πεποίθησις: 7:6-16. (Comfort by the arrival of Titus.)
   a. The arrival of Titus: 7:6-7.
   b. The effect of the interim epistle: 7:8-13a.
   c. The reception of Titus at Corinth: 7:13b-15.
   d. Paul's confidence: 7:16.

The key words in this section are:

καυχᾶσθαι: 7:14 (cf. 5:12; 9:2; 10:8, 13, 15-17; 11:12, 16, 18, 30; 12:1, 5f., 9).

καύχησις: 1:12; 7:4, 14 (cf. 8:24; 9:4 [v. 1]; 11:10, 17).

καύχημα: 1:14 (cf. 5:12; 9:3).

πεποιθέναι: (1:9); 2:3; (10:7).

πεποίθησις: 1:15 (cf. 3:4; 8:22; 10:2).

θαρρεῖν: 7:16 (5:6, 8; 10:1f.), (μη ἐγκακεῖν, 4:1, 16).

εἰλικρίνεια: 1:12 (2:17) (cf. ἀλήθεια, 4:2; 6:7; 7:14; 11:10; 12:6; 13:8; ἀληθής, 6:8).

1. The theme of καύχησις (πεποίθησις) and εἰλικρίνεια (The reproach of boasting and untruthfulness): 1:12-14

For our boast is this, the testimony of our conscience that we have behaved in the world, and still more toward you, with holiness and godly sincerity, not by earthly wisdom but by the grace of God. For we write you nothing but what you can read and understand; I hope you will understand fully, as you have understood in part, that you can be proud of us as we can be of you, on the day of the Lord Jesus.

Verse 12: ἡ γὰρ καύχησις ἡμῶν αὕτη ἐστίν. The theme of Paul's καύχησις appears abruptly, is strongly accented — in this consists my καύχησις —[1] and is evidently directed against reproaches that Paul is accustomed to boast. Paul corrects the reproaches. That he speaks as if he were a defendant is shown in his calling of a witness — **τὸ μαρτύριον τῆς συνειδήσεως ἡμῶν.** According to the formulation, the witness of his conscience — this concept is not problematic here or in need of explanation — is thus the object of his καύχησις.[2] Actually, Paul boasts of what his conscience testifies—**ὅτι . . . ἀνεστράφημεν ἐν τῷ κόσμῳ**—which actually means, "my boast is that I can say with good conscience, I conducted myself. . . ." If the reference is truly to boasting, then Paul allows a witness to speak which cannot be suborned, his conscience.

Paul boasts of his ἀναστραφῆναι,[3] his behavior or conduct of life (the term is used only here in Paul; cf. Eph. 2:3; 1 Tim. 3:15; 1 Peter 1:7, etc.), and, of course, as a conduct of life **ἐν ἁγιότητι καὶ εἰλικρινείᾳ τοῦ θεοῦ** the term is used with both nouns. The two nouns form a hendiadys, and both denote purity. (ἁπλότητι would mean the same thing, a term which appears in ℵ D G pl lat and sy instead of ἁγιότητι. ἁγιότης does not occur elsewhere in Paul; ἁπλότης appears also in 8:2; 9:11, 13; 11:3; and Rom. 12:8. But τοῦ θεοῦ seems to suit ἁγιότης better.)

Since in the antithesis (ἐν σοφίᾳ) σαρκικῇ equals κατὰ σάρκα (cf. v. 17), τοῦ θεοῦ must be the equivalent of κατὰ τὸν θεόν, thus, according to God's norm, conforming to God's requirement (cf. Ign. Magn. 6:1: ἐν ὁμονοίᾳ θεοῦ,[4] and Ign. Pol. 7:1: ἐν ἀμεριμνίᾳ θεοῦ). It is not used after

---

[1] So it is of little consequence whether καύχησις is intended as a *nomen actionis* equivalent to boasting, or as a *nomen rei actae* equivalent to the boast; cf. v. 14, καύχημα.

[2] συνείδησις is the knowledge of myself concerning myself, thus also my conforming to the divine requirement.

[3] The ἐν with ἀναστραφῆναι first of all denotes manner, Bl.-D. para. 219, 4, and latterly area. Paul elsewhere writes περιπατεῖν, 4:2; 5:7; 10:2f.; 12:18, etc. So the ἐν τῷ κόσμῳ indicates both the apostolic consciousness of Paul, who is aware of himself as an apostle of the κόσμος (Rom. 15:19), as well as his eschatological consciousness, insofar as he is aware of himself as over against the κόσμος and must worthily represent this over-against-ness; cf. Phil. 2:15 (1 Cor. 4:9: he is exposed to the gaze of the κόσμος).

[4] Likewise in Magn. 15; Phld. inscr. Pol. 1:3; Magn. 6:2: ὁμοήθεια θεοῦ; Phld. 1:2: ἐπιείκεια θεοῦ; 8:1: ἑνότης θεοῦ.

the analogy of δικαιοσύνη τοῦ θεοῦ — which God gives[5] (this feature later comes into its own in the ἐν χάριτι θεοῦ), or as a genitive of quality — as God possesses it, cf. on 11:2, p. 200.

The more precise meaning of integrity derives from the contrast οὐκ ἐν σοφίᾳ σαρκικῇ.[6] This cannot mean, "not from the ethical and aesthetic motifs of the sages," that is, of the popular philosophers (Williger, Hagios, 91). For in the context, the σοφία ἀνθρώπων of 1 Cor. 2:5 is certainly not intended. Indeed, the contrast with ἁγιότης (ἁπλότης) and εἰλικρίνεια, and the defense in face of the reproach of ἐλαφρία in 1:17 (the πανουργία of 4:2 and the δόλος in 4:2; 12:16) indicate that it is a matter of the moral conduct of life, that therefore the σοφία σαρκική is cunning, calculation, the "wisdom" of egoism. Paul has been reproached for such egoism; cf. 10:2: ἐπί τινας τοὺς λογιζομένους ἡμᾶς ὡς κατὰ σάρκα περιπατοῦντας.[7]

Integrity is thus honesty and selflessness. But how can Paul boast of these without destroying them? Naturally, there cannot be swaggering, and naturally, Paul does not intend to say, "I am used to boasting of my integrity." But now he must boast of it, speak of it, in order not to be mistaken. Just as, in order to establish κοινωνία, he had to appear to the community in his preparedness for his death, in his πεποίθησις in God, and in his παράκλησις, now he must appear in the good conscience of his integrity. Indeed, they should understand him (v. 13). And they must do so above all because he is an apostle. For the Corinthians, the judgment concerning Paul's person — and he stands before the community as though one accused — is at issue only insofar as he is a proclaimer and in his person may give the gospel no offense (cf. 1 Cor. 9:12), not because the community would be a competent forum before which he had to give answer (cf. 1 Cor. 2:15; 4:3). But the misunderstanding that he is boasting of his integrity is also set aside by the addition of the antithetical ἀλλ᾽ ἐν χάριτι θεοῦ.

χάρις here cannot be the grace of office which gives to Paul his commission and authority (Rom. 1:5; 12:3; 15:15; 1 Cor. 3:10). It is rather the power granted by God for a genuine ἀναστρέφεσθαι (cf. 1 Cor. 15:10; 2 Cor. 12:8f.), essentially identical with δύναμις (cf. the antithesis in 1 Cor. 2:5:

---

[5] Kümmel, p. 197: "Here Paul assumes divine predicates [!] because he knows he is borne by the grace of God."

[6] σαρκικός equals κατὰ σάρκα, which as such does not mean "sinful," but simply "human."

[7] Cf. the parallels in Herm. sim. IX, 25:2: ἀπόστολοι καὶ διδάσκαλοι οἱ κηρύξαντες εἰς ὅλον τὸν κόσμον καὶ διδάξαντες σεμνῶς καὶ ἁγνῶς τὸν λόγον τοῦ κυρίου καὶ μηδὲν ὅλως νοσφισάμενοι εἰς ἐπιθυμίαν πονηράν, ἀλλὰ πάντοτε ἐν δικαιοσύνῃ καὶ ἀληθείᾳ πορευθέντες, καθὼς καὶ παρέλαβον τὸ πνεῦμα τὸ ἅγιον. ("Apostles and teachers who preached to all the world, and taught reverently and purely the word of the Lord, and kept nothing back for evil desire, but always walked in righteousness and truth, even as they had received the Holy Spirit.")

μὴ . . . ἐν σοφίᾳ ἀνθρώπων ἀλλ᾽ ἐν δυνάμει θεοῦ, and cf. the alternation of χάρις and δύναμις in 2 Cor. 12:8f.).

It is possible that Paul has conceived χάρις in Hellenistic fashion as a mysterious something at work in him (Wetter, *Charis*), but what is decisive is that he knows he is borne by God in his activity and destiny (cf. χάρισμα in v. 11). He understands his integrity as God's gift.

By means of the antithesis ἀλλ᾽ ἐν χάριτι θεοῦ, the definition of σοφία as σαρκική, which first of all meant κατὰ σάρκα, that is, according to the norm of the σάρξ, takes on the connotation of being inspired by the σάρξ.

The additional **περισσοτέρως δὲ πρὸς ὑμᾶς**[8] also corresponds to the defense posture from which Paul is speaking, for it includes the idea, "certainly you must be aware of it!" It is thus almost an appeal to the conscience of the Corinthians (cf. 4:2; 5:11).

To what extent has Paul behaved in an especially genuine fashion toward the Corinthians? Naturally, the word "especially" is to be taken *cum grano salis,* for of course Paul has not behaved less genuinely elsewhere. But it would have to have been especially clear to the Corinthians. Why? Certainly not because he worked for a long time at Corinth (according to Acts 18:11, over a year and a half). A better explanation is that because at Corinth he did not allow himself to be supported by the community (11:7; 1 Cor. 9:6), because the relationships were exceptionally difficult and gave occasion for misinterpretations. Thus Paul was not especially honest at Corinth, but especially cautious.

To what extent, then, is what is said in verse 12 a reason for the summons to intercession in verse 11? The last word in verse 11 states that ὑπὲρ ἡμῶν the community's thanksgiving should redound to God. Does this not again express the καύχησις for which he is reproached? No! It is a matter of boasting of what God does. If God acts mightily in Paul, then one must thank God ὑπὲρ αὐτοῦ. There is no personal boasting contained here. But Paul can require boasting, since he is aware of his integrity which he owes to the χάρις of God. He can require it precisely because he does not personally take to boasting. So in the last analysis the ἡ γὰρ καύχησις ἡμῶν αὕτη ἐστίν means, "my boast is that I do not boast of myself, but of the χάρις τοῦ θεοῦ."[9]

Verse 13: This verse assures the Corinthians of Paul's integrity, and especially toward the community with regard to a particular reproach, that is, that his letters are equivocal — **οὐ γὰρ ἄλλα γράφομεν ὑμῖν ἀλλ᾽ ἢ ἃ ἀναγινώσκετε.**[10] The meaning is just as he writes. The reproach had perhaps been raised because of the change in his travel plans. Another

---

[8] An antithesis?
[9] Cf. 1 Cor. 15:10.
[10] οὐκ ἄλλο ἀλλ᾽ ἤ means "nothing (else) than" also in classical Greek; cf. Bl.-D. para. 448, 8.

reproach regarding his epistles appears in 10:10: ὅτι αἱ ἐπιστολαὶ μέν, φησίν, βαρεῖαι καὶ ἰσχυραί. The ἢ καὶ ἐπιγινώσκετε merely heightens the ἀναγινώσκετε — "not otherwise, than as you read and understand." Since the Corinthians actually misunderstand him or certainly only half understand him, the ἢ καὶ ἐπιγινώσκετε means, "as you with good intent can and must understand."

That the Corinthians actually do not or do not fully understand Paul, is expressed in the ἐλπίζω δὲ ὅτι ἕως τέλους ἐπιγνώσεσθε,[11] in which Paul's struggle to help the Corinthians' arrive at an understanding is again at issue.

Verse 14 gives the basis of this hope: καθὼς καὶ ἐπέγνωτε ἡμᾶς ἀπὸ μέρους. According to Windisch, 57, in the contrast between ἀπὸ μέρους and ἕως τέλους two ideas are mingled: 1) till now, and till finally; 2) in part, and fully. The meaning is that now Paul is partially known by the Corinthians (this is a reference to 1 Cor. 13:12, where, however, an ἄρτι appears with γινώσκω ἐκ μέρους, and the contrast is stated in the τότε), but one day, that is, in the consummation, they will fully understand him. Affectation! The meaning is simply, as they understand him now at least in part, they will — the sooner, the better! — fully understand him. And it is precisely with this that Paul is concerned in his letter.

The clause ὅτι καύχημα ὑμῶν ἐσμεν indicates in what respect they should understand him, that is, simply by the fact that he is their apostle (the argument is similar in 5:12ff.). The apostle is the community's boast, just as the community is the apostle's boast — καθάπερ καὶ ὑμεῖς ἡμῶν which means, "as surely as I think to boast of you on the day. . . ."

Indeed, Windisch, 58 (just as Luther), wants to construe the ὅτι as a "because," and writes: "Paul is certain that the Corinthians will retain their proper understanding to the end (of this life), because he is sure that on the day of the Lord he will be for them and they for him a reason for boasting." But do they already have the proper understanding? And above all, Paul writes that right now they should (as in 5:12) learn to understand the καύχημα. To understand him (v. 12) is indeed nothing else than to understand his καύχημα (that he is an apostle). ὅτι can only be explicative. It is directly dependent on ἐπέγνωτε, but as regards content also on the ἐπιγνώσεσθε.

Paul's καύχημα . . . ἐν τῇ ἡμέρᾳ τοῦ κυρίου ἡμῶν Ἰησοῦ[12] consists in his being able to point to the community. Cf. 1 Thess. 2:19 and Phil. 2:16. On that ἡμέρα, he need not refer to what he is, but to what they are.

---

[11] ἕως τέλους as the opposite of ἀπὸ μέρους means "perfectly," "totally" (Windisch, 57, and Bauer on the v.; indeed, it means "to the end").

[12] Does the ἐν τῇ ἡμέρᾳ etc. belong only with καθάπερ? On ἡμέρα τοῦ κυρίου ἡμῶν Ἰησοῦ cf. 1 Cor. 1:8 etc.

Neither the apostle nor the community can boast of themselves before God. But since they recognize that God is at work in the other and acknowledges the other, each may know he is recognized and acknowledged by God. On the other hand, humiliation occurs when God does not confirm the work (cf. 12:21). Each one boasts in God, and the boasting is basically a thanksgiving, for it is obvious to Paul that he does not owe his activity to his own power. Cf. the ἐν χάριτι θεοῦ in verse 12. In addition, cf. 1 Cor. 3:8f.: θεοῦ γὰρ ἐσμεν συνεργοί· θεοῦ γεώργιον, θεοῦ οἰκοδομή ἐστε (v. 9), and 1 Cor. 15:10: χάριτι δὲ θεοῦ εἰμι ὅ εἰμι . . . οὐκ ἐγὼ δὲ ἀλλὰ ἡ χάρις τοῦ θεοῦ σὺν ἐμοί.

2. Apostolic πεποίθησις and εἰλικρίνεια in Paul's behavior (The reproach of the unreliability of his promises): 1:15—2:4

Because I was sure of this, I wanted to come to you first, so that you might have a double pleasure; I wanted to visit you on my way to Macedonia, and to come back to you from Macedonia and have you send me on my way to Judea. Was I vacillating when I wanted to do this? Do I make my plans like a worldly man, ready to say Yes and No at once? As surely as God is faithful, our word to you has not been Yes and No. For the Son of God, Jesus Christ, whom we preached among you, Silvanus and Timothy and I, was not Yes and No; but in him it is always Yes. For all the promises of God find their Yes in him. That is why we utter the Amen through him, to the glory of God. But it is God who establishes us with you in Christ, and has commissioned us; he has put his seal upon us and given us his Spirit in our hearts as a guarantee. But I call God to witness against me — it was to spare you that I refrained from coming to Corinth. Not that we lord it over your faith; we work with you for your joy, for you stand firm in your faith. For I made up my mind not to make you another painful visit. For if I cause you pain, who is there to make me glad but the one whom I have pained? And I wrote as I did, so that when I came I might not suffer pain from those who should have made me rejoice, for I felt sure of all of you, that my joy would be the joy of you all. For I wrote you out of much affliction and anguish of heart and with many tears, not to cause you pain but to let you know the abundant love that I have for you.

a. In principle: The altering of travel plans does not spell unreliability: 1:15-22.

Verse 15: καὶ ταύτῃ τῇ πεποιθήσει. Paul had conceived his travel plans in the πεποίθησις expressed in verse 14, thus in the trust which he believes he can place in the Corinthians in light of his sincere behavior characterized in verse 12. It is therefore not a πεποίθησις ἐν σαρκί (Phil. 3:4).

ἐβουλόμην πρότερον πρὸς ὑμᾶς ἐλθεῖν. The πρότερον (in the sense of "earlier") is of course not linked to ἐβουλόμην, but rather to πρὸς ὑμᾶς ἐλθεῖν — first to you and then to Macedonia (τὸ πρότερον occurs in ℜ, τὸ δεύτερον in K, and is omitted in ℵ*).

ἵνα δευτέραν χάριν σχῆτε. In place of χάριν, B bo L P min and Thdt read χαράν, which is certainly a correction according to verse 24 and 2:3.

The choice here (Windisch, 63) between χάρις as denoting "pleasure," "friendliness" in the secular sense (Acts 24:27; 25:3, 9), or "proof of grace" is to be rejected, since for Paul both meanings coincide. It is naturally a proof of grace. Cf. Rom. 1:11: ἐπιποθῶ γὰρ ἰδεῖν ὑμᾶς, ἵνα τι μεταδῶ χάρισμα ὑμῖν πνευματικὸν εἰς τὸ στηριχθῆναι ὑμᾶς, and Rom. 15:29: οἶδα δὲ ὅτι ἐρχόμενος πρὸς ὑμᾶς ἐν πληρώματι εὐλογίας Χριστοῦ ἐλεύσομαι.

Yet with his visit Paul also pays the Corinthians a kindness, and personal joy is to result from it, cf. verse 24; 2:2f. But if the visit by which Paul shows his good will to the Corinthians is a χάρις, then it is God, as it were, who shows such good will through his visit. Paul thus speaks — since he knows he is only an instrument — with a humility which indeed is easily understood as human pride.

δευτέραν: Since Paul in 12:14 and 13:1f. announces a third visit to Corinth (in the interim epistle, however!), Lietzmann, 102 thinks that the δευτέρα χάρις is reckoned from the first visit (founding of the community), and that it denotes the interim visit already made, and referred to in 2:1f. But this certainly cannot be the meaning — instead of ἐβουλόμην . . . ἐλθεῖν, the reading would have to be ἦλθον. The idea must rather be that Paul wanted to visit the Corinthians twice, first, on the journey from Asia to Macedonia (πρότερον), then on the return journey from Macedonia (the δευτέρα χάρις). The fact that the ἵνα-clause does not follow the καὶ δι᾽ ὑμῶν διελθεῖν εἰς Μακεδονίαν (which of course would be the correct reading), is no argument against it. For Paul, the intention to visit Corinth twice stands in the foreground, and the added καὶ δι᾽ ὑμῶν explains the plan.

Verse 16: καὶ δι᾽ ὑμῶν διελθεῖν εἰς Μακεδονίαν, καὶ πάλιν ἀπὸ Μακεδονίας ἐλθεῖν πρὸς ὑμᾶς (cf. on v. 15). The plan developed in the ἐβουλόμην κτλ. of verse 15 is other than that communicated in 1 Cor. 16:5-9, according to which Paul intends to journey from Asia first to Macedonia and from there to visit Corinth. This plan was not carried out. Rather, according to 2:1f., Paul meanwhile journeyed directly from Asia to Corinth, a visit which resulted ἐν λύπῃ. At that time he must have written the interim epistle, to which 2:4, 9; 7:12 refer (and of course the letter from which 2:14—7:4; 10:1—13:10 derive; cf. 12:21: μὴ πάλιν ἐλθόντος μου[13] ταπεινώσῃ με ὁ θεός μου πρὸς ὑμᾶς). In this letter (or otherwise,

---

[13] [οὐ]?

[14] He must certainly have communicated the plan to the Corinthians before his interim visit; for he could only make the decision of 2:1 after the interim visit.

perhaps through Titus, who delivered the letter?) he must have communicated the plan[14] of verses 15f., which also was not carried out, and for which reason the Corinthians reproached him. Rather, the plan of 1 Corinthians was carried out, since Paul journeyed to Macedonia (2:12f.; 7:5), from where he will now arrive a third time in Corinth (12:14; 13:1f.).

καὶ ὑφ' ὑμῶν προπεμφθῆναι εἰς τὴν Ἰουδαίαν (cf. 1 Cor. 16:6; Rom. 15:24). The utterance concerns the equipment for the journey. εἰς τὴν Ἰουδαίαν thus indicates the final goal of the journey as in 1 Cor. 16:4 and Rom. 15:24.

Verse 17: τοῦτο οὖν βουλόμενος μήτι ἄρα τῇ ἐλαφρίᾳ ἐχρησάμην; ἢ ἃ βουλεύομαι κατὰ σάρκα βουλεύομαι. The clause contains two parallel rhetorical questions in self-defense, which respond to the reproaches of the Corinthians who described Paul's promises as lightly made and unreliable. τῇ ἐλαφρίᾳ with the article (!) thus means, "in the frivolousness with which I am reproached." ἐχρησάμην is the equivalent of χρῆσθαι which means "to make use of," just as in 3:12 (thus the customary usage). κατὰ σάρκα, scarcely distinguishable from τῇ ἐλαφρίᾳ, means at best perhaps "not uprightly," in any event as one acts who does not belong to Christ and does not have the πνεῦμα (v. 22; cf. Schauf, *Sarx*, 126f.). Cf. the reproach in 10:2: ἐπί τινας τοὺς λογιζομένους ἡμᾶς ὡς κατὰ σάρκα περιπατοῦντας, and the defense in 1:12: οὐκ ἐν σοφίᾳ σαρκικῇ.

ἵνα ᾖ παρ' ἐμοὶ τὸ ναὶ ναὶ καὶ τὸ οὒ οὔ. The ἵνα-clause clearly explains the τῇ ἐλαφρίᾳ and κατὰ σάρκα. The ἵνα is thus not final, but consecutive (Bl.-D, para. 391, 5) or epexegetical. The meaning of the clause is, "as though I had said Yes and No at the same time." Cf. James 5:12: ἤτω δὲ ὑμῶν τὸ ναὶ ναί, καὶ τὸ οὒ οὔ. On the double "Yes, yes," "No, no" cf. Matthew 5:37; Sl Enoch 49:1 and Str.-B. I, 337.[15] It is impossible to assume with Windisch, 66, that Paul believed he had already fulfilled his promise by coming to Corinth at all. Then of course his ναί would also have been a ναὶ κατὰ σάρκα. But Paul maintains it is a ναί, even when not outwardly fulfilled.

Verse 18: πιστὸς δὲ ὁ θεὸς ὅτι ὁ λόγος ἡμῶν ὁ πρὸς ὑμᾶς οὐκ ἔστιν ναὶ καὶ οὔ. Since a ὅτι-clause is dependent on the πιστὸς δὲ ὁ θεός, the meaning is not "God is true," as in 1 Cor. 1:9; 10:13; 1 Thess. 5:24; and 2 Thess. 3:3 (cf. 1 John 1:9). It is rather an oath formula — "as surely as God is true," "by God's faithfulness," or "God is my witness, that. . . ." The phrase is a solemn declaration as in verse 23; Gal. 1:20, etc.[16]

---

[15] Together with P⁴⁶ min and vg Kümmel, 197, wants to read τὸ ναὶ καὶ τὸ οὔ, and traces the doubling to an assimilation to Matt. 5:37. Kümmel correctly rejects the interpolation of a μή behind the ἵνα (Nissen, *Philologus*, XCII, 1937, 247f.).

[16] According to Kümmel, 197f., the λόγος would denote Paul's missionary preaching, for the purpose of accenting its reliability. But does this fit in the context?

Verses 17f. repulse the accusation of unreliability, first of all by only a reproachful counter-question — the Corinthians should have trusted him! — then by appeal to God as witness. The reply is therefore not a refutation, but a purely personal repulse. Only verses 19-22 contain a refutation, which is of course "dogmatic" in nature. That is, Paul does not explain the situation and does not give the reasons which led him to alter his plan (these are given only in 1:23—2:4), but merely indicates that the Yes or No of one who is united to Christ cannot possibly be unreliable. Since the Corinthians are united to Christ with Paul, they should have trusted him. Only on the basis of this fundamental reflection follows the concrete refutation of the reproach. "An ordinary man would have allowed this explanation to follow right after verse 17" (Windisch, 74, on vv. 23ff.). But Paul has corrected the misunderstanding in this way, as though he were obliged or wished to defend himself before the Corinthians as a competent forum! He first requires Christian trust, but then also makes possible human understanding.

Verse 19: ὁ τοῦ θεοῦ γὰρ υἱὸς Χριστὸς Ἰησοῦς . . . οὐκ ἐγένετο ναὶ καὶ οὔ, ἀλλὰ ναὶ ἐν αὐτῷ γέγονεν. Jesus Christ is the incarnate Yes (ἐγένετο is used of his mission, γέγονεν of his presence in the kerygma, or in the community). We might suppose it would be more logical to say that Christ's No is really a No, and that his Yes is a reliable Yes. But at issue in this context is that a promise (a Yes) is proved to be reliable, and the idea is this, that whoever is in Christ (v. 22) is reliable because his Yes is a Yes, since Christ is the incarnate Yes. What is at stake, then, is not a Yes or No which Christ utters, but the Yes which he is. He is an unequivocal Yes which God has spoken in him.

The phrase, ὁ ἐν ὑμῖν δι' ἡμῶν κηρυχθείς, δι' ἐμοῦ καὶ Σιλουανοῦ καὶ Τιμοθέου, is evidently intended to give the statement more weight — you have learned no other Christ from us than just this one — and, of course, with a side-glance at other missionaries who proclaim an ἄλλος Ἰησοῦς (11:4). No doubt for this reason Paul adds the δι' ἐμοῦ καὶ Σιλουανοῦ καὶ Τιμοθέου. The meaning is, therefore, not my personally invented Christ, but the Christ proclaimed by apostolic preaching.[17] "The listing of names" is basically intended to be an "emphatic reminder of the days of first inspiration and love" (Lietzmann, 103). It is a thrust against Paul's rivals at Corinth, on whom the reproaches finally fall — "opposed to them it is precisely I who am reliable; my Christ is the Yes!"

Verse 20: ὅσαι γὰρ ἐπαγγελίαι θεοῦ, ἐν αὐτῷ τὸ ναί (an anticipated nominative instead of πάσαις ταῖς ἐπαγγελίαις τοῦ θεοῦ, ὅσαι γὰρ εἰσίν, γέγονεν ἐν αὐτῷ τὸ ναί, cf. Bl.-D, para. 466, 2).

---

[17] Thus also Kümmel, 198.

Support now follows for the proposition that Christ is the Yes. He is such because the Old Testament promises are fulfilled in him (cf. Rom. 15:8). He has proved that his promises are reliable. This is corroborated by the community's liturgical practice — διὸ καὶ δι' αὐτοῦ τὸ ἀμὴν τῷ θεῷ πρὸς δόξαν δι' ἡμῶν — "you yourselves acknowledge it by the Amen offered to God through him!"[18]

The liturgical custom of speaking the Amen in worship is assumed (1 Cor. 14:16), and by way of the formula διὰ τοῦ κυρίου ἡμῶν Ἰησοῦ Χριστοῦ, just as Paul himself uses it in expressions of prayer, cf. Rom. 1:8; 7:25, etc.[19]

The δι' αὐτοῦ marks Christ as mediator of the prayers, that is, not in the primitive sense of advocate, but in the sense that he is the access to God for those who pray (cf. Rom. 5:2). Christ is not conceived as the one who inspires prayers, who is "mystically present" (thus Windisch, 70).

Verse 21: Verse 21 now conveys the idea which really gives the reason. In this Christ, who is the incarnate Yes, Paul and the community are joined in a unity, and both have received the Spirit. Therefore — what is now not expressed, but is obvious from what precedes — what is true of Christ is true of us, and thus both share in the Yes. That is, a Yes uttered by Paul must be understood by the community as a true Yes, because it is Christ's Yes, and he cannot be reproached for a κατὰ σάρκα βουλεύεσθαι (v. 17).

ὁ δὲ βεβαιῶν ἡμᾶς σὺν ὑμῖν εἰς Χριστὸν καὶ χρίσας ἡμᾶς θεός. (θεός is a predicate as in 4:6; 5:5): "Thus it is God himself who. . . ." βεβαιοῦν means to ratify a purchase legally, and can be a juridical term (cf. Windisch, 71, and Deissmann, B.S. 100ff., especially 104f.) just as ἀρραβών which denotes a payment on account, or earnest money. Legal βεβαίωσις[20] of course does not occur through the payment of an ἀρραβών, but the payment of an ἀρραβών still makes the purchase valid. The application of legal language here is incorrect, since for Paul βεβαιοῦν is clearly identical with διδόναι τὸν ἀρραβῶνα, and since, above all, it is not a purchase which is validated here but rather persons who are "established." That is, they are given a firm stand, they are secured in Christ. Paul thus uses βεβαιοῦν in a way similar to 1 Cor. 1:6, 8; cf. Col. 2:7 (βεβαιούμενοι τῇ πίστει, alongside ἐρριζωμένοι καὶ ἐποικοδομούμενοι ἐν αὐτῷ).[21]

---

[18] Since the δι' ἡμῶν naturally does not refer to Paul and his comrades, but to the community.

[19] 'αμήν is the formula of assent, of the Yes, and is connected with ναί in Rev. 1:7 and 22:20.

[20] "Corresponding perhaps to our *Quittung* (receipt)," Windisch, 71, thus written out by the seller.

[21] Gnostic terminology is reflected in the βεβαιοῦν which is the equivalent of στηρίζειν; cf. 2 Thess. 2:17 with Heb. 13:9, and cf. 1 Cor. 1:8 and Od Sol 38:17: "For I was established and lived and was redeemed, And my foundations were laid on account of the Lord's hand." Cf. Schlier in *TDNT* I, 602f., who sees a possible blend with juridical terminology — Christ is conceived as an Aion or field of force, as it were, into which the individual is set by Baptism.

The Christians are established εἰς Χριστόν, so that they belong to Christ. In the context, this means that their action and speech is determined by Christ. And Paul emphasizes, ἡμᾶς σὺν ὑμῖν. In Christ, therefore, Paul and the community are united, so that the community can and therefore must acknowledge and understand him as determined by Christ.

καὶ χρίσας ἡμᾶς. χρίειν appears alongside βεβαιοῦν, and is used in the Old Testament of kings, priests and prophets. Naturally, the ἡμᾶς cannot refer to Paul alone. Rather, the σὺν ὑμῖν dominates the entire statement — clearly, the καρδίαι ἡμῶν are the hearts of all Christians. Obviously in mind is Baptism, which incorporates us into Christ (1 Cor. 12:13; Gal. 3:26-28). It can be characterized as an anointing, because it grants the Spirit. We need not think of a special act of anointing at Baptism (thus since Tertullian, cf. Lietzmann, 103, and thus, of course, also Reitzenstein, *Taufe,* 183f.; on the other hand, cf. Goguel, RHPhR 10, 1930, 198).[22]

Verse 22: ὁ καὶ σφραγισάμενος ἡμᾶς καὶ δούς. These two participles are evidently intended to explain the two which precede — ὁ βεβαιῶν and ὁ χρίσας — perhaps as visible signs of the invisible βεβαιοῦν and χρίειν. In any event, σφραγίζειν also denotes Baptism, namely insofar as it is a "sealing" by naming the ὄνομα Χριστοῦ.

σφραγίζειν here is certainly not an eschatological term as in Ezekiel 9:4ff.; the Ps. of Sol. 15:8, 10 (σημεῖον τοῦ θεοῦ, σημεῖον τῆς ἀπωλείας); 4 Ezra 6:5; 8:51ff.; Rev. 7:2ff. and 14:1ff. (and, of course, construed in this sense by Schweitzer, *Mysticism,* 230, 1, and by Käsemann, *Leib,* 129), or at least not primarily, but rather has the connotation of taking into possession. σφραγίς is really the sign which corroborates, takes into possession, or proves to whom it belongs. At this date it appears to have been a sign of Jewish circumcision (Rom. 4:11; Barn. 9:6; Str.-B. III, 495; IV, 31ff.), and is also a term used in the mysteries (cf. Heitmüller, ΣΦΡΑΓΙΣ, Heinrici-FS., 40-59; Windisch, 73). Since Herm. Sim. IX, 16:3-5 and 2 Clem. 7:6[23] it can positively be demonstrated as applied to Baptism (cf. Lietzmann, 103f.) and in this fashion is perhaps already assumed by Paul.

In any event σφραγισάμενος here means "he who has made you Christ's possession through naming the name of Christ in the Baptism." That this σφραγίζεσθαι is determinative for eschatological salvation (cf. Eph. 1:13f.: ἐν ᾧ [sc. Χριστῷ] καὶ πιστεύσαντες ἐσφραγίσθητε τῷ πνεύματι τῆς ἐπαγγελίας τῷ ἁγίῳ, ὅς ἐστιν ἀρραβὼν τῆς κληρονομίας ἡμῶν, and 4:30: τὸ πνεῦμα τὸ ἅγιον τοῦ θεοῦ, ἐν ᾧ ἐσφραγίσθητε εἰς ἡμέραν ἀπολυτρώσεως), is not considered in this context, nor is attention given to the purpose for which the πνεῦμα is an ἀρραβών. The latter is rather of import in 5:5.[24]

---

[22] God "anointed" Jesus in Luke 4:18; Acts 4:27, clearly with the πνεῦμα, as expressly stated in Acts 10:38 (cf. Heb. 1:9). The χρῖσμα in 1 John 2:20, 27 is the πνεῦμα.

[23] Cf. Knopf, *Apostolische Väter* I, 162, on 2 Clem. 6:9, and Preisigke, *Gotteskraft,* 25ff.

[24] Obviously of course for eschatological salvation.

τὸν ἀρραβῶνα τοῦ πνεύματος ἐν ταῖς καρδίαις ἡμῶν. Just as God's βεβαιοῦν and χρίειν is demonstrated or made visible in the sealing by the ὄνομα, so also by the granting of the ἀρραβὼν τοῦ πνεύματος, insofar as it is experienced in the individual's Baptism and demonstrated by the pneumatic conditions of the χαρίσματα.

ἀρραβὼν τοῦ πνεύματος occurs as in 5:5 and Eph. 1:14, and ἀπαρχή is used in the same sense in Rom. 8:23.[25]

On the bestowal of the Spirit in Baptism cf. 1 Cor. 6:11; 12:13; Acts 2:38; 10:44ff.; and 19:6. διδόναι is used of the πνεῦμα in Rom. 5:5 (cf. λαμβάνειν in Rom. 8:15; 1 Cor. 2:12; 2 Cor. 11:4; Gal. 3:2, 14). On ἐν ταῖς καρδίαις ἡμῶν, cf. Gal. 4:6: ἐξαπέστειλεν ὁ θεὸς τὸ πνεῦμα τοῦ υἱοῦ αὐτοῦ εἰς τὰς καρδίας ἡμῶν. Cf. also Rom. 5:5; 8:27.

Verses 20-22 have thus shown that for Paul a Yes and No at the same time are impossible (v. 17), and that the community, united with him in Christ, should have known that. So it follows that Paul's Yes is a Yes even when circumstances seem to make it a No. In this case Paul has said Yes to his promises precisely by not coming to Corinth, for his coming would not have been a χάρις, but a judgment, not a coming in and for χαρά, but in and for λύπη. This is stated in 1:23—2:4. After all, the Corinthians themselves are responsible for the fact that his Yes seemed to be a No, for because of the λύπη which his previous visit evoked, they have made it impossible to carry out that plan (v. 15f.).

b. In fact: The apostle's relation to the community was determinative in the altering of travel plans: 1:23 — 2:4

Verse 23: Now Paul finally gives the actual reason for the change in his travel plans.

ἐγὼ δὲ μάρτυρα τὸν θεὸν ἐπικαλοῦμαι ἐπὶ τὴν ἐμὴν ψυχήν. The sentence is a formula of protestation.[26] Similar formulas occur with μάρτυς in Josephus (cf. Schlatter, *Josephus,* 56. Deissmann, *L. v. O.,* 258, draws a comparison with the formula of cursing in Ditt Or II, Nr. 532, 29ff.: ἐπαρῶμαι αὐτός τε κατ' ἐμοῦ καὶ σ[ώμα]τος τοῦ ἐμαυτοῦ καὶ ψυχῆς καὶ βίου κα[ὶ τέ]κνων. ἐπὶ τὴν ἐμὴν ψυχήν. On ἐπικαλεῖσθαι ἐπὶ (= against), cf. the prayers from Rheneia for vengeance in Deissmann, *L. v. O.,* 355.

ὅτι φειδόμενος ὑμῶν οὐκέτι ἦλθον εἰς Κόρινθον. The οὐκέτι alludes to the period following the interim visit, to which 2:1 refers.

Verse 24: οὐχ ὅτι κυριεύομεν ὑμῶν τῆς πίστεως. οὐχ ὅτι may mean, "by that I do not intend to say that" (Lietzmann, 104). In that case, verse 24 corrects the self-conscious utterance of verse 23, as if Paul had wanted to insist that as lord of the Corinthians he could deal harshly or

---

[25] τοῦ πνεύματος is an explicative genitive.

[26] It cannot be argued that Paul's oaths correspond to Matt. 5:33-37.

mildly with them. The οὐχ ὅτι is used thus in Phil. 4:17. Or, it may mean, "but it is not such that" (thus in 3:5). In that case, verse 24 gives the reason for verse 23 — it was precisely in order not to be compelled to lord it over them, but in order to spare them, that Paul did not come to Corinth. So much the better!

In any case, Paul defends himself against his opponents' reproach that he tyrannizes the community (cf. 4:5; 10:8; 13:10; 1 Cor. 7:35).

Windisch, 77, thinks that οὐχ ὅτι κυριεύομεν can only have relative force; that is, that it applies only to the extent the community displays an established life of faith, for elsewhere Paul certainly does "rule," for example in 13:5,9b; 12:20f.; 10:6b; cf. 2:9; 7:15. But the governing and ruling, which Paul exercises as apostle, is not at all the κυριεύειν spurned here. (It is rather a serving, 1 Cor. 3:5.) But here, in face of the reproaches, he intends to deny that he is personally fond of power.

Windisch, 76f., draws a comparison with the Stoic tenet that the wise man has no κύριος. But Epictetus in Diss IV, 5, 4 (οὐδεὶς ἀλλοτρίου ἡγεμονικοῦ κυριεύει; "No one is master over another's governing principle. . . .") and in 12:7 (προαιρέσεως ἀλλοτρίας κύριος οὐδείς; "No man is master of another's moral purpose. . . .") states the principle impossibility, not the intended possibility which rests on a decision!

ἀλλὰ κτλ. Lietzmann, 104, is surprised that Paul does not simply say, "I indeed am only a coworker, not a lord." Instead, πίστεως appears, which is foreign to the context! But what is at issue is the apostle's relationship to the community, not a relationship of personal friendship. The Corinthians face him as Christians, and ὑμῶν τῆς πίστεως means, "over you as Christians." Cf. the identical τῇ γὰρ πίστει ἑστήκατε — "you are indeed independent Christians."

ἀλλὰ συνεργοί ἐσμεν τῆς χαρᾶς ὑμῶν. The πίστις, which Paul will not rule, is distinguished from χαρά, on behalf of which he will be a coworker. χαρά is the state of faith necessarily flowing from πίστις, the joy in which πίστις is actualized.

On the one hand, cf. Rom 14:17: οὐ γάρ ἐστιν ἡ βασιλεία τοῦ θεοῦ βρῶσις καὶ πόσις, ἀλλὰ δικαιοσύνη καὶ εἰρήνη καὶ χαρὰ ἐν πνεύματι ἁγίῳ, and Galatians 5:22: ὁ δὲ καρπὸς τοῦ πνεύματός ἐστιν ἀγάπη, χαρά, εἰρήνη κτλ. On the other, cf. Phil. 1:25: καὶ τοῦτο πεποιθὼς οἶδα, ὅτι μενῶ καὶ παραμενῶ πᾶσιν ὑμῖν εἰς τὴν ὑμῶν προκοπὴν καὶ χαρὰν τῆς πίστεως. Cf. also the imperative χαίρετε in 13:11; 1 Thess. 5:16; Phil. 2:18; 3:1, and 4:4. In addition, cf. Gulin, *Freude* I, 183f., who of course somewhat narrowly emphasizes that Paul assumes the right to punish moral deficiencies in the community. In that case, χαρά is only in its prime when the community's moral behavior conforms to its faith. But Gulin correctly points out that in what follows λύπη becomes the theme.

The formulation συνεργοὶ τῆς χαρᾶς ὑμῶν is chosen precisely with a view to what will be said in 2:1ff. "Because I have joint responsibility for your χαρά I did not come, so long as my coming would only have led to λύπη."

The fundamental Christian joy of 1:24 could be distinguished from the personal joy of 2:3. Actually, the joy of 2:3 is a personal joy, and yet a joy which Paul has as apostle and which corresponds to the community's Christian joy: ὅτι ἡ ἐμὴ χαρὰ πάντων ὑμῶν ἐστιν, 2:3. He will rejoice precisely as apostle, which of course actually coincides with his personal joy.

τῇ γὰρ πίστει ἐστήκατε first of all gives the reason for the negative statement: οὐχ ὅτι κυριεύομεν ὑμῶν τῆς πίστεως. The Corinthians are independent Christians, and over them as such Paul enjoys no personal lordship.

On ἑστάναι cf. 1 Cor. 10:12; 15:1; 16:13; 7:37; Rom. 11:20; and 1 Thess. 3:8. τῇ πίστει is not an instrumental, but a local dative (cf. Col. 1:23: εἴ γε ἐπιμένετε τῇ πίστει): "You have truly gained your status in faith."

Verse 1: ἔκρινα δὲ ἐμαυτῷ τοῦτο.[27] ἔκρινα is used here as in 1 Cor. 2:2: "I decided" (in contrast to ἐβουλόμην in 1:15). ἐμαυτῷ (a dative of advantage, or παρ' ἐμοί, ἐν ἐμοί as in 1 Cor. 7:37 and 11:13) emphasizes what is conscious, reflected upon.

τὸ μὴ πάλιν ἐν λύπῃ πρὸς ὑμᾶς ἐλθεῖν. The ἐν is the equivalent of בְּ which means "with." ἔρχεσθαι ἐν means "to bring" (cf. Gulin, *Freude*, I, 264, 1). Cf. 1 Cor. 4:21: ἐν ῥάβδῳ ἐλθεῖν, and Rom. 15:29: ἐν πληρώματι εὐλογίας ἔρχεσθαι. Cf. also Rom. 15:32: ἐν χαρᾷ ἐλθεῖν.

As the position indicates, the πάλιν does not merely belong with ἐλθεῖν ("I did not want to come a second time, and then of course in λύπη"). Rather, πάλιν ἐν λύπῃ belong together. Thus one visit ἐν λύπῃ has already taken place, and since it cannot have been his first sojourn at the community's founding, Paul must have been in Corinth again during the interim. On 1:16 cf. pages 38f. and the τρίτον in 12:14 and 13:1f. So΄ Paul did not want to cause pain (v. 2), but this naturally assumes that he did not want to suffer pain (v. 3), for the community's joy and the joy of the apostle correspond (cf. v. 3) — likewise the λύπη, as its position indicates.

Verse 2: εἰ γὰρ ἐγὼ λυπῶ ὑμᾶς, καὶ τίς ὁ εὐφραίνων με εἰ μὴ ὁ λυπούμενος ἐξ ἐμοῦ. καὶ τίς means "who then" (on καί in the apodosis as an interrogative clause, cf. Bl.-D, para. 442, 8). The translation, "who then is (would be) there to make me glad, but the one whom I have pained?" would be absurd. Verse 2 thus gives the basis for verse 1. The Corinthians are his only joy; how then can he give them pain, from whom he awaits joy! In that case he would destroy his own joy. According to Windisch, 79, the τίς ὁ εὐφραίνων με sounds egotistical. As if this were not his love speaking!

---

[27] B min P⁴⁶ read γάρ instead of δέ, which according to Kümmel, 198, was actually the original. Illuminating!

Verse 3: καὶ ἔγραψα τοῦτο αὐτὸ ἵνα. Is τοῦτο αὐτό the object of ἔγραψα? In any event, ἔγραψα is not linked as an epistolary aorist to this letter just written, so that we would have to locate the τοῦτο αὐτό in a clause just written (1:23;[28] 2:1f.) or in one like it (ἵνα κτλ.).[29] ἔγραψα rather refers to the interim letter (7:8) clearly named in verses 4 and 9, and which the τοῦτο αὐτό denotes in its entirety.[30]

The ἔγραψα would refer to the interim letter, even if τοῦτο αὐτό were intended adverbially — "for this very reason" (cf. 2 Peter 1:5, and Bl.-D. para. 160; 290, 4). Of course, what militates against this reading is that in verse 9 Paul uses εἰς τοῦτο for "therefore." And elsewhere, the adverbial τοῦτο αὐτό appears with intransitive verbs (such as "to come"), and with transitive verbs only where they have their own object (as in 2 Peter 1:5).

Or, can the τοῦτο αὐτό be an intensified μόνον? "I wrote (sc. the interim letter) only in order not to have to come"? **ἵνα μὴ ἐλθὼν σχῶ** means, "that I might not suffer λύπη at my coming" — as Paul feared when he wrote 12:20, and **ἀφ᾽ ὧν ἔδει με χαίρειν** means, exactly as the apostle of the community, cf. 1:14 and 1 Thess. 2:19f. On **πεποιθὼς ἐπὶ πάντας ὑμᾶς**, cf. 1:15 in connection with 1:14. The **ὅτι ἡ ἐμὴ χαρὰ πάντων ὑμῶν ἐστιν** indicates that the apostle's joy and that of the community correspond as personal experiences of joy; in essence they are identical. It is not that Paul's joy is the prior and the Corinthians' joy the result (Windisch, 81), though the identity can be described factually in personal experiences of joy which follow.

Of course, Paul could also have written ὅτι ἡ ἐμὴ λύπη πάντων ὑμῶν ἐστιν (Bachmann, 94), for the one is given with the other. But it is characteristic that he writes just χαρά — it is χαρά which is at issue.

Verse 4: ἐκ γὰρ πολλῆς θλίψεως καὶ συνοχῆς καρδίας ἔγραψα ὑμῖν. The θλῖψις and the συνοχὴ καρδίας are that very grief over the λύπη of the interim visit, not the θλῖψις of 1:8. In any case, the διὰ πολλῶν δακρύων must refer to that λύπη. And the clause gives the basis for the ἔγραψα τοῦτο αὐτό in verse 3: "I already had enough grief and wanted no more of it." On συνοχή which denotes distress or anguish, cf. συνέχειν in 5:14 and Phil. 1:23. (Cf. θλῖψις καὶ στενοχωρία in Rom. 2:9; ἀνάγκη καὶ θλῖψις in 1 Thess. 3:7.)

διὰ πολλῶν δακρύων means "with many tears." διά describes manner, as in 3:11; 5:7; and Romans 14:20; cf. Bl.-D. para. 223, 2.

Since the letter in mind here cannot be 1 Corinthians (or one prior to it),

---

[28] If 1:23f. is meant, then the sense would be: "I wrote ἀλλὰ συνεργοί ἐσμεν τῆς χαρᾶς ὑμῶν — indeed, because I would not have λύπη, but rather χαρά; but my joy is truly also yours."

[29] The ἵνα-clause can certainly not explain an ἔγραψα τοῦτο!

[30] The sense is, when I wrote that letter I did it so that I could work for your joy; for when I wrote to spare myself λύπη (at my visit), it was done for the sake of your joy, since my joy and yours coincide.

it is an interim letter which Paul sent to Corinth after that visit ἐν λύπῃ (cf. 7:8), obviously delivered by Titus and of whose effect he first awaits (v. 13) and then receives (7:6ff.) a report.

οὐχ ἵνα λυπηθῆτε. This statement is not in contradiction to 7:8, for Paul of course desired a λύπη εἰς μετάνοιαν (7:8ff.), and not a λύπη for its own sake, a merely personal sorrow as recompense for the λύπη caused him by the community. He has not acted from pique or a desire for revenge, but out of ἀγάπη as an apostle: ἀλλὰ τὴν ἀγάπην ἵνα γνῶτε ἣν ἔχω περισσοτέρως εἰς ὑμᾶς. Is the περισσοτέρως used in half jesting fashion — "all too abundantly" — or as one loves the sick child "more" than the healthy (cf. Luke 15:29-32)?

Insofar as the λύπη of the community was mere grief and pain, Paul did not wish it. For as an apostle he was obliged to rejoice in the community, not be its judge. For this very reason he wrote that letter and merely wrote. And that letter which caused pain (as is indirectly clear from v. 4, and directly from 7:8), was written from love, not from bad temper or desire for vengeance. The pain caused him (v. 5) is really a pain caused the community, for it disturbs the relationship between the apostle and the community. If the community has not allowed this relationship to be disturbed, or if it has eliminated the disturbance by drawing back from the offender (v. 6), forgiveness must now prevail (v. 7). Where there is no readiness to forgive, there Satan finds entry (v. 11). This thought is explicated in verses 5-11.

3. Elimination of the quarrel (πεποίθησις and εἰλικρίνεια are determinative also in the present relation to the community): 2:5-11

But if anyone has caused pain, he has caused it not to me, but in some measure — not to put it too severely — to you all. For such a one this punishment by the majority is enough; so you should rather turn to forgive and comfort him, or he may be overwhelmed by excessive sorrow. So I beg you to reaffirm your love for him. For this is why I wrote, that I might test you and know whether you are obedient in everything. Any one whom you forgive, I also forgive. What I have forgiven, if I have forgiven anything, has been for your sake in the presence of Christ, to keep Satan from gaining the advantage over us; for we are not ignorant of his designs.

After the mere allusions in verses 1-4, what was actually at issue in the λύπη of the interim visit in verse 1 comes to light somewhat more clearly.

Verse 5: εἰ δέ τις λελύπηκεν. A member of the community must have offended Paul personally. At the same time, the community did not unequivocally take Paul's side, but (as vv. 6-10; 7:11 indicate) only did so later, so that the offense took on the character of a principle, and disturbed the relationship between Paul and the community.

The τις is no doubt the ἀδικήσας of 7:12, and the affair can only have occurred at the interim visit (at best, in connection with it later on). It is not possible to establish a connection with 1 Corinthians. Under no circumstances can the ἀδικήσας be the "incestuous person" of 1 Cor. 5, for his behavior was not a personal offense against Paul, but a direct offense against the community — quite apart from the fact that Paul could not have been content with ἐπιτιμία (v. 6) instead of the excommunication demanded in 1 Cor. 5:5, or that he would have been able to settle the case by personal forgiveness (v. 10).

οὐκ ἐμὲ λελύπηκεν, ἀλλὰ . . . πάντας ὑμᾶς. The pain which Paul experienced should no more be construed as a personal insult against the apostle than the λύπη which he gave the community should be understood as a personal affront to the community on his part (v. 4). For the community Paul is the apostle; its existence depends on him. Thus what affects Paul affects the community (though it has understood this only in part or to a certain degree), whether it be χαρά (v. 3) or λύπη (v. 5).

The ἀπὸ μέρους is restrictive — the community as a whole was not affected by the λύπη. But this can only mean that the λύπη, on principle aimed at the community as a whole, was not at all felt or construed as such by one part of the community. Only the other part really suffered from it — the πλείονες of verse 6.

It is hardly likely that the λελύπηκεν and not the ἀπὸ μέρους should limit the πάντας, and thus should mean "to a certain extent" (identical to ὀλίγον, cf. Windisch, 85).[31]

ἵνα μὴ ἐπιβαρῶ is a parenthesis which furnishes motivation for the ἀπὸ μέρους. ἐπιβαρεῖν elsewhere means "to burden" (1 Thess. 2:9 and 2 Thess. 3:8). But "in order not to burden him (the λυποῦντα) more severely" (thus already Chrysostom) yields no sense, since it would certainly not be a burden for the offender to have pained the community only in part. Is the clause ironic — "in order to exert no pressure on the minority" (v. 6), or, may we construe ἐπιβαρεῖν absolutely, in a sense which of course has not been documented — "to heap up a great weight of words," "to exaggerate," "in order not to say too much"? The context appears to require it.

Verse 6: ἱκανὸν τῷ τοιούτῳ ἡ ἐπιτιμία αὕτη ἡ ὑπὸ τῶν πλειόνων. The majority of the community, therefore, has taken the apostle's side by meting out an ἐπιτιμία (reproach, reprimand, penalty)[32] to the λυπήσας

---

[31] Kümmel, 198, following Schlatter, states that the ἀπὸ μέρους here "restricts the sinking into pain and suffering to what is varied in degree and unlike in extent." But does ὑμᾶς belong before πάντας? And in v. 6 the reference is clearly to the majority!

[32] ἐπιτιμία in this sense is not used classically. In classical usage the term denotes the status of the ἐπίτιμος, the citizen in possession of all his rights. The classical term for punishment is τὸ ἐπιτίμιον, τὰ ἐπιτίμια. But in the papyri ἐπιτιμία already appears as a term for punishment. Chrysostom and others construe the term after ἐπιτίμησις to mean reproach, reproof.

(αὕτη is the punishment reported by Titus, 7:11). The ὑπὸ τῶν πλειόνων indicates that a minority of the community still persists in opposition.

This ἐπιτιμία should suffice, that is, the ἱκανόν is to be construed temporally — now, forgiveness should follow the ἐπιτιμία.

Verse 7: ὥστε τοὐναντίον μᾶλλον ὑμᾶς χαρίσασθαι καὶ παρακαλέσαι. The ὥστε is dependent on the ἱκανόν in verse 6, which is the same as to say ἀνάγκη or πρέπον (Windisch, 87). τοὐναντίον μᾶλλον is in contrast to the ἐπιτιμία which was appropriate till now — "so that contrariwise you must rather forgive him" (Lietzmann, 106). χαρίζεσθαι in the sense of "to forgive" is Pauline (v. 10; 12:13; Col. 3:13; and Eph. 4:32). The term really means "to show a favor," "to give" (cf. Josephus Ant IV 144: ἁμαρτήματα χαρίζεσθαι),[33] corresponding to the term ἀφιέναι.

μή πως τῇ περισσοτέρᾳ λύπῃ καταποθῇ ὁ τοιοῦτος. According to this statement, the ἐπιτιμία had its effect on the λυπήσας, and he has now been grieved. In 1 Peter 5:8 καταπίνειν is used of devouring by the διάβολος (for further material, cf. Windisch, 88). As verse 9 (cf. 7:11, 15) indicates, Paul himself had desired the offender's punishment. So now he also has the right to declare the punishment meted out as sufficient.

Verse 8: διὸ παρακαλῶ ὑμᾶς κυρῶσαι εἰς αὐτὸν ἀγάπην. κυροῦν is a technical term for "confirm," or "conclude." Does Paul have an official decision by the community in mind?

Verse 9: εἰς τοῦτο γὰρ καὶ ἔγραψα ἵνα γνῶ τὴν δοκιμὴν ὑμῶν. There is no contradiction between Paul's earlier demand to punish the λυπήσας and his present mildness. What was at issue for him was not a personal matter, but only his relation as apostle to the community. δοκιμή here denotes confirmation, just as in Phil. 2:22. Lietzmann, 106, writes: "That I might put you to the test." The εἰ εἰς πάντα ὑπήκοοί ἐστε indicates that the community stood the test, for in the meantime Titus reported its ὑπακοή (7:15) to Paul.

What is misleading in Paul's situation emerges again in this verse, since as apostle and in spite of 1:24, Paul is lord of the community, the one who can demand obedience (cf. 7:15; 10:6; Phil. 2:12; Philemon 21; and 2 Thess. 3:14).

Verse 10: ᾧ δέ τι χαρίζεσθε, κἀγώ. The community need not suppose it would have to proceed further for Paul's sake. He had written only that it adopt the proper attitude (v. 9). If the community has now settled the matter by properly conceiving its relationship to Paul as its apostle and by drawing the consequence from that, then the matter is settled also for Paul. He too forgives, to the extent he had anything at all to forgive: **καὶ γὰρ ἐγὼ ὃ κεχάρισμαι, εἴ τι κεχάρισμαι, δι' ὑμᾶς ἐν προσώπῳ Χριστοῦ.** The clause accents most strongly that for Paul the question is one of principle, not personal. To the extent he forgave, he did so not because he was given personal satisfaction, but solely for the community's sake. So it is doubtful

---

[33] Translator's note: Bultmann's reference is incorrect.

whether for his part there can be any talk of "forgiving," since he was in no way personally offended!

For this reason Paul did not write, "if I forgive, then you must do so." Rather, the forgiveness of the community must precede, because Paul's "forgiveness" (to the extent it can be called such) is the forgiveness of the apostle for whom the matter is settled only when the community acts in corresponding fashion — "my forgiveness is included in yours."

In the context, the view implicit in Bousset's suggestion (*Schriften N.T.* 179) that the κεχάρισμαι be construed as passive, is impossible. He translates: "For what forgiveness I have received — if I really am forgiven — has occurred for your sake," which means, "it does not at all touch me personally, for truly, I have been shown grace from the Lord only for your sake. How could I insist on atonement for injury?" The restrictive "if I really am forgiven" would already be unlikely. Above all, the clause would give no reason at all for the harmony of action — ᾧ δέ τι χαρίζεσθε, κἀγώ).

Windisch is surprised (as early as p. 88 on v. 7) that Paul does not speak of the divine forgiveness which the offender must receive. But this does not at all affect the relationship between Paul and the community! Of sole relevance here is that "Paul (looks) only to the offense which the sinner has given to persons, and (reflects on) the tangled state of affairs only to the extent persons are affected by it" (p. 91). For 1) if Paul's forgiveness is genuine, he may not make it depend on the prior divine forgiveness, and 2) he certainly lays all the stress on treating the offense and entanglement not as a personal concern, but as a matter between himself and the Corinthians, as between an apostle and his community. The forgiveness is intended precisely to exclude the personal element. And this is what the ἐν προσώπῳ Χριστοῦ means — "I have appeared in spirit before Christ, and called him to witness my forgiveness" (Lietzmann, 107). The interpretation of Dibelius, *Geisterwelt,* 52, "that you may stand before the face of Christ" (and need not fear the charges of Satan before his judgment seat) is hardly correct.

Verse 11: ἵνα μὴ πλεονεκτηθῶμεν ὑπὸ τοῦ σατανᾶ. Just as Paul, so also the community must regard the matter as settled, for if one were now to act from personal motives, thus subjectively, Satan would gain power (in saying this Paul need not have imagined how that would actually be). This would hardly mean in order that the offender not become Satan's booty. The reference to Satan as lurking in the background also appears in 1 Cor. 7:5. πλεονεκτεῖν means "to take advantage of," "to outwit," cf. 7:2; 12:17; and 1 Thess. 4:6.

οὐ γὰρ αὐτοῦ τὰ νοήματα ἀγνοοῦμεν. The νοήματα refer to aspirations, plans, intentions, cf. 3:14; 4:4; 10:5; and 11:3 (cf. Eph. 6:11: στῆναι πρὸς τὰς μεθοδείας τοῦ διαβόλου).

1:23—2:11 indicates Paul's objectivity. He excludes elements of personal pique from the pertinent question. At issue is the apostle's relation to the community. Objectivity as such is not specifically Christian (however much at issue in the present instance). But for the Christian it is an indispensable duty and is an easy task for him, since the ἀγάπη which he should let prevail is established in him through God's ἀγάπη (cf. Rom. 5:5). He can exclude the question of his own person, can forgive, since he knows he stands ἐν προσώπῳ Χριστοῦ.

1:15-22: Trust must of necessity arise from union with Christ. Even the requirement of mutual trust is as such not specifically Christian, but has special urgency for the Christian, and is a new possibility for the one who belongs to God and has the Spirit.

In Christ, all moral demands retain their value (cf. Phil. 4:8), and receive new foundation (renewal of the creation).

4. Paul's yearning for the community: 2:12-13; 7:5

When I came to Troas to preach the gospel of Christ, a door was opened for me in the Lord; but my mind could not rest because I did not find my brother Titus there. So I took leave of them and went on to Macedonia. . . . For even when we came into Macedonia, our bodies had no rest but we were afflicted at every turn — fighting without and fear within.

2:12 turns back to the report, and to that extent takes up 1:15f.—2:3 again. It is not as though Paul now wanted to report on the interim. Rather, by way of the report he speaks of his longing to hear about the community. It should learn to understand him ever better — his apostolic relation to it has really determined his personal experience and action.

Verse 12: ἐλθὼν δὲ εἰς τὴν Τρῳάδα. So, after the θλῖψις of 1:8, Paul came to Troas from Asia (elsewhere Τρῳάς denotes the district of Troas; but it could denote the port city of Alexandria-Troas as in Acts 16:8, 11 and 20:5f.; cf. Lietzmann, 107). The name is used with the article, cf. Bl.-D. para. 261, 1.

εἰς τὸ εὐαγγέλιον τοῦ Χριστοῦ. τοῦ Χριστοῦ used with εὐαγγέλιον is an objective genitive (cf. εὐαγγελίζεσθαι αὐτόν in Gal. 1:16). εὐαγγέλιον here is used as an action noun equivalent to εἰς τὸ εὐαγγελίζεσθαι Χριστόν.

καὶ θύρας μοι ἀνεῳγμένης ἐν κυρίῳ. The figure is used as in 1 Cor. 16:9 and Col. 4:3 for the expression, "when a possibility (for work) was offered to me." The figure is Rabbinic: "To open a door," to give opportunity, cf. Str.-B. III, 484f.; cf. Josephus Bell VI, 295: τὴν τῶν ἀγαθῶν πύλην ("the gate of blessings"). The ἐν κυρίῳ is formula-like, cf. verses 14, 17 and Rom. 16:3-9, etc.

Verse 13: οὐκ ἔσχηκα ἄνεσιν τῷ πνεύματί μου. ἔσχηκα appears in the perfect rather than the aorist, cf. 1:9 and Bl.-D. para. 343, 2. The πνεῦμα is the "I" of Paul as in Rom. 1:9, 2 Cor. 7:13, and 1 Cor. 16:18. 7:5 is completely identical with it: οὐδεμίαν ἔσχηκεν ἄνεσιν ἡ σάρξ ἡμῶν. τῷ μὴ εὑρεῖν με Τίτον τὸν ἀδελφόν μου. The dative of the infinitive without the preposition occurs only here in the New Testament (Bl.-D. para. 401), and με is used with it as subject (Bl.-D. para. 406, 3).

It is clear from 7:5ff. that Paul waited for Titus from Corinth with news of how the community had received his letter. ἀλλὰ ἀποταξάμενος αὐτοῖς ἐξῆλθον εἰς Μακεδονίαν. As to sense, αὐτοῖς means "the people from Troas" (Lietzmann, 107). So great was Paul's tension and yearning that he dispensed with his activity in Troas.

7:5: καὶ γὰρ ἐλθόντων ἡμῶν εἰς Μακεδονίαν οὐδεμίαν ἔσχηκεν ἄνεσιν ἡ σάρξ ἡμῶν. The γὰρ stems from the redactor, who joined the pieces of the various letters. Lietzmann, 131, arguing for the original sequence of 7:5ff. after 7:4 appeals to the correspondence between παρακλήσει in verse 4 and παρακαλῶν in verse 6; between παρεκάλεσεν in verse 6 and παρακλήσει in verse 7; between χαρᾷ in verse 4 and χαρῆναι in verse 7, and between θλίψει in verse 4 and θλιβόμενοι in verse 5. But this proves only the intelligence of the redaction, which also attached the γάρ. Windisch, 233ff., wants to connect 7:5-16 with 2:1-13 or actually accept the following order as original: 2:1-4 — Paul's non-appearance and his letter; 2:12f. — the journey to Macedonia; 7:5-16 — the arrival of Titus, and 2:5-11 — the matter of the λυπήσας.

Weiss, *Urchristentum*, 265, and Loisy, *Rev. d'hist. et de litt. rel.* 7, 1921, 111, also remove 2:14—7:4 from the context of 2:13 and 7:5 and connect it with chapters 10–13. (That 2:14—7:4 is written as if the reconciliation had not occurred, would in itself be no compelling proof. For even after what Titus achieved Paul could still write as persuasively and vigorously for the community's understanding as he does in 2:14—7:4.)

Schnedermann's view, 341, that Titus arrived right between 7:3 and 4 is unintelligible. But 7:5 after 7:4 is too harsh!

οὐδεμίαν ἔσχηκεν ἄνεσιν occurs here just as in 2:13. The τῷ πνεύματί μου there corresponds to the ἡ σάρξ ἡμῶν here without any difference in meaning. σάρξ is used in the neutral sense of the "I" in its corporeality, cf. 12:7; 1 Cor. 7:28; and Gal. 4:13f. The situation is described in exclamations heaped up without connection — ἀλλ' ἐν παντὶ θλιβόμενοι (sc. ἦμεν); ἔξωθεν μάχαι, ἔσωθεν φόβοι (sc. ἦσαν). If μάχαι refers to external opposition and difficulties, then φόβοι of course refers only to the anxiety plaguing Paul respecting the Corinthian community. Added to this there is still the delicate external situation, and the lively representation of this situation furnishes the foil for verse 6.

5. Justification for the πεποίθησις (Comfort by the arrival of Titus): 7:6-16

But God, who comforts the downcast, comforted us by the coming of Titus, and not only by his coming but also by the comfort with which he was comforted in you, as he told us of your longing, your mourning, your zeal for me, so that I rejoiced still more. For even if I made you sorry with my letter, I do not regret it (though I did regret it), for I see that that letter grieved you, though only for a while. As it is, I rejoice, not because you were grieved, but because you were grieved into repenting; for you felt a godly grief, so that you suffered no loss through us. For godly grief produces a repentance that leads to salvation and brings no regret, but worldly grief produces death. For see what earnestness this godly grief has produced in you, what eagerness to clear yourselves, what indignation, what alarm, what longing, what zeal, what punishment! At every point you proved yourselves guiltless in the matter. So although I wrote to you, it was not on account of the one who did the wrong, nor on account of the one who suffered the wrong, but in order that your zeal for us might be revealed to you in the sight of God. Therefore we are comforted. And besides our own comfort we rejoiced still more at the joy of Titus, because his mind has been set at rest by you all. For if I have expressed to him some pride in you, I was not put to shame; but just as everything we said to you was true, so our boasting before Titus has proved true. And his heart goes out all the more to you, as he remembers the obedience of you all, and the fear and trembling with which you received him. I rejoice, because I have perfect confidence in you.

a. The arrival of Titus: 7:6-7.

Verse 6: ἀλλ᾽ ὁ παρακαλῶν τοὺς ταπεινοὺς παρεκάλεσεν ἡμᾶς ὁ θεός. ὁ παρακαλῶν τοὺς ταπεινούς is very likely a traditional predication, enclosed as it were in quotation marks. Paul chose it because it is true to say of God that παρεκάλεσεν ἡμᾶς (corresponding to 1:3f.). On the participial style of the predication, cf. what was said on 1:4.

As to content, cf. Isa. 49:13: καὶ τοὺς ταπεινοὺς τοῦ λαοῦ αὐτοῦ παρεκάλεσεν; Ps. 112:6: (ὁ θεὸς ἡμῶν ὁ . . .) καὶ τὰ ταπεινὰ ἐφορῶν, and Job 5:11: τὸν ποιοῦντα ταπεινοὺς εἰς ὕψος (ταπεινός is the equivalent of עָנִי).[34]

ἐν τῇ παρουσίᾳ Τίτου. The ἐν is instrumental. Here, then, the long awaited Titus finally met him from Corinth.

Verse 7: οὐ μόνον δὲ ἐν τῇ παρουσίᾳ, αὐτοῦ ἀλλὰ καὶ ἐν τῇ παρακλήσει ᾗ παρεκλήθη ἐφ᾽ ὑμῖν. The essential thing is not that Titus arrived, but rather that he came with comforting news. By means of this peculiar formula Paul, as it were, gives all the credit to the community which appears as actor,

---

[34] Not primarily "humble" but "inferior."

while Titus is passively involved. For Paul does not say, "by the comfort which he brought me from you," but "by the comfort which he received among you"[35] (Lietzmann, 131). This comfort with which Titus is, so to speak, laden or filled, now comes to Paul.

Now, how this actually took place is stated in what follows: ἀναγγέλλων ἡμῖν (the circumstantial participle is used instead of the finite verb) τὴν ὑμῶν ἐπιπόθησιν — the Corinthians' longing (the word appears again only in v. 11; cf. Aquila Ez. 23:11; Clem. Al. Strom IV, 21, 131; Damascius, de principiis, 38; in place of this term, Rom. 15:23 reads ἐπιποθία, a hapax legomenon).

τὸν ὑμῶν ὀδυρμόν describes the Corinthians' lament over the offense given to Paul, or their lament of remorse, cf. verses 9ff. τὸν ὑμῶν ζῆλον ὑπὲρ ἐμοῦ[36] denotes the Corinthians' zeal for Paul, that is, the attempt to rectify their error, as is then reported in verse 11, where ζῆλος occurs among a profusion of expressions to describe this zeal.

ἐπιπόθησις, ὀδυρμός and ζῆλος indicate a gradation from mood to act.

ὥστε με μᾶλλον χαρῆναι. Does the μᾶλλον mean "still more" (Bl.-D. para. 244, 2), not only about Titus' arrival, but also about the news he brought; not only about the ἐπιπόθησις and the ὀδυρμός of the Corinthians but also about their ζῆλος? Or does it mean "rather, on the contrary," that is, in contrast to the former λύπη?

b. The effect of the interim epistle: 7:8-13a

Verse 8: ὅτι εἰ καὶ ἐλύπησα ὑμᾶς ἐν τῇ ἐπιστολῇ, οὐ μεταμέλομαι. This phrase explains the ὥστε με μᾶλλον χαρῆναι in verse 7, which becomes fully intelligible only through what follows — I rejoiced, for the very fact that I grieved you earlier (and thus also myself had λύπη) has led to joy.

Naturally, the ἐπιστολή is that of 2:3f., 9, which Titus then obviously brought to Corinth. Despite 2:4, it was of course clear to Paul that it had to grieve the Corinthians, cf. pp. 46f. on 2:4. But since it had the desired result (since the λύπη according to v. 9 was a λύπη κατὰ θεόν) Paul does not regret it but rather rejoices over it.

The εἰ καὶ μετεμελόμην added to the οὐ μεταμέλομαι affords an understanding of Paul's restlessness, his φόβος (2:13 and 7:5). It could certainly grieve him to have written that letter, for he was not sure of the outcome. Had it actually hurt him? In any case he does not regret it now, but rather is glad.

βλέπω ὅτι ἡ ἐπιστολὴ ἐκείνη εἰ καὶ πρὸς ὥραν ἐλύπησεν ὑμᾶς. The general sense is clear; the construction is certainly not. It would be simplest to read a γάρ behind the following βλέπω together with ℵ C 𝕽 G pl it and sy.

---

[35] Does ἐφ' ὑμῖν mean concerning you, for your sake, or among you?
[36] ὑπὲρ ἐμοῦ is without the repeated article, cf. Bl.-D. para. 272.

The γάϱ is missing in B D* sa and Ambst. Then the εἰ καὶ μετεμελόμην may simply be a qualification attaching to the preceding οὐ μεταμέλομαι. (The γάϱ might have been omitted because it was supposed one had to connect εἰ καὶ μετεμελόμην with what follows.) Then, of course, we need assume no interruption of the clause, as does Lietzmann, 131: "I see that that letter, though it grieved you for a time (sc. it has had its salutary results)." Rather, ἐλύπησεν is not the predicate of the εἰ-clause, but of the ὅτι-clause, and the parenthesis is not πϱὸς ὥϱαν, but εἰ καὶ πϱὸς ὥϱαν. The meaning is thus, "for I see that that letter — though only for a while — grieved you." Then of course the asyndetic continuation νῦν χαίϱω is harsh.[37]

So it is probably better to take the βλέπω (without the γάϱ?) up to the ἐλύπησεν ὑμᾶς as a parenthesis, in which εἰ καὶ πϱὸς ὥϱαν is in turn a parenthesis: "Though it grieved me — I see (indeed) that the letter grieved you (though only for a while) — yet now I rejoice."[38]

πϱὸς ὥϱαν is used as in Gal. 2:5 [1 Thess. 2:17] and Philemon 15.

Verse 9: νῦν χαίϱω, οὐχ ὅτι ἐλυπήθητε. The νῦν χαίϱω refers to the report of Titus, and corresponds to the ὥστε μᾶλλον χαϱῆναι in verse 7.

οὐχ ὅτι ἐλυπήθητε. This phrase corresponds to the statement of 2:4 that Paul has not written from personal injury in order to grieve the Corinthians (cf. p. 47). The ἀλλ᾿ ὅτι ἐλυπήθητε εἰς μετάνοιαν corresponds to the positive ἵνα γνῶ τὴν δοκιμὴν ὑμῶν (2:9). (On μετάνοια cf. Windisch, 233f.). In Paul, μετάνοια occurs only here and in Rom. 2:4, and in that passage in the technical sense of Jewish and Christian mission preaching (corresponding to the Hebrew שוב for which the LXX most often has ἐπιστϱέφειν; Paul uses this term only in 3:16 in a quotation from Ex. 34:34, and in 1 Thess. 1:9 in the technical sense of "repentance"). Just as μετάνοια is used here of remorse within the Christian life, so also μετανοεῖν in 12:21. μετάνοια appears in Plutarch and other moralists. It was taken over by Jewish Hellenism,[39] but is most often avoided by Paul, possibly because it subjects the concept of πίστις to a moralistic misunderstanding.

The positive character of such a λύπη εἰς μετάνοιαν is explained by the **ἐλυπήθητε γὰϱ κατὰ θεόν.** The κατὰ θεόν does not mean effected by God, but rather corresponding to God's will;[40] cf. Gal. 1:4: κατὰ τὸ θέλημα τοῦ θεοῦ, and Rom. 8:27: κατὰ θεὸν ἐντυγχάνει ὑπὲϱ ἁγίων. Its counterpart would be κατὰ σάϱκα, which would be synonymous with λύπη τοῦ κόσμου (v. 10).

ἵνα ἐν μηδενὶ ζημιωθῆτε ἐξ ἡμῶν. ζημιοῦσθαι means to be injured,

---

[37] Lietzmann, 130, translates: "For though I grieved you in that letter, I do not regret it; (indeed) though I did regret it, I (nevertheless) see that that letter, though it grieved you for a time — now (however) I rejoice, not because you. . . ."
[38] vg and P⁴⁶ facilitate the reading with a βλέπων (*videns*) instead of a βλέπω.
[39] Especially in Philo.
[40] Cf. Test. Gad 5:7 (cf. p. 56 on v. 10).

Paul's Boasting

cf. Phil. 3:8.[41] The ἵνα is probably intended as consecutive (thus also Lietzmann, 132), but since the result complies with the divine intention, it is also final (thus also Windisch, 231). The result, therefore, is that Paul's conduct has only led to the community's advantage.

Verse 10: If in verse 9 the λύπη εἰς μετάνοιαν was characterized as λύπη κατὰ θεόν, its positive sense is made still more clear in verse 10:

ἡ γὰρ κατὰ θεὸν λύπη μετάνοιαν εἰς σωτηρίαν ἀμεταμέλητον ἐργάζεται.

If the λύπη κατὰ θεόν produces μετάνοια, then this indicates the identity of λύπη εἰς μετάνοιαν and λύπη κατὰ θεόν. But μετάνοια is now given positive definition by the εἰς σωτηρίαν (sc. ἄγουσιν), σωτηρία of course construed in the unconditionally eschatological sense, just as θάνατος in the antithesis which follows.

As a result, λύπη as genuine sorrow does not have its meaning in itself as a mood. Its meaning lies in the fact that it brings one to a resolution, to μετάνοια which leads to σωτηρία. For this reason, this μετάνοια is characterized by an oxymoron, as ἀμεταμέλητος, as a remorse which one need not regret — precisely because it leads to σωτηρία.[42]

On the subject itself, cf. Test. Gad 5:7: ἡ γὰρ κατὰ Θεὸν ἀληθὴς μετάνοια [ἀναιρεῖ τὴν ἄγνοιαν καὶ] φυγαδεύει τὸ σκότος, καὶ φωτίζει τοὺς ὀφθαλμοὺς καὶ γνῶσιν παρέχει τῇ ψυχῇ, καὶ ὁδηγεῖ τὸ διαβούλιον πρὸς σωτηρίαν (Windisch, 232): "For true repentance after a godly sort [destroyeth ignorance, and] driveth away the darkness, and enlighteneth the eyes, and giveth knowledge to the soul, and leadeth the mind to salvation." (Charles, II, 341).

Cf. Philo Leg All III, 211f. where στεναγμός is distinguished in a twofold manner — from unjust desire or from moral regret. Cf. further Hierocl Carm Aur XIV (Mullach, p. 98): ἡ δὲ μετάνοια αὕτη φιλοσοφίας ἀρχὴ γίνεται, καὶ τῶν ἀνοήτων ἔργων τὲ καὶ λόγων φυγή, καὶ τῆς ἀμεταμελήτου ζωῆς ἡ πρώτη παρασκευή ("Now this repentance is the beginning of philosophy; the banishment both of senseless deeds and words, and the first step toward life without regret." R. A. H. cf. Windisch, 233).[43]

The idea is further accented by the antithesis — ἡ δὲ τοῦ κόσμου λύπη θάνατον κατεργάζεται. κόσμος, of course, is construed in the specifically Pauline sense of the godless or anti-godly world, so that the λύπη τοῦ κόσμου is identical to λύπη κατὰ σάρκα. If it leads to death (naturally, not to despair or suicide, but rather to unconditionally eschatological death; θάνατος is the end of sin, Rom. 6:16, 21, 23 and 7:5), that does not need

---

[41] Is ζημιωθῆναι a party cry and an allusion to a reproach from the community?

[42] But it is pointless to link ἀμεταμέλητος with σωτηρίαν, as does Schlatter in *Bote*, 587.

[43] In addition to the parallels in Windisch, 232, cf. Herm mand X 2:4: αὕτη οὖν ἡ λύπη (sc. ἡ μετάνοια) δοκεῖ σωτηρίαν ἔχειν, ὅτι τὸ πονηρὸν πράξας μετενόησεν. ("Therefore this grief seems to bring salvation, because he repented of having done wickedly.") A Christian addition? Cf. Spitta, *Urchristentum*, 2, 432.

especially to mean that it leads to taking personal offense, or to anger and hate, but merely that it is something purely negative, that it looks backward rather than forward.

Christian behavior is therefore not the suppression of the affective states, as though λύπη as πάθος were something evil in itself. For the Christian the issue is rather the intentionality of the πάθη, that is, the question of whereof and whither they lead. They are therefore understood from the perspective of the historicity of *Dasein* (for the Stoa, λύπη together with ἡδονή, ἐπιθυμία and φόβος belong to the πάθη).

Verse 11: This next verse indicates how the statement in verse 10 (genuine sorrow produces μετάνοια toward σωτηρία) has been verified in the present instance— **ἰδοὺ γὰρ αὐτὸ τοῦτο τὸ κατὰ θεὸν λυπηθῆναι πόσην κατειργάσατο ὑμῖν σπουδήν, ἀλλὰ ἀπολογίαν, ἀλλὰ ἀγανάκτησιν, ἀλλὰ φόβον, ἀλλὰ ἐπιπόθησιν, ἀλλὰ ζῆλον, ἀλλὰ ἐκδίκησιν.** Since according to verse 10 the λύπη κατὰ θεόν produces μετάνοια, the κατειργάσατο thus identifies the true μετάνοια. The description once more takes up the concepts ἐπιπόθησις and ζῆλος from verse 7 and adds σπουδή, ἀπολογία, ἀγανάκτησις, φόβος, and ἐκδίκησις, so that seven concepts are named. (Is the number seven intentional? Hardly.)

One concept is joined to the other by an ἀλλά, which has the force of heightening (sc. οὐ μόνον, cf. Bl.-D. para. 448, 6).

σπουδή[44] denotes zeal for settling the matter, for giving Paul satisfaction, or for reconciling him.

Regarding the term ἀπολογία or apology, it is of little consequence whether Paul means that the Corinthians indicate their zeal by apologizing as such, or by adducing good reasons for their apology.

ἀγανάκτησις denotes the indignation or irritation of the Corinthians, whether over the ἀδικήσας, or over their own earlier behavior.

φόβος is the fear of Paul's indignation, or of his breaking off relations with the community. The term φόβος makes clear that they have a bad conscience.

ἐπιπόθησις denotes the yearning (cf. on v. 7) or desire to be reconciled to Paul.

ζῆλος or zeal is scarcely distinguishable from σπουδή and means, at least in the more specialized sense of the term, to give Paul satisfaction so that ἐκδίκησις immediately results.

ἐκδίκησις is the equivalent of atonement or punishment of the ἀδικήσας (cf. ἐπιτιμία in 2:6). ἀπολογία and ἐκδίκησις are concepts from criminal law. Paul, therefore, does not conceive the relationship of the congregation to its apostle as personal, but as legal. This is indicated by the following

---

[44] Lietzmann, 132, defines it as "a good will;" Weizsäcker, *Neues Testament,* as "effort."

clause—ἐν παντὶ συνεστήσατε ἑαυτοὺς ἁγνοὺς εἶναι τῷ πράγματι⁴⁵—since ἁγνός (innocent) and πρᾶγμα (suit) are also legal terms.

Use of the accusative (ἁγνούς) with the infinitive (εἶναι) for the same subject is poor Greek. Classical Greek would read ὄντας (Bl.-D. para. 406, 1). Is εἶναι corrupted from ἐν, which 𝔎 and pl placed behind εἶναι? In any event the dative of relation, τῷ πράγματι, is also poor Greek, cf. Bl.-D. para. 197.

If Paul does not simply intend to say that as a result of its μετάνοια, its σπουδή, etc. the community is now innocent, then the sense must be that by the ἐκδίκησις meted out to the ἀδικήσας, the community has proved that it was innocent of that ἀδικία from the outset. But it was just this proof which was required as recognition of Paul's authority, and the community had first been prompted to it by his letter. Now the Corinthians had complied with it by taking a position against the ἀδικήσας, and only now has their σπουδή become clear. In this case also there was need of μετάνοια.

Verse 12: This, then, settles the matter for Paul. Again he emphasizes that he has not written from personal pique, but only to establish the right relationship to the community, to bring the community to the state of mind worthy of it and required of it. The verse corresponds to 2:9.

ἄρα εἰ καὶ ἔγραψα ὑμῖν. The reference is to the very letter cited in verse 8 and 2:3f., 9. **οὐχ ἕνεκεν τοῦ ἀδικήσαντος οὐδὲ ἕνεκεν τοῦ ἀδικηθέντος.** So the meaning is very clear — persons are not at issue in the entire affair. Naturally, the ἀδικήσας is the λυπήσας of 2:5, and the ἀδικηθείς is Paul, whom that one λελύπηκεν, according to 2:5.

What the ἀδικήσας actually did cannot be determined. Windisch, 237ff. wants to assume a suit analogous to 1 Cor. 6:1-11, in which Paul was only indirectly involved since the community had denied the very principle of 1 Cor. 6:1-11. But there is more reason for assuming a direct, personal offense against Paul, and the polemic of the interim epistle (the details which it must have contained concerning the ἀδικήσας are of course not preserved) certainly allows us to assume just that, cf. 10:12ff., 11:5f., 7ff., and 12:11ff.

Nothing can be gleaned from the usage of ἀδικεῖν. In general, it means to do someone an injustice, to injure someone;⁴⁶ in particular, it means through legal violation to injure someone respecting his rights or business (especially in monetary affairs; cf. Windisch, 238). It does not expressly mean "to offend," but the injustice attached to it may still be an offense. **ἀλλ' ἕνεκεν τοῦ φανερωθῆναι τὴν σπουδὴν ὑμῶν τὴν ὑπὲρ ἡμῶν πρὸς ὑμᾶς ἐνώπιον τοῦ θεοῦ.** The ἐνώπιον τοῦ θεοῦ perhaps belongs to the

⁴⁵ Lietzmann, 132, translates the συνεστήσατε ἑαυτούς, "you have given proof that you are clean. . . ." συνιστάναι as well may be a juridical term meaning to fix, corroborate, prove.
⁴⁶ Paul may have construed it after the terms ἄδικος, ἀδικία, as meaning "to do ill" (cf. 1 Cor. 6:7f., 9, and especially 6:1), "to injure."

φανερωθῆναι (Lietzmann, 133). Then it would be clear that the court to which the Corinthians are answerable is not the person of Paul but God, whose apostle he is. Of course, it is also possible that the ἐνώπιον τοῦ θεοῦ is meant to characterize the σπουδή, so that ἐνώπιον τοῦ θεοῦ would amount to κατὰ θεόν (cf. vv. 9-11). The meaning, then, is that since the Corinthians strive in the presence of God, earnestly and uprightly, they do so κατὰ θεόν. In this fashion, Paul's behavior is described in 4:2 as ἐνώπιον τοῦ θεοῦ, which then is synonymous with ἐν προσώπῳ Χριστοῦ in 2:10.

The σπουδή is described as ὑμῶν ὑπὲρ ἡμῶν. Of course, Ambrosiaster, Chrysostom, Theodoret, and others read ἡμῶν ὑπὲρ ὑμῶν. In that case, the statement would correspond with 2:4: ἔγραψα ὑμῖν . . . τὴν ἀγάπην ἵνα γνῶτε ἣν ἔχω περισσοτέρως εἰς ὑμᾶς. (The variants, ὑμῶν ὑπὲρ ὑμῶν in ℵ D* and F, and ἡμῶν ὑπὲρ ἡμῶν in G d* and g are not totally senseless, but the second especially is scarcely tolerable). But since verse 11 referred to the Corinthians' σπουδή (cf. also τὸν ὑμῶν ζῆλον ὑπὲρ ἐμοῦ in v. 7), and entirely on account of verse 13a — διὰ τοῦτο παρακεκλήμεθα — then ὑμῶν ὑπὲρ ἡμῶν must certainly be read, so that the verse corresponds to 2:9 (ἵνα γνῶ τὴν δοκιμὴν ὑμῶν). The variants will have arisen as a result of the πρὸς ὑμᾶς which can only mean "among you" (cf. 1 Thess. 3:4; Gal. 1:18; Matt. 13:56 and Bl.-D. para. 239, 1.2), and belongs with (φανερωθῆναι) τὴν σπουδήν.

Verse 13a: The **διὰ τοῦτο παρακεκλήμεθα** forms the conclusion, which closes the ring, cf. verses 6f.

c. The reception of Titus at Corinth: 7:13b-15

These verses form a new beginning after verses 5-7. They refer not only to the joy that the matter in dispute is disposed of, but also that a personal, friendly mood has been created. Together with the apostolic relationship the personal relationship has also been settled. The heightening in verses 13b-15 is expressed in the θαρρῶ of verse 16, over against the παρακεκλήμεθα of verse 13a.

Verse 13b: ἐπὶ δὲ τῇ παρακλήσει ἡμῶν. A special joy attaches to the παράκλησις which Titus' report brought. The first ἐπί or "at" has the sense of "besides," while the second, dependent on ἐχάρημεν, has the sense of "concerning."

περισσοτέρως μᾶλλον ἐχάρημεν. The περισσοτέρως is heightened by μᾶλλον (Bl.-D. para. 60, 3 and para. 246), or means "still much more," cf. Mark 7:36 and Phil. 1:23.

The **ἐχάρημεν ἐπὶ τῇ χαρᾷ Τίτου** is analogous to the παρεκάλεσεν ἡμᾶς ὁ θεὸς . . . ἐν τῇ παρακλήσει ᾗ παρεκλήθη ἐφ᾽ ὑμῖν (v. 6f.). Just as the comfort which Titus received is Paul's reason for comfort, so Titus' joy is the basis for Paul's.

ὅτι ἀναπέπαυται τὸ πνεῦμα αὐτοῦ ἀπὸ πάντων ὑμῶν. The ὅτι-clause is grammatically dependent upon the τῇ χαρᾷ Τίτου, and as to content is also the object of ἐχάρημεν.

As in 2:13, τὸ πνεῦμα is used of the person. The ἀναπαύειν τὸ πνεῦμα is used as in 1 Cor. 16:18 and Philemon 20. The phrase is from the LXX, cf. Str.-B. III, 486, and Nägeli, *Wortschatz*, 64f. The meaning is "he was refreshed." ἀπό is the equivalent of ὑπό, cf. Acts 4:36; 15:4 and Bl.-D. para. 210, 2.

Verse 14: ὅτι εἴ τι αὐτῷ ὑπὲρ ὑμῶν κεκαύχημαι, οὐ κατῃσχύνθην. The κεκαύχημαι refers to the time when Paul sent Titus (with the letter) to Corinth. Had Titus then not been in Corinth before, and did he not know the Corinthians? οὐ κατῃσχύνθην not only means "I did not need to be ashamed," but also "I was not ruined." The Old Testament καταισχυνθῆναι (נִכְלַם) contains the thought that the one concerned must rightly be ashamed.

ἀλλ᾽ ὡς πάντα ἐν ἀληθείᾳ ἐλαλήσαμεν ὑμῖν. This remark, in itself without any motivation, evidently derives from suspicion regarding Paul's truthfulness, cf. 1:13f., 15ff.

οὕτως καὶ ἡ καύχησις ἡμῶν ἐπὶ Τίτου (D G P al lat sy read πρὸς T.) The force of the ἀληθείᾳ ἐγενήθη is that the καύχησις presented itself as truth, as a true word, and thus, as it were, first became truth.

Verse 15: καὶ τὰ σπλάγχνα αὐτοῦ περισσοτέρως εἰς ὑμᾶς ἐστιν ἀναμιμνησκομένου τὴν πάντων ὑμῶν ὑπακοήν. Just as in 6:12 etc., τὰ σπλάγχνα means "heart." The usage is also Greek, and in the LXX translates רַחֲמִים. The meaning of περισσοτέρως εἰς ὑμᾶς ἐστιν is "all the more (quite especially) devoted (inclined) toward you," cf. εἶναι εἰς in 1 Cor. 8:6 and Rom. 11:36. The force of the ἀναμιμνησκομένου τὴν πάντων ὑμῶν ὑπακοήν is that Paul can require the ὑπακοή described in the ὡς μετὰ φόβου καὶ τρόμου ἐδέξασθε αὐτόν, because he is an apostle and represents the authority of God; cf. 2:9, p. 55.

μετὰ φόβου καὶ τρόμου is used in accordance with Isa. 19:16, etc. just as in 1 Cor. 2:3; Phil. 2:12 and Eph. 6:5

d. Paul's confidence: 7:16

Verse 16. χαίρω is used as in verses 4, 7, 9, and 13. The stage of grief is thus passed, and when Paul comes to Corinth again the visit can be ἐν χαρᾷ, cf. 2:1-3.

ὅτι ἐν παντὶ θαρρῶ ἐν ὑμῖν. The ἐν ὑμῖν is the equivalent of εἰς ὑμᾶς in 10:1. Paul can be confident, and now not only because of his apostolic παρρησία (5:6,8), but because of the community's behavior. The desired effect of his letter has been realized.

Chapter 2

The Apostolic Office

[Letter C] 2:14–7:4

1. Paul's παρρησία: 2:14—4:6.
   a. The apostle's ἱκανότης: 2:14—3:6.
      The ἱκανότης theme: 2:14-17.[1]
      Paul's work proves he is a διάκονος χριστοῦ: 3:1-3.
      His office proves he is a διάκονος of the καινὴ διαθήκη: 3:4-6.
   b. From this διακονία results παρρησία: 3:7-18.
      The διακονία of the καινὴ διαθήκη as a διακονία of πνεῦμα and ζωή: 3:7-11.
      The καινὴ διακονία is accordingly one of παρρησία, or ἐλευθερία: 3:12-18.
   c. Actualizing παρρησία in apostolic activity: 4:1-6.
      διακονία establishes openness (εἰλικρίνεια and πεποίθησις in 2:17 and 3:1, cf. 1:12-14, 15): 4:1-2.
      It establishes accessibility (thus 2:14-16 is made intelligible—the apostle's activity is the φανέρωσις of γνῶσις, 2:14 and 4:6, or of ἀλήθεια, 4:2, and of course in a peculiar duality, 2:15f. and 4:3f.): 4:3-6.
2. ζωή (δόξα) as hidden and revealed: 4:7—6:10.
3. The plea for trust: 6:11—7:4 [6:14—7:1].

1. Paul's παρρησία: 2:14—4:6

a. The apostle's ἱκανότης: 2:14—3:6

But thanks be to God, who in Christ always leads us in triumph, and

---

[1] Grounding the apostle's πεποίθησις in the apostolic task, and in the εἰλικρίνεια which conforms to it.

through us spreads the fragrance of the knowledge of him everywhere. For we are the aroma of Christ to God among those who are being saved and among those who are perishing, to one a fragrance from death to death, to the other a fragrance from life to life. Who is sufficient for these things? For we are not, like so many, peddlers of God's word; but as men of sincerity, as commissioned by God, in the sight of God we speak in Christ. Are we beginning to commend ourselves again? Or do we need, as some do, letters of recommendation to you, or from you? You yourselves are our letter of recommendation, written on your hearts, to be known and read by all men; and you show that you are a letter from Christ delivered by us, written not with ink but with the Spirit of the living God, not on tablets of stone but on tablets of human hearts. Such is the confidence that we have through Christ toward God. Not that we are competent of ourselves to claim anything as coming from us; our competence is from God, who has made us competent to be ministers of a new covenant, not in a written code but in the Spirit; for the written code kills, but the Spirit gives life.

The ἱκανότης theme: 2:14-17

Verse 14: τῷ δὲ θεῷ χάρις. The expression is similar to that in 8:16, 1 Cor. 15:57, and Rom. 7:25. Usually it refers to what directly precedes, by introducing a contrast or a new element organically attached to what precedes (8:16). Here there is no such reference. The context is lost. The redactor, who inserted the piece, took from verses 12f. only the idea of Paul on a missionary journey, although in verses 12f. this idea is merely the foil for Paul's tension and yearning. In any case 2:14-17 expresses what Paul calls his πεποίθησις in 3:4, and thus formulates the theme in what follows.

The expression is liturgical, and just as in 8:16 and 1 Cor. 15:57 a τῷ διδόντι is attached, so here a τῷ . . . θριαμβεύοντι . . . καὶ . . . φανεροῦντι. . . .

τῷ πάντοτε θριαμβεύοντι ἡμᾶς ἐν τῷ Χριστῷ. It is clear that the θριαμβεύειν, analogous to φανεροῦν, indicates that God allows Paul to work as his apostle. The exact meaning is not certain.

Apart from the intransitive "to triumph," the first meaning of θριαμβεύειν (according to Windisch, 96f.) is to allow to triumph. Though not documented as such, it may derive from θρίαμβος (cf. the Hymn to Dionysus, hence "triumph"), or θριαμβευτής (the one who celebrates a triumph) after the analogy of μαθητεύειν, which can also change from the intransitive to the causative, cf. Bl.-D. para. 148, 3; 309, 1.2). The second meaning of the term is "to lead in triumphal procession" (as vanquished or prisoners) as in Plutarch. From this derives the more general meaning "to conquer," cf. Col. 2:15: (God) ἀπεκδυσάμενος τὰς ἀρχὰς καὶ τὰς ἐξουσίας ἐδειγμάτισεν ἐν παρρησίᾳ, θριαμβεύσας αὐτοὺς ἐν αὐτῷ. The third meaning is "to lead (an apprehended criminal) about in the streets." This use is attested late, cf.

Lietzmann, 108. In the diminished sense it means "to expose someone to scorn" (Gregory of Nyssa and others), or "to shame" (Windisch, 97, L.-S.). The fourth meaning is "to conduct publicly," "to send hither and yon," or "to make publicly known," cf. Lietzmann, 108; Windisch, 97, and L.-S.

The first definition would somewhat suit the context, the second is not impossible, the third is out of the question. But perhaps the fourth suffices, to which Lietzmann and Windisch (the latter offers the second and fourth definitions as options) incline. Gulin, *Freude* I, 257, 2 opts for the second definition and wants to construe verse 14 as Colossians 2:15 — Paul regards himself as the one defeated (the enemy) of God, who now is forced (cf. the ἀνάγκη of 1 Cor. 9:16) to stride before Christ's triumphal car, in order to magnify the victory of his Lord. "Here he praises God's rule which can convert even apparent defeats into victories, and weaknesses into triumph" (Gulin, *op. cit.*, p. 258).[2]

Paul writes ἐν τῷ Χριστῷ, since he belongs to Christ, or since his activity occurs within the sphere of Christ, that is, within the area of the history determined by Christ, within the new world (cf. 5:17). The ἐν Χριστῷ in verse 17 is used in the same way (cf. p. 70).

καὶ τὴν ὀσμὴν τῆς γνώσεως αὐτοῦ φανεροῦντι δι᾽ ἡμῶν ἐν παντὶ τόπῳ.[3] φανεροῦν is used of God's action in Christ in Rom. 3:21 (the object is the δικαιοσύνη θεοῦ), in 16:25 (the object is the μυστήριον), and in Col. 1:26 (the object is the μυστήριον). It occurs in the eschatological sense in 1 Cor. 4:5 (τὰς βουλὰς τῶν καρδιῶν), and in Col. 3:4 (ὁ Χριστός). It is used of missionary preaching in Col. 4:3 (αὐτὸ sc. τὸ μυστήριον), and Titus 1:3 (τὸν λόγον αὐτοῦ ἐν κηρύγματι).

The three meanings together form a unity — God's action in Christ is an eschatological event which continues to occur in the preaching. One meaning dominates depending upon the context. What is meant here is the φανεροῦν through the preaching, which, however, as verse 15 indicates, is an eschatological event.

In any event, the τὴν ὀσμὴν τῆς γνώσεως denotes the knowledge of God spread abroad by the preaching of the gospel. It is the γνῶσις τῆς δόξης τοῦ θεοῦ ἐν προσώπῳ Χριστοῦ in 4:6. But while γνῶσις is set forth under the figure of light in 4:6, here it is under the figure of aroma. In the context,

---

[2] Kümmel, p. 198, thinks the fourth definition is too bland and prefers the second, but in such a way that the factor of being conquered is omitted. Schlatter's translation in *Bote,* 495, is improbable, to the effect that Paul describes himself as conquered by God. Liechtenhan's interpretation in *Mission,* 66, is impossible, to the effect that "Paul confesses here that he ran from God by his departure for Macedonia, but that God conquered him again, so that now he marches along in God's triumphal procession as a vanquished enemy" (cited according to Kümmel, 198). If the first meaning of θριαμβεύοντι should be intended, then the ἐν could also be construed instrumentally, but scarcely in connection with the second and fourth meaning.

[3] φανεροῦν means "to show (itself)" without thought for whether anyone sees it, "to make visible."

this figure can hardly be linked to θριαμβεύειν (to lead as in a triumphal procession), as though Paul had in mind the incense which, for example, Appian in his Rom. Hist. Pun. 66 (Mendelsohn, I, p. 205f.) mentions at the triumph of Scipio Africanus minor. And, he scarcely has in mind the aroma which streams over him as sacrifice,[4] though in Phil. 4:18 he describes the gift of the Philippian community as an ὀσμὴν εὐωδίας, a θυσίαν δεκτήν.[5] Gulin, of course, in *Freude* I, 258f., 2, writes that Paul, in his work for Christ, is offered as a sacrifice to God (cf. Phil. 2:17). But here the ὀσμή is certainly not the aroma of sacrifice which rises to God. According to verse 15, the aroma applies to persons.[6]

The expression rather rests on the ancient idea[7] that fragrance is a sign of the divine presence and the divine life[8] (cf. Wettstein, N.T.G. II, 181, and Lohmeyer, *Wohlgeruch,* 32ff.). Cf. for example, Eur. Hipp. 1392. When Artemis appears to him at his death, Hippolytus says: ὦ θεῖον ὀσμῆς πνεῦμα; "O divine spirit of fragrance" (R.A.H.).

Cf. Plutarch's Isis et Osiris 15. On her search for Osiris, Isis comes to Byblos and there sits down by a spring. She has spoken with no one there τῆς δὲ βασιλίδος τὰς θεραπαινίδας ἀσπάζεσθαι καὶ φιλοφρονεῖσθαι τήν τε κόμην παραπλέκουσαν αὐτῶν καὶ τῷ χρωτὶ θαυμαστὴν εὐωδίαν ἐπιπνέουσαν ἀφ' ἑαυτῆς. ἰδούσης δὲ τῆς βασιλίδος τὰς θεραπαινίδας ἵμερον ἐμπεσεῖν τῆς ξένης τῶν τε τριχῶν (πλοκῆς ἕνεκα) τοῦ τε χρωτὸς ἀμβροσίαν πνέοντος. The queen orders Isis fetched and makes her the nurse of her little boy. ("Save only that she welcomed the queen's maidservants and treated them with great amiability, plaiting their hair for them and imparting to their persons a wondrous fragrance from her own body. But when the queen observed her maidservants, a longing came upon her for the unknown woman and for such hairdressing and for a body fragrant with ambrosia." Plutarch, Moral Essays, V, 41.)

The Rabbinic passages in Str.-B. III, 497, are scarcely true parallels. They refer to the fragrance of the pious (רֵיחַ of Abraham, the three men in the fiery furnace, and of Daniel) which ascends or spreads like the fragrance of apples, or of the merit of the righteous, as sweet to God as the scent of balsam (כְּרֵיחַ בַּלְסָמוֹן).[9] The passages from Sirach are more appropriate.[10] Sir. 24:12-15 (wisdom is speaking):

---

[4] The notion is impossible, for according to v. 15 it is a Χριστοῦ εὐωδία.
[5] Cf. Eph. 5:2: Χριστὸς . . . παρέδωκεν ἑαυτὸν ὑπὲρ ἡμῶν προσφορὰν καὶ θυσίαν τῷ θεῷ εἰς ὀσμὴν εὐωδίας.
[6] Dupont, *Gnosis,* 41, also interprets from out of Old Testament sacrificial terminology (ὀσμὴ εὐωδίας in Gen. 8:21, etc.), but not as though Paul were the sacrifice. Rather, the γνῶσις (Χριστοῦ) is compared with the aroma of sacrifice.
[7] Cf. Ign. Eph. 17:1, and Bauer on that passage.
[8] Accordingly, the devil stinks.
[9] Cf. Knox, *St. Paul,* 129f.
[10] Cf. Harder, *Gebet,* 103f.

So I took root in an honored people,
in the portion of the Lord, who
is their inheritance.
I grew tall like a cedar in Lebanon,
and like a cypress on the heights
of Hermon.
I grew tall like a palm tree in
Engedi,
and like rose plants in Jericho;
like a beautiful olive tree in the
field,
and like a plane tree I grew tall.
Like cassia and camel's thorn I
gave forth the aroma of spices (LXX: δέδωκα ὀσμήν)
and like choice myrrh I spread (LXX: διέδωκα εὐωδίαν)
a pleasant odor,
like galbanum, onycha, and stacte,
and like the fragrance of frankincense in the tabernacle.

Sir. 39:13f.:
Listen to me, O you holy sons,
and bud like a rose growing by
a stream of water;
send forth fragrance like (LXX: ὡς λίβανος εὐωδιάσατε ὀσμήν)
frankincense,
and put forth blossoms like a lily.
Scatter the fragrance, and sing a
hymn of praise;
bless the Lord for all his works.

In Ethiopic Enoch 24, Enoch sees on the seventh mountain an extraordinarily sweet smelling tree whose fruit (according to 25) will some day give life to the elect.

Syr. Baruch 67:6 reads: "And the vapour of the smoke of the incense of the righteousness which is by the law is extinguished in Zion."

Gnosticism offers true parallels:

In Hippolytus, *Refutatio* V 19, 3, the πνεῦμα of the Sethians (in midst of φῶς and σκότος) is not ὡς ἀνέμου ῥιπὴ ἢ λεπτή τις αὔρα νοηθῆναι δυναμένη, but οἱονεὶ μύρου τις ὀσμὴ ἢ θυμιάματος ἐκ συνθέσεως κατεσκευασμένου λεπτὴ διοδεύουσα δύναμις ἀνεπινοήτῳ τινὶ καὶ κρείττονι ἢ λόγῳ ἔστιν ἐξειπεῖν εὐωδία; ". . . as a current of wind, or some gentle breeze that can be felt; but, as it were, some odour of ointment or of incense formed out of a compound. (It is) a subtle power, that insinuates itself by means of some impulsive quality in a fragrance, which is inconceivable and better than could be expressed by words." The Ante-Nicene Fathers, V, 65.

In VII 22, 14f., the "second sonship" of Basilides at its ascension leaves the πνεῦμα in the midst. The πνεῦμα retains in itself the fragrance of sonship (ἔχει δὲ ἐν ἑαυτῷ μύρου παραπλησίως τὴν δύναμιν [τῆς υἱότητος τὴν] ὀσμήν; ". . . and has in itself, similarly with ointment, its own power, a savour of Sonship." The Ante-Nicene Fathers, V, 105). Psalm 132:2 (LXX) is then interpreted in this fashion (the oil from the head which flows down on Aaron's beard).

Irenaeus, Haereses I, 21, 3 (the Migne enumeration, but in Harvey I, 14, 2; Vol. I, p. 185 — the Sacrament of the Marcosians) writes: ἔπειτα μυρίζουσι τὸν τετελεσμένον τῷ ὀπῷ τῷ ἀπὸ [τοῦ] βαλσάμου. τὸ γὰρ μύρον τοῦτο τύπον τῆς ὑπὲρ τὰ ὅλα εὐωδίας εἶναι λέγουσιν. ("After this they anoint the initiated person with balsam; for they assert that this unguent is a type of that sweet odour which is above all things." The Ante-Nicene Fathers, I, 346.)

The Ginza, pp. 58, 23ff. reads:

I am the one sent of light;
> Everyone who smells its fragrance, receives life. . . .

The adulterers scented me,
> then they quickly abandoned their adultery.

Their adultery they quickly abandoned,
> came and surrounded themselves with my aroma.

They said:
> When we were without knowledge (γνῶσις), we committed adultery;

now that we have knowledge, we no longer commit adultery.
> (Then the same is said of liars, murderers, magicians and others.)

From the Mandaean Liturgies II, XXX, 1ff. (p. 199):

The fragrance came from its place,
> the truth came from its site,

the fragrance came from its place,
> He came and descended on the house.

He calls and livens the dead,
> He rouses and brings forth those lying there.

He wakens the souls,
> who are zealous and worthy of the place of light.

This, this did the one who is good
> and raised up the sign of life.

The πάντοτε in the first part and the ἐν παντὶ τόπῳ in the second part of verse 14 correspond to the liturgical-hymnal character of the verse and indicate the apostle's self-consciousness.

Verse 15: ὅτι Χριστοῦ εὐωδία ἐσμὲν τῷ θεῷ. In the causal clauses of verses 15f. the figure alternates. In verse 14 the gospel was the fragrance, while in verses 15f. it is the apostle himself who is thus identical with the λόγος τοῦ θεοῦ which he proclaims (v. 17). This is not the self-consciousness of the pneumatic but is based upon the fact that God's Word is not a universal truth, an idea, but rather the spoken, accosting Word which as such does not exist without its bearer. As the Word, so the apostle himself belongs to the eschatological saving event described in verse 16. (In 6:1 the συνεργεῖν [τῷ θεῷ] expresses the idea that the apostle himself belongs to the revelation.)

Weiss wants to strike the τῷ θεῷ (*Aufgaben,* 32). It would be in the way if it had to be specially linked to εὐωδία, after the analogy of the ὀσμή (or εἰς ὀσμήν) εὐωδίας τῷ κυρίῳ (= for God) frequent in the LXX; cf. Eph. 5:2; p. 64, n. 5. Then Paul would be construed as the offering whose fragrance ascends to God, cf. pp. 63f. But the offering motif suits neither the figure of the θριαμβεύειν nor, above all, the context, since the εὐωδία is certainly not supposed to benefit God, but rather humans (cf. v. 14: ὀσμὴ τῆς γνώσεως αὐτοῦ, and vv. 15-16). For this reason they are also Χριστοῦ εὐωδία! If the τῷ θεῷ is original, then it can only mean "to God's glory" (or, "in God's service").

ἐν τοῖς σῳζομένοις καὶ ἐν τοῖς ἀπολλυμένοις. This clause alludes to the dual effect of the proclamation, which at first sight is not intelligible but rather obscure, since it cannot be seen to what extent the apostle should be an εὐωδία for the ἀπολλύμενοι. But verse 16 carries the motif further.

Verse 16: οἷς μὲν ὀσμὴ ἐκ θανάτου εἰς θάνατον, οἷς δὲ ὀσμὴ ἐκ ζωῆς εἰς ζωήν. The two ἐκ's are lacking in the Western tradition and in ℜ. This simplifies the thought, but scarcely correctly, since Paul loves to play rhetorically with prepositions. The ἐκ — εἰς is intended merely to describe the radical effect of the ὀσμή, or in any event its gradual effect (Lietzmann, 109). Cf. Rom. 1:17: δικαιοσύνη γὰρ θεοῦ ἐν αὐτῷ ἀποκαλύπτεται ἐκ πίστεως εἰς πίστιν; 2 Cor. 3:18: μεταμορφούμεθα ἀπὸ δόξης εἰς δόξαν, and 2 Cor. 4:17: τὸ γὰρ παραυτίκα ἐλαφρὸν τῆς θλίψεως καθ' ὑπερβολὴν εἰς ὑπερβολὴν αἰώνιον βάρος δόξης κατεργάζεται ἡμῖν. Cf. also Ps. 83:8: πορεύσονται ἐκ δυνάμεως εἰς δύναμιν, and Jer. 9:3: ἐκ κακῶν εἰς κακὰ ἐξήλθοσαν. (Cf. Jülicher, *Einleitung,* 102, on Rom. 1:17: "Faith (is) the beginning . . . and the end.") The ἐκ then is hardly to be explained from the idea of predestination,[11] though it is already lurking in the τοῖς ἀπολλυμένοις. The meaning then would be, "for those who come forth from death (or life) and 'have fallen prey' to it 'each in his own way' (Bousset, Schriften N.T. 180)."[12]

Clearly, Paul is thinking only of the actual effect of the proclamation, without reflecting psychologically or physiologically on the dual effect of

---

[11] And, as regards the ἐκ θανάτου and the ἐκ ζωῆς, reference to Christ's death and resurrection is out of the question.

[12] For it is certainly the ὀσμή which is described, not the hearers.

the fragrance, or on the peculiarity of the fragrance of death. Thus the ὀσμὴ ἐκ θανάτου is hardly the smell of a corpse, of decomposition, or of a plague. And the amply attested notion that a fragrance which in itself is salutary under certain conditions has a ruinous effect (Windisch, 98, with examples from Aristotle) is scarcely present here. ὀσμή is a paled figure for "effect," as then the ἀπολλύμενοι are described as blinded in 4:3f.

A similar figure appears in Rabbinic literature (Str.-B. III, 498f.) where the dual effect of the Torah is compared to the dual effect of סם (Aramaic: סמא), that is, of balsam or other medicine (for example, "since he busies himself with the Torah for its own sake, it becomes a medicine of life . . . but for every one who does not busy himself with the Torah for its own sake, it becomes a medicine of death").[13]

The idea appears without the figure in Philo Mut Nom 202: τῶν δὲ θείων δογμάτων οἱ μὲν ἀκούουσιν ἐπ' ὠφελείᾳ, οἱ δ' ἐπὶ βλάπῃ αὐτῶν τὲ καὶ ἑτέρων. (". . . but the divine truths are heard by some to their profit, by some to the harm of themselves and others.")

The dual effect of the gospel is described in 1 Cor. 1:18: ὁ λόγος γὰρ ὁ τοῦ σταυροῦ τοῖς μὲν ἀπολλυμένοις μωρία ἐστιν, τοῖς δὲ σῳζομένοις ἡμῖν δύναμις θεοῦ ἐστιν. Cf. Phil. 1:28: For the ἀντικείμενοι, the Christian's courage is an ἔνδειξις ἀπωλείας, ὑμῶν δὲ σωτηρίας. 1 Peter 2:7 describes the dual effect of the stone laid by God in Zion.

The gospel is thus not equivocal, and hearing spells decision (cf. 4:2f.). In the separation which it brings about between the σῳζόμενοι and the ἀπολλύμενοι there occurs the eschatological event, the judgment.

Käsemann, *Leib,* 181f., correctly states that the administration of the sacrament and the charismatic preaching supplement one another. In Baptism, sinful worldliness is sacramentally destroyed, and on this basis the charismatic preaching again and again destroys seductive worldliness and confirms the sacramental existence of the baptized. "The preaching is effective, because the sacrament has been effective. For primitive Christianity, the sacrament is not the *verbum visibile.* Conversely, one might say that for Paul the preaching is the *sacramentum audibile.* As preacher the apostle is 'liturgist,' who dispenses God's salvation in priestly fashion and brings the world as sacrifice to God. (Rom. 15:16: εἰς τὸ εἶναί με λειτουργὸν Χριστοῦ Ἰησοῦ εἰς τὰ ἔθνη, ἱερουργοῦντα τὸ εὐαγγέλιον τοῦ θεοῦ, ἵνα γένηται ἡ προσφορὰ τῶν ἐθνῶν εὐπρόσδεκτος, ἡγιασμένη ἐν πνεύματι ἁγίῳ.) As such he is Χριστοῦ εὐωδία for life or death, a representative of the divine triumphal march through all the world."

This is surely an exaggeration. It is true, of course, that the preaching has sacramental character, that it is not a lecture concerning a universal

---

[13] In addition cf. Kümmel, 198, who correctly states that the Rabbinic passages all speak of medicine, not of fragrance.

truth, but rather an event. But this event is not grounded in the sacrament of Baptism, which really cannot apply to missionary preaching. Rather, preaching and sacrament are alike grounded in the saving event. On this basis, preaching and sacrament are effective. Thus the preaching can indeed be described as *sacramentum audibile,* but the sacrament may also be described as *verbum visibile.*

On the basis of the hymnic description of the apostle's activity the question now is: καὶ πρὸς ταῦτα τίς ἱκανός? Windisch, 99f. is surprised at this suddenly posed question. Since to this point the reference was not only to the office, but also to Paul, the bearer of the office, we would perhaps expect the question "Who belongs to us?" But there was no reference at all to the bearer as a man with human qualities! The question certainly means, "Who can be such a bearer of the Word, or how can I be such a bearer?" Thus the answer in verse 17 (which again of course surprises Windisch) which does not enumerate the qualities required but is rather a confession. But the question is clearly occasioned by the fact that at Corinth Paul's ἱκανότης was contested, as 3:1ff. and particularly 3:5f. indicate, and, of course, as the polemic in verse 17 already shows.

Verse 17: This verse answers the question, since Paul is speaking of himself. First, the answer is given in the negative: οὐ γάρ ἐσμεν ὡς οἱ πολλοὶ καπηλεύοντες τὸν λόγον τοῦ θεοῦ. The λόγος τοῦ θεοῦ is the gospel, the preaching, which spreads the ὀσμὴ τῆς γνώσεως (v. 14). On ὁ λόγος τοῦ θεοῦ cf. 1 Cor. 14:36; 1 Thess. 2:13; Acts 4:29, etc.

καπηλεύειν means to be a κάπηλος (small dealer). Occurring in the Greek since Plato (in polemic against sophistry) the term was current in the figurative sense for hawking spiritual goods, for "dealing in," that is, teaching philosophy, offering spiritual goods, etc. for the sake of material gain and not for the essential reasons (cf. Wettstein, N.T.G. II, 183, and Windisch, 100).

The καπηλεύειν τὸν λόγον τοῦ θεοῦ, therefore, does not mean to falsify the preaching[14] (Luther) but to make capital from it. And, it does not mean to offer through advertising, to make palatable (Barth-Thurneysen, *Come Holy Spirit,* 219), however much this idea may be linked to it. It is, therefore, a selfish activity which would be ἐν σοφίᾳ σαρκικῇ ἀναστρέφεσθαι (1:12; on the whole, 2:17 is essentially parallel to 1:12).

Thus, the less the community can call the apostle to account, since he is not answerable to it but rather to God, the more he himself is κατέναντι θεοῦ obliged to a personal behavior which conforms to the Word. The principle put positively reads: ἀλλ' ὡς ἐξ εἰλικρινείας. εἰλικρίνεια is used here as in 1:12, and the ὡς is not comparative, but causal. Accordingly, the meaning is "as such who acts ἐξ εἰλικρινείας."

---

[14] Thus indeed the δολοῦν τὸν λόγον in 4:2.

70   *The Apostolic Office*

The εἰλικρίνεια is described thusly: ἀλλ᾽ ὡς ἐκ θεοῦ κατέναντι θεοῦ ἐν Χριστῷ λαλοῦμεν. The ἐκ θεοῦ denotes the preaching or the apostle's task as derived from God. The κατέναντι θεοῦ denotes the apostle as speaking before God's eyes, answerable to God, cf. 4:2: ἐνώπιον τοῦ θεοῦ, and 12:19: κατέναντι θεοῦ ἐν Χριστῷ λαλοῦμεν. The ἐν Χριστῷ is used in a locative sense, as in verse 14 (p. 63) and denotes a new creature belonging to the new world of Christ.

Verse 17 is joined to verse 16 by a γάρ, which allows us to infer an ἐγώ. The answer to the question in verse 16 (τίς ἱκανός) thus reads "I am!" At the same time it indirectly refers to whomever selflessly proclaims the Word. May Paul say this of himself? As he is aware (3:1), his opponents will immediately accuse him of συνιστάνειν ἑαυτόν. Why is that not so, and why has Paul the right to speak thus?

3:1—4:6 as a whole gives the answer. In particular, the answer is given first of all in 3:1-6. Paul's answer of course is that 1) his work (that is, God's activity through him, 3:1-3), and 2) his office (that is, God's activity toward him, 3:4-6) give him the right.

Paul's ἱκανότης is thus not a qualification to be demonstrated before assuming office, the proof of the fulfillment of various conditions. It is not to be established outside of and alongside his apostolic activity. The one who is ἱκανός is called, and through the calling becomes ἱκανός.

Basically, only 3:4-6 gives the answer to 2:16f. 3:1-3 is really a digression, occasioned by the thought of the opponents' censure, and, of course, contains an indirect reply.

Paul's work proves he is a διάκονος Χριστοῦ: *3:1-3*

2:14-17 had provocatively expressed the apostle's proud self-consciousness[15] — his πεποίθησις, as 3:4 states. Naturally, Paul must have in mind his opponents' reproach, and just as the reproach of καύχησις was repudiated in 1:12-14 following verse 11, so here the reproach of συνιστάνειν ἑαυτόν.

Verse 1: ἀρχόμεθα πάλιν ἑαυτοὺς συνιστάνειν. The πάλιν indicates that Paul is accustomed to hearing such a reproach, cf. 4:2; 5:12; 10:12; and 18, where the slogan συνιστάνειν recurs.

The rhetorical question naturally intends to expose the reproach as unjustified, but the second question allows it to appear in a certain sense correct! For when Paul further asks ἢ μὴ χρῄζομεν ὥς τινες συστατικῶν ἐπιστολῶν, then he certainly intends to say that he has no need of letters of recommendation from the other side, since he can recommend himself — as indeed is stated in verses 2f. and cf. 4:2! On συστατικὴ ἐπιστολή (a technical term for a letter of recommendation) cf. Lietzmann, 110, and

---

[15] Cf. Knox, *St. Paul*, 129ff.

Windisch, 103. Naturally, Paul does not reject letters of recommendation as such (the accent is on the χρῄζομεν). He himself writes them under certain circumstances (Rom. 16:1ff. and Philemon).

By inserting the ὥς τινες, Paul attacks his opponents, who need letters of recommendation for their activity. The πρὸς ὑμᾶς indicates that missionaries from elsewhere have come to Corinth, "certain people" who work against Paul. From whence they have letters of recommendation cannot be known. Nothing points to Jerusalem (not even 11:22, Lietzmann, 110). The ἢ ἐξ ὑμῶν makes clear that these people allow themselves to be further recommended from Corinth.[16] That they are also people who recommend themselves is indicated in 10:12 and 18.[17]

Verse 2: Verses 2f. fix the meaning of verse 1. Of course, Paul needs no letters of recommendation. He recommends himself, not, however, through words but through his activity. ἡ ἐπιστολὴ ἡμῶν ὑμεῖς ἐστε — precisely the Corinthian community is his letter of recommendation!

ἐγγεγραμμένη ἐν ταῖς καρδίαις ἡμῶν, γινωσκομένη καὶ ἀναγινωσκομένη ὑπὸ πάντων ἀνθρώπων. According to Lietzmann, 110, assuming that ἡμῶν is to be read (instead of ὑμῶν in ℵ 33 pc), two figures are blended here: 1) "You are written on my heart;" and 2) "you are my letter of recommendation from Christ to all men." In the context, however, the first idea is without any motivation. A letter written on Paul's heart certainly cannot be regarded as a letter of recommendation. γινωσκομένη καὶ ἀναγινωσκομένη cannot be said of him, and the exegesis given in verse 3 (the φανερούμενοι ὅτι) does not suit.[18]

7:3 is no proof of the ἡμῶν (προείρηκα γὰρ ὅτι ἐν ταῖς καρδίαις ἡμῶν ἐστε εἰς τὸ συναποθανεῖν καὶ συζῆν), for the προείρηκα need not refer to 3:2, but to a written or oral utterance now lost. Only the ὑμῶν makes sense. When the Corinthians reflect on themselves, then they must recognize that they are Paul's work, and as such known far and wide — γινωσκομένη καὶ ἀναγινωσκομένη ὑπὸ πάντων ἀνθρώπων. (That they were Christians is as well known as it was of the Roman and Thessalonian community, 1 Thess. 1:8; Rom. 1:8).

Verse 3: φανερούμενοι ὅτι ἐστὲ ἐπιστολὴ Χριστοῦ διακονηθεῖσα ὑφ᾽ ἡμῶν. The clause is appended without syntactical connection, is loosely appended to the preceding ὑμεῖς, and gives the reason for the γινωσκομένη. On the notion of a letter written by a god to humans, cf. Ezekiel 2:9ff.;

---

[16] Would Jerusalem emissaries do this?

[17] "It lies in the nature of the case that (Paul) . . . can furnish no unequivocal proof, or proof visible to all, of his apostleship, but on his own must demand the authority he deserves" (Hanna Grothmann. The quotation could not be verified).

[18] Weiss, *Aufgaben*, 32, may be correct in wanting to omit the ἐγγεγραμμένη ἐν ταῖς καρδίαις ἡμῶν. If it is to be retained, then certainly it can only mean, since you are Christians. For the notion that they who are the letter are written in their own heart is absurd.

Revelation 2–3; Herm visio II, 1–2, and the Odes of Solomon 23; cf. also Stübe, *Himmelsbrief,* and Deissmann, *L.v.O.,* 321. With Paul, however, the mythological figure is hardly in force. The figure was evidently conceived by him on the spur.

The ἐπιστολή Χριστοῦ makes clear that Paul's work is basically not his own, but that of Christ (whose δοῦλος he is, according to 4:5), for which he merely assumes the role of διάκονος. Note the διακονηθεῖσα ὑφ᾽ ἡμῶν, which contains a slogan developed later in the text, cf. below. διακονηθεῖς denotes a placement (procurement) by virtue of office (or duty). Kümmel, 199, mistakenly wonders whether διακονηθεῖσα means written by Paul.

The character of the ἐπιστολή as a divine work is further described in two antitheses:

First of all, in the **ἐγγεγραμμένη οὐ μέλανι ἀλλὰ πνεύματι θεοῦ ζῶντος.** On θεὸς ζῶν cf. 1 Thess. 1:9 and 2 Cor. 6:16, etc. It is the אֵל חַי of the Old Testament-Jewish tradition. In this expression the πνεῦμα θεοῦ ζῶντος as the miraculously working power of God is contrasted with human letters of recommendation written in ink. How vastly superior to that of his rivals is Paul's letter of recommendation!

Second, the character of the ἐπιστολή is described in the **οὐκ ἐν πλαξὶν λιθίναις ἀλλ᾽ ἐν πλαξὶν καρδίαις σαρκίναις.** Paul's letter of recommendation is thus contrasted not only with human letters of recommendation, but also with the Old Testament law, and of course (as is indicated in what follows), because the apostle's activity which founded the community occurred in the service of the new covenant. This epistle thus proves that the apostle is a διάκονος καινῆς διαθήκης (v. 6). This is the leading idea, and not the notion that a genuine letter of recommendation can only be written on the hearts of living persons. The context might support a contrast between the hearts of living persons and human letters of recommendation (μέλανι), but then there would be no reason for the contrast with the πλάκες λίθιναι. So the καρδίαι σάρκιναι are not regarded as human and animate over against the inanimate, but rather as wakened to life over against the law of Moses.

The second antithesis is thus occasioned by the thought in verse 6 anticipated here, and takes its formulation from Old Testament passages;

Exod. 31:18: καὶ ἔδωκεν Μωυσεῖ . . . τὰς δύο πλάκας τοῦ μαρτυρίου, πλάκας λιθίνας γεγραμμένας τῷ δακτύλῳ τοῦ θεοῦ.

Jer. 38(31):33: ὅτι αὕτη ἡ διαθήκη, ἣν διαθήσομαι τῷ οἴκῳ Ἰσραηλ μετὰ τὰς ἡμέρας ἐκείνας, φησὶν κύριος·Διδοὺς δώσω νόμους μου εἰς τὴν διάνοιαν αὐτῶν καὶ ἐπὶ καρδίας αὐτῶν γράψω αὐτούς.

Ezek. 11:19: καὶ δώσω αὐτοῖς καρδίαν ἑτέραν καὶ πνεῦμα καινὸν δώσω ἐν αὐτοῖς καὶ ἐκσπάσω τὴν καρδίαν τὴν λιθίνην ἐκ τῆς σαρκὸς αὐτῶν καὶ δώσω αὐτοῖς καρδίαν σαρκίνην.

Ezek. 36:26: καὶ δώσω ὑμῖν καρδίαν καινὴν καὶ πνεῦμα καινὸν δώσω ἐν ὑμῖν καὶ ἀφελῶ τὴν καρδίαν τὴν λιθίνην ἐκ τῆς σαρκὸς ὑμῶν καὶ δώσω ὑμῖν καρδίαν σαρκίνην.

(Admonition to the pupil in Prov. 7:3:
  περίθου δὲ αὐτοὺς σοῖς δακτύλοις,
  ἐπίγραψον δὲ ἐπὶ τὸ πλάτος τῆς καρδίας σου).

With Paul, then, two ideas intertwine — the letters are not written on stone, but on hearts, and fleshly hearts are substituted for stony ones.

The Old Testament expression has its analogy in the Greek. Thucydides II 43, 2 writes of the fallen whose fame is their gravestone: ἀνδρῶν γὰρ ἐπιφανῶν πᾶσα γῆ τάφος, καὶ οὐ στηλῶν μόνον ἐν τῇ οἰκείᾳ σημαίνει ἐπιγραφή, ἀλλὰ καὶ ἐν τῇ μὴ προσηκούσῃ ἄγραφος μνήμη παρ᾽ ἑκάστῳ τῆς γνώμης μᾶλλον ἢ τοῦ ἔργου ἐνδιαιτᾶται. ("For the whole world is the sepulchre of famous men, and it is not the epitaph upon monuments set up in their own land that alone commemorates them, but also in lands not their own there abides in each breast an unwritten memorial of them, planted in the heart rather than graven on stone.")

Isocrates Areopagus 41 writes that one should οὐ τὰς στοὰς ἐμπιπλάναι γραμμάτων, ἀλλ᾽ ἐν ταῖς ψυχαῖς ἔχειν τὸ δίκαιον. (". . . not fill the stoas with inscriptions but have what is right in their hearts." [R.A.H.])

Plato Phaedrus 276 a.c. writes: Ὅς (λόγος sc.) μετ᾽ ἐπιστήμης γράφεται ἐν τῇ τοῦ μανθάνοντος ψυχῇ, δυνατὸς μὲν ἀμῦναι ἑαυτῷ, ἐπιστήμων δὲ λέγειν τε καὶ σιγᾶν πρὸς οὓς δεῖ. . . . ("The word which is written with intelligence in the mind of the learner, which is able to defend itself and knows to whom it should speak, and before whom to be silent.")

And again: Οὐκ ἄρα σπουδῇ αὐτὰ ἐν ὕδατι γράψει μέλανι σπείρων διὰ καλάμου μετὰ λόγων ἀδυνάτων μὲν αὐτοῖς λόγῳ βοηθεῖν, ἀδυνάτων δὲ ἱκανῶς τἀληθῆ διδάξαι. ("Then he will not, when in earnest, write them in ink, sowing them through a pen into words which cannot defend themselves by argument and cannot teach the truth effectually.")

Cf. Hirzel, Ἄγραφος Νόμος, 51:3, and Rudberg, ThStKr., 94, 1922, 179f., together with further parallels regarding the "inner script on tablets of the heart" in Greek literature.

Paul certainly is not thinking of letters and honorary decrees publicly displayed on marble tablets, but not because the οὐκ ἐν πλαξὶν λιθίναις is coordinated with the οὐ μέλανι (Lietzmann, 110). The parallel is only formal, and in regard to content, the second antithesis contains a new idea. The reason is rather that, as verses 6ff. indicate, Paul is thinking of the Old Testament tablets of the law which of course cannot be coordinated with μέλαν.

The text of the second antithesis is doubtful. The reading of most majuscules—ἐν πλαξὶν καρδίαις σαρκίναις, according to which καρδίαις σαρκίναις would be an appositive — is difficult to translate: "on tablets which are human hearts" (Lietzmann, 110).

The reading of Marcion F K Irenaeus and Origen — ἐν πλαξὶν καρδίας σαρκίναις — would be grammatically smoother, but to connect σαρκίναις with πλαξίν instead of with καρδίαις is scarcely possible. Bo sa vg pc read ἐν πλαξὶν καρδιῶν σαρκίναις ("which however gives no evidence of their exemplar, since they want to render the clause intelligible," Lietzmann, 111), which is no improvement. Among the conjectures is the omission of the καρδίαις (thus Weiss, *Aufgaben*, 32, and others) but hardly with justification, since ἐν πλαξὶν σαρκίναις is scarcely intelligible without an explanation. It would be best to omit the πλαξίν (with Lachmann and Holsten, cited in Windisch, 106, and others). Then the antithesis is simple and clear.

Verse 3, the formulation of which is already determined by verses 6ff., contains the key words in what follows: διακονηθεῖσα — διακονία or διάκονος in verses 6, 7ff.; πνεύματι — πνεῦμα in verses 6, 7ff. and ἐν πλαξὶν λιθίναις — ἐντετυπωμένη λίθοις in verse 7.

Conversely, the language of verses 6, 7ff. is not occasioned by verse 3, for the formulation of verse 3 is unclear, and the juxtaposition of antitheses is tortured. The second antithesis indicates that the idea of the διαθήκη (v. 6) is in mind. Verse 3 is thus determined by verses 6, 7ff. which means that Paul's letter of recommendation corresponds to the fact that he is the διάκονος καινῆς διαθήκης, a διαθήκη which is not of λίθος, but of the πνεῦμα.

His office proves he is a διάκονος *of the* καινὴ διαθήκη: *3:4-6.*

If 2:17 stated that Paul's ἱκανότης rests on his εἰλικρίνεια, now 3:4-6 states that his ἱκανότης rests on the character of the καινὴ διαθήκη — a διαθήκη which grants life — to the service of which God has called him. From it Paul derives his πεποίθησις.

Paul thus traces his moral behavior back to the πεποίθησις (sc. καύχησις) given through the gospel, though the εἰλικρίνεια would really be a matter of the will which hearkens to the gospel. But for him obedience too derives from the fact that God ἱκάνωσεν him as a διάκονος καινῆς διαθήκης (cf. 2:16f. with 3:5). From his character as διάκονος of the καινὴ διαθήκη follows the denial of the κρυπτὰ τῆς αἰσχύνης, along with the assertion that his activity is the φανέρωσις τῆς ἀληθείας (4:2).

Paul's message is open, and veiled only to those who are perishing. Just as the gospel, so the apostle can only be understood by the hearer's συνείδησις (4:2).

Paul thus regards his ἱκανότης as a gift. It is not granted on the basis of human qualities, and it is not to be judged according to criteria visible in his person. So the Corinthians need not test Paul's person but his proclamation, or test themselves by the proclamation, and from that point arrive at a judgment about Paul.

The character of the καινὴ διαθήκη is described in 3:7-18, so that the meaning of 3:4-6 is clear. It is the διαθήκη of ζωή and δόξα and to this fact corresponds its public character, while the old covenant was and still is characterized by a veiling. But in accordance with this public character, the διάκονοι τῆς καινῆς διαθήκης have παρρησία (v. 12), that is, ἐλευθερία (v. 17), which is nothing else than πεποίθησις (v. 4). In this way, therefore, Paul's πεποίθησις is established, and for this reason he can make evident the γνῶσις (2:14 and 4:6) and act ἐξ εἰλικρινείας (2:17).

Now, just as 3:4 (7)-18 establishes Paul's πεποίθησις, so 4:1-6 infers his πεποίθησις from 3:4 (7)-18; that is, resumes the theme of 3:7-18. Paul is thus not one who veils but who makes evident — εἰλικρινής has to do with the person as well as the subject matter (4:2) — and through this φανέρωσις he recommends himself.

What God has done to Paul leads to the φωτισμὸς τῆς γνώσεως through him (4:6), a thought which harks back to 2:14 and closes the ring. But a second ring is drawn — 4:7—6:10 shows the paradox of the φανέρωσις which is at the same time a concealing.

Verse 4: πεποίθησιν δὲ τοιαύτην ἔχομεν διὰ τοῦ Χριστοῦ πρὸς τὸν θεόν. The meaning of τοιαύτην was stated in verses 1-3, and was thematically formulated in 2:14-17. It is a πεποίθησις πρὸς τὸν θεόν, that is, not "in God" (Lietzmann, 110), but rather toward God, in reference to God (cf. Rom. 15:17: ἔχω οὖν τὴν καύχησιν ἐν Χριστῷ Ἰησοῦ τὰ πρὸς τὸν θεόν). πεποίθησις of course is the καύχησις, the pride, courage, self-consciousness which does not spring from need for recognition. Paul possesses it in reference to God, not persons. Before God he is comforted and proud, of course, διὰ τοῦ Χριστοῦ, cf. Gal. 5:10: ἐγὼ πέποιθα εἰς ὑμᾶς ἐν κυρίῳ, and Phil. 2:24: πέποιθα δὲ ἐν κυρίῳ ὅτι καὶ αὐτὸς ταχέως ἐλεύσομαι. In Gal. 5:10 and Phil. 2:24, however, the term is more formula-like, denoting trust as "devout," and in those passages the πεποιθέναι is not pride, but trust directed to the future. Here the idea is more concrete. Paul has this πεποίθησις through Christ, that is, through his calling and being entrusted with the office of διάκονος, just as verse 5 states. Thus, the πεποίθησις which he has πρὸς τὸν θεόν actually derives from God himself.

Verse 5: οὐχ ὅτι ἀφ' ἑαυτῶν ἱκανοί ἐσμεν. The meaning is, "not that we were competent of ourselves." Surprisingly, the λογίσασθαί τι ὡς ἐξ ἑαυτῶν yields the whither of the ἱκανότης. We would have expected, "to proclaim the Word of God (2:17)," or the like. But the λογίσασθαί τι is more general and is intended to indicate Paul's radical incapacity for any independent activity. But the formulation certainly derives from the fact that Paul has in mind his opponents' reproaches, or their boasting in their capacity for λογίζεσθαι, cf. 10:2, 7; 11:5 and 12:6 (cf. 1 Cor. 4:1). Accordingly, λογίζεσθαι does not mean to think something through to the end, to plan or design (the βουλεύεσθαι of 1:17), but rather to make judgments, to evaluate something.

The ἀφ' ἑαυτῶν denotes independence. Because the accent lies here, it is repeated in the ὡς ἐξ ἑαυτῶν (the ὡς is used as in 2:17: "As those who do this of themselves"). ἀλλ᾿ ἡ ἱκανότης ἡμῶν ἐκ τοῦ θεοῦ. In the New Testament, in the Bible as a whole, and in early Christian literature, "fitness" occurs only here, but it does appear in Plato.

Human insufficiency and the divine power are contrasted here as in 1 Cor. 15:10. There are Jewish parallels in Windisch, 108, particularly from Philo, cf. the Ebr. 166. Som II 25 states that without God mankind is not ἱκανός for knowledge and purity. But Philo lacks the Pauline dialectic, that is, the idea that it is exactly God's mightiest deed which is a gift, and the view developed in Ebr. 167-202 is not at all that of religious humility but of scepticism.

The last statement is set forth in detail in verse 6, which not only states that but also gives the purpose for which God has made Paul ἱκανός.

Verse 6: ὃς καὶ ἱκάνωσεν ἡμᾶς.[19] The καί does not mean "also," but "really" (Lietzmann, 111, writes that καί is used merely to emphasize the following word; then it would mean "actually").

διακόνους καινῆς διαθήκης. διάκονος designates Paul as apostle; cf. 1 Thess. 3:2 (the τοῦ θεοῦ is attested by ℵ* A P Ψ vg, etc.; D* 33 and it read differently); 2 Cor. 3:6 (καινῆς διαθήκης); 6:4 (θεοῦ); 11:15 (δικαιοσύνης); 11:23 (Χριστοῦ); cf. also Col. 1:25 (of the ἐκκλησία); Eph. 3:7 (of the εὐαγγέλιον), and 1 Tim. 4:6 (Χριστοῦ Ἰησοῦ). Is the usage terminological? In any case not in 1 Cor. 3:5: (Παῦλος and Ἀπολλῶς) διάκονοι δι᾿ ὧν ἐπιστεύσατε.

καινῆς διαθήκης. In the Greek διαθήκη means "testament." In the LXX it is a translation of בְּרִית or covenant, and in this sense most often appears in Paul and the New Testament. At any rate it appears in that sense here.[20] The concept καινὴ διαθήκη as of the new covenant derives from Jer. 38:31-33, already alluded to in 3:3. Evidently, the community already took up the concept prior to Paul. Cf. Mark 14:24 and parallels; 1 Cor. 11:25; cf. in addition Heb. 8:8, 9:15, and 12:24. The antonym is παλαιὰ διαθήκη in verse 14: cf. 1 Cor. 5:7 (παλαιὰ ζύμη); Rom. 7:6 (παλαιότης γράμματος) and Gal. 4:24 (the δύο διαθῆκαι).

The καινὴ διαθήκη is characterized as **οὐ γράμματος ἀλλὰ πνεύματος** (a genitive of quality with διαθήκη). γράμμα denotes the Old Testament Mosaic law, as verses 7ff. show, and is the characteristic of the παλαιὰ διαθήκη. Cf. Rom. 2:27: καὶ κρινεῖ ἡ ἐκ φύσεως ἀκροβυστία τὸν νόμον τελοῦσα σὲ τὸν διὰ γράμματος καὶ περιτομῆς παραβάτην νόμου.

This clause indicates that the law is called γράμμα in a specific sense, that is, in the way it encounters the Jew who fulfills it legally, obedient to the letter, and thus may transgress it insofar as it expresses the divine

---

[19] Does the ἡμᾶς here denote the apostles in general?

[20] Thus not, "unilateral disposition" (as in Kümmel, 199, following Behm).

will, while the Gentile who does not possess it as γράμμα, can fulfill it. Cf. Rom. 2:29: ἀλλ' ὁ ἐν τῷ κρυπτῷ Ἰουδαῖος (is a true Jew), καὶ περιτομὴ καρδίας ἐν πνεύματι οὐ γράμματι, and Rom. 7:6: ὥστε δουλεύειν [ἡμᾶς] ἐν καινότητι πνεύματος καὶ οὐ παλαιότητι γράμματος.

πνεῦμα, on the other hand, is the divine power, and in contrast to it γράμμα may be described as human capability, or as the principle of human ability. The contrast γράμμα — πνεῦμα does not coincide with the contrast between form and content, between formulated, legal regulation and the real intention of the law.[21] The Greek contrast between νόμος γεγραμμένος and ἄγραφος is totally different. In it the νόμος ἄγραφος is the origin and basis of a law which is historically fixed, a νόμος which of course aspires to fulfill its intent, but never expresses it purely and thus always has its critical principle in the νόμος γεγραμμένος. The Pauline contrast between γράμμα and πνεῦμα[22] does not contrast the real intent of the law with its inadequate expression in what is historically fixed in writing, but rather denotes two tendencies, two principles or powers. The law is the power which, encountering one as requirement, directs one to its performance in his own strength. The Spirit is the power of God which, encountering one as gift, enables one to do what he cannot in his own strength (Käsemann, *Leib*, 129).

Cf. Luther on Rom. 7:6 (Römerbrief I 62, 28ff.): 'Litera' hic non debet accipi tantum pro figuralibus, ut copiose b. Augustinus c. 4 de spi. et lit. disserit. Fallit ergo Lyra, quando dicit Christum legem evacuasse quoad iudicialia et ceremonialia, sed non quoad moralia: immo quoad moralia hic loquitur aperte, quod sit lex mortis et litere. And again (II, 166, 12ff.): 'Litera' apud apostolum Paulum est non tantum figuralis scriptura aut doctrina legis, sed prorsus omnis doctrina, que precipit ea, que sunt bone vite, sive sit evangelica sive Mosaica. Hec enim si cognoscantur et memoria teneantur et non assit spiritus gratie, sunt tantum litera vacua et mors anime (cf. II 168, 1ff.). ("The term 'letter' must here not be taken to mean only the symbolic parts of Scripture, as Augustine shows in an extensive discussion in chapters 4 and 6 of *On the Spirit and the Letter*. Lyra is therefore mistaken in saying that Christ made the law of no effect in so far as it deals with judicial and ceremonial matters but not in so far as it deals with moral issues. As a matter of fact, the apostle speaks here obviously of the law in so far as it deals with moral issues, and as such it is the law of death and of the letter." And again: "The apostle means by 'letter' not merely those parts of Scripture that have a symbolical significance and the teaching of the law, but, rather, every teaching that prescribes what constitutes the good life whether it is to be found in the Gospel or in Moses.

---

[21] Idea and concretization in the empirical reality.
[22] Cf. Frank, *Philosophical Understanding and Religious Truth*, p. 148ff.

78

The Apostolic Office

For when one learns it and keeps it in one's memory and the Spirit of grace is not present, it is merely an empty letter and the soul's death." The Library of Christian Classics, XV, 196f.)

Windisch, 110, thinks Paul could only have spoken thus because in his day the καινὴ διαθήκη was not yet fixed in writing, but existed only in personal, oral proclamation. It may be true that on another occasion Paul would not have given shape to his ideas in just this way. In any event, Paul's statement holds true for the period of the written New Testament only when the latter in turn is not misconstrued as γράμμα, that is, as a demanding power and principle of performance, but rather as a kerygma which sets one under the creative power of God. The statement which for Paul already contains the idea that the new covenant is one of life, has its basis in the τὸ γὰρ γράμμα ἀποκτέννει, τὸ δὲ πνεῦμα ζωοποιεῖ. This expresses Paul's idea that the way of the law necessarily leads to death, since the law as a power which demands and summons to human performance or, insofar as it equals human capability, awakens the σάρξ or the sin which slumbers in it, which of necessity renders man a transgressor of the law, whether through transgression of concrete commandments or through guileful fulfillment for the sake of καύχησις.[23] Cf. Rom. 7:7ff. and Rom. 7:5: ὅτε γὰρ ἦμεν ἐν τῇ σαρκί, τὰ παθήματα τῶν ἁμαρτιῶν τὰ διὰ τοῦ νόμου ἐνηργεῖτο ἐν τοῖς μέλεσιν ἡμῶν εἰς τὸ καρποφορῆσαι τῷ θανάτῳ. Cf. Rom. 8:2: ὁ γὰρ νόμος τοῦ πνεύματος τῆς ζωῆς ἐν Χριστῷ Ἰησοῦ ἠλευθέρωσέν σε ἀπὸ τοῦ νόμου τῆς ἁμαρτίας καὶ τοῦ θανάτου, and 1 Cor. 15:56: τὸ δὲ κέντρον τοῦ θανάτου ἡ ἁμαρτία, ἡ δὲ δύναμις τῆς ἁμαρτίας ὁ νόμος.

How is this statement the foundation for what precedes? Simply for the reason (if the γάρ is not a mere continuation) that for Paul καινὴ διαθήκη from the outset signifies a covenant which leads to life; for this very reason it must be a διαθήκη πνεύματος.

The contrast between the διαθῆκαι and the character of the καινὴ διαθήκη is explained by the fact that from it results the character of Paul's apostolate. This is spelled out in 3:7-18.[24]

b. From this διακονία results παρρησία: 3:7-18

Now if the dispensation of death, carved in letters on stone, came with such splendor that the Israelites could not look at Moses' face because of its brightness, fading as this was, will not the dispensation of the Spirit be attended with greater splendor? For if there was splendor in the dispensation of condemnation, the dispensation of righteousness must far exceed it in splendor. Indeed, in this case,what once had splendor has come to have no splendor at all, because of the splendor

---

[23] Cf. Gogarten, *Die Verkündigung Jesu Christi*, 1948.
[24] It is thus not a polemic against Judaism.

that surpasses it.For if what faded away came with splendor, what is permanent must have much more splendor. Since we have such a hope, we are very bold, not like Moses, who put a veil over his face so that the Israelites might not see the end of the fading splendor. But their minds were hardened; for to this day, when they read the old covenant, that same veil remains unlifted, because only through Christ is it taken away. Yes, to this day whenever Moses is read a veil lies over their minds; but when a man turns to the Lord the veil is removed. Now the Lord is the Spirit, and where the Spirit of the Lord is, there is freedom. And we all, with unveiled face, beholding the glory of the Lord, are being changed into his likeness from one degree of glory to another; for this comes from the Lord who is the Spirit.

In 3:7-11, first by comparison of the διακονίαι which correspond to the two διαθῆκαι, the character of the διάκονος καινῆς διαθήκης is made clear. Just as the παλαιὰ διαθήκη γράμματος kills, so the διακονία which corresponds to it is a διακονία τοῦ θανάτου (v. 7), τῆς κατακρίσεως (v. 9), a καταργούμενον (v. 11). And just as the καινὴ διαθήκη πνεύματος makes alive, so the διακονία corresponding to it is a διακονία τοῦ πνεύματος (v. 8), τῆς δικαιοσύνης (v. 9), a μένον (v. 11). The new διακονία is thus far superior to the old in δόξα.

In 3:12-18 the conclusion is drawn: The διάκονος of the καινὴ διαθήκη is characterized by παρρησία (v. 12), by ἐλευθερία (v. 17). At the same time, Paul abandons the strict course of the context, since in verse 12 he still has in mind the παρρησία of the apostle, but in verses 17f. no longer only the apostle, but the entire community of the καινὴ διαθήκη. The character of this διαθήκη is imparted not only to the apostle, but to all believers. In 4:1ff. he of course returns to the theme of the apostolate.

The διακονία of the καινὴ διαθήκη as a διακονία of πνεῦμα and ζωή (The comparison of the two διακονίαι): 3:7-11

The comparison in verses 7-11 leads to three conclusions *a minori ad maius* (on the Jewish drawing of conclusions קַל וָחוֹמֶר or "easy and hard," cf. Str.-B. III, 223-226): In verses 7f: εἰ δὲ . . . πῶς οὐχὶ μᾶλλον; in verse 9: εἰ γὰρ . . . πολλῷ μᾶλλον, and in verse 11: εἰ γὰρ . . . πολλῷ μᾶλλον.

Verses 7f.: The first conclusion comprises two verses, because the immediate consequence of the εἰ δὲ . . . πῶς οὐχὶ μᾶλλον clauses is interrupted by the ὥστε-clause attached to ἐν δόξῃ. That clause is designed to portray the greatness of the δόξα of the old διακονία, so that the greatness of the δόξα of the new covenant emerges more strikingly.

εἰ δὲ ἡ διακονία τοῦ θανάτου. Just as the διακονία of the καινὴ διαθήκη is the apostolic office, so the διακονία of the παλαιὰ διαθήκη is the office of Moses, as is shown by the ὥστε-clause and what follows. No thought is given here to Moses' office finding its continuation, for example, in the synagogue preaching. But, as verse 14 shows, that idea is assumed. Just as now the old διαθήκη is, according to verse 6, a covenant of the letter which kills, so it may also be simply described as a διακονία τοῦ θανάτου, and it is of little consequence whether the ἐν γράμμασιν is linked to the διακονία τοῦ θανάτου (which would yield the motive for the description διακονία τοῦ θανάτου, since according to verse 6, τὸ γράμμα ἀποκτείνει) or to the ἐντετυπωμένη λίθοις. In any event, the intention is to accent the idea of the λίθος in reminiscence of verse 3, and the ἐντετυπωμένη λίθοις as well as the ἐν γράμμασιν are intended to characterize the inferiority of the old διαθήκη and its διακονία. But the expression is incorrect to the extent it was of course not the διακονία, but rather the διαθήκη which was ἐντετυπωμένη λίθοις.

ἐγενήθη ἐν δόξῃ means either "attained to δόξα" or "appeared in δόξα." The latter perhaps better corresponds with the ἔσται ἐν δόξῃ of verse 8 and with the διὰ δόξης and ἐν δόξῃ of verse 11. The ὥστε-clause and what follows make clear that the ἐγενήθη ἐν δόξῃ (v. 7a) refers to Exod. 34:29ff.: **ὥστε μὴ δύνασθαι ἀτενίσαι τοὺς υἱοὺς Ἰσραὴλ εἰς τὸ πρόσωπον Μωϋσέως.** Cf. Exod. 34:29-35:

> When Moses came down from Mount Sinai, with the two tables of the testimony in his hand as he came down from the mountain, Moses did not know that the skin of his face shone because he had been talking with God. And when Aaron and all the people of Israel saw Moses, behold, the skin of his face shone, and they were afraid to come near him. But Moses called to them; and Aaron and all the leaders of the congregation returned to him, and Moses talked with them. And afterward all the people of Israel came near, and he gave them in commandment all that the Lord had spoken with him in Mount Sinai. And when Moses had finished speaking with them, he put a veil on his face; but whenever Moses went in before the Lord to speak with him, he took the veil off, until he came out; and when he came out, and told the people of Israel what he was commanded, the people of Israel saw the face of Moses, that the skin of Moses' face shone; and Moses would put the veil upon his face again, until he went in to speak with him.

In his Vit Mos II 70, Philo writes: κατέβαινε πολὺ καλλίων τὴν ὄψιν ἢ ὅτε ἀνῄει, ὡς τοὺς ὁρῶντας τεθηπέναι καὶ καταπεπλῆχθαι καὶ μηδ' ἐπὶ πλέον ἀντέχειν τοῖς ὀφθαλμοῖς δύνασθαι κατὰ τὴν προσβολὴν ἡλιοειδοῦς φέγγους ἀπαστράπτοντος. (". . . he descended with a countenance far more beautiful than when he ascended, so that those who saw him were filled with awe and amazement; nor even could their eyes continue to stand the dazzling brightness that flashed from him like the rays of the sun.")

According to Rabbinic exegesis (Str.-B. III, 515f.), the Israelites could not look upon Moses because of their sin with the golden calf. This explains the ὥστε-clause. The **τὴν καταργουμένην** joined to the **διὰ τὴν δόξαν τοῦ**

προσώπου αὐτοῦ calls to mind the inferiority of this mighty δόξα, just as the ἐντετυπωμένη λίθοις calls to mind the inferiority of the old διακονία. The idea is accented in verse 11 and spelled out in verses 13f.

Just as in verse 11, the καταργούμενος is perhaps not meant to be a true participle (passing away), but rather a substitute for the verbal adjective (transitory); cf. Bl.-D. para. 65, 3.

Verse 8: πῶς οὐχὶ μᾶλλον ἡ διακονία τοῦ πνεύματος ἔσται ἐν δόξῃ. The ἔσται is not a genuine future (referring to the Parousia), but the future of logical inference (Bl.-D. para. 349, 1), for according to verse 18 the δόξα is already present in character and parallel to the περισσεύει of verse 9.[25]

The question is naturally not deliberative or one of doubting, but rather rhetorical: How great the δόξα of the new must be, if the old διακονία had such a mighty δόξα!

The discussion of δόξα in Windisch, 115, is insufficient; cf. v. Gall, *Herrlichkeit*; Schneider, *Doxa,* and Kittel, *Herrlichkeit.* In the LXX δόξα is the translation of כָּבוֹד. It describes the manifestation of God, sensuously appearing as brilliance (glory), in which the sense of physical (exaltation) and of social power (demand) are united. As early as in the Old Testament the concept of the כָּבוֹד is historicized. Yahweh's כָּבוֹד is manifest (or will be manifest) as judgment and grace in the people's history.

In his use of δόξα, Paul proceeds from the basic meaning of כָּבוֹד as the manifestation of God's power (cf. Rom. 6:4: ἠγέρθη Χριστὸς ἐν νεκρῶν διὰ τῆς δόξης τοῦ πατρός,[26] and 1 Thess. 2:12: εἰς τὴν ἑαυτοῦ βασιλείαν καὶ δόξαν; cf. also Rom. 9:23).

For Paul, too, δόξα denotes "brilliance" or "glory," as verse 7 indicates, corresponding with the fact that at his conversion Christ showed himself to him in the brilliance of δόξα. But Paul claims the same δόξα for the gospel (cf. 4:4ff.) and for the existence of believers (3:18), though there is nothing of brilliance to be seen here. For Paul, then, it is not this sense which makes up the concept, but rather that basic meaning of a manifestation of power — just as in Isa. 6 only the cherubim see the "Kabod" of God which fills the whole earth, and not the prophet himself.

If Paul thus retains the concept of δόξα as manifestation of divine power, and by doing so follows not only the Old Testament pattern of thought but also Hellenistic conceptuality, according to which δόξα denotes the divine miraculous power synonymously with δύναμις, φῶς, and πνεῦμα, he has nevertheless radically historicized the concept. The δόξα manifest in Christ or the gospel determines the individual's historical life, not of course as a fluid working magically and uniformly in all the baptized, but as differentiated,

[25] The διακονία τοῦ πνεύματος is the opposite of διακονία τοῦ θανάτου. πνεῦμα is thus synonymous with ζωή.
[26] Cf. 1 Cor. 6:14: ὁ δὲ θεὸς καὶ τὸν κύριον ἤγειρεν καὶ ἡμᾶς ἐξεγερεῖ διὰ τῆς δυνάμεως αὐτοῦ.

visible in the charism, that is, in individual gifts and tasks, while the "Kabod" as eschatological glory extends to the community of people. According to Paul, the gift of the δόξα conveys the individual into the eschatological situation in which what is worldly has been fundamentally destroyed, so that, paradoxically, the δόξα can be manifest even in death, cf. 4:7ff.

According to Windisch, 115, Paul unconsciously gives to the term δόξα another nuance, insofar as in his statements regarding the Mosaic legend he has in mind the mythological view of δόξα, but when he speaks of the δόξα of the new covenant he has in mind the "essence of all the blessings of salvation, especially purely religious blessings such as fellowship with God or sonship with God." False! The meaning of δόξα as manifestation of power is uniformly retained, though with Moses it is apparent to the senses, but not in the new covenant. In the new covenant δόξα does not denote the essence of the blessings of salvation, but rather the life-producing power of God from which follow παρρησία and ἐλευθερία (vv. 12, 17), πεποίθησις (3:4) and the συνιστάνειν ἑαυτόν, or the Christian καύχησις (4:2; cf. 1:12).

The Christian δόξα is no doubt an eschatological phenomenon (as the καινὴ διαθήκη as such), but it is not first and foremost future (as indeed the αἰώνιον βάρος δόξα in 4:17), as surely as it is also that. For, according to verse 12, the believer, by virtue of this δόξα has τοιαύτην ἐλπίδα, namely, that the δόξα already present will remain. It already effects in the believer the μεταμορφοῦσθαι ἀπὸ δόξης εἰς δόξαν, verse 18. 4:7ff. indicates how such a transformation is manifested. God's δύναμις is proved ἐν ἀσθενείαις (12:9ff.). In verse 10 Paul does not add τῆς μελλούσης ἀποκαλυφθῆναι εἰς ἡμᾶς (Rom. 8:18) to the εἴνεκεν τῆς ὑπερβαλλούσης δόξης — which according to Windisch, 117, he might have done.

δόξα as God's eschatological manifestation of power rests on the καινὴ διαθήκη, to which corresponds the διακονία illustrated by the contrasts between θάνατος (v. 7) and πνεῦμα (v. 8); κατάκρισις (v. 9) and δικαιοσύνη (v. 9); and τὸ καταργούμενον (v. 11) and τὸ μένον (v. 11).

The concepts in each of the two series are thus almost synonymous; they agree on the concept of ζωή. The πνεῦμα is the ζωοποιοῦν (v. 6); the δικαιοσύνη is the acquittal to life in contrast to the κατάκρισις (v. 9); and the μένον is that very life not destroyed by death.

Verse 9: εἰ γὰρ ἡ διακονία τῆς κατακρίσεως δόξα, πολλῷ μᾶλλον περισσεύει ἡ διακονία τῆς δικαιοσύνης δόξῃ. The verse is an abbreviation in face of verses 7f. The ἡ διακονία . . . δόξα is identical to the ἐγενήθη ἐν δόξῃ in verse 7. P⁴⁶ ℵ D* G al it and sy read τῇ διακονίᾳ instead of ἡ διακονία, and ℵ D G and pl add an ἐν to the δόξῃ.

The second conclusion (cf. p. 79) has the same force as the first. From this and from the parallelism of concepts in the three series it follows that δικαιοσύνη is not a "righteousness which takes effect as a walking according to the Spirit" (Ritschl, in Windisch 116), and it is also not a righteousness of God which utters acquittal (Windisch). It is rather the acquittal itself, that is, the righteousness awarded by God (Rom. 1:17), and which spells ζωή in contrast to κατάκρισις and θάνατος.

κατάκρισις (in the Greek Bible only here and in 7:3; a synonym of κατάκριμα in Rom. 5:16, 18, and 8:1) denotes judgment, the judgment unto death, corresponding to the θάνατος of verse 7 and the τὸ γὰρ γράμμα ἀποκτείνει in verse 6. Cf. the result of service to the law according to Rom. 3:19f.; 5:16, 18; Gal. 3:10, and on the other hand, the freedom from κατάκριμα in Rom. 8:1, 34.

Windisch, 116, correctly states that δικαιοσύνη as such could also designate the παλαιὰ διαθήκη (cf. Rom. 10:5: τὴν δικαιοσύνην τὴν ἐκ νόμου, and Gal. 3:21). But the blessing of salvation denoted by δικαιοσύνη (this and not a human quality is intended) is precisely what is not effected by the νόμος. περισσεύει is used here as in 1:5 and elsewhere and means "to be rich in, to have abundance."

Verse 10: This verse is not at all disturbing in the context (Windisch, 116). It does not at all negate the idea of the recurring protasis that the old covenant had a δόξα, but rather states that this δόξα (which, according to v. 7, was still a mighty one) is nothing in face of the δόξα of the new covenant. Thus the clause most appropriately belongs in the context and gives the reason for the πολλῷ μᾶλλον in verse 9.[27]

καὶ γὰρ οὐ δεδόξασται τὸ δεδοξασμένον. The τὸ δεδοξασμένον denotes the old διακονία. It is true of this διακονία that οὐ δεδόξασται, that is to say, **ἐν τούτῳ τῷ μέρει,** "in this respect," in other words, when the old δόξα is compared with the new (cf. 3:9, and parallels in Windisch, 117), while in other respects, according to verse 7, it is great indeed.

εἵνεκεν τῆς ὑπερβαλλούσης δόξης, sc. of the new διαθήκη. (Windisch, 116, foolishly asks whether perhaps a more precise definition such as τῆς ἐν Χριστῷ has been omitted; the context automatically yields this sense). The old δόξα means nothing for the reason that the new is so luxuriant. (ὑπερβάλλειν is a favorite with Paul; cf. 9:14; ὑπερβαλλόντως in 11:23; ὑπερβολή in 1:8; 4:7, 17; Rom. 7:13; 1 Cor. 12:31 and Gal. 1:13; cf. also Lietzmann, 112). Weiss in *Aufgaben,* 32, needlessly states that ἐν τούτῳ τῷ μέρει is a gloss on εἵνεκεν κτλ.

Verse 11: **εἰ γὰρ τὸ καταργούμενον διὰ δόξης, πολλῷ μᾶλλον τὸ μένον ἐν δόξῃ.** This is the third conclusion (cf. p. 79) in which the formulation is varied: διὰ δόξης (sc. ἐγενήθη in v. 7). διά characterizes manner as in 2:4 (Bl.-D. para. 223, 3), and alternates with ἐν δόξῃ (sc. ἔσται as in v. 8;

---

[27] Lietzmann, 112, incorrectly adds, "that which was glorified (through the law)." No! What was glorified is the law itself!

cf. 1 Cor. 12:8f., etc.). The τὸ καταργούμενον denotes the παλαιὰ διαθήκη which is at an end once the new is present (καταργούμενον here is a genuine participle, no doubt in contrast to v. 7, cf. p. 81). τὸ μένον means "to remain," that is, in the eschatological future, just as in 1 Cor. 13:13.

The καινὴ διακονία *is accordingly one of* παρρησία, *or* ἐλευθερία: *3:12-18*

According to Windisch, 112, 3:7-18 is a "Christian midrash" on Exod. 34:29-35, conceived independently of the epistle's situation and easily loosed from the context, though not an interpolation. But this could at most be true of 3:7-11, for 3:12-18 most intimately coheres with the train of thought. The παρρησία, which Paul is concerned to maintain is grounded in the unveiled character of the καινὴ διαθήκη. But even 3:7-11 is firmly joined to the context by 3:6 (διακονία καινῆς διαθήκης). It is really necessary to show that παρρησία results from the nature of the new covenant. What is correct in Windisch's exposition is merely that 3:7-18 is not anti-Jewish in motivation, but rather contrasts Christianity with Judaism.

Verse 12: The **ἔχοντες οὖν τοιαύτην ἐλπίδα** is the hope grounded in knowledge of the μένον (v. 11), or it is knowledge of the πνεῦμα (v. 8) and δικαιοσύνη (v. 9).

Why does Paul not write (as in 4:1) ἔχοντες οὖν τοιαύτην διακονίαν, rather than replace διακονία with ἐλπίς? In regard to content, the terms are identical. Were Paul to write τοιαύτην διακονίαν, then the τοιαύτην would imply what is expressed by ἐλπίς. He intends to say, since our διακονία has this ἐλπίς-character, since as διάκονοι we have such a hope. . . .[28]

It follows from the ἔχοντες — ἐλπίδα that the δόξα given the διάκονοι of the new covenant is not a simple possession (any more than it is merely a hope for the future). The διάκονος possesses the δόξα, but he has not been magically changed. He is set within a life-movement, the goal of which he does not have at his disposal, but which he may hope for. But in this hope, and this is what is essential to the context, he has παρρησία — **πολλῇ παρρησίᾳ χρώμεθα.**

παρρησία was originally a political concept, denoting the right to say anything, the title to openness in public, a right which the δοῦλος or φυγάς did not possess (Eur. Phoen. 390ff.).

Political led to ethical usage (in φιλία), παρρησία then denoting openness as the courage to say anything (whence then the arrogance of slaves). Among Epicureans and Cynics παρρησία became an ethical concept in terms of the right to the public character of one's entire conduct of life.[29]

In Jewish Hellenism παρρησία is the right to openness toward God, and

---

[28] The reason for Paul's speaking of ἐλπίς lies in the last antithesis: τὸ καταργούμενον — τὸ μένον.

[29] Cf. Peterson, *Zur Bedeutungsgeschichte von* παρρησία, Seeberg-FS, 283-297.

has its basis in the συνείδησις.[30] The same is true of Christian usage. παρρησία is expressed in prayer (1 John 3:21; 5:14); the Christian has παρρησία toward God (Eph. 3:12; Heb. 4:16), and will have it especially at the judgment, 1 John 2:28; 4:17.[31]

παρρησία is thus related to ἐλευθερία and ἐξουσία. The meaning of παρρησία also moves over into the public sphere. Cf. John 7:4, 13, 26; 11:54; 18:20; and perhaps also Phil. 1:20.

In 2 Cor. 3:12 παρρησία is almost synonymous with πεποίθησις in 3:4. It is the courage for openness and accessibility, its right established in the ἐλπίς of the διάκονος of the καινὴ διαθήκη. For it is precisely of the new covenant that accessibility and thus openness are characteristic, in contrast to the old covenant characterized by veiledness, as verses 13f. state.

But the fact that Paul uses παρρησία and not πεποίθησις as in verse 4, is due to his opponents' reproaches, as 4:1-4 clearly show. The posture of παρρησία is contrasted with ἐγκακεῖν (cowardice), with τὰ κρυπτὰ τῆς αἰσχύνης (the secrecy of shame), and with πανουργία and δολοῦν. It is maintained in τῇ φανερώσει τῆς ἀληθείας, and keeps nothing veiled. In the context, then, παρρησία is not openness toward God (Windisch, 118), but rather the apostle's openness toward his hearers in his public activity. It is the practice of the εἰλικρίνεια of 2:7 over against the δόλος of 4:2. The πολλῇ παρρησίᾳ χρώμεθα corresponds to the οὐ γὰρ ἐπαισχύνομαι τὸ εὐαγγέλιον in Rom. 1:16.

χρώμεθα (χρῆσθαι means to deal with, as in 1:17) is naturally an indicative, not a subjunctive, for the intention, of course, is to describe actual behavior, as in the parallel of 4:1.

Verse 13: The παρρησία is grounded in the δόξα of the new covenant, for as μένον this δόξα does not require veiling as did that of the old. By indicating veiledness as the character of the Mosaic covenant, verses 13f. assert that this παρρησία is peculiar to the διάκονος of the new. **καὶ οὐ καθάπερ Μωϋσῆς ἐτίθει κάλυμμα ἐπὶ τὸ πρόσωπον αὐτοῦ.** There is an aposiopesis here. The sentence should begin, "and it is not so (as with Moses, who. . . ."), cf. Bl.-D. para. 482.[32] In contrast to verse 7, Moses' activity is described according to Exod. 34:33-35, the description motivated by the Old Testament text. **πρὸς τὸ μὴ ἀτενίσαι τοὺς υἱοὺς Ἰσραήλ** — the Israelites were not to look **εἰς τὸ τέλος τοῦ καταργουμένου,**[33] at the end of what was passing away, at the transitory (on καταργουμένου, cf. vv. 7, 11), that is, they were not to notice that Moses' δόξα was at an end.[34]

---

[30] So also Preis Zaub. XII 187.

[31] Cf. the προσαγωγή in Rom. 5:2!

[32] Cf. Ljungvik, ZNW 32, 1933, 207f., and Fridrichsen, ZNW 34, 1935, 307f.

[33] A vg and Ambst read: εἰς τὸ πρόσωπον τοῦ καταργουμένου — a correction. Likewise, a few mss. from the bo read: εἰς τὴν δόξαν τοῦ προσώπου αὐτοῦ τὴν καταργουμένην.

[34] Goettsberger (BZ 16, 1924, 1ff.) and Schlatter, Bote, 514 incorrectly add τοῦ καταργουμένου νόμου. (As to content, the addition is of course correct.)

To the fact, then, that the δόξα of the old διακονία is transitory and already superceded corresponds the fact that it was veiled. But for Paul this means that the old covenant or old διακονία as such is characterized by veiling, by its contrast with παρρησία.

Verse 14: ἀλλὰ ἐπωρώθη τὰ νοήματα αὐτῶν. With the ἀλλά, the idea takes on an about face. To the veiling of the δόξα, the object of beholding, corresponds the obduracy and delusion of those beholding, who do not perceive that Moses' δόξα is extinguished, so that the κάλυμμα can be said to lie both on Moses' face (v. 13) or on the reading of the Old Testament (v. 14), as well as on the καρδία of the Israelites (v. 15). The ἀλλά means, "indeed, still more!" Cf. 1 Cor. 3:2; Phil. 1:18, and Bl.-D. para. 448, 6. The ἐπωρώθη means, "it was hardened, made stubborn," cf. Rom. 11:7; Mark 6:52; 8:17; and John 12:40 (according to Isa. 6:10). πώρωσις occurs in Rom. 11:25; Eph. 4:18, and Mark 3:5. τὰ νοήματα denotes their ideas as in 4:4 and 11:3, but which for Paul always includes an "aspiring to," "a being set on," cf. 2:11, p. 50. The term is not strictly distinguished from καρδία (cf. πώρωσις τῆς καρδίας in Eph. 4:18; ἡ καρδία πεπωρωμένη in Mark 6:52 and 8:17). Both terms are connected in Phil. 4:7: φρουρήσει τὰς καρδίας ὑμῶν καὶ τὰ νοήματα ὑμῶν, for just as according to verse 15, the κάλυμμα ἐπὶ τὴν καρδίαν αὐτῶν κεῖται.

ἄχρι γὰρ τῆς σήμερον ἡμέρας τὸ αὐτὸ κάλυμμα ἐπὶ τῇ ἀναγνώσει τῆς παλαιᾶς διαθήκης μένει. The event of Exod. 34 is therefore typical. As the veil lay on Moses' face, so in future it lies on the "Moses" of the Torah, or, as is stated now in a totally nonfigurative use of the image, on the reading of the παλαιὰ διαθήκη (this concept appears here for the first time), that is to say, in the synagogue worship at which Moses is always present. (The idea of course is not that the Torah rolls were veiled; for this veiling is removed at the reading.)

μὴ ἀνακαλυπτόμενον ὅτι ἐν Χριστῷ καταργεῖται. In the context, the clause must in any case mean that the removal of the veil would indicate the disappearance of the old δόξα. The subject of the καταργεῖται can therefore only be the παλαιὰ διαθήκη[35] (or its δόξα). The veil hides the fact that this covenant is abrogated, just as the veil on the πρόσωπον of Moses concealed that his δόξα was at an end.[36] So it is impossible to translate the clause, "which is not unlifted because (only) in (fellowship) with Christ is it taken away" (Windisch, 122).[37] The destruction of the veil is of no consequence.

The μὴ ἀνακαλυπτόμενον cannot simply attach to μένει as a predicate

---

[35] It is this of course which was characterized as καταργούμενον in vv. 11 and 13.

[36] The καταργεῖσθαι of the veil is not at all the issue, rather that of the old δόξα (v. 11). As to the veil, the question is merely how it relates to the ἀνακαλύπτεσθαι or περιαιρεῖσθαι (v. 16).

[37] Likewise Schlatter, *Bote,* 515f., and Kümmel, 200, while Lietzmann, 113, preferred παλαιὰ διαθήκη as the subject.

("it remains unlifted," Luther), for then it would have to read οὐ! And the μὴ ἀνακαλυπτόμενον cannot be an accusative absolute — "since it is not disclosed that the παλαιὰ διαθήκη is abrogated" — for then it would have to read μὴ ἀποκαλυπτόμενον! μὴ ἀνακαλυπτόμενον[38] is rather a subjunctive participle and means, "it remains without being lifted." The ὅτι is causal and means, "because the παλαιὰ διαθήκη is abrogated in (or through) Christ." It is precisely that καταργεῖσθαι ἐν Χριστῷ which furnishes the reason why the veil is not lifted but remains.

Oepke (*TDNT,* 3, 560) finds the transition to verse 14 abrupt, because he construes the verse to read that the δόξα, which Israel should see but does not because of its obduracy, is the δόξα of Christ, not that of Moses. "But since Paul does not call into question the identity of the Old and New Testament God of salvation, the glory of Christ can also be seen in the Old Testament covenant word when correctly understood." For this reason he takes the verse to mean that to this day the veil remains; it is not taken away because it is put aside (only) in (and through) Christ.

But, in the context, this is a totally misleading reflection. In the context, the παλαιὰ διαθήκη comes into question only as a διαθήκη of death, of κατάκρισις, as that which is καταργούμενον. In the context, Paul neither reflects on the fact that the Old Testament as a book of revelation contains prophecies of Christ and thus when "correctly understood" reveals Christ's δόξα, nor on the fact that the law is the παιδαγωγὸς εἰς Χριστόν (Gal. 3:24) and to that extent has positive significance for the history of salvation. He reflects only on the fact that the law leads to death and that it has its τέλος in Christ (Rom. 10:4).

Thus Barth is also incorrect when in *Evangelium und Gesetz,* 18, and by appeal to 2 Cor. 3:15, he writes that "we do not recognize that the law proclaims our justification by God," due, of course to the deceit of sin, by virtue of which we use the law to justify ourselves before God. Cf. also p. 13: "The law, to be sure, attests to the grace of God;" it is "the necessary form of the Gospel, whose content is grace" (p. 11).

The latter is rather the opposite of what Paul says.

In the context, Paul has not reflected further on the question of the original meaning of the law. The veiling veils that the law is passing away, that it has its end (Rom. 10:4: τέλος, not goal as with Barth!) in Christ. The question as to the positive significance of the law is not discussed, and in the context the law is at issue only insofar as it is the law of Moses, demanding in its mode of encounter and thus leading to death and judgment, transitory. At the root here is neither the idea of Gal. 3:19-25 (of the νόμος as παιδαγωγός) and Rom. 5:20 (νόμος δὲ παρεισῆλθεν), nor the idea of the νόμος as ἅγιος (Rom. 7:12).

---

[38] Cramer thus correctly states in Cat 370, 9: "Μὴ ἀνακαλυπτόμενον" εἰς τὸ γνῶναι αὐτοὺς ὅτι ἐν Χριστῷ καταργεῖται ὁ νόμος. ("[He writes] 'unveiled' so that they know the law is abolished in Christ.")

For Paul, the place of the νόμος in salvation history is certainly that of promise, and he recognizes the original intent of the law as the original will of God made valid through Christ (Gal. 5:14; Rom. 13:8-10).

For Paul the law as a way of salvation is no longer at issue, however important to him the Old Testament is as promise. Its meaning as promise has of course become clear only from the perspective of its fulfillment. Paul indeed interprets the Old Testament in forced fashion (allegory, typology, etc.; cf. von Harnack, AT, 124ff.).[39] It is axiomatic for Paul that:

The Old Testament as law is abrogated by the doctrine of justification.

The Old Testament as prophecy is abrogated by allegory.

The revelation in the Old Testament is God's activity in the national history.

The revelation in the New Testament is God's eschatological activity in Christ.

The enduring significance of the Old Testament is its explication of the historical understanding of existence.[40]

The law is paradigmatic (the correlation of law and gospel).

The Old Testament thus is a permanent παιδαγωγός. But is it necessary in its specifically Old Testament character? No! (Cf. Rom. 2:14f.) The law presupposed by the gospel need not be the actual Old Testament. But nowhere is the human situation under law so explained as in the Old Testament (creation, God in history, humans in their temporality and historicality, knowledge of sin and grace, the eschatological hope). Authority is ceded the Old Testament, however, only from the perspective of the New. Since faith sees that here a person under the law is understood as typical, it grasps the Old Testament in a new way as promise by construing the law as promise of the gospel (which the Old Testament itself did not do, though of course Paul does with his construct of salvation history, which is foreign to the Old Testament). Thus the church again directs the Old Testament word to people as a present and continually valid word of God,[41] but understood from the New Testament (that is, not allegorized, but in such fashion that the law is construed as promise, as with Barth). Note the variety in the New Testament with such a procedure. It illustrates that the extreme is possible *in abstracto,* without preaching the Old Testament, but it likewise illustrates that preaching should not be directed toward abstract considerations, but toward history, and that the affirmation of Jesus as historical and eschatological includes the affirmation of that history which leads to him as revelation — though newly seen.

Verse 15: ἀλλ᾽ ἕως σήμερον ἡνίκα ἂν ἀναγινώσκηται Μωϋσῆς κάλυμμα

---

[39] Does the Old Testament revelation have independent force alongside the New?

[40] Why does the church retain the Old Testament against Gnosticism and Marcion? Because it construes human existence as historical, construes God as Creator and Lord of history and construes the eschatological event as an historical fact.

[41] Use of the Old Testament in thankfulness and freedom.

ἐπὶ τὴν καρδίαν αὐτῶν κεῖται. The idea is the same as in verse 14, but with a nuance, again marked by the ἀλλά. To the veiledness of the ἀνάγνωσις of the παλαιὰ διαθήκη corresponds the veiledness of the καρδία of the hearers, as was already stated in the ἐπωρώθη τὰ νοήματα αὐτῶν of verse 14 (p. 86) — "yes, rather, the veil does not really lie over the object, but over the subject." With a characteristic modification, verse 16 marks the contrast between the Christian and Jewish religion by a quotation from Exod. 34:34.

Verse 16: ἡνίκα δὲ ἐὰν ἐπιστρέψῃ πρὸς κύριον, περιαιρεῖται τὸ κάλυμμα. In the LXX, Exod. 34:34 reads: ἡνίκα δ' ἂν εἰσεπορεύετο Μωϋσῆς ἔναντι κυρίου λαλεῖν αὐτῷ, περιῃρεῖτο τὸ κάλυμμα.

Israel is very likely conceived as subject of the ἐπιστρέψῃ.[42] Paul construes the ἐπιστρέφειν (did he read ἐπέστρεψεν instead of εἰσεπορεύετο in his LXX text? Cf. Windisch, 123) in the technical sense of "conversion," as a turning to Christian faith, such as in 1 Thess. 1:9 (cf. 1 Peter 2:25; Acts 9:35; 11:21; 14:15; and 15:19, etc.).

The imperfect is boldly altered to the future tense.

Paul thus sees in Moses' activity in Exod. 34 the prefiguration of a new possibility which is then described in verse 18.

Characteristically, verses 14-16, just as verse 18, have in mind not only the διάκονος, that is to say, the lawgiver or apostle, but Jews and Christians in general. At bottom, for the apostle as for all believers, the παρρησία or ἐλευθερία is grounded in the gospel. Only at 4:1 does Paul return to the context.

Now, before the Christian position is described in verse 18, follows a parenthesis in verse 17.

Verse 17: ὁ δὲ κύριος τὸ πνεῦμά ἐστιν· οὗ δὲ τὸ πνεῦμα κυρίου, ἐλευθερία. Verse 17a gives the exegetical justification for drawing the consequence from Exod. 34:34. Turning to the κύριος (Χριστός) means a turning to the πνεῦμα. The "κύριος" of the text denotes "πνεῦμα"; on this exegetical ὁ δέ cf. Eph. 4:9 and Heb. 2:9.

Verses 6 and 8 had characterized the καινὴ διαθήκη primarily as that of the πνεῦμα. The question thus remained, May the Christian proclamation of the κύριος be described as the διακονία τοῦ πνεύματος? By all means! For by the κύριος of Exod. 34:34 nothing but the πνεῦμα is meant. So there is no simple identification of κύριος and πνεῦμα here, since there is immediate reference to the πνεῦμα of the κύριος, cf. 13:13.[43]

Verse 17b then draws the consequence for the context: ἐλευθερία is given with the πνεῦμα.[44] The assumption is that the intimate connection

---

[42] According to Allo, 92: ἡ καρδία αὐτῶν follows v. 15, a reading which Kümmel, 200, deems possible.

[43] Cf. Kümmel, *Kirchenbegriff*, 46, note 19a.

[44] Cf. Frank, *Philosophical Understanding and Religious Truth*, p. 155f. Corresponding to the idea assumed in v. 12 that where there is δόξα, there is παρρησία.

between πνεῦμα and ἐλευθερία is not uncontested. This is true not only of the Corinthian pneumatics, for whom πνεῦμα and ἐλευθερία are catchwords, but also for Paul. Cf. Rom. 8:1f.: οὐδὲν ἄρα νῦν κατάκριμα τοῖς ἐν Χριστῷ Ἰησοῦ. ὁ γὰρ νόμος τοῦ πνεύματος τῆς ζωῆς ἐν Χριστῷ Ἰησοῦ ἠλευθέρωσέν σε ἀπὸ τοῦ νόμου τῆς ἁμαρτίας καὶ τοῦ θανάτου. For the connection between ἐλευθερία and πνεῦμα cf. Gal. 5:13ff.

As things stand, Paul could conclude the train of thought with verse 17. The ἐλευθερία which verse 17 demonstrated as unique to Christians is, of course, also the παρρησία of verse 12. 4:1ff. then could be attached right here. But in verse 17 Paul is not thinking especially of the apostle and his παρρησία, but of Christians generally, and he wants first of all to expand the idea of verse 16 from the positive side. Verse 18 is attached to verse 16 by way of verse 17.

Verse 18: ἡμεῖς δὲ πάντες. The πάντες clearly shows that here Paul is thinking of Christians in general. We Christians (in contrast to the Jews, v. 15) are those to whom what was said in verse 16 (and explained in v. 17) applies. A Christian self-consciousness then is expressed in verse 18.

ἀνακεκαλυμμένῳ προσώπῳ τὴν δόξαν κυρίου κατοπτριζόμενοι τὴν αὐτὴν εἰκόνα μεταμορφούμεθα ἀπὸ δόξης εἰς δόξαν.

Since the clause does not read ἀνακεκαλυμμένη καρδίᾳ (cf. v. 15), but rather ἀνακεκαλυμμένῳ προσώπῳ, it is easy to assume that the Christians are not seen in parallel with the Jews, but with Moses himself. In this case the κατοπτρίζεσθαι[45] would not have to mean "behold," but rather "to throw an image of," "to reflect." Moses of course does not behold the divine δόξα. It is rather reflected in his face touched by the divine δόξα. This interpretation, however, is contradicted by the following:

First of all, κατοπτριζόμενοι is in the middle voice. Only the active means "to reflect," whereas the middle means "to look in a mirror" — naturally, in order to see oneself in the mirror — thus also "to mirror oneself." Cf. Zeus (v. Arnim, Stoic Vet Frag I 66, 35ff.) concerning a καλλωπιζόμενος, who while loitering walks over a grave — δικαίως . . . ὑφορᾷ (he regards with annoyance) τὸν πηλόν. οὐ γὰρ ἔστιν ἐν αὐτῷ κατοπτρίζεσθαι. ἐσοπτρίζεσθαι also means "to mirror oneself."

Cf. Plut Praec Coniug 141 D: ὁ Σωκράτης ἐκέλευε τῶν ἐσοπτριζομένων νεανίσκων τοὺς μὲν αἰσχροὺς ἐπανορθοῦσθαι τῇ ἀρετῇ, τοὺς δὲ καλοὺς μὴ καταισχύνειν τῇ κακίᾳ τὸ εἶδος. ("Socrates used to urge the ill-favored among the mirror-gazing youth to make good their defect by virtue, and the handsome not to disgrace their face and figure by vice.") Cf. Jamblichus Protr c. XXI κδ' concerning the Pythagorean σύμβολον: παρὰ λύχνον μὴ ἐσοπτρίζου. ἐνοπτρίζεσθαι is used in the same fashion. Cf. Porphyr Marc

---

[45] For κατοπτρίζεσθαι as meaning "to reflect," cf. Dupont, RB 56, 1949, 392-411, and *Gnosis,* 119f., 121.

13: (one should not pray God for material things of which one has no need when one is freed from the body, but rather for virtue, for spiritual blessings): δι᾿ ὧν μάλιστα καὶ αὐτὸς ἐνοπτρίζεσθαι πέφυκεν, οὔτε διὰ σώματος ὁρατὸς ὢν οὔτε διὰ ψυχῆς αἰσχρᾶς καὶ ὑπὸ τῆς κακίας ἐσκοτισμένης ("Hereby can God best be reflected, who cannot be seen by the body, nor yet by an impure soul darkened by vice." *Porphyry The Philosopher To His Wife Marcella,* p. 63). This means, then, that God is mirrored in the virtue — but naturally the idea is not that God observes himself, but that his image is reflected by the virtue, so that one may see his reflected image in the virtuous soul. He is "reflected."[46] The conclusion of Porphyr Marc 13 must be correspondingly interpreted. The conclusion reads: ἐπέσθω τοίνυν ὁ μὲν νοῦς τῷ θεῷ ἐνοπτριζόμενος τῇ ὁμοιώσει θεοῦ ("Let then thy mind follow after God," and "[Now the wise man . . . is known by God], and is reflected by his likeness to him." *Porphyry The Philosopher To His Wife Marcella,* p. 64). Thus the νοῦς should follow after God as one who, by resembling God (by means of virtue, cf. Porphyr Marc 16: ἡ δὲ ὁμοίωσις ἔσται διὰ μόνης ἀρετῆς; "Thou wilt best honor God by making thy mind like unto Him, and this thou canst do by virtue alone," *Porphyry The Philosopher To His Wife Marcella,* p. 65), reflects God. The ἐνοπτριζόμενος now takes on active sense, surely required by the fact that ἐνοπτριζόμενος has an accusative object (it is not a reflexive!).

Thus Corssen, ZNW 19, 1919/20, 2-6, is no doubt correct in his opposition to Reitzenstein, Hist. Mon., 143-255 (cf. Reitzenstein, FS. Andreas, 48-50), who reads ἐνοπτριζόμενος τῇ ὁμοιώσει θεοῦ with Mai and Nauck against the manuscript tradition, and construes the clause to mean, "since he beholds (looks at) himself in God and thus becomes like him." But aside from the conjecture θεοῦ, can this sense be supported grammatically?

Secondly, the context demands the meaning "to behold" for κατοπτρίζεσθαι. All the old versions render the term in this fashion (the vg reads *speculantes*). According to the context, the Christians can certainly not be paralleled with Moses, but only with Jews, and for good or ill the ἀνακεκαλυμμένῳ προσώπῳ must be construed in terms of the ἀνακεκαλυμμένη καρδίᾳ in verse 15.

Thirdly, only when the κατοπτρίζεσθαι denotes a beholding can we understand the μεταμορφούμεθα, for the idea of transformation through

---

[46] Certainly Wisdom 7:26 is also to be understood in this sense. (Of σοφία):
ἀπαύγασμα γάρ ἐστιν φωτὸς ἀιδίου
καὶ ἔσοπτρον ἀκηλίδωτον τῆς τοῦ θεοῦ ἐνεργείας
καὶ εἰκὼν τῆς ἀγαθότητος αὐτοῦ.
"For she is an effulgence from everlasting light
And an unspotted mirror of the working of God,
And an image of his goodness."
Wisdom is the pure reflection of God; it represents God (in the world as the πνεῦμα νοερόν, v. 22, which διήκει δὲ καὶ χωρεῖ διὰ πάντων, cf. v. 24).

reflection is not intelligible, though indeed the idea of transformation through beholding is, and particularly through beholding in a mirror.

On this point, cf. Reitzenstein, FS. Andreas, 48-50, and particularly Zosimos' report of the magic mirror of Alexander the Great: Whoever is mirrored in it, becomes pure and spiritual.[47]

The idea does not occur in James 1:23ff. where Reitzenstein (Hist. Mon. 248) wishes to find it: ὅτι εἴ τις ἀκροατὴς λόγου ἐστὶν καὶ οὐ ποιητής, οὗτος ἔοικεν ἀνδρὶ κατανοοῦντι τὸ πρόσωπον τῆς γενέσεως αὐτοῦ ἐν ἐσόπτρῳ· κατενόησεν γὰρ ἑαυτὸν καὶ ἀπελήλυθεν, καὶ εὐθέως ἐπελάθετο ὁποῖος ἦν. ὁ δὲ παρακύψας εἰς νόμον τέλειον τὸν τῆς ἐλευθερίας καὶ παραμείνας, οὐκ ἀκροατὴς ἐπιλησμονῆς γενόμενος ἀλλὰ ποιητὴς ἔργου, οὗτος μακάριος ἐν τῇ ποιήσει αὐτοῦ ἔσται. Here in this passage, the νόμος τέλειος is in no way compared to a magic mirror, looking into which works transformation. The comparison is rather a simple one: Just as looking into a mirror is a transient, fleeting moment without effect, so a mere hearing of the law without doing it is ineffectual.

Further, this idea is not present in Wisdom 7:22. (Reitzenstein, *op. cit.,* p. 247). The idea of transformation through looking in a mirror may underlie the Odes of Solomon 13:1-4:

Behold, the Lord is our mirror.
    Open (your) eyes and see them in Him.
And learn the manner of your face,
    Then declare praises to His Spirit.
And wipe the paint from your face,
    And love His holiness and put it on.
Then you will be unblemished at all times with Him.

(Charlesworth, p. 64)

If present at all, the idea is nonetheless used in an ethical, paraenetic fashion. Thus also in Philo Vit Mos II, 139, the brass wash beaker of the holy place is constructed of mirrors: "ὑπομιμνησκέσθω μέντοι" φησί "καὶ ὁ μέλλων περιρραίνεσθαι, ὅτι τοῦδε τοῦ σκεύους ἡ ὕλη κάτοπτρα ἦν, ἵνα καὶ αὐτὸς οἷα πρὸς κάτοπτρον αὐγάζῃ τὸν ἴδιον νοῦν καί, εἴ τι ὑπαφαίνοιτο αἶσχος . . . , τοῦτο θεραπεύῃ τὲ καὶ ἰᾶται τοῦ γνησίου καὶ ἀνόθου μεταποιούμενος κάλλους." "Let him," he means, "who shall be purified with water, bethink him that the mirrors were the material of this vessel, to the end that he himself may behold his own mind as in a mirror; and, if some ugly spot appear . . . then he may salve and heal the sore and hope to gain the beauty which is genuine and unalloyed" (that is, the beauty of virtue).

Cf. Philo Migr Abr 190: ἀναχωρήσας γὰρ ὁ νοῦς καὶ τῶν αἰσθήσεων καὶ τῶν ἄλλων ὅσα κατὰ τὸ σῶμα ὑπεξελθὼν ἑαυτῷ προσομιλεῖν ἄρχεται ὡς πρὸς κάτοπτρον ἀφορῶν ἀλήθειαν, καὶ ἀπορρυψάμενος πάνθ' ὅσα

---

[47] Cf. also Knox, *St. Paul,* 131f.; Dibelius, *Mystik,* 6f.

ἐκ τῶν κατὰ τὰς αἰσθήσεις φαντασιῶν ἀπεμάξατο τὰς περὶ τῶν μελλόντων ἀψευδεστάτας διὰ τῶν ὀνείρων μαντείας ἐνθυσιᾷ:[48] "In deep sleep the mind quits its place, and, withdrawing from the perceptions and all other bodily faculties, begins to hold converse with itself, fixing its gaze on truth as on a mirror, and, having purged away as defilements all the impressions made upon it by the mental pictures presented by the senses, it is filled with Divine frenzy and discerns in dreams absolutely true prophecies concerning things to come." The spirit thus looks into itself as its mirror; obviously a figure of self-examination.

The same idea is present in Spec Leg I 219, in the description of the liver as a mirror (cf. Plat Tim 71b): ἵν' ἐπειδὰν τῶν ἡμερινῶν φροντίδων ἀναχωρήσας ὁ νοῦς, ὕπνῳ μὲν παρειμένου τοῦ σώματος, μηδεμιᾶς δὲ τῶν αἰσθήσεων ἱσταμένης ἐμποδών, ἀνακυκλεῖν αὐτὸν ἄρξηται καὶ τὰ νοήματα καθαρῶς ἐφ' αὑτοῦ σκοπεῖν, οἷα εἰς κάτοπτρον ἀποβλέπων τὸ ἧπαρ ἕκαστα εἰλικρινῶς καταθεᾶται τῶν νοητῶν καὶ περιβλεπόμενος ἐν κύκλῳ τὰ εἴδωλα, μή τι πρόσεστιν αἶσχος, [ἵνα] τὸ μὲν φύγῃ, τὸ δ' ἐναντίον ἕληται, καὶ πάσαις ταῖς φαντασίαις εὐαρεστήσας προφητεύῃ διὰ τῶν ὀνείρων τὰ μέλλοντα: "In consequence when the mind, withdrawing from its daytime cares, with the body paralyzed in sleep and the obstruction of every sense removed, begins to turn itself about and concentrate upon the pure observation of its concepts, it looks into the liver as into a mirror where it gains a lucid view of all that mind can perceive and, while its gaze travels round the images to see whether they contain any ugly defect, it eschews all such and selects their opposites, and so, well satisfied with all the visions presented to it, prophesies future events through the medium of dreams."[49]

On the other hand, in the Acts of John 95f., p. 198, 12ff., transformation occurs by looking through a mirror at the divine nature. (Jesus says) Ἔσοπτρόν εἰμί σοι τῷ νοοῦντί με . . . ἴδε σεαυτὸν ἐν ἐμοὶ λαλοῦντι.[50] ("I am a mirror to you who know me . . . see yourself in me who am speaking. . . ." Hennecke, *New Testament Apocrypha*, II, 230.)

In the Acts of Thomas 111–113, the king's son who sets out from Egypt and has doffed his filthy garment, is given his splendid native robe at the border of his father's kingdom:

But suddenly, when I saw it over against me,
    The (splendid robe) became like me, as my reflection in a mirror;
I saw it (wholly) in me,
    And in it I saw myself (quite) apart (from myself),
So that we were two in distinction

---

[48] Cf. Knox, *St. Paul*, 131f. (132.3).
[49] Cf. Plat Tim 70d-72; also in Leisegang, *Geist* I, 196f.
[50] Cf. Käsemann, *Leib*, 166f.

And again one in a single form.
And again I saw that all over it
The motions of (knowledge) were stirring.
And I saw too
That it was preparing as for speech.
And with its royal movements
It poured itself entirely toward me. . . .[51]

But it appears that κατοπτρίζεσθαι may not only mean "to mirror oneself" (or to be reflected and thus throw a reflected image), but also "to behold in a likeness."[52] ἐσοπτρίζεσθαι is used in this fashion in Lydus, de Magistratibus, III, 1: λόγον . . . δι' οὗ ἄν τις ἀμυδρῶς (faintly) ἐσοπτρίσαιτο τὴν πάλαι κρατήσασαν . . . λαμπρότητά τε καὶ εὐταξίαν. (". . . a word . . . by which anyone should faintly see what was mastered of old . . . both splendor and order." [R.A.H.]) Here the meaning of ἐσοπτρίζεσθαι is no doubt "to see (as) in a mirror," thus not the thing itself, but a likeness of it, cf. 1 Cor. 13:12: βλέπομεν γὰρ ἄρτι δι' ἐσόπτρου ἐν αἰνίγματι, τότε δὲ πρόσωπον πρὸς πρόσωπον.

For ἐνοπτρίζεσθαι cf. 1 Clement 36:2: διὰ τοῦτο (sc. through Jesus Christ) ἀτενίζομεν εἰς τὰ ὕψη τῶν οὐρανῶν, διὰ τούτου ἐνοπτριζόμεθα τὴν ἄμωμον καὶ ὑπερτάτην ὄψιν αὐτοῦ, διὰ τούτου ἠνεῴχθησαν ἡμῶν οἱ ὀφθαλμοὶ τῆς καρδίας, διὰ τούτου ἡ ἀσύνετος καὶ ἐσκοτωμένη διάνοια ἡμῶν ἀναθάλλει εἰς τὸ φῶς, διὰ τούτου ἠθέλησεν ὁ δεσπότης τῆς ἀθανάτου γνώσεως ἡμᾶς γεύσασθαι. "Through him we see (as in a mirror?) the reflection of his (that is, God's) faultless and lofty countenance (appearance). . . ."

For κατοπτρίζεσθαι, cf. Philo Leg All III, 101 on Exod. 33:13. (Moses says to God) μὴ γὰρ ἐμφανισθείης μοι δι' οὐρανοῦ ἢ γῆς ἢ ὕδατος ἢ ἀέρος ἢ τινος ἁπλῶς τῶν ἐν γενέσει, μηδὲ κατοπτρισαίμην ἐν ἄλλῳ τινὶ τὴν σὴν ἰδέαν ἢ ἐν σοὶ τῷ θεῷ αἱ γὰρ ἐν γενητοῖς ἐμφάσεις διαλύονται, αἱ δὲ ἐν τῷ ἀγενήτῳ μόνιμοι καὶ βέβαιοι καὶ ἀίδιοι [ἂν] διατελοῖεν — "For I would not that Thou shouldst be manifested to me by means of heaven or earth or water or air or any created thing at all, nor would I find the reflection of Thy being in aught else than in Thee Who art God." Certainly, the meaning here is not "nothing created shall reflect you toward me, O God, but you yourself shall be the mirror in which I see you," so that God would be regarded as the mirror of himself (thus Lietzmann, 113). Rather, for the ἤ-clause an ἰδοίμην is to be inferred from the κατοπτρισαίμην.

On ἐνοπτρίζεσθαι cf. in addition Hierocl. Carm Aur, Mullach p. 22, 8ff.: ὥσπερ γὰρ ὀφθαλμῷ λημῶντι καὶ οὐ κεκαθαρμένῳ τὰ σφόδρα φωτεινὰ ἰδεῖν οὐχ οἷόν τε, οὕτω καὶ ψυχῇ μὴ ἀρετὴν κεκτημένη τὸ τῆς ἀληθείας

[51] The text according to R. Mcl. Wilson in Hennecke-Schneemelcher (1965), II, 502f.
[52] When there is an accusative object (except for the reflexive ἑαυτόν), another interpretation is certainly not possible.

ἐνοπτρίσασθαι κάλλος ἀμήχανον ("For just as it is not possible for the eye which is blurred and unclean to see what brightly shines, so it is impossible for the soul which has not acquired virtue to see the beauty of truth." R.A.H.).

Here, certainly, ἐνοπτρίζεσθαι has totally lost the sense of "to see in a reflected image," and means merely "to see." Did Paul use κατοπτρίζεσθαι in this attenuated sense so that it means merely "to behold," with the result that the idea of looking through a mirror is not to be considered at all? Does κατοπτρίζεσθαι thus equal ἀτενίζειν in verses 7 and 13?

τὴν αὐτὴν εἰκόνα μεταμορφούμεθα: "We are being changed into the same likeness." The μεταμορφοῦσθαι denotes the change into a new shape, that is, a new essence. μορφή of course is that which appears toward the outside (in the LXX synonymous with εἶδος, ὁμοίωμα, ὅρασις, ὄψις, cf. Lohmeyer on Phil. 2:6; p. 91, note 5), but it is contrasted with "essence," for which the Old Testament and Paul lack a term. Rather, "shape" is the very expression of "essence." In Hellenistic usage, μορφή (just as ὄνομα) becomes the name for the (divine) essence, cf. Reitzenstein, HMR, 357f.

The εἰκών is the very δόξα-image of the kyrios which we behold. Naturally, the meaning is not that we are changed into a "likeness" of the Kyrios, but rather that we are made like his essence, thus also become δόξα. The reason why Paul does not simply say τὴν αὐτὴν δόξαν, but τὴν αὐτὴν εἰκόνα, lies of course in the fact that he has in mind the κύριος and his δόξα as the object of sight, thus as εἰκών. We are changed into that which we behold. The sense is thus the same as in Rom. 8:29: ὅτι οὓς προέγνω, καὶ προώρισεν συμμόρφους τῆς εἰκόνος (the shape) τοῦ υἱοῦ αὐτοῦ; cf. verse 30: τούτους καὶ ἐδόξασεν. Cf. also Phil. 3:21: ὃς μετασχηματίσει τὸ σῶμα τῆς ταπεινώσεως ἡμῶν σύμμορφον τῷ σώματι τῆς δόξης αὐτοῦ.

This aspect is expressed here in the ἀπὸ δόξης εἰς δόξαν. The transformation is thus a process occurring in stages or without cessation. That this process occurs not only in an eschatological future, but now in the eschatological present follows from the fact that the beholding is a present activity.[53] But this is also indicated in 4:4, where the reference is to seeing τοῦ εὐαγγελίου τῆς δόξης τοῦ Χριστοῦ, which according to 4:6 enlightens the hearts. It is indicated above all in 4:7, according to which we have this θησαυρός already in the hull of earthly life. And, of course, this inner possession is at work in us as the life of Christ, 4:8ff. He is the ἔσω (ἄνθρωπος) ἡμῶν, who ἀνακαινοῦται ἡμέρᾳ καὶ ἡμέρᾳ, 4:16.

The transformation, then, does not take place as a magical process, but as the divine power's coming into effect in the historical life of the believer

---

[53] This is also due to the fact that the μεταμορφούμεθα reflects appropriation of a term from the mysteries.

in whom that power becomes his own for labor and for suffering (cf. pp. 81f.). In addition, cf. Rom. 12:2: μεταμορφοῦσθε τῇ ἀνακαινώσει τοῦ νοός, εἰς τὸ δοκιμάζειν ὑμᾶς τί τὸ θέλημα τοῦ θεοῦ.

Paul is not thinking of a cultic or mystical beholding, though for him — analogous to the beholding with veiled face at the synagogue reading — the moment of beholding is primarily the Christian worship, in which the gospel is proclaimed (on the relation of worship to life, cf. Col. 3:15-17).

And, of course, the ἀνάγνωσις of the νόμος does not involve a real beholding. Just as in that reading the sight of God is not veiled but rather the νοήματα are hardened and the καρδίαι covered, so the Christian "beholding" is nothing but the clarity and certainty with which the believers' νοήματα and καρδίαι grasp God's grace and will. Cf. a similar, spiritualizing interpretation of the transforming vision in the mysteries, Emped Fr B. 110.

Kümmel, 201, correctly emphasizes that the idea of present transformation through beholding Christ is a mystical idea which appears only here in Paul but which is divested of its authentically mystical sense, since the transformation is the working of Christ who (as Lord of the Spirit) has given the πνεῦμα as guarantee; and since Paul on the other hand regards sight as a matter of reason (5:7; Rom. 8:24f.), and describes the believer's life in the world as distinct from Christ (Phil. 1:23; cf. 2 Cor. 5:6, 8!).

How then is the transformation to be understood? As the ἀνακαινοῦσθαι of the ἔσω ἄνθρωπος of 4:16, the occurrence of which is described in 4:7-16,[54] or as a walking in the Spirit, as the εὐάρεστοι αὐτῷ (τῷ κυρίῳ) εἶναι in 5:9, by which the gulf between now and then is neutralized.

A reason is added, confirming the certainty of the μεταμορφοῦσθαι asserted — **καθάπερ ἀπὸ κυρίου πνεύματος**, sc. perhaps εἰκός ἐστιν. Accordingly, it (the μεταμορφοῦσθαι) proceeds from the κύριος πνεύματος. Lietzmann, 112, translates, "as (it) is (worked) by the Lord of the Spirit."

ἀπὸ κυρίου πνεύματος can scarcely mean, "from the Spirit of the Lord" (that would certainly have to read ἀπὸ πνεύματος κυρίου). Very likely the better reading is, "from the Lord of the Spirit." In any event the πνεῦμα could be an appositive — "from the Lord, who is the Spirit." It is highly improbable that κυρίου is adjectival (Knox, *St. Paul*, 131, 4), meaning "from the lordly Spirit."

Excursus: κύριος and πνεῦμα

Naturally, the ὁ δὲ κύριος τὸ πνεῦμά ἐστιν in verse 17 is an exegetical comment, not a definition of κύριος, though it of course assumes a certain identity of κύριος and πνεῦμα. In this regard, cf. especially the alternation of πνεῦμα (and of course πνεῦμα τοῦ θεοῦ as well as πνεῦμα τοῦ Χριστοῦ)

---

[54] Cf. Rom. 12:2.

and Χριστός in Rom. 8:9-11, and the parallelism of the formulae ἐν Χριστῷ (or κυρίῳ) and ἐν πνεύματι.

Paul clearly shaped the ἐν Χριστῷ in analogy with the pre-Christian formula ἐν πνεύματι (a formula of ecstasy). He thus construed the κύριος in analogy with the πνεῦμα as the wondrous power effective in faith, and by doing so decisively altered the character of the Jewish and primitive Christian Christology, that is, of the apocalyptic Son of Man doctrine. By doing so he was not only able to make contact with the Hellenistic Kyrios-cult (cf. Bousset, *Kyrios Christos,* and also Guignebert, RHphR 7, 1927, 253-264, especially 260), but also with the primitive community, insofar as it already clearly regarded the exalted Jesus in a specific way as King of the present age who inspired the prophets. But above all, Paul could combine πνεῦμα and κύριος, since for him both were eschatological entities. As κύριος, Christ is eschatological ruler, and the πνεῦμα (according to the Jewish view) is the gift of the end-time.

The Hellenistic-Jewish Sophia-doctrine hardly served Paul as a means (Windisch, 125; Knox, *St. Paul,* 71ff.). It furnishes an analogy to the extent that in Wisdom 7:2ff. the mythological heavenly hypostasis of Wisdom is interpreted as the Stoic πνεῦμα pervading the world (cf. 7:22: πνεῦμα νοερόν, ἅγιον — "a spirit quick of understanding, holy;" v. 23: διὰ πάντων χωροῦν πνευμάτων — "penetrating through all spirits;" v. 24: διήκει δὲ καὶ χωρεῖ διὰ πάντων — "she pervadeth and penetrateth all things;" v. 25: ἀπόρροια τῆς τοῦ παντοκράτορος δόξης εἰλικρινής — "a clear effluence of the glory of the Almighty;" and v. 26: ἀπαύγασμα . . . φωτὸς ἀϊδίου . . . εἰκὼν τῆς ἀγαθότητος αὐτοῦ — "an effulgence from everlasting light . . . an image of his goodness;" Charles, I, 546f.). But for Paul Christ is not (at least not primarily) a cosmic, but a historical force. Clearly, it is not the Stoic, but rather the Hellenistic-Gnostic idea of the πνεῦμα on which Paul is leaning, and according to which the πνεῦμα (in the context of a dualistic world view) is a supernatural divine power and gift. But if he has taken up this idea and shaped the ἐν Χριστῷ in analogy with the ἐν πνεύματι, then conversely the ἐν πνεύματι must be interpreted according to the ἐν Χριστῷ. Since for Paul Christ is the eschatological salvation event, ἐν Χριστῷ as well as ἐν πνεύματι denotes the total determination of life by Christ or the πνεῦμα, but not a mysterious quality or higher nature.

ἐλευθερία is thus not the Stoic independence of the ἡγεμονικόν or νοῦς from the σῶμα and the ἔξω (as Windisch, 126, supposes by appeal to Philo[55] Deus imm 46-48; on Stoic freedom, cf. Bultmann, ZNW 13, 1912, 100f., 104, and Schlier, *TDNT* 2, 487-502, cf. further Jonas, *Augustin*). Rather, the Pauline concept of freedom is related to the Gnostic idea as freedom from the αἰὼν οὗτος, though for Paul Gnostic freedom from

---

[55] In the above cited passage, Philo himself is influenced by the Gnostic concept of freedom.

εἱμαρμένη becomes freedom from νόμος and ἁμαρτία (Rom. 6:18, 20, 22; 8:1f., and Gal. 2:4; 5:1, 13), which includes a δουλεύειν in love (Gal. 5:13). It is thus also freedom from death (Rom. 8:21) and from all human conditions (1 Cor. 7:21-24; 9:19; 10:29; 12:13, and Gal. 3:28). Freedom thus occurs in concrete historical existence in which the believer already exists eschatologically as καινὴ κτίσις. And it is operative in the παρρησία of the proclaimer, in his εἰλικρίνεια and πεποίθησις.

In the matter of adopting the conceptuality of the Hellenistic mysteries, the conceptuality of Jewish-Christian apocalyptic Christology and soteriology fails to express how salvation determines life in the present, but rather renders faith as essentially hope. This conceptuality aims at indicating that the change of the aeons is imminent and has not yet taken place. On the other hand, contemporaneity can be expressed in the terminology of the mysteries. What is peculiar to Paul is that he understands the presence of salvation as an eschatological phenomenon, or that he construes the eschatological event as present.[56]

c. Actualizing παρρησία in apostolic activity: 4:1-6

Therefore, having this ministry by the mercy of God, we do not lose heart. We have renounced disgraceful, underhanded ways; we refuse to practice cunning or to tamper with God's word, but by the open statement of the truth we would commend ourselves to every man's conscience in the sight of God. And even if our gospel is veiled, it is veiled only to those who are perishing. In their case the god of this world has blinded the minds of the unbelievers, to keep them from seeing the light of the gospel of the glory of Christ, who is the likeness of God. For what we preach is not ourselves, but Jesus Christ as Lord, with ourselves as your servants for Jesus' sake. For it is the God who said, "Let light shine out of darkness," who has shone in our hearts to give the light of the knowledge of the glory of God in the face of Christ.

3:7-18 demonstrates that the διάκονος of the καινὴ διαθήκη has and must have παρρησία (v. 12) or πεποίθησις (v. 4), that therefore the characterization of the apostle in 2:14-16 is appropriate, and thus that Paul acts ἐξ εἰλικρινείας (2:17). His office confirms his πεποίθησις (3:4), and gives him παρρησία (3:12). He must thus speak as boldly as he did in 2:14-17. If he were not to do so, he would indicate that he was not ἱκανός (2:16; 3:5f.), that he did not understand his office. His consciousness of office gives him his sincerity (4:2 is the equivalent of ἐξ εἰλικρινείας in 2:17), and whoever doubts it should look to what he proclaims. He is not one who veils but who makes evident. He thus commends himself by nothing else than the φανέρωσις τῆς ἀληθείας (4:2), and in doing that very thing also

---

[56] Cf. also pp. 74f.

commends himself by his activity, which of course is grounded in nothing else than in the φανέρωσις (4:6) given to him.

The close connection between 4:1-6 and 3:7-18, by which Paul returns to his apostolic character and activity after digressing on the general Christian situation (3:16-18), is indicated in the following particulars:

1. In 4:1, the ἔχοντες κτλ. again takes up the ἔχοντες of 3:12, and the οὐκ ἐγκακοῦμεν . . . τὰ κρυπτὰ τῆς αἰσχύνης corresponds to the πολλῇ παρρησίᾳ χρώμεθα in 3:12.

2. The διακονία in 4:1 corresponds to the διακονία in 3:7.

3. The καθὼς ἐλεήθημεν corresponds to the διὰ Χριστοῦ in 3:4.

4. The discussion of the κεκαλυμμένον in 4:3f. harks back to the κάλυμμα of 3:13-18, and the blinded νοήματα of 4:4 correspond to the hardened νοήματα in 3:14f., just as the αὐγάσαι in 4:4 corresponds to the ἀτενίσαι in 3:13.

διακονία *establishes openness: 4:1-2*

Verse 1: The **διὰ τοῦτο** is connected with everything said in 3:7-18. Because it is true that the new covenant has a superior δόξα, and its διακονία possesses παρρησία, and all believers enjoy ἐλευθερία and thus a share in the δόξα, therefore . . . But the **ἔχοντες τὴν διακονίαν ταύτην** which explains the διὰ τοῦτο, limits what was stated in 3:7-18 insofar as the object of reflection is not the ἐλευθερία and δόξα which belong to all Christians but rather the apostle — which resumes the context dominant since 2:14.

The **καθὼς ἠλεήθημεν** (because we have experienced [God's] mercy) resumes the διὰ τοῦ Χριστοῦ of 3:4, or the expression of humility in 3:5.

In the New Testament, ἔλεος (cf. Bultmann, *TDNT*, 2, 477-487, and *Theology of the New Testament*, 282f.) frequently has the original Old Testament sense of goodness, and often the special meaning of pity or mercy. Used of God it has the Old Testament sense of faithfulness and grace, especially in reference to his salvation-historical and eschatological deed. For this reason ἐλεηθῆναι is used of the call to salvation in Rom. 11:30f. and 1 Peter 2:10, particularly of the calling of an apostle in 1 Cor. 7:25; 2 Cor. 4:1, and 1 Tim. 1:13, 16; cf. also 1 Cor. 15:10, and Gal. 1:15.

In the context οὐκ ἐγκακοῦμεν (just as in v. 16) cannot mean "we do not become weary"[57] (Luther), or "we do not become weary, careless" (Windisch, 132), but conforming to the πολλῇ παρρησίᾳ χρώμεθα in 3:12 means, "we do not despair"[58] (Lietzmann, 114), "we do not draw in our horns," "we are not cowardly" (as in 4:16).[59] Cf. Polyb IV, 19, 10 where the meaning is to behave cowardly, and thus equals the οὐκ ἐπαισχύνομαι in Rom. 1:16.

---

[57] Thus the LXX; Gal. 6:9; 2 Thess. 3:13.
[58] Thus Eph. 3:13.
[59] The antonym is θαρροῦμεν in 5:8.

Verse 2: ἀλλὰ ἀπειπάμεθα τὰ κρυπτὰ τῆς αἰσχύνης. Regarding ἀπειπεῖν as a term of renunciation, cf. Windisch, 132. Windisch, however, errs in construing ἀπειπεῖν in this passage as an expression of conversions terminology.

αἰσχύνη may denote 1) τὸ αἶσχος, the infamous, the disgrace, the disgraceful, or 2) *pudor,* the shame, being ashamed of oneself.

Thus τὰ κρυπτὰ τῆς αἰσχύνης has several possible meanings:

1. If αἰσχύνη is the equivalent of αἶσχος, and the genitive is one of quality, then the meaning is "what is hidden, secrets of infamous character which bring disgrace or are disgraceful."[60]

2. If αἰσχύνη is the equivalent of αἶσχος, and the genitive is subjective, then the meaning is "secrets which belong to disgrace, that is, hidden disgraceful things." Both meanings turn out to be the same, more or less.

3. If αἰσχύνη is equal to shame and the genitive is subjective, the meaning is "secrets which shame hides."[61]

4. If αἰσχύνη equals shame, but the genitive is one of quality, the meaning is "secrets of which one is ashamed."[62]

5. If αἰσχύνη equals shame, but the genitive is explicative, then the meaning is, "the secrets of being ashamed, that is, a shame which must be hidden."

Since the antonym is the παρρησία of 3:12, αἰσχύνη must certainly be understood as shame, and only possibilities three through five are relevant. Very likely the best translation is, "we renounce all cowardly secret action" (thus according to meaning number five).

In connection with 4:2, Windisch, 132, refers to Philo Spec Leg I, 321, and to Epict Diss III, 22, 14.

In Spec Leg I 321 Philo writes: οἱ μὲν γὰρ τὰ βλαβερὰ πράττοντες αἰσχυνέσθωσαν καὶ καταδύσεις ἐπιζητοῦντες καὶ γῆς μυχοὺς καὶ βαθὺ σκότος ἐπικρυπτέσθωσαν τὴν πολλὴν ἀνομίαν αὐτῶν ἐπισκιάζοντες, ὡς μηδεὶς ἴδοι· τοῖς δὲ τὰ κοινωφελῆ δρῶσιν ἔστω παρρησία καὶ μεθ' ἡμέραν διὰ μέσης ἴτωσαν ἀγορᾶς ἐντευξόμενοι πολυανθρώποις ὁμίλοις, ἡλίῳ καθαρῷ τὸν ἴδιον βίον ἀνταυγάσοντες καὶ διὰ τῶν κυριωτάτων αἰσθήσεων τοὺς συλλόγους ὀνήσοντες. . . . ("For virtue has no room in her home for a grudging spirit. Let those who work mischief feel shame and seek holes and corners of the earth and profound darkness, there lie hid and keep the multitude of their iniquities veiled out of the sight of all. But let those whose actions serve the common weal use freedom of speech and walk in daylight through the midst of the market-place, ready to converse with crowded gatherers, to let the clear sunlight shine upon their own life

---

[60] Cf. Eph. 5:12: τὰ γὰρ κρυφῇ γινόμενα ὑπ' αὐτῶν αἰσχρόν ἐστιν καὶ λέγειν.

[61] Cf. τὰ κρυπτὰ τῆς καρδίας in 1 Cor. 14:25.

[62] Thus τὰ κρυπτὰ τοῦ σκότους in 1 Cor. 4:5. As in possibility number four, note the πάθη ἀτιμίας in Rom. 1:26, and the πνεῦμα ἁγιοσύνης in Rom. 1:4. Cf. also Rom. 6:21: τίνα οὖν καρπὸν εἴχετε τότε; ἐφ' οἷς νῦν ἐπαισχύνεσθε.

and through the two most royal senses, sight and hearing, to render good service to the assembled groups. . . ."

Epict Diss III, 22, 13ff. writes that the genuine Cynic must be without μῆνις, φθόνος, lustful desires, desire for fame, etc. ἐκεῖνο γὰρ εἰδέναι σε δεῖ, ὅτι οἱ ἄλλοι ἄνθρωποι τοὺς τοίχους προβέβληνται καὶ τὰς οἰκίας καὶ τὸ σκότος, ὅταν τι τῶν τοιούτων ποιῶσιν, καὶ τὰ κρύψοντα πολλὰ ἔχουσιν . . . (15) ὁ Κυνικὸς δ᾽ ἀντὶ πάντων ὀφείλει τὴν αἰδῶ προβεβλῆσθαι· εἰ δὲ μή, γυμνὸς καὶ ἐν ὑπαίθρῳ ἀσχημονήσει (he makes a miserable figure). ("For this you ought to know: Other men have the protection of their walls and their houses and darkness, when they do anything of that sort, and they have many things to hide them . . . (15) But the Cynic, instead of all these defenses, has to make his self-respect his protection; if he does not, he will be disgracing himself naked and out of doors.")

On this view, the participles which follow give the reason: We can renounce secrets, because . . . **μὴ περιπατοῦντες ἐν πανουργίᾳ.** As in 5:7; 10:2f. and 12:18, etc., περιπατεῖν (just as ἀναστρέφεσθαι in 1:12) is frequently used of the conduct of life. πανουργία denotes slyness, cunning, craftiness; cf. 11:3 (in 12:16 the adverb is used), and Eph. 4:14, etc.

Paul thus need not be ashamed, because he does nothing disgraceful. μὴ περιπατεῖν ἐν πανουργίᾳ is the equivalent of οὐκ ἐν σοφίᾳ σαρκικῇ in 1:12!

μηδὲ δολοῦντες τὸν λόγον τοῦ θεοῦ. δολοῦν means to falsify (for example, wine, in Luc Hermot 59; cf. the ἄδολον γάλα in 1 Peter 2:2). The clause is a defense against the reproach of δόλος in 12:16 and 1 Thess. 2:3, as well as against the reproach of a lack of εἰλικρίνεια, cf. 1:12 and 2:17.[63] It is clear that Paul turns to the reproaches of his opponents who accuse him of acting from mean motives, hypocritically, of dissembling. Such reproofs thus match the reproach that he συνιστάναι ἑαυτόν (3:1), as what follows directly shows. These reproaches aimed at the apostle concern his motives as well as his preaching.

If Paul defends himself here by repudiating mean motives, then of course he does so only on the basis of the description of his apostolate as a διακονία τῆς καινῆς διαθήκης which excludes all insincere motives. After all, he does not say, "I am not ashamed becuase I have no poor motives," but rather, "since I need not be ashamed, I have no poor motives." Indeed, it is psychologically conceivable that in that case he is saying, "I need not be ashamed because I have no poor motives."

If anyone were to object, "Why cannot a deceiver also recruit for a good cause?" the answer would be, "Believe in the cause, and your question will vanish!" This is the sense of what follows — **ἀλλὰ τῇ φανερώσει τῆς ἀληθείας συνιστάνοντες ἑαυτούς.** By the proclamation of the gospel Paul proves his εἰλικρίνεια, his selfless sincerity.

---

[63] It is thus more vigorous or more specific than the reproach of καπηλεύειν in 2:17 (p. 69).

The ἀλήθεια which he proclaims (as in 2:14, φανεϱοῦν is used of the preaching), is not his personal truthfulness, but that very λόγος τοῦ θεοῦ which he does not falsify. It is the gospel which according to verse 3 he does not veil. It is the ὀσμὴ τῆς γνώσεως of 2:14, to the φωτισμός of which he is called, according to verse 6.

Thus Paul commends himself, as stated in reference to 3:1, and of course πϱὸς πᾶσαν συνείδησιν ἀνθϱώπων. "When people search their conscience, then they must agree with me" (Lietzmann, 115). Then it is clear why the teaching of right doctrine can prove the proclaimer's εἰλιϰϱίνεια. ἀλήθεια is not grasped by reflection, but by the συνείδησις. That is, the unbiased hearer is so shaped by the quality of ἀλήθεια, that he himself becomes the εἰλιϰϱινής and thus can see that the proclaimer of such ἀλήθεια is also shaped by εἰλιϰϱίνεια.

For this reason, the following statement by Windisch, 134, is incorrect: "The συνείδησις of 'men' furnishes an important point of contact for the gospel. The chief thing, however, is not the winning of men for the truth itself, but rather their recognition of the disinterestedness and legitimacy of its proclaimer."[64]

But could not the proclaimer be blind or a liar? The hearer must not ask! He must ask himself how he stands with respect to ἀλήθεια. A liar — he must then tell himself — would proclaim another gospel, not at all able to affect the hearers' συνείδησις. Only the εἰλιϰϱινής is ἱϰανός, according to 2:17. Thus, in conscience's being affected by the proclamation lies the criterion for the truth of that proclamation and for the εἰλιϰϱίνεια of the proclaimer. Where the proclamation can no longer touch the hearers' conscience, the proclaimer is not ἱϰανός. And Paul expressly writes ἀνθϱώπων, because he already has in mind the ἐνώπιον τοῦ θεοῦ equal to the ϰατέναντι θεοῦ in 2:17, and which means "answerable to God."[65]

διαϰονία *establishes accessibility: 4:3-6*

Verse 3: εἰ δὲ ϰαὶ ἔστιν ϰεϰαλυμμένον τὸ εὐαγγέλιον ἡμῶν. τὸ εὐαγγέλιον ἡμῶν is contrasted with the τὸ εὐαγγέλιον τοῦ Χϱιστοῦ of 2:12, because the apostle's preaching is at issue here — the gospel of Christ as we proclaim it.

It may be that the apostolic preaching appears veiled, that is — since we must of course interpret from out of the historical situation — that for the Gnostics at Corinth Paul's preaching does not seem to demonstrate the

---

[64] Langerbeck's argument in *Gnosis,* 132, note 2, is impossible: "By revealing (sc. proclaiming) the truth we are united to God, (and of course) in all accessibility, so that all men know it (that is, without its hiding anything)." He supports his statement with an appeal to Wisdom 7:14: διὰ τὰς ἐϰ παιδείας δωϱεὰς συσταθέντες — "those who get it (σοφία) obtain friendship with God, commended for the gifts that come from instruction."

[65] ἐνώπιον τοῦ θεοῦ is naturally not linked to πϱὸς . . . ἀνθϱώπων, but to συνιστάνοντες ἑαυτούς, cf. 7:12.

δόξα or mediate the πνεῦμα and ἐλευθερία, as they claim to do.⁶⁶ The gospel is thus equivocal, but it is so precisely because it is addressed to the συνείδησις (otherwise than in the formal parallel in Corp Herm 16, 1). In its accessibility it is also hidden, hidden from curious and imperious inquiry. For understanding does not rest on the reasoning sense, but on the yielding resolution of the one whose conscience is touched. For this reason the very thing which constitutes the gospel's accessibility, namely, that each may understand it in his συνείδησις, also establishes its hiddenness — ἐν τοῖς ἀπολλυμένοις ἐστὶν κεκαλυμμένον.⁶⁷

The ἀπολλύμενοι (2:15; 1 Cor. 1:18, and 2 Thess. 2:10) are the hardened (v. 4). It is not stated (Kümmel, 201) that Paul includes his Corinthian opponents among them (Lietzmann, 115). The formulation is quite basic, just as in 2:15f.

Objectively, the hiddenness of the gospel is different from that of the παλαιὰ διαθήκη, whose vanity was intended to remain hidden. Subjectively, of course, the hiddenness is the same to the extent that now, with the existence of the καινὴ διαθήκη, hearers may identify the hiddenness of the old's passing away with the hiddenness of the new's appearing. In both instances there is hiddenness for the hardened νοήματα (3:14 and 4:4). In both instances they will not surrender their own security, and hence in the one case veil themselves from the nothing in despair, and in the other presumptuously veil themselves from the Lord.

Verse 4: The ἀπολλύμενοι are described in verse 4: **ἐν οἷς ὁ θεὸς τοῦ αἰῶνος τούτου ἐτύφλωσεν τὰ νοήματα τῶν ἀπίστων.**⁶⁸ The ἀπολλύμενοι are not simply erring or foolish ones, but have fallen to ruin, to Satan Naturally, this is not stated from the perspective of deterministic speculation, but in order to make clear the seriousness of the decision. What is at stake in the question of faith is the either-or, God or Satan. There is no third thing between.

The phrase ὁ θεὸς τοῦ αἰῶνος τούτου⁶⁹ occurs only here in Paul. Elsewhere he uses ὁ σατανᾶς (2:11; 11:14, etc.; cf. ὁ διάβολος in Eph. 4:27; 6:11; and the Pastorals; cf. also Βελιάρ in 2 Cor. 6:15). Related to it is the phrase οἱ ἄρχοντες τοῦ αἰῶνος τούτου in 1 Cor. 2:6,8 (cf. Eph. 2:2: ὁ

---

⁶⁶ Thus we certainly need not "at best decipher" (Lietzmann, 115) what evoked the reproach; cf. the opinions enumerated by Windisch, 134. In contrast to the opinion of Fridrichsen, *Apostle,* 14f., that the indictment against Paul is that the gospel supposedly revealed to him is actually his own invention and thus is "veiled" to others, Kümmel, 201, is correct.

⁶⁷ Cf. the Messianic Mystery in John.

⁶⁸ Cf. Wisdom 2:21: ταῦτα ἐλογίσαντο, καὶ ἐπλανήθησαν· ἀπετύφλωσεν γὰρ αὐτοὺς ἡ κακία αὐτῶν. ("Thus reasoned they, being far astray, for their wickedness blinded them." Charles, I, 538.)

⁶⁹ ὁ αἰὼν οὗτος appears in Paul in Rom. 12:12; 1 Cor. 1:20; 2:6,8; 3:18; 2 Cor. 4:4; and Gal. 1:14.

ἄρχων τῆς ἐξουσίας τοῦ ἀέρος, and John 12:31; 14:30; 16:11:[70] ὁ ἄρχων τοῦ κόσμου τούτου. **And cf. Test Jud 19:4:** ἐτύφλωσεν γάρ με ὁ ἄρχων τῆς πλάνης, καὶ ἠγνόησα ὡς ἄνθρωπος [καὶ ὡς σάρξ] ἐν ἁμαρτίαις φθαρείς).

On designating the antigodly power as God, cf. Jonas, *Gnosis* I, 166, who states that such is to be understood from the process of profanizing the astral sphere: "The stars remain what they were in the monistic system — the gods of the world. As such they are included in the bracketing, and because they are the highest and most significant beings of the cosmos, they undergo transvaluation in the most heightened form. As gods of the world they become the antigods of the real God."

Paul can take up the Gnostic concept of the θεὸς τοῦ αἰῶνος τούτου, since for him the seductive and ruinous power of this aeon or "world" is a positively active power in opposition to God, not something relatively inferior or basically harmless. The world is not "imperfect" but evil. People experience it as seductive and ruinous. It is seductive by the fact that it offers itself to them as available to their desires and performances, their "fame." It is ruinous because it enslaves those who yield to it under the illusion that they have it at their disposal. They fall prey to it and thus lose grasp of themselves.

The "god of this aeon," however much Paul will have conceived it as a personal "evil," is not a causative power back of the human will, but is at work in the will's deciding for evil. Apparent recourse is had to supernatural factors when it is a matter of final decisions or an ultimate fate, for whose explanation there are no clear grounds, or whose importance towers above all individual decisions or events. There are analogies in Homer's Iliad IX 628f. (When Odysseus and Ajax together with Phoenix vainly attempt to urge Achilles to leave off his anger) Ajax says to Odysseus:

. . . αὐτὰρ Ἀχιλλεὺς
ἄγριον ἐν στήθεσσι θέτο μεγαλήτορα θυμόν,
σχέτλιος . . .

"But Achilles hath wrought to fury the proud heart within him, cruel man! neither recketh he of the love of his comrades. . . ."

Then in 636f., Ajax turns to Achilles:

. . . σοὶ δ' ἄλληκτόν τι κακόν τε
θυμὸν ἐνὶ στήθεσσι θεοὶ θέσαν εἵνεκα κούρης
οἴης . . .

"But as for thee, the gods have put in thy breast a heart that is obdurate and evil by reason of one only girl!"

In XII 292ff. Ajax says (the Trojans would not have breached the wall)
εἰ μὴ ἄρ' υἱὸν ἑὸν Σαρπηδόνα μητίετα Ζεὺς
ὦρσεν ἐπ' Ἀργείοισι, λέονθ' ὣς βουσὶν ἔλιξιν.

---

[70] Cf. Windisch, 135.

"Had not Zeus the counsellor roused his own son, Sarpedon, against the Argives, as a lion against sleek kine. . . ."

But in 307f. he states:

ὥς ῥα τότ᾽ ἀντίθεον Σαρπηδόνα θυμὸς ἀνῆκε
τεῖχος ἐπαίξαι διά τε ῥήξασθαι ἐπάλξεις.

"So did his spirit then urge godlike Sarpedon to rush upon the wall, and break down the battlements."

Cf. Sophocles Oed Tyr 1329ff.:

Ἀπόλλων τάδ᾽ ἦν, Ἀπόλλων, φίλοι,
ὁ κακὰ κακὰ τελῶν ἐμὰ τάδ᾽ ἐμὰ πάθεα.
ἔπαισε δ᾽ αὐτόχειρ νιν οὔ τις, ἀλλ᾽ ἐγὼ τλάμων.

"Apollo, friends, Apollo, he it was That brought these ills to pass; But the right hand that dealt the blow was mine, none other."

Cf. also Sophocles Oed Col 371f. (Ismene concerning her brothers):

νῦν δ᾽ ἐκ θεῶν τοῦ κἀλιτηρίου φρενὸς
εἰσῆλθε τοῖν τρὶς ἀθλίοιν ἔρις κακή . . .

"But now some god and an infatuate soul Have stirred betwixt them a mad rivalry."

Cf. again Sophocles El 199f.: εἴτ᾽ οὖν θεὸς εἴτε βροτῶν ἦν ὁ ταῦτα πράσσων; "whether a god or mortal wrought the woe" (that is, the murder of Agammemnon).

τῶν ἀπίστων. The ἐν οἷς . . . τῶν ἀπίστων would properly mean, among the ἀπολλύμενοι in the special group of the ἄπιστοι. But that cannot possibly be meant. The ἀπολλύμενοι and ἄπιστοι are rather identical. The τῶν ἀπίστων thus appears in place of an αὐτῶν, in order to describe the persons concerned. Or is it a gloss (Schmiedel, 231 and elsewhere) for the purpose of marking the difference between those who do not believe the gospel and the υἱοὶ Ἰσραήλ of 3:13?[71] What follows states that the ἀπολλύμενοι are indeed unbelievers.

εἰς τὸ μὴ αὐγάσαι τὸν φωτισμόν.[72] The φωτισμὸς τοῦ εὐαγγελίου τῆς δόξης τοῦ Χριστοῦ is merely a plerophoric expression for the τὴν δόξαν τοῦ εὐαγγελίου, or the τοῦ Χριστοῦ which we would expect following 3:18.

[71] Elsewhere, of course, ἄπιστοι is a special term for the Gentiles! 1 Cor. 6:6, etc.
[72] Wisdom 7:25f.: ἀτμὶς γάρ ἐστιν τῆς τοῦ θεοῦ δυνάμεως
καὶ ἀπόρροια τῆς τοῦ παντοκράτορος δόξης εἰλικρινής·
διὰ τοῦτο οὐδὲν μεμιαμμένον εἰς αὐτὴν παρεμπίπτει.
ἀπαύγασμα γάρ ἐστιν φωτὸς ἀιδίου
καὶ ἔσοπτρον ἀκηλίδωτον τῆς τοῦ θεοῦ ἐνεργείας
καὶ εἰκὼν τῆς ἀγαθότητος αὐτοῦ.
"For she is a breath of the power of God,
And a clear effluence of the glory of the Almighty;
Therefore can nothing defiled find entrance into her.
For she is an effulgence from everlasting light
And an unspotted mirror of the working of God,
And an image of his goodness." R. H. Charles, I, 547.

(It is nonsense that in this passage Paul ignores the "Χριστὸς ἐσταυρωμένος, entirely deprived of δόξα" and is thinking only of the Risen One [Windisch, 136f.]. Christ also as crucified is the κύριος τῆς δόξης [1 Cor. 2:8]. The δόξα is a paradox, as of course 4:7ff. at once makes clear).

φωτισμός is thus clearly active in sense, and denotes radiating, shining, brilliance. τοῦ εὐαγγελίου is a subjective genitive (that which belongs to the gospel) or a genitive of author (the brilliance proceeding from the gospel). τῆς δόξης is very likely a genitive of quality, and τοῦ Χριστοῦ is a subjective genitive (belonging to τῆς δόξης, or to τοῦ εὐαγγελίου?). αὐγάσαι must mean "to see," not, as is usual, "to radiate" (cf. Nägeli, *Wortschatz*, 25f.). If "to radiate" were meant (the ancient versions except for sa construe it in this fashion), then an αὐτοῖς (which 𝔐 vg and sy add) would hardly be superflous. Indeed, for αὐγάσαι as meaning "to see," an αὐτούς would be desirable, but for all that quite superfluous. But the meaning of αὐγάσαι as "to see" is secured by the fact that the μὴ αὐγάσαι is the consequence of blinding by the "god of this world," as well as by the parallelism of αὐγάσαι with ἀτενίσαι in 3:13.[73]

ὅς ἐστιν εἰκὼν τοῦ θεοῦ. The relative clause explains why the gospel is an εὐαγγέλιον τῆς δόξης. It is such because it is the εὐαγγέλιον τῆς δόξης τοῦ Χριστοῦ for he is the εἰκὼν τοῦ θεοῦ. Finally, then, it is the δόξα of God himself which shines in the gospel.

Christ is also referred to as εἰκὼν τοῦ θεοῦ in 1 Cor. 11:7, where the connection between εἰκών and δόξα is clear. εἰκών is thus understood primarily as ἀπαύγασμα (cf. above, note 72, Wisdom 7:25f., and cf. Heb. 1:3: ὃς ὢν ἀπαύγασμα τῆς δόξης καὶ χαρακτὴρ τῆς ὑποστάσεως αὐτοῦ).

The concept of Christ as the primal man who is God's εἰκών (thus Adam according to Gen. 1:27), and the oriental view that the king is the son and image of God, will have influenced the idea; cf. Windisch, 137; Dibelius, RGG I², 1602, and Kleinknecht, *TDNT* 2, 389f., who states that the εἰκών is not something inferior, but an equivalent phenomenon.[74]

Verse 5: οὐ γὰρ ἑαυτοὺς κηρύσσομεν ἀλλὰ Χριστὸν Ἰησοῦν κύριον. The clause establishes that those who regard Paul's gospel as κεκαλυμμένον are actually blinded by Satan. Paul really proclaims the εὐαγγέλιον τῆς δόξης; he does not proclaim himself, but Christ Jesus. "Not ourselves" — this does not repel the charge that Paul makes himself the object of his

[73] Incidentally, the same would be true even if the εἰς τὸ μή should not yield the result, but rather the purpose of the ἐτύφλωσεν. Windisch, 136, construes the phrase as denoting purpose, and refers to Corp Herm 7:3: τοιοῦτός ἐστιν ὃν ἐνεδύσω ἐχθρὸν χιτῶναι ἄγχων σε κάτω πρὸς αὐτόν, ἵνα μὴ ἀναβλέψας καὶ θεασάμενος τὸ κάλλος τῆς ἀληθείας καὶ τὸ ἐγκείμενον ἀγαθόν, μισήσῃς τὴν τούτου κακίαν (that is, in the ἀληθεία). "Such is the hateful cloak thou wearest — that throttles thee [and holds thee] down to it, in order that thou may'st not gaze above, and, having seen the Beauty of the Truth, and Good that dwells therein, detest the bad of it. . . ." *Thrice-Greatest Hermes*, II, 77.

[74] Cf. the cosmological sense of εἰκών in Col. 1:15f.

preaching, but rather the charge of egoistic motives. For Paul, however, to preach the gospel from egoistic motives would be precisely to preach himself, to set himself in Christ's place.

Paul proclaims Χριστὸν Ἰησοῦν κύριον.[75] The κύριον, as the following ἑαυτοὺς δὲ δούλους ὑμῶν διὰ Ἰησοῦν indicates, is predicative — "as Lord." The reason for this addition does not lie in the statement about the character of preaching as of the εὐαγγέλιον τῆς δόξης τοῦ Χριστοῦ (v. 4) — otherwise it might have to read τὸν κύριον τῆς δόξης (or δεδοξασμένον) — but in the rejection of egoistic motives in antithesis to the οὐ . . . ἑαυτούς. This thought is immediately given positive expression in the **ἑαυτοὺς δὲ δούλους ὑμῶν διὰ Ἰησοῦν**. We would have expected δούλους αὐτοῦ. But this thought is expressed by the διὰ Ἰησοῦν, "for Jesus' sake," that is, as his slaves and thus (along with that) also as yours. The διὰ Ἰησοῦν is thus not to be paraphrased — "in imitation of the model of Jesus" or "in order to win you for Jesus" (Windisch, 138). But the turn of phrase lying in the ὑμῶν is motivated by the situation. Paul's opponents, of course, assert that he slyly labors only for himself, to make himself lord of the community, cf. 1:24; 10:8; 13:10; and 1 Cor. 7:35 (cf. p. 44).

Grammatically, ἑαυτοὺς δὲ δούλους ὑμῶν is dependent on κηρύσσομεν, so that the apostle — in his role as servant of the communities — would belong to the content of the gospel. But it is highly questionable whether Paul has this in mind and does not simply intend to say that in such proclamation we are only your slaves.

In actuality, of course, the apostle also belongs to the gospel, and in 2:14ff. Paul, as it were, proclaims himself.[76,77] Cf. pp. 66f.: The apostle is himself the εὐωδία Χριστοῦ, and by the very fact that the gospel does not exist without him, since it is the accosting word of God in which the saving event in Christ is further accomplished, the apostle is liable to the misunderstanding that he proclaims himself (in terms of his opponents' reproofs). As a true proclaimer he must risk this misunderstanding. He must speak in Christ's or in God's stead to his hearers (5:18f.), precisely when he intends to speak as δοῦλος Χριστοῦ and of the communities.

Verse 6: ὅτι ὁ θεὸς ὁ εἰπών . . . ὃς ἔλαμψεν. If there is no anacoluthon here, then ὁ θεός must be a predicate, just as in 1:21 and 5:5 (though in these passages it appears without the article). The subject is ὁ εἰπών, "it is God who has said." Or, ὁ εἰπών is in apposition to ὁ θεός, and the relative

---

[75] Luther translates ". . . that he may be the Lord."
[76] Cf. Dio Chrys Or 13, 11f.: οἱ μὲν γὰρ πολλοὶ τῶν καλουμένων φιλοσόφων αὐτοὺς ἀνακηρύττουσιν, ὥσπερ οἱ Ὀλυμπίασι κήρυκες. ("Now the great majority of those styled philosophers proclaim themselves such, just as the Olympian heralds proclaim the victors. . . .")
[77]Synesios of Cyrene, De dono astrolabii, MPG 66, 1580A writes: τὸ κηρύττειν ἑαυτόν, καὶ πάντα ποιεῖν ὑπὲρ ἐπιδείξεως, οὐ σοφίας, ἀλλὰ σοφιστείας ἐστίν. (". . . to proclaim oneself and to do everything for display is not the part of wisdom but of sophistry." [R.A.H.] Cf. Heinrici, 151.)

clause is the subject — "God who has said . . . is the one who has let light shine."

In D* G 81 it Mcion and Chr the ὅς is omitted, so that ὁ θεός becomes the subject and ἔλαμψεν the predicate.

ὁ εἰπών· **ἐκ σκότους φῶς λάμψει**. The phrase is modeled after Gen. 1:3 which reads, καὶ εἶπεν ὁ θεός Γενηθήτω φῶς. Cf. Ps. 11:4: ἐξανέτειλεν ἐν σκότει φῶς τοῖς εὐθέσιν (the use is figurative!). In this phrase, the λάμπειν is clearly intransitive.

ὃς ἔλαμψεν ἐν ταῖς καρδίαις ἡμῶν. The λάμπειν here can hardly be intended as intransitive ("who radiated"). It is rather transitive due to the definition of purpose in the πρὸς φωτισμόν — "who has let light shine," "who has let it be light." In any event, the definition of purpose is clear: **πρὸς φωτισμὸν τῆς γνώσεως τῆς δόξης τοῦ θεοῦ ἐν προσώπῳ Χριστοῦ**. In the context, of course, Paul's γνῶσις cannot be at issue, but only the γνῶσις spread through his preaching (2:14). The πρὸς φωτισμὸν τῆς γνώσεως corresponds to the τῷ . . . τὴν ὀσμὴν τῆς γνώσεως αὐτοῦ φανεροῦντι δι' ἡμῶν of 2:14, or to the τῇ φανερώσει τῆς ἀληθείας of verse 2. The φωτισμός is Paul's activity, or its purpose, its effect. Paul spreads the word of God, the truth (v. 2) or the γνῶσις made possible by it. φωτισμός is therefore active just as in verse 4 — the shining, the brilliance (in v. 4 of course under the aspect that it is seen; in v. 6 under the aspect that it shines).[78]

φωτισμός then denotes neither the radiance of the γνῶσις before us, nor the radiance within us (cf. Windisch, 139; so also Lietzmann, 114, translates "so that the knowledge dawned," that is, in our hearts — and, so it appears, do almost all exegetes). The meaning is rather that "God has let it lighten in our hearts, so that (through the preaching) we bring to light the γνῶσις of the δόξα of God."[79] The meaning is therefore the same as in Gal. 1:16: ἀποκαλύψαι τὸν υἱὸν αὐτοῦ ἐν ἐμοί, ἵνα εὐαγγελίζωμαι αὐτὸν ἐν τοῖς ἔθνεσιν. The ὃς ἔλαμψεν κτλ. thus refers to Paul's conversion. (Cf. Wetter, FS. Jülicher, 80-92.) For this reason ἐν ταῖς καρδίαις ἡμῶν cannot apply to Christians as such (in that case they would have to be viewed under the aspect of cooperating also in the spread of the gospel), but only to Paul himself, or to Paul and his co-workers. Why not simply πρὸς τὸν φωτισμὸν τῆς δόξης, rather than . . . τῆς γνώσεως τῆς δόξης? Because φωτισμός occurs in the proclamation, the result of which is that very γνῶσις. δόξα is not a perceptible phenomenon. The fact that the spreading of γνῶσις is described as φωτισμός does not derive from Gen. 1:3. Rather, Gen. 1:3 is cited because the proclamation is taken for φωτισμός. This is the language of Gnosticism, cf. below.

This γνῶσις is described as τῆς δόξης τοῦ θεοῦ, whereas after verse 4

[78] Only in this way can v. 6 furnish the basis for v. 5, cf. below.
[79] Dupont, *Gnosis*, 37, 1, also recognizes the active sense of φωτισμός, but wants to construe God as subject. But then it is still identical to ἔλαμψεν!

and 3:18 we might expect τῆς δόξης τοῦ Χριστοῦ. But the δόξα Χριστοῦ is ultimately God's δόξα. According to verse 4, Christ is of course the image of God, the εἰκὼν τοῦ θεοῦ, and thus God's δόξα appears ἐν προσώπῳ Χριστοῦ — whoever sees Christ, sees God (cf. John 14:9).[80] Obviously, the πρόσωπον Χριστοῦ is not visible in ecstatic vision, but by faith in the proclaimed word.

Paul, then, first of all parallels his conversion with the creation. But since his conversion in turn is only for the purpose of spreading the φωτισμός of God's δόξα, his conversion is only one element of that event parallel to creation, in which now "light shines out of darkness." That is, creation and saving event are made parallel, just as according to 5:1 the believer is a καινὴ κτίσις. The formulation may be influenced by Jewish belief in the end-time as equal to the beginning-time. On this subject, cf. Staerk, *Erlösererwartung,* 21f.[81]

Verse 6 furnishes the basis for verse 5 (ὅτι!). The intent behind it is not to account for the general statement "we preach Christ" by the notion that Paul can do so because he has seen Christ (Windisch, 140), or to explain "why his gospel brightly shines for unblinded eyes" (Lietzmann, 115). Rather, verse 6 furnishes the exact basis for verse 5, that is, for the assertion that Paul preaches Jesus as κύριος, and himself as δοῦλος. This is so because (by his conversion) he is commissioned to spread the very knowledge of the δόξα of God manifest in Christ.[82] Thus what was asserted in 2:14-17 is proven from the character of the gospel. The ring is closed.

2. δόξα or ζωή as hidden and revealed: 4:7–6:10

a. The hiddenness of ζωή under cover of the old aeon: 4:7–5:10.
   ζωή in θάνατος: 4:7-18.
   1. The paradox: 4:7-12.
   2. ζωή in proclamation: 4:13-15.
   3. The character of ζωή as future: 4:16-18.
   Determination of the present by the future: 5:1-10.
   1. The temporariness of the present as an indication of the future: 5:1-5.
   2. Life as a being determined by the future: Faith, yearning and responsibility: 5:6-10.
b. The revelation of ζωή in proclamation: 5:11–6:10.
   Proclamation as the breaking in of the new creation: 5:11-19.

[80] He is of course the εἰκών of v. 4.
[81] Dupont, *Gnosis,* 37f., stresses that Paul is speaking of his conversion, and polemicizes against deriving φωτισμὸς τῆς γνώσεως from Hellenistic mysticism. But cf. Corp Herm 7, 2; 10, 21; 13, 18; Ascl 41 (Nock-Festugiere II, pp. 352ff.), Corp Herm 1, 32, and in addition Festugiere, *Revelation* I, 281, 3.
[82] This corroborates our interpretation of φωτισμός, cf. above.

1. The new criterion for judgment: 5:11-15.
2. The basis for proclamation in the saving event: 5:16-19.
The practice of proclamation.
1. Proclamation as eschatological event: 5:20-6:2.
2. The apostle in the power of the eschatological event: 6:3-10.

a. The hiddenness of ζωή under cover of the old aeon: 4:7–5:10

ζωή in θάνατος: 4:7-18

But we have this treasure in earthen vessels, to show that the transcendent power belongs to God and not to us. We are afflicted in every way, but not crushed; perplexed, but not driven to despair; persecuted, but not forsaken; struck down, but not destroyed; always carrying in the body the death of Jesus, so that the life of Jesus may also be manifested in our bodies. For while we live we are always being given up to death for Jesus' sake, so that the life of Jesus may be manifested in our mortal flesh. So death is at work in us, but life in you. Since we have the same spirit of faith as he had who wrote, "I believed, and so I spoke," we too believe, and so we speak, knowing that he who raised the Lord Jesus will raise us also with Jesus and bring us with you into his presence. For it is all for your sake, so that as grace extends to more and more people it may increase thanksgiving, to the glory of God. So we do not lose heart. Though our outer nature is wasting away, our inner nature is being renewed every day. For this slight momentary affliction is preparing for us an eternal weight of glory beyond all comparison, because we look not to the things that are seen but to the things that are unseen; for the things that are seen are transient, but the things that are unseen are eternal.

The φανέρωσις of ἀλήθεια (4:2), or the φωτισμός of γνῶσις (4:6) occurs in the νέκρωσις of the ἔξω ἄνθρωπος (v. 16). This section is not at all a "contemplation" or "confession" (Windisch, 141), but rather a new treatment of the old theme struck in 2:14-17 (Lietzmann, 115: "Continuation of the apology begun in 3:4").

The catchword is φανέρωσις in verse 10f., as well as in 2:14 and 4:2, but with a nuance. Till now the reference was to the φανέρωσις of γνῶσις (2:14), of ἀλήθεια (4:3), or of the φωτισμὸς τῆς γνώσεως (4:6) occurring through the apostle's preaching. Now the reference is to the φανέρωσις of ζωή, and indeed of the φανερωθῆναι of the ζωὴ τοῦ Ἰησοῦ in the body of the preaching apostle. But this φανέρωσις results in the hearers' reception of ζωή (v. 12), and occurs in the λαλεῖν of the apostle (v. 13). The presupposition for the ζωή of the communities is that the φανέρωσις of the ζωὴ τοῦ Ἰησοῦ takes place in his body.

Finally, then, it is one and the same φανέρωσις. Since preaching spreads γνῶσις, it works ζωή in the hearers.[83] The reason why the accent falls on this aspect now is that it is the φανέρωσις of the δόξα which is effected by the preaching. But where there is δόξα there is also ζωή. And just as the Jews' question to the assertion in Romans 3:21–4:25 that the δικαιοσύνη τοῦ θεοῦ is a present reality reads, "Where then are the ζωή and ἁγιασμός?" So the Corinthian Gnostics' question to the assertion that Paul's preaching works the φανέρωσις of δόξα must read, To what extent is the ζωή mediated by this preaching, a ζωή of which the Gnostics boast on the basis of their gospel, and in contrast to which Paul's preaching appears to them contemptible?

While the section in 2:14–4:6 thus had in view the apostle's office with respect to his person and defended his παρρησία, the basic issue in 4:7-18 (or up to 5:10) is the content of the apostolic preaching, hence not the person but the subject matter. Just as 2:14–4:6 made clear the inner connection between person and subject matter, so 4:7-18 (or up to 5:10) makes clear the inner connection between subject matter and person, and this emerges with full clarity in 5:11–6:10.

1. The paradox: 4:7-12

The fact that ζωή is now the theme indicates that the meaning of the Christian concept of ζωή is not clear, not a concept of natural thought. Just as φανέρωσις was not a clear concept (the εὐαγγέλιον can be veiled, 4:3), and just as it is two-edged, for life or for death (2:15f.), so also ζωή is equivocal — externally it appears as θάνατος. But this paradoxical character of ζωή corresponds precisely with its divine nature. It is, of course, the ζωή τοῦ Ἰησοῦ to which the νέκρωσις τοῦ Ἰησοῦ corresponds, and the one can only be had together with the other.

But the reason why Paul first speaks of himself as apostle in order to explain the concept of ζωή is that the Corinthian Gnostics fail to see the σημεῖα τοῦ ἀποστόλου (12:12) precisely in him, the apostle, that they regard him as weak (10:10), that according to their lights he does not appear to be a pneumatic. For them, too, apostle and preaching are a unity. The preaching of the contemptible apostle seems to them contemptible.

Verse 7: ἔχομεν δὲ τὸν θησαυρὸν τοῦτον ἐν ὀστρακίνοις σκεύεσιν. As to the diction, θησαυρός is used in the figurative sense in Sirach 1:25 (θησαυροὶ σοφίας), and likewise in Barnabas 11:4.[84]

The ὀστράκινα σκεύη[85] denote the weak, transitory body. Cf. Lam. 4:2:

---

[83] As indeed was already stated in 2:15f., and indirectly also in the description of the καινὴ διακονία as a διακονία τοῦ πνεύματος τῆς δικαιοσύνης, as μένον in 3:7-11, cf. also Phil. 3:8-10. To attain to the knowledge of Christ Jesus is to participate in his resurrection.

[84] Wisdom 7:14 (ἀνεκλιπὴς γὰρ θησαυρός ἐστιν ἀνθρώποις, sc. σοφία) "For she is unto men a treasure that faileth not." Charles, I, 546.

[85] On the inferiority of earthly vessels, cf. Str.-B. III, 516.

πῶς ἐλογίσθησαν εἰς ἀγγεῖα ὀστράκινα, ἔργα χειρῶν κεραμέως, and Isa. 64:8 (in the Hebrew, v. 7): καὶ νῦν, κύριε, πατὴρ ἡμῶν σύ, ἡμεῖς δὲ πηλὸς ἔργον τῶν χειρῶν σου πάντες. A similar figure is used in Ta ᾿an 7a (Str.-B. I, 861): "The daughter of the emperor (Hadrian) said to R. Jehoshua b. Hananiah [ca. 90 B.C.]" — that is, in reference to his scholarship — "Ah, such lordly wisdom in such an ugly vessel!"[86]

The reference is to Paul as apostle. The θησαυρός is thus not the Christian γνῶσις τῆς δόξης which the apostle spreads; it is not "the gospel and its *doxa*" (Lietzmann, 115, and Windisch, 141f.) — or is such only by implication. What is explicit is that the θησαυρός is Paul's διακονία as a διακονία τῆς δόξης, which lends him his "status." τοῦτον of course refers to verse 6, which described that status. It is Paul's very status which appears in an unworthy garment. But just this contradiction between status and appearance has its reason and sense: ἵνα ἡ ὑπερβολὴ τῆς δυνάμεως ᾖ τοῦ θεοῦ καὶ μὴ ἐξ ἡμῶν. The ἵνα . . . ᾖ means, this proves that. . . . (Lietzmann, 114: "that one may know"). On δύναμις cf. 6:7; 12:9; 13:4; 1 Cor. 1:18,24; 2:4f., etc. ὑπερβολή is a favorite with Paul, cf. verse 17; 1:8; 4:17; 12:7; 1 Cor. 12:31; Rom. 7:13 and Gal. 1:13 (cf. ὑπερβαλλόντως in 11:23; ὑπερβάλλειν in 3:10; 9:14; elsewhere in the New Testament it appears only in Eph. 1:19; 2:7; and 3:19). It expresses the οὐχ ἀφ᾿ ἑαυτῶν of 3:5, the ἐκ θεοῦ of 2:17, the διὰ τοῦ Χριστοῦ of 3:4, or the καθὼς ἠλεήθημεν of 4:1.[87]

The misconception that faith depends on the brilliant, fascinating shape of the preacher must be guarded against. What renders the apostle's πεποίθησις liable to misunderstanding — his external appearance and condition which contradict his καύχησις — is precisely what establishes it, for this condition and appearance give free play to the activity of God whose δύναμις is made perfect in ἀσθένεια (12:3).

On 4:7 Windisch, 143, refers to the contrast between God and man accented in 4 Ezra 4:11; Epict Diss II 19, 27, and especially in Plato Ion 533dff. (cf. in Leisegang, *Geist* I,1, 126ff.). But the parallels merely indicate that the idea of God as such is not specifically Pauline. The contrast with Plato, however, lies in the latter's identification of the divine in man despite human weakness. Man with his capacity has no share in the divine revelation, he does not contribute to it (thus Plato's orientation to the psychological phenomenon of ecstasy, in which man's νοῦς is silent; on the other hand, cf. 1 Cor. 14:13ff.).[88] For Plato, then, there is not as for Paul that causal

---

[86] The comparison of the body with a breakable vessel is Hellenistic. Cf. Windisch, 142, and Knox, *St. Paul*, 135. Barn 7:3 reads (the κύριος) ἔμελλεν τὸ σκεῦος τοῦ πνεύματος (= his body) προσφέρειν θυσίαν (". . . was going to offer the vessel of the spirit as a sacrifice for our sins. . . ."). 11:9 likewise reads: τὸ σκεῦος τοῦ πνεύματος.

[87] Cf. 1 Cor. 15:10.

[88] On the other hand, cf. the Pauline paradox that God is at work in human effort.

connection between ἀσθένεια and δύναμις, grounded in the cross of Christ. Further, for Plato the revelation consists in the genesis of the work (of art) performed by man, while for Paul God's ζωή is revealed precisely in the historical life of man.

Verse 8. Verses 8-11 unfold the idea of verse 7, first in four brief, then in two longer antitheses. The theme is the contradiction between status and appearance as the paradoxical revelation of ζωή.

ἐν παντὶ θλιβόμενοι ἀλλ᾽ οὐ στενοχωρούμενοι, ἀπορούμενοι ἀλλ᾽ οὐκ ἐξαπορούμενοι. The meaning is "afflicted, but not crushed, perplexed, but not driven to despair!" The ἐν παντί (sc. καιρῷ, καὶ τόπῳ, καὶ πράγματι. Cf. Theophylact's Expositio in epist. ad Cor. 264, MPG 124, 841) naturally belongs to all the antitheses in verses 8f., and is taken up again by the πάντοτε in verse 10 and the ἀεί in verse 11. The temporal aspect in the ἐν παντί is thus dominant.

The antitheses[89] (linked by paronomasia in v. 8) are ranged in the style of the diatribe; cf. Bultmann, *Diatribe*, 25ff., 79ff., and especially Epict Diss II 19, 24:

δείξατέ μοί τινα νοσοῦντα καὶ εὐτυχοῦντα,
    κινδυνεύοντα καὶ εὐτυχοῦντα,
    ἀποθνήσκοντα καὶ εὐτυχοῦντα,
    πεφυγαδευμένον καὶ εὐτυχοῦντα,
    ἀδοξοῦντα καὶ εὐτυχοῦντα.

("Show me a man who though sick is happy, though in danger is happy, though dying is happy. . . .") Cf. also Windisch, 143.[90]

On the lavishness of the list, cf. the peristasis-catalog in Bultmann, *Diatribe*, 19. In the antithesis, ἀλλ᾽ οὐ is used with the participle because the individual concept is negated; cf. Bl.-D. para. 430,3.

Verse 9: διωκόμενοι ἀλλ᾽ οὐκ ἐγκαταλειπόμενοι, καταβαλλόμενοι ἀλλ᾽ οὐκ ἀπολλύμενοι. "Persecuted,[91] but not forsaken; struck down, but not destroyed." The ἐγκαταλειπόμενοι is naturally used of God.

Cf. Josh. 1:5 (God speaks to Joshua): ὥσπερ ἤμην μετὰ Μωυσῆ, οὕτως ἔσομαι καὶ μετὰ σοῦ καὶ οὐκ ἐγκαταλείψω σε οὐδὲ ὑπερόψομαί σε; Ps. 36:25: καὶ οὐκ εἶδον δίκαιον ἐγκαταλελειμμένον; Ps. 36:28: ὅτι κύριος

---

[89] Plutarch's Moralia, 1057E, in Fridrichsen, CN IX, 1944, 30.
[90] Cf. also A. v. Droste-Hülshoff:
    "Verlassen, aber einsam nicht,
    Erschüttert, aber nicht zerdrückt,
    So lange noch das heilge Licht
    Auf mich mit Liebesaugen blickt!" (Lebt wohl, p. 234).
    "Forsaken, but not alone,
    Shaken, but not bowed down,
    So long as still the holy light
    With eyes of love keeps me in sight." [R.A.H.]
[91] Fridrichsen, *op. cit.*, writes that διωκόμενοι ἀλλ᾽ οὐκ ἐγκαταλειπόμενοι may mean "pursued (by a rival in the match) but not overtaken (outdistanced)" (?)

. . . οὐκ ἐγκαταλείψει τοὺς ὁσίους αὐτοῦ, and Sirach 2:10: ἢ τίς ἐνέμεινεν τῷ φόβῳ αὐτοῦ καὶ ἐγκατελείφθη. God's "not forsaking" thus belongs to devotional language, and appears also in Deut. 31:6-8; Ps. 15:10 and 1 Chron. 28:20.

Naturally, the antitheses do not mean, "it goes badly with us but not entirely." "We always find a way out, and are preserved from the worst" (Windisch, 143).[92] The meaning is rather that "in all affliction things do not really and finally go badly for us. We can say Yes to it all (εὐδοκεῖν, 12:10)." It is just this which the δύναμις of God brings about, that all suffering loses its desperate character, that, as verses 10f. state, it becomes a φανέρωσις τῆς ζωῆς τοῦ Ἰησοῦ.

This also explains the formal contradiction between the οὐκ ἐξαπορούμενοι in verse 8 and the ὥστε ἐξαπορηθῆναι ἡμᾶς καὶ τοῦ ζῆν in 1:8. According to Windisch, 143, what is at issue in 1:8 is merely the subjective consciousness of greatest distress, while the οὐκ ἐξαπορούμενοι in 4:8 is objective as well, and in this sense, then, also applies to 1:8.[93] The ἐξαπορηθῆναι in 1:8 is uttered from the human point of view, and in the ἀλλὰ ἐν ἑαυτοῖς of 1:9 Paul adopts the divine point of view toward it, or he subjects himself to God's judgment and for this very reason is not in despair. Likewise, the οὐκ ἐξαπορούμενοι of 4:8 is the judgment of faith.

Formally comparable is the attitude of the Stoic as in Epict Diss II 19, 24, or in Seneca's Ep 41, 4: Si hominem videris interritum periculis, intactum cupiditatibus, inter adversa felicem, in mediis tempestatibus placidum, ex superiore loco homines videntem, ex aequo deos, non subibit te veneratio eius? non dices, "ista res maior est altiorque quam ut credi similis huic in quo est corpusculo possit"?[94] ("If you see a man who is unterrified in the midst of dangers, untouched by desires, happy in adversity, peaceful amid the storm, who looks down upon men from a higher plane, and views the gods on a footing of equality, will not a feeling of reverence for him steal over you? Will you not say: 'This quality is too great and too lofty to be regarded as resembling this petty body in which it dwells? . . .'")

For Paul, however, the ἔσω ἄνθρωπος (v. 16) — for which the paradoxical ζωή is active in sufferings — is not the inwardness of the Stoic who shuts himself off from whatever happens, whom no occurrence can affect, but which also means nothing. Rather, the ἔσω ἄνθρωπος is the person drawn in faith toward the future, not given with spiritual states or with disposition, but only believed and constituted by faith amid occurrences.

---

[92] Certainly, Jesus found no escape from the cross!

[93] Quite the reverse! 1:8 is a judgment on the situation, and 4:8 on Paul as master of it.

[94] Cf. also Seneca Ep 30:3: hoc philosophia praestat, in conspectu mortis hilarem [esse] et in quocumque corporis habitu fortem laetumque nec deficientem quamvis deficiatur = "this is what he (Bassus) owes to philosophy: (It makes) one cheerful in view of death, brave in every bodily condition, without weakness amid all weakness."

Cf. Luther on Heb. 2:9 (WA 57, Hebräerbrief [Ficker] 122) with reference to Rom. 6:6: oportet enim "destrui corpus peccati" et legem carnis seu membrorum, cum sit impossibile "aliquod inquinatum intrare regnum celorum" [Rev. 21:27]. Talis autem destruccio fit per cruces, passiones, mortes et ignominias. Ideo Deus mortificat, ut vivificet, humiliat, ut exaltet etc. Et hoc est, quod Apostolus gloriatur se nihil nosse nisi Ihesum Christum et hunc ipsum non gloriosum, sed crucifixum [1 Cor. 2:2], portans stigmata Domini sui in corpore suo [Gal. 6:17]. Christum enim crucifixum in se habere est vivere plenum temptacionibus et passionibus, et ideo fit carnalibus "signum, cui contradicitur" etc. [Luke 2:34]. Consilium ergo est omnem temptacionem, eciam ipsam mortem obviis ulnis [with open arms] non secus ac ipsum Christum excipere in laude et leticia. ("For it is necessary that 'the body of sin' and the law of the flesh or the members 'be destroyed' [Rom. 6:6], since it is impossible for 'anything unclean to enter the kingdom of heaven' [cf. Rev. 21:27]. But such destruction comes about through crosses, sufferings, deaths, and disgraces. Therefore God kills in order to make alive; He humiliates in order to exalt, etc. And this is what the apostle glories in when he says that he knows nothing except Jesus Christ, and Him not glorified but crucified [cf. 1 Cor. 2:2]. He bears on his body the marks of his Lord [cf. Gal. 6:17]. For to bear Christ crucified in oneself is to live a life full of trials and sufferings, and for this reason He becomes for carnal men 'a sign that is spoken against' [Luke 2:34]. Therefore one should resolve to receive with open arms every trial, even death itself, with praise and joy, just as one should receive Christ Himself." Luther's Works, Vol. 29, 130.)

Verse 10: The antithetical clause in verses 10f. are no longer linked by an ἀλλ᾽ οὐ as in verses 8f., but by a ἵνα, so that the paradox in the concept of life becomes more clear. The very death at work in outward existence must bring the inner life to light. πάντοτε τὴν νέκρωσιν τοῦ Ἰησοῦ ἐν τῷ σώματι περιφέροντες, ἵνα καὶ ἡ ζωὴ τοῦ Ἰησοῦ ἐν τῷ σώματι ἡμῶν φανερωθῇ. Lietzmann, 115f. translates: "I am in continual peril of my life, and suffer bodily from my wearisome vocation, just as Jesus suffered (Gal. 6:17), that like Jesus at his resurrection I may some day also have life bodily, as verse 14 expressly states."

First of all, however, the τὴν νέκρωσιν τοῦ Ἰησοῦ περιφέρειν does not mean to be in peril of life, but to be actually dying, that is, actually διαφθείρεσθαι respecting the σῶμα (the ἔξω ἄνθρωπος), to be delivered up to the power of death.[95] It is this which occurs in the θλίβεσθαι, ἀπορεῖσθαι, διώκεσθαι and καταβάλλεσθαι of verses 8f. And it is this very event as described in verses 8f. which Paul in verse 10 and on his own

---

[95] As indeed the παθήματα τοῦ Χριστοῦ in 1:5 are not the perils of suffering, but the suffering itself!

terms calls a περιφέρειν of the νέκρωσις τοῦ Ἰησοῦ (thus not simply as Lietzmann's interpretation, 115f. assumes, of νέκρωσις or θάνατος in general). For this reason, the antitheses in verses 8f. have validity, since for Paul all sufferings are not sufferings in the human sense, but a νέκρωσις τοῦ Ἰησοῦ, because in them he shares the death of Jesus, because in them occurs the κοινωνία παθημάτων αὐτοῦ, the συμμορφίζεσθαι τῷ θανάτῳ αὐτοῦ (Phil. 3:10). Of course, there are sufferings which are also such from a human point of view. The συμμορφίζεσθαι τῷ θανάτῳ αὐτοῦ thus does not take place in mystical contemplation, but in what is destined for a person's life.

But again, it is not that the apostle's fellowship with Jesus would be established by his effort on behalf of Jesus and his cause, or that the dying of Jesus would be a figurative expression for the suffering which comes upon the one who sides with him. For just as participation in Jesus' life does not consist in sharing the victory of his cause, but proceeds from Jesus' resurrection as an effective power (Phil. 3:10: τοῦ γνῶναι αὐτὸν καὶ τὴν δύναμιν τῆς ἀναστάσεως αὐτοῦ), so sharing the death of Jesus is the actual experience of the power of death at work in his death.

What Paul says here of himself as apostle is of course fundamentally true of all believers, not, say, merely of those who labor for Jesus as apostles. In Phil. 3:4-11 Paul is not speaking as an apostle, but sets himself as a type of believer in whom faith as surrender of the πεποιθέναι ἐν σαρκί becomes visible. In the same way, the statements in 2 Cor. 12:5-10 about God's δύναμις in ἀσθένεια are on principle and not especially oriented to the apostle. In particular, the σκόλοψ τῇ σαρκί is clearly a bodily malady and not a consequence of Paul's apostolic activity. After all (when correctly understood), human life is already a participation in Christ's death, for his passion begins with his incarnation.

The sufferings in which the νέκρωσις τοῦ Ἰησοῦ is at work are therefore sufferings which may happen to anyone, the Christian in particular, since he must suffer precisely as Christian. The apostle, of course, must suffer all the more. These sufferings become the sufferings of Christ, the νέκρωσις τοῦ Ἰησοῦ by the fact that the one who suffers is in fellowship with Christ and thus can understand his sufferings as those of Christ, can appropriate them in understanding (by faith).

One enters into fellowship with Christ by means of the baptism which is εἰς τὸν θάνατον αὐτοῦ. The idea of verses 10f. is the same as that of Rom. 6:3-11: The Christian shares in Jesus' death in order by this to obtain a share in his life. Of course, the purpose of 2 Cor. 4:10f. is far from Rom. 6:3-11, namely, that participation in the ζωή of Jesus is demonstrated in freedom from ἁμαρτία. And the idea essential to 2 Cor. 4:10f., that the sacrament stands not only at the beginning of the Christian life but gives to one's entire life sacramental character, is only alluded to in Rom. 6:6. But because 2 Cor. 4:10f. is concerned to allow fellowship with Jesus' death to emerge as a fellowship which embraces and determines all of life, Paul uses the expression νέκρωσις here instead of θάνατος.

νέκρωσις (a Hellenistic term) is a word used by physicians for the mortification or dying away of the body or a part of it. In Epictetus it is used figuratively, to denote the ἀπονέκρωσις of the ψυχή, the ἀπονεκρωθῆναι of the ἐντρεπτικόν and αἰδῆμον, thus in a spiritual sense (*TDNT,* 4, 893f.).

Paul uses νέκρωσις in the sacramental sense, and of course writes νέκρωσις instead of θάνατος, since in this passage dying with Christ is not meant in that basic sense of a once for all (anticipatory) event in the Baptism, but in the sense that it continually occurs in concrete historical life. The Christian's (or apostle's) suffering is that continual process in which the death of Jesus is at work in the Christian (or apostle) as a continual killing off or continual dying away, such as the εἰς θάνατον παραδίδοσθαι in verse 11.

There is no mystical talk here. νέκρωσις occurs and ζωή is thus revealed in the very living of life and its encounters, not in inwardness or in the experience and enjoyment of the soul, for this can be known only by faith, verse 13, and naturally not in an external *imitatio.* For the sufferings are not hunted out, but appear of their own accord.

On the other hand, it is clear that the Gnostic idea of σῶμα underlies the conceptual formulation. Baptism indeed incorporates the baptized into the σῶμα Χριστοῦ, cf. 1 Cor. 12:13 (as does the Lord's Supper in 1 Cor. 10:16). Cf. also Rom. 7:4: καὶ ὑμεῖς ἐθανατώθητε τῷ νόμῳ διὰ τοῦ σώματος τοῦ Χριστοῦ, εἰς τὸ γενέσθαι ὑμᾶς ἑτέρῳ, τῷ ἐκ νεκρῶν ἐγερθέντι. This is an abbreviation for "you were given into death by the fact that the σῶμα Χριστοῦ was given into death," by which statement Paul assumes a sharing in the σῶμα Χριστοῦ. The σῶμα Χριστοῦ is a "cosmic" entity, and the connection of the baptized with this body is cosmic. "Cosmic" powers are at work in the baptized for the διαφθείρεσθαι of the ἔξω ἄνθρωπος and for participation in the ἀνάστασις. But while in Gnosticism these powers are actually understood as cosmic and effect a natural transformation of the baptized, for Paul God's δύναμις is his grace at work in the proclaimed word, grasped by faith and effective in the believers' historical existence, since the believer understands his destiny anew *sub specie* Christ's death and resurrection. That is, he understands all suffering as a διαφθείρεσθαι of the ἔξω ἄνθρωπος, which likewise frees the ἔσω ἄνθρωπος for the future, just as by his death Christ was freed for ἀνάστασις. But Christ's death and resurrection are the efficient cause, insofar as they are further transmitted through the word and believed. On the "Godhead of God" in Luther, cf. Gogarten, *Verkündigung,* 332ff., and 371: The reality of the revelation is given with God's action and not with human subjective feelings (Luther, WA 10, 1, 2, 82: Therefore "one person may well cling more firmly to Christ than another, just as one loves him more and more strongly believes, but he has no more than the other on that account. In matters which belong to salvation, Christ is one and the same Christ for all, for which reason he is also really Christ").

The ζωή is present only in the event and is not a psychic disposition gained through remaining aloof from bodily life. The killing off of bodily life does not occur in renunciatory concentration on inwardness, but occurs "of itself," that is, through that destiny in which the annihilating power of death is at work. The question is merely whether, by virtue of fellowship with Christ, a person understands this being destroyed as a sharing in the death of Christ, and thus believes that the resurrection life is at work in him.

The conception is thus entirely different from that in Plato. Cf. the Phaedo 66e and 67a: εἰ γὰρ μὴ οἷόν τε μετὰ τοῦ σώματος μηδὲν καθαρῶς γνῶναι, δυοῖν θάτερον, ἢ οὐδαμοῦ ἔστιν κτήσασθαι τὸ εἰδέναι ἢ τελευτήσασιν· τότε γὰρ αὐτὴ καθ᾽ αὑτὴν ἡ ψυχὴ ἔσται χωρὶς τοῦ σώματος, πρότερον δ᾽ οὔ. καὶ ἐν ᾧ ἂν ζῶμεν, οὕτως, ὡς ἔοικεν, ἐγγυτάτω ἐσόμεθα τοῦ εἰδέναι, ἐὰν ὅτι μάλιστα μηδὲν ὁμιλῶμεν τῷ σώματι μηδὲ κοινωνῶμεν, ὅτι μὴ πᾶσα ἀνάγκη (insofar as it is not absolutely necessary), μηδὲ ἀναπιμπλώμεθα τῆς τούτου φύσεως, ἀλλὰ καθαρεύωμεν ἀπ᾽ αὐτοῦ, ἕως ἂν ὁ θεος αὐτὸς ἀπολύσῃ ἡμᾶς· καὶ οὕτω μὲν καθαροὶ ἀπαλλαττόμενοι τῆς τοῦ σώματος ἀφροσύνης, ὡς τὸ εἰκὸς μετὰ τοιούτων τι ἐσόμεθα καὶ γνωσόμεθα δι᾽ ἡμῶν αὐτῶν πᾶν τὸ εἰλικρινές· τοῦτο δ᾽ ἐστὶν ἴσως τὸ ἀληθές. 67e: τῷ ὄντι ... οἱ ὀρθῶς φιλοσοφοῦντες ἀποθνῄσκειν μελετῶσι, καὶ τὸ τεθνάναι ἥκιστα αὐτοῖς ἀνθρώπων φοβερόν. ("For, if pure knowledge is impossible while the body is with us, one of two things must follow, either it cannot be acquired at all or only when we are dead; for then the soul will be by itself apart from the body, but not before. And while we live, we shall, I think, be nearest to knowledge when we avoid, so far as possible, intercourse and communion with the body, except what is absolutely necessary, and are not filled with its nature, but keep ourselves pure from it until God himself sets us free. And in this way, freeing ourselves from the foolishness of the body and being pure, we shall, I think, be with the pure and shall know of ourselves all that is pure, — and that is, perhaps, the truth ... 67e: 'the true philosophers practice dying, and death is less terrible to them than to any other men.'") Cf. 64a and 80e.

Accordingly, Philo writes in Gig 14 (to which Windisch refers, 147): αὗται μὲν οὖν εἰσι ψυχαὶ τῶν ἀνόθως φιλοσοφησάντων, ἐξ ἀρχῆς ἄχρι τέλους μελετῶσαι τὸν μετὰ σωμάτων ἀποθνῄσκειν βίον, ἵνα τῆς ἀσωμάτου καὶ ἀφθάρτου παρὰ τῷ ἀγενήτῳ καὶ ἀφθάρτῳ ζωῆς μεταλάχωσιν. ("These last, then, are the souls of those who have given themselves to genuine philosophy, who from first to last study to die to the life in the body, that a higher existence immortal and incorporeal, in the presence of Him who is himself immortal and uncreated, may be their portion.") In Det Pot Ins 49,

Philo writes: ὁ μὲν δὴ σοφὸς τεθνηκέναι δοκῶν τὸν φθαρτὸν βίον ζῇ τὸν ἄφθαρτον, ὁ δὲ φαῦλος ζῶν τὸν ἐν κακίᾳ τέθνηκε τὸν εὐδαίμονα. ("What we arrive at is this: the wise man, when seeming to die to the corruptible life, is alive to the incorruptible; but the worthless man, while alive to the life of wickedness, is dead to the life happy.")

Secondly (cf. pp. 115f.) Lietzmann overlooks the fact that the ἵνα καὶ ἡ ζωὴ τοῦ Ἰησοῦ κτλ. applies not only to the future resurrection life, but to the present, as verse 11 already shows (ἵνα καὶ ἡ ζωὴ τοῦ Ἰησοῦ φανερωθῇ ἐν τῇ θνητῇ σαρκὶ ἡμῶν). This is also clear from the description in verse 10 of the meaning of the antitheses in verses 8f. In that very οὐ στενοχωρούμενοι, οὐκ ἐξαπορούμενοι, οὐκ ἐγκαταλειπόμενοι, οὐκ ἀπολλύμενοι the ζωὴ τοῦ Ἰησοῦ is revealed. Naturally, the φανερωθῆναι of the ζωὴ τοῦ Ἰησοῦ is not limited to the present, for the ζωὴ τοῦ Ἰησοῦ is the resurrection life. But the point is that this already makes itself felt in the present; this is the paradox.

Verse 11: ἀεὶ γὰρ ἡμεῖς οἱ ζῶντες εἰς θάνατον παραδιδόμεθα διὰ Ἰησοῦν, ἵνα καὶ ἡ ζωὴ τοῦ Ἰησοῦ φανερωθῇ ἐν τῇ θνητῇ σαρκὶ ἡμῶν. Materially, the statement is the same as in verse 10, but it gives the basis for verse 10, since the περιφέρειν τὴν νέκρωσιν τοῦ Ἰησοῦ is now explained as a παραδίδοσθαι εἰς θάνατον διὰ Ἰησοῦν. The διὰ Ἰησοῦν must therefore have a sense which explains the concept of the νέκρωσις τοῦ Ἰησοῦ; it must define the παραδιδόναι εἰς θάνατον as an event which allows for the experience of θάνατος as a sharing in the death of Jesus. In any case, the meaning is not, "so that I witness to him," but either "because we share in Jesus' death" or "so that we obtain a share in Jesus' death." The first would correspond more exactly with verse 10 and conform to Phil. 3:8: ἡγοῦμαι πάντα ζημίαν εἶναι διὰ τὸ ὑπερέχον τῆς γνώσεως Χριστοῦ Ἰησοῦ — on the basis of the γνῶσις of Christ Jesus, that is, because I have known, laid hold of Christ Jesus. The second would correspond to Phil. 3:10: τοῦ γνῶναι αὐτὸν κτλ. — in order that I might know him. Since verse 11 gives the reason for verse 10, the former is probably intended.

ἡμεῖς οἱ ζῶντες, which means, of course, we who have life in the body (not, who are alive in Christ). If as such we are given into death, then it is clear that death is not conceived as threateningly imminent, but as presently at work.

The ἐν τῇ θνητῇ σαρκὶ ἡμῶν explains the ἐν τῷ σώματι ἡμῶν in verse 10 (just as σάρξ may stand for σῶμα when the intent is to accent the mortality of the body; cf. Käsemann, *Leib*, 123f., and Bultmann, *Theology of the New Testament*, 200, 233). This formulation expresses still more pointedly the paradox of the φανέρωσις.[96] Lietzmann, 116, thinks that the φανέρωσις

---

[96] The ἐν τῇ θνητῇ σαρκὶ ἡμῶν clearly shows that the ζωή is revealed in the present. According to Windisch, 146f., Paul would really have had to speak only of the future life in the ἵνα-clause!

of the ζωή τοῦ Ἰησοῦ occurs "as the replacement of the σάρξ by a pneumatic σῶμα, whose essence the Christian indeed already bears here on earth . . . and which in the end totally annihilates the sarkic σῶμα." This is correct insofar as the φανέρωσις is synonymous with the ἀνακαινοῦσθαι.of the ἔσω ἄνθρωπος (v. 16), but the idea of an already existent though latent σῶμα is, according to 5:1ff., clearly incorrect. In any event, the φανέρωσις not only occurs in a mysterious event of transformation, an idea which Paul may also have appropriated, but above all in the μὴ στενοχωρεῖσθαι, etc. of verses 8f., and, as verse 12 shows, it occurs in positive fashion in the activity of Paul — the ζωή becoming evident in him is demonstrated in the believers, cf. 6:4-10.

Verse 12: ὥστε ὁ θάνατος ἐν ἡμῖν ἐνεργεῖται, ἡ δὲ ζωὴ ἐν ὑμῖν. The sentence is naturally not ironic as in 1 Cor. 4:8f., but rather a seriously intended conclusion drawn from verses 10f.

Now, when it is said that ὁ θάνατος ἐν ἡμῖν, ἡ δὲ ζωὴ ἐν ὑμῖν, then this of course does not deny that in Paul also the ζωή is at work, as verses 10f. precisely stated. But surprisingly enough, the formulation in verse 12 completely ignores this thought. Verse 12 speaks as though only death is at work in Paul, as though the life evident in his deathly fate is proved only to the hearers of his proclamation who believe. On the one hand, this sharpens the paradox that the revelation of life requires death — since Paul is given unto death, life emerges among his hearers. And on the other, it is clear that the ζωή revealed in Paul's body is not a condition perceptible in him, but an event, his very activity as proclaimer. The ζωή is present only in his proclamation and, to put it as crassly as possible, he says, only with the hearers of the proclamation! Among these, of course, it cannot be perceived in worldly, unequivocal fashion but, as verse 14 states, will be proven only at their resurrection. But Paul can still require it of the community if it intends to be Christian. For the believer, of course, it is a certainty, verses 13f.

Fuchs, *Christus,* 83, thinks he can infer from verse 12 that the statements in verses 8-11 apply only to the apostle, not to all believers. He writes that there is a parallel between the history of Christ Jesus and that of Paul himself "which, however, may not be confused with the nature of Christian existence as such." Paul carries about the dying of Jesus in his body, his sufferings are Christ's sufferings, etc. Fuchs continues: "If these statements applied to every believer, then martyrdom would be the only Christian possibility of existence; our task would consist in an exact imitation of Jesus. But Paul knows how to differentiate. While the death (of Jesus) is operative in him, the life (of Jesus) is operative in his hearers."

Still, verses 10f. have their parallel in Phil. 3:10, and Phil. 3:10 is paradigmatic for Christian existence as such.

2. ζωή in proclamation: 4:13-15

Verses 13-15 explain verse 12. The connection is contradictory: Though death is at work in Paul, he still speaks, that is, he is active as proclaimer. In fact, he speaks in the certainty that though he now has fallen prey to death, in the future he can be certain of life, for God will raise him up. By adding καὶ παραστήσει σὺν ὑμῖν to the καὶ ἡμᾶς σὺν Ἰησοῦ ἐγερεῖ, the second half of verse 12 gets its due — ἡ δὲ ζωὴ ἐν ὑμῖν. This becomes the prevailing idea in the τὰ γὰρ πάντα δι᾿ ὑμᾶς of verse 15. In verses 13-15, then, the λαλοῦμεν (v. 13) and the δι᾿ ὑμᾶς (v. 15) have the chief stress, and the theme is that of ζωή becoming effective in the proclamation, which leads the hearers as well as Paul himself toward resurrection.

Verse 13: ἔχοντες δὲ τὸ αὐτὸ πνεῦμα τῆς πίστεως, κατὰ τὸ γεγραμμένον· ἐπίστευσα, διὸ ἐλάλησα, καὶ ἡμεῖς πιστεύομεν, διὸ καὶ λαλοῦμεν. The τὸ αὐτὸ πνεῦμα τῆς πίστεως can only refer to what follows, since there was yet no reference to the πνεῦμα τῆς πίστεως — we have the very same spirit of faith as is described in the scriptural word.

κατὰ τὸ γεγραμμένον is a formula-quotation, and appears only here in the New Testament. Is it a juridical formula? Cf. Deissmann N.B., 78.[97] Ps. 11:1 is cited according to the LXX (in Hebrew, Ps. 116:10 reads: "I believe [trust], when I speak [pray]." The text is uncertain, and Gunkel, *Psalmen,* 503, totally alters it). πνεῦμα τῆς πίστεως is used instead of simply πίστιν. The connection can hardly be as Windisch, 148, weighs it; that is, either the Spirit which the believer receives, or the Spirit which is operative in faith, which constitutes its essence. The genitive is subjective[98] — the Spirit as it is peculiar to faith. Basically, the πνεῦμα describes the type of faith, its "how." Paul has just that type of faith which the Psalm word describes, that is, he has a spirit of faith which moves to speech. The quotation thus confirms that there is a faith which moves to speech — for Paul, to proclamation. It is just this faith which Paul possesses, and thus he speaks.

The final clause should simply read καὶ ἡμεῖς λαλοῦμεν. But in analogy with the scriptural word Paul expands the final clause — καὶ ἡμεῖς (that is, as the psalmist so we πιστεύομεν, διὸ καὶ λαλοῦμεν) — in order once more to accent the inseparability of faith and speech (or because the idea of this inseparability forces itself on him).

The clause thus makes clear that 1) Paul possesses the ζωή in faith (this and nothing else gives the basis for his activity); and that 2) the ζωή is effective in activity, in proclamation (in his παρρησία). How can it be such in a life which is not apostolic? By analogy! That is, in an existence for others, in service, and naturally also in παρρησία as freedom from anxiety.

---

[97] There are similar rabbinic formulas, cf. Bonsirven, *Exegese,* 32, and Schrenk, *TDNT,* 1,749.
[98] Cf. 1 Cor. 4:21: ἐν . . . πνεύματί τε πραΰτητος, and Gal. 6:1: ἐν πνεύματι πραΰτητος.

122   The Apostolic Office

Verse 14: εἰδότες ὅτι ὁ ἐγείρας τὸν κύριον Ἰησοῦν καὶ ἡμᾶς σὺν Ἰησοῦ ἐγερεῖ.[99] Verse 14 describes the content of faith, but now in such a way that its content is not the present but rather the future ζωή. The formulation is very likely fashioned according to the tradition (Windisch, 149: "A fixed catechetical maxim").[100] Cf. Rom. 8:11: εἰ δὲ τὸ πνεῦμα τοῦ ἐγείραντος τὸν Ἰησοῦν ἐκ νεκρῶν οἰκεῖ ἐν ὑμῖν, ὁ ἐγείρας ἐκ νεκρῶν Χριστὸν Ἰησοῦν ζωοποιήσει καὶ τὰ θνητὰ σώματα ὑμῶν διὰ τοῦ ἐνοικοῦντας αὐτοῦ πνεύματος ἐν ὑμῖν.

1 Cor. 6:14 reads: ὁ δὲ θεὸς καὶ τὸν κύριον ἤγειρεν καὶ ἡμᾶς ἐξεγερεῖ διὰ τῆς δυνάμεως αὐτοῦ.

1 Cor. 15:22f. reads: ὥσπερ γὰρ ἐν τῷ Ἀδὰμ πάντες ἀποθνήσκουσιν, οὕτως καὶ ἐν τῷ Χριστῷ πάντες ζωοποιηθήσονται. ἕκαστος δὲ ἐν τῷ ἰδίῳ τάγματι· ἀπαρχὴ Χριστός, ἔπειτα οἱ τοῦ Χριστοῦ ἐν τῇ παρουσίᾳ αὐτοῦ. It is characteristic of Paul (in contrast to the aphorisms of the mysteries, cf. Windisch, 149) that God and not Jesus is the subject of the clause.

Is the σὺν Ἰησοῦ also traditional, or is it Paul's addition? It indicates that though the acts of raising are temporally distinct (cf. 1 Cor. 15:23), in face of the essential unity (or, conceived in Gnostic terms, in face of the cosmic unity) the temporal distinction disappears — Christ's raising and that of believers is an eschatological event. So it is incorrect to paraphrase, "we who are united with Jesus," or even, "so that we then are united with Jesus."[101] At best we might paraphrase, "like Jesus," but in such a way that Jesus' resurrection provides the basis for our own.

The continuation, καὶ παραστήσει σὺν ὑμῖν, is an addition to the traditional formula. In this passage, the παριστάναι is not a presentation before the βῆμα of God (Rom. 14:10; cf. 2 Cor. 5:10) where judgment is first meted out, but a presentation of the justified, just as in 11:2; 1 Cor. 8:8; Col. 1:22, 28; and Eph. 5:27.[102] Cf. the Odes of Solomon 21:6f.: "And I was raised up to the light and went past before his countenance. And I came near to him, while I praised and confessed him." Cf. the Odes of Solomon 36:2; the Act Thom 113, and the προσαγωγή in Rom. 5:2; Eph. 2:18; 3:12; 1 Peter 3:18; and Heb. 6:18-20; 7:25; 10:19-22. The idea is traditional, but what is essential for Paul is the σὺν ὑμῖν, cf. 1:14; 1 Thess. 2:19 and Phil. 2:16. One is not saved as individual, but rather in community.

In addition, the δι' ὑμᾶς in verse 15 makes absolutely clear that the meaning of verses 13f. in relation to verse 12 is not, "now of course life is at work in you, but death in me; but one day I also will receive life with you." Rather, the idea is explained that the ζωὴ τοῦ Ἰησοῦ at work

[99] κύριον is omitted in P⁴⁶ B 33 vg Or and Tert.
[100] Cf. the characteristic εἰδότες in 1:7; 5:6; Rom. 5:3; 6:9; 13:11, etc.; cf. the οἴδαμεν in 5:1 and also p. 130.
[101] Thus Kümmel, 202, who attacks Lietzmann's notion that eschatology dissolves the concept of time.
[102] Str.-B. has no parallels for this thought.

in Paul effects life for the community (v. 12). The faith which supports Paul's proclamation has just this for its content, that one day a living community will stand before God. And precisely for the community's sake the ζωή at work in Paul proves itself out in his life as passion.

But how can faith in the future of ζωή appear without mediation in verses 13f. instead of faith in its present character (vv. 7-12)? Because the ζωή to which verses 7-12 referred is from the outset the future life evident in the present. It is the resurrection life, just as Jesus' resurrection corresponds to his death (cf. Phil. 3:10f.). So, to a certain extent, the νέκρωσις τοῦ Ἰησοῦ which Paul experiences is also future, since it is the imminent death present in all suffering.[103]

The ζωή of verses 7-12 is certainly not the animation of Paul's soul, the power of inwardness, a character formed by fate. All this which, of course, thrives also in Paul (cf. vv. 8f. and 6:4-10), thrives only on the basis of the life already his by faith, but which is not his as a spiritual possession.[104] It exists outside him in Christ, and ahead of him in the resurrection; it is his by faith. The future, however, is not simply an imminent state but a power determining the present and to that extent already present. It becomes a determining power, present by faith in it. Thus the present character of ζωή consists in a being oriented to and open for the future by faith.

Verse 15: τὰ γὰρ πάντα δι᾽ ὑμᾶς. τὰ πάντα refers to the λαλεῖν of verse 13 and everything which it includes (vv. 8-11). The δι᾽ ὑμᾶς explains the σὺν ὑμῖν. This concludes the giving of reasons for verse 12 in verses 13f.

The subsequent ἵνα-clause stands in a certain tension with the preceding clause — ἵνα ἡ χάρις πλεονάσασα διὰ τῶν πλειόνων τὴν εὐχαριστίαν περισσεύσῃ εἰς τὴν δόξαν τοῦ θεοῦ. Paul's ultimate motive is thus the glory of God for whose sake he labors for the community. The idea of God's glory as the ultimate goal of the saving event occurs in Phil. 1:11; 2:11; 2 Cor. 1:20; 1 Cor. 10:31; and Rom. 15:6f.[105]

As to the grammatical construction, the πλεονάσασα may be transitive (as in 1 Thess. 3:12, etc.) and περισσεύσῃ intransitive (as in 1:5; 8:2, 7, and especially in 9:12!), in which case the τὴν εὐχαριστίαν is dependent on πλεονάσασα. The translation would thus be, "in order that grace may increase thanksgiving, and thus abound to the glory of God." Then διὰ τῶν πλειόνων (by further or several, cf. Bl.-D. para. 244, 3, that is, by a greater number) belongs to πλεονάσασα, "so that grace may increase thanksgiving by an ever growing number (of believers). . . ." Or, on the other hand, πλεονάσασα may be intransitive (as in Rom. 6:1), and περισσεύσῃ transitive (as in 9:8, etc.), in which case the τὴν εὐχαριστίαν is dependent upon περισσεύσῃ. The translation would then be, "so that grace, growing through

---

[103] Whoever has lost anxiety for what is ahead, is (either absolutely dead, or) truly alive.
[104] "Aliena vita"!
[105] That God's glory may be acknowledged in thanksgiving, cf. 1:11; 9:12f., and cf. p. 30.

more and more believers, may increase thanksgiving to God." But this also allows for a connection between διὰ τῶν πλειόνων and περισσεύσῃ (Lietzmann, 116) — "so that grace may grow and through an ever greater number (of those converted) may increase thanksgiving to the glory of God!"

The χάρις is identical in content with the δύναμις of God in verse 7 (cf. the alternation of χάρις and δύναμις in 12:8f., and cf. pp. 34f. on 1:12). By proving itself salutary, God's δύναμις is conceived as χάρις, and since God's redemptive activity occurs in the saving work of Christ and apostolic preaching, it can appear as it were independently. It becomes ever greater and richer as a result of the apostle's activity; it is itself at work in him to the glory of God.

3. The character of ζωή as future: 4:16-18

Verses 7-12 had described the paradoxical contemporaneity of ζωή under cover of the destiny of death. Verses 13-15 had shown that the present ζωή is at work in the apostle's preaching, since it conducts believers and the apostle himself toward future resurrection. But ζωή was one-sidedly conceived as the future resurrection life, and to the apostle's present existence only the ὁ θάνατος ἐν ἡμῖν ἐνεργεῖται seemed to apply. Now, however, verses 16-18 indicate that the future ζωή is at the same time present (v. 16), and that it demonstrates its present character in a certain hope (vv. 17f.).

Verse 16: διὸ οὐκ ἐγκακοῦμεν. The διό does not attach to verse 12 by way of verses 13-15 (Windisch, 151) but is a conclusion drawn from verse 15. Precisely because Paul's activity which is undertaken in view of the future must lead to the glory of God, he does not lose heart.

The οὐκ ἐγκακοῦμεν is used here as in 4:1 and means, we do not lose heart, are not cowardly (equal to the θαρροῦμεν in 5:8). The transition corresponds to 3:12 and 4:1 regarding the general idea that Paul's confidence results from his being entrusted with the διακονία of the καινὴ διαθήκη. But here it appears with the special nuance that Paul derives his confidence from the fact that his διακονία leads to the δόξα τοῦ θεοῦ.

ἀλλ᾽ εἰ καὶ ὁ ἔξω ἡμῶν ἄνθρωπος διαφθείρεται, ἀλλ᾽ ὁ ἔσω ἡμῶν ἀνακαινοῦται ἡμέρᾳ καὶ ἡμέρᾳ. As to grammar, the ἡμῶν is possessive, Bl.-D. para. 184; 284, 1.[106] Is ἡμέρᾳ καὶ ἡμέρᾳ a Hebraism (יוֹם וָיוֹם)? Cf. Bl.-D. para. 200, 1.

On the one hand, the contrast between the ἔξω and ἔσω ἄνθρωπος was given shape in philosophy since Plato, was developed in the Stoa as well as in Plotinus, and on the other was formed in Gnosticism. In both instances the ἔσω ἄνθρωπος denotes the authentic person and the contrast derives from the knowledge that man, as he is first of all present to

---

[106] The final clause is introduced by ἀλλά just as in Rom. 6:5; 1 Cor. 9:2, etc.; cf. Bl.-D. para. 448, 5.

himself and others, is not authentic man. It thus derives from the awareness of man's authenticity and his being moved by the question regarding it. In philosophy the ἔσω ἄνθρωπος as the authentic person is contrasted with the ἔξω ἄνθρωπος as the one imprisoned by sensuousness in the external world, and thus ruled by passion and anxiety. Conversely, the ἔσω ἄνθρωπος is the spiritual person who penetrates the essence of things, lives by self-discipline, and becomes independent of external occurrence.[107] In Gnosticism the inner person can really only be defined in a negative way, since in contrast to psychic life it too is transcendent. It is the pneumatic light-spark dwelling in man as substance, the reality of which can only be experienced in ecstasy.

For Paul, the ἔσω ἄνθρωπος is not the life of the human spirit[108] in contrast to its sensuousness, just as the ἔξω ἄνθρωπος is not sensuousness from which the spirit must distance itself. The ἔξω ἄνθρωπος is not the σάρξ against which the πνεῦμα strives (Gal. 5:17), just as the ἔσω ἄνθρωπος is not the πνεῦμα, of whose ἀνακαινοῦσθαι it would be senseless to speak. The ἔξω ἄνθρωπος is, of course, the θνητὴ σάρξ of verse 11 construed as the transitory σῶμα subject to fate; it is a person seen within the sphere of the σάρξ as that which is present-at-hand within the world. From this ἔξω ἄνθρωπος the ἔσω ἄνθρωπος of course can distance itself, but not by a withdrawal into its spirit, its inwardness, but only by faith in what one will be or already is in union with Christ. The parallel is Gal. 2:20: ζῶ δὲ οὐκέτι ἐγώ, ζῇ δὲ ἐν ἐμοὶ Χριστός (= the ἔσω ἄνθρωπος); ὁ δὲ νῦν ζῶ ἐν σαρκί (= the ἔξω ἄνθρωπος). . . .[109]

The ἔσω ἄνθρωπος of 2 Cor. 4:16 is thus not identical with the ἔσω ἄνθρωπος of Rom. 7:22: συνήδομαι γὰρ τῷ νόμῳ τοῦ θεοῦ κατὰ τὸν ἔσω ἄνθρωπος — or it is such only in a formal way, to the extent that here too the ἔσω ἄνθρωπος is the authentic person, not empirically realized but unredeemed under the law. He is thus the old person to the extent he is aware of God's claim, while the ἔσω ἄνθρωπος of 2 Cor. 4:16 is the new person who, as Christ, lives in the believer (Gal. 2:20).

In Paul the concept of the ἔσω ἄνθρωπος is not related to that of philosophy, but it is related to Gnosticism, insofar as the ἔσω ἄνθρωπος is an absolutely supernatural, transcendent entity. Paul may also have conceived it mythologically, as a mysterious something in people. But the ἔσω ἄνθρωπος is not something merely negative or experienceable, say, only in ecstasy. Of course it is never empirically realized, but it is still something actually at work in life. When Paul writes ἀνακαινοῦται ἡμέρᾳ

---

[107] Cf. for example Iren Haer I, 21, 4.

[108] Cf. Bultmann, *Theologie NT,* 204.

[109] It is thus related to Gnosticism by the fact that from the "world's" viewpoint the authentic person can only be negatively described. He cannot be empirically realized as Gnosticism, however, would wish (in the psychological phenomenon of ecstasy).

καὶ ἡμέρᾳ, the meaning is the same as the μεταμορφοῦσθαι ἀπὸ δόξης εἰς δόξαν in 3:18 (pp. 95f.).

The ζωή peculiar to the ἔσω ἄνθρωπος is thus only in process, in becoming — provided it is not misconstrued as a "development" after the analogy of plant and animal life, that is, as a continual advance on the basis of something already attained. It is rather viewed from the ever invisible future. If one's gaze is directed to the past (instead of to the future), then the ζωή has disappeared. It is always *aliena vita*! It is a continual renewal in withstanding the encounters of fate, a getting ahead of them (the ὑπερνικᾶν of Rom. 8:37) by dint of the power to understand them. In other words, it is the νέκρωσις τοῦ 'Ιησοῦ in one's self-understanding as a sharing in the ζωὴ τοῦ 'Ιησοῦ as the Risen One. In contrast to development as growth from germinal structure, it is a growth from out of the future, from out of the goal which of course cannot be described from perception, just as verses 17f. characterize its imperceptibility in obviously mythological language. The mode of existence of the ἔσω ἄνθρωπος is described in Phil. 3:12-14 as a being on the way between a no longer and a not yet. From this it is clear that the ἀνακαινοῦσθαι does not occur as a natural process, but takes place in the historical vitality of a moment-by-moment enduring of encounters, in other words, that faith is open to the future and lives from out of the future by seizing it anew in the given moment.

This living from out of the future characterizes eschatological existence, because existence is not an endless process, but has its goal which is outwardly visible in death, beyond which lies resurrection which cannot be perceived. The ἀνακαινοῦσθαι is thus an ever new and ever changing growth not only in the formal sense, but in the material sense as well, insofar as καινός is "new" in the eschatological sense (on καινός as an eschatological predicate, cf. *TDNT* 3, 449, and Bultmann, *The Gospel of John,* 527, on Jn. 13:34). According to 5:17, the one united to Christ (ἐν Χριστῷ) is a καινὴ κτίσις (cf. Gal. 6:15). For this reason Rom. 6:4 applies: ἵνα ὥσπερ ἠγέρθη Χριστὸς ἐκ νεκρῶν . . . οὕτως καὶ ἡμεῖς ἐν καινότητι ζωῆς περιπατήσωμεν; or Rom. 7:6: ἀποθανόντες ἐν ᾧ κατειχόμεθα (sc. τῷ νόμῳ), ὥστε δουλεύειν [ἡμᾶς] ἐν καινότητι πνεύματος καὶ οὐ παλαιότητι γράμματος; or Rom. 12:2: καὶ μὴ συσχηματίζεσθε τῷ αἰῶνι τούτῳ, ἀλλὰ μεταμορφοῦσθε τῇ ἀνακαινώσει τοῦ νοός. Cf. also Col. 3:10 and 3:4.

Our understanding of ἀνακαινοῦσθαι ἡμέρᾳ καὶ ἡμέρᾳ scarcely requires those religious-historical parallels to which Windisch (153f.) refers.[110]

There is an analogous use in the Midrash on Ps. 25, para. 2 (105b) (cf. Str.-B. I, 897), which reads that overnight God renews the soul which

---

[110] Of σοφία, Wisdom 7:27 writes:
μία δὲ οὖσα πάντα δύναται
καὶ μένουσα ἐν αὐτῇ τὰ πάντα καινίζει.
("And she, though but one, hath power to do all things;
And remaining in herself, reneweth all things. . . ." R. H. Charles, I, 547.)

has become weary and used up with the day's work, and by appeal to Lam. 3:23, where it is said of God's חֶסֶד and רַחֲמִים, "they are new every morning" (the LXX omits this verse).

Egyptian myths of the (ritually enacted) daily renewal of the sun or of the king, and of the continual (daily) death and rebirth of the earth serpent identified with the dead, scarcely offer an analogy.

The eschatologically "new" is common to the Old Testament-Jewish hope since the time of Isa. 65:17: "Behold, I create new heavens and a new earth" (cf. *TDNT*, 3, 449). And "Behold, I am doing a new thing" (Isa. 43:19) is echoed in Rev. 21:5: ἰδοὺ καινὰ ποιῶ πάντα.

Gnosticism offers parallels to the idea that this eschatological change already occurs in the present. Cf. Ig Eph 19:2f. on the shining star, whose καινότης causes astonishment: (3) ὅθεν ἐλύετο πᾶσα μαγεία καὶ πᾶς δεσμὸς ἠφανίζετο κακίας. ἄγνοια καθηρεῖτο, παλαιὰ βασιλεία διεφθείρετο θεοῦ ἀνθρωπίνως φανερουμένου εἰς καινότητα ἀϊδίου ζωῆς· ἀρχὴν δὲ ἐλάμβανεν τὸ παρὰ θεῷ ἀπηρτισμένον. ἔνθεν τὰ πάντα συνεκινεῖτο διὰ τὸ μελετᾶσθαι θανάτου κατάλυσιν. ("By this all magic was dissolved and every bond of wickedness vanished away, ignorance was removed, and the old kingdom was destroyed, for God was manifest as man for the 'newness' of eternal life, and that which had been prepared by God received its beginning. Hence all things were disturbed, because the abolition of death was being planned.") Cf. 20:1 on Ἰησοῦς Χριστός as ὁ καινὸς ἄνθρωπος. Cf. Schlier, *Untersuchungen*, 28ff., Excerpta ex Theodoto 74: ἀνέτειλεν ξένος ἀστὴρ καὶ καινός, καταλύων τὴν παλαιὰν ἀστροθεσίαν, καινῷ φωτί, οὐ κοσμικῷ, λαμπόμενος, ὁ καινὰς ὁδοὺς καὶ σωτηρίους τρεπόμενος. ("a strange and new star arose doing away with the old astral decree, shining with a new unearthly light, which revolved on a new path of salvation. . . ." The Excerpta Ex Theodoto Of Clement Of Alexandria, 87.)

If in 2 Cor. 4:16 Paul is actually influenced by Gnostic usage, in any event he has reinterpreted the cosmic process in terms of the individual and historical.

Verse 17: τὸ γὰρ παραυτίκα ἐλαφρὸν τῆς θλίψεως. Verse 17 does not furnish the basis for the positive half of verse 16, but for the οὐκ ἐγκακοῦμεν. Despondency is out of place because the misery of the present is nothing in face of the glory to come.

Contrast between the wretched present and the glorious future is an idea common to Paul, Jewish and Gnostic eschatology, as well as to Hellenistic belief in immortality. Even the particular nuance here has Hellenistic parallels, cf. Seneca's Dial IX, XVI, 4; Windisch, 155): omnes isti (Hermes, Regulus, Cato) levi temporis impensa invenerunt, quo modo aeterni fierent, et ad immortalitatem moriendo venerunt. ("All these by a slight sacrifice of time found out how they might become eternal, and by dying reached immortality.")

The θλῖψις is described as ἐλαφρόν (Paul frequently uses the neuter singular of the adjective for an abstract term; cf. Rom. 2:4: τὸ χρηστὸν τοῦ θεοῦ, and 2 Cor. 8:8: τὸ γνήσιον τῆς ἀγάπης, etc., cf. also Bl.-D. para. 263, 2). It is such, because it is παραυτίκα (the adverb is used instead of the adjective), that is momentary, present, thus temporary; it is "only for the present," corresponding to the πρόσκαιρα in verse 18. Knowledge of what is temporary naturally passes from the theoretical to the existential, if it actually is knowledge of the one who stands within the life movement of the ἔσω ἄνθρωπος of verse 16. For when that understanding is appropriated ever anew, then with such a "training in Christianity" it will become more and more certain or self-evident. And though every θλῖψις must be overcome, it may still be greeted, because it draws sense away from the βλεπόμενα (v. 18), and ὑπομονὴν κατεργάζεται, so that it may be said: ἀλλὰ καὶ καυχώμεθα ἐν ταῖς θλίψεσιν in Rom. 5:3.[111]

The fruit of θλῖψις is **καθ᾿ ὑπερβολὴν εἰς ὑπερβολὴν αἰώνιον βάρος δόξης**. On ὑπερβολή cf. verse 7 (p. 112). With Paul, καθ᾿ ὑπερβολὴν εἰς ὑπερβολήν is a favorite rhetorical use of the preposition, cf. pp. 67f. on 2:16. The meaning is, "most abundantly" (Lietzmann's translation, 116, is perhaps correct: "In ever new abundance;" in any event the phrase means "in never-ending abundance").

Reitzenstein, HMR, 355, thinks the reference to βάρος δόξης is odd, and perhaps not to be explained by the fact that the stem כבד means "to be heavy" (the meaning of כָּבוֹד as "heaviness" or "weight" is not usual). There may be Gnostic usage here, as attested in the Mandaean writings. The Book of John, p. 204, 24ff. reads, "He is raptured by prayer at night, raptured in brilliant garments come from the great (life). Uthras fill him with what he lacks, and what is empty in him they heap up. When he bears a pure burden, he is reckoned among men of tested piety. [Reckoned is he] among men of tested piety who separate themelves at the name of Jawar. The treasury of life rested on them, it illumined their shape, and for them is established a way to the house of the Great One."

Ginza, p. 528, 9ff. reads: "When you behold something ugly, do not give up your burden. Again, when you behold something ugly, do not slacken, but do more than is needed. For whoever is burdened, ascends, whoever is empty is here cut off. I am burdened and ascend, my works and gift of reward go before me, and I lean upon my well doing."

Windisch, 155, refers to the description of the brightness beyond in the Pseudo-Clementine Homilies 17, 16 (p. 238), and in Seneca Ep 102, 28.

The **κατεργάζεται ἡμῖν** may not be construed in terms of the idea of reward. What is characteristic is that the subject is the ἐλαφρὸν τῆς

---

[111] The idea here is as in Rom. 8:18: λογίζομαι γὰρ ὅτι οὐκ ἄξια τὰ παθήματα τοῦ νῦν καιροῦ πρὸς τὴν μέλλουσαν δόξαν ἀποκαλυφθῆναι εἰς ἡμᾶς.

θλίψεως, not a "we." Without the assistance of the "I," outside of it, as it were, this κατεργάζεται occurs. The αἰώνιον βάρος δόξης is not the motive for self-surrender to the death of Christ, but indeed its fruit.[112]

It is this fruit which is alluded to in the αἰώνιον βάρος δόξης, which is not described from perception, for this δόξα cannot at all be spoken of so as to be perceived, and a greater or lesser βάρος of δόξα is not conceivable at all. For just as the ζωή is not an accessible phenomenon, so also the δόξα cannot be conceived as an accessible state or condition. But if believing understanding always occurs in struggle, in conquest, in an ἀνακαινοῦσθαι which conforms to a διαφθείρεσθαι, then faith may hope in a future in which a total self-understanding is realized without enigma and anxiety — τότε δὲ ἐπιγνώσομαι καθὼς καὶ ἐπεγνώσθην, 1 Cor. 13:12.

Verse 18: μὴ σκοπούντων ἡμῶν τὰ βλεπόμενα ἀλλὰ τὰ μὴ βλεπόμενα. A genitive absolute is joined to the ἡμῖν of Bl.-D., para. 423, 5. In this clause, the condition or assumption is named under which what was said (vv. 16f.) applies. In the context it is very likely meant to be an assumption come true — "for us who. . . ," or "since we. . . ." In essence, this naturally also implies an "if we. . . ."

The σκοπεῖν τὰ μὴ βλεπόμενα may be conceived as paradox. In any event, it is not a seeing with the ὄμμα τῆς ψυχῆς (cf. the Hellenistic parallels in Windisch, 156), not a "seer's gaze." Rather, σκοπεῖν is a "keeping-in-view," a taking as a point of orientation; cf. for example Gal. 6:1 and Phil. 2:4. Phil. 3:14 is parallel — κατὰ σκοπὸν διώκω εἰς τὸ βραβεῖον τῆς ἄνω κλήσεως. τὰ μὴ βλεπόμενα is intended in the original sense. The sphere of the βλεπόμενα is the sphere of the σάρξ, of the φανερόν in contrast to the πνεῦμα, the κρυπτόν, cf. Rom. 2:28f.

If Paul spoke of himself as apostle in verses 7-15, and if the οὐκ ἐγκακοῦμεν in verse 16 still applies to his behavior as apostle, in verse 17 he is thinking of the common Christian hope, as is clear from verse 18, especially if the supporting clause should be a quotation, which is not improbable — τὰ γὰρ βλεπόμενα πρόσκαιρα, τὰ δὲ μὴ βλεπόμενα αἰώνια. In any event, in Judaism as in Hellenism, we encounter numerous gnomon-like sentences with the same sense (cf. Windisch, 156).

Clearly, 5:1-5 does not refer to the apostle and his hope as apostle, but to the common Christian hope. Only 5:6 and 5:11 in its entirety return to the apostle.

Determination of the present by the future: 5:1-10

For we know that if the earthly tent we live in is destroyed, we have a building from God, a house not made with hands, eternal in the

---

[112] A misunderstanding arising from the fact that a person's self should concern him, since God will have him himself. But for this very reason he may not acquire the self. It is a matter *of* the self, but not *for* the self!

heavens. Here indeed we groan, and long to put on our heavenly dwelling, so that by putting it on we may not be found naked. For while we are still in this tent, we sigh with anxiety; not that we would be unclothed, but that we would be further clothed, so that what is mortal may be swallowed up by life. He who has prepared us for this very thing is God, who has given us the Spirit as a guarantee. So we are always of good courage; we know that while we are at home in the body we are away from the Lord. For we walk by faith, not by sight. We are of good courage, and we would rather be away from the body and at home with the Lord. So whether we are at home or away, we make it our aim to please him. For we must all appear before the judgment seat of Christ, so that each one may receive good or evil, according to what he has done in the body.

5:1-5 is actually a digression, since the apostolic office is not in view here. The statements are evidently occasioned by a close association with 4:17f. Their basic idea is polemic, that is, directed against the Corinthian Gnostics who reject Paul's picture of the future. Nevertheless, 5:6-10 again incorporate the thought of 5:1-5 within the main theme. Verse 6 again takes up 4:16. From the hope established in verse 1-5 results Paul's θαρρεῖν, just as the μὴ ἐγκακεῖν[113] resulted from the hope developed in 4:14f. But the general orientation of verses 1-5 retains its effect until verse 11, since the clauses speak more and more of the common Christian attitude, as it finally emerges clearly in the τοὺς γὰρ πάντας ἡμᾶς of verse 10.

1. The temporariness of the present as an indication of the future: 5:1-5

Verse 1: οἴδαμεν γὰρ ὅτι ἐὰν ἡ ἐπίγειος ἡμῶν οἰκία τοῦ σκήνους καταλυθῇ, οἰκοδομὴν ἐκ θεοῦ ἔχομεν, οἰκίαν ἀχειροποίητον αἰώνιον ἐν τοῖς οὐρανοῖς. οἴδαμεν, like the εἰδότες in 4:14 (cf. p. 122), introduces a generally recognized tenet of Christian faith, which in this case, of course, the Corinthian Gnostics seem not to have recognized. Cf. the οἴδαμεν in Rom. 2:2; 3:19; 7:14; 8:22, 28; 1 Cor. 8:4 and 1 Tim. 1:8.

The clause gives the reason for (γάρ) the certainty of 4:17f., particularly for the τὰ δὲ μὴ βλεπόμενα αἰώνια, and by hope in the οἰκία αἰώνιος.

ἡ ἐπίγειος ἡμῶν οἰκία τοῦ σκήνους. τὸ σκῆνος is an epexegetical genitive. The earthly habitation is only a tent, not a massive construction. In contrast to the tent, the heavenly dwelling is called an οἰκοδομή. The σῶμα is naturally intended, as verses 6 and 8 show. The figurative description of the body as tent is frequent in Hellenistic literature (since Pythagoras and Plato), cf. Windisch, 158; Kroll, *Hermes Trismegistos,* 341, 5, and Leisegang, *Pneuma,* 30f.; especially 30, 2; 31, 4.5.[114] In the Hebrew Old Testament it occurs only in Isa. 38:12 where the sick Hezekiah laments: "My dwelling

---

[113] Since the οὐκ ἐγκακοῦμεν in v. 16 was not explained, but the basis for it laid again in vv. 17f., it is taken up once more in 5:6, and 5:6 could really be attached to 4:18.

[114] Knox, *St. Paul,* 136, 8.

is plucked up and removed from me like a shepherd's tent" (other images follow). The LXX reads: κατέλιπον τὸ λοιπὸν τῆς ζωῆς μου· ἐξῆλθεν καὶ ἀπῆλθεν ἀπ᾽ ἐμοῦ ὥσπερ ὁ καταλύων σκηνὴν πήξας.

Rabbinic literature lacks the figure of the tent, and the figure of the house for the body is also not common, cf. Str.-B. III, 517; cf. on the other hand Wisdom 9:15: φθαρτὸν γὰρ σῶμα βαρύνει ψυχήν, καὶ βρίθει τὸ γεῶδες σκῆνος νοῦν πολυφρόντιδα. Cf. also Corp Herm 13:12, 15: καλῶς σπεύδεις λῦσαι τὸ σκῆνος.

Among the Mandaeans the description of the body as structure, dwelling or house ("defective house") is very frequent, as also of its counterpart in the heavenly structure or dwelling, cf. Vielhauer, *Oikodome*, 35ff.[115]

In verses 2ff. the figure of the garment abruptly alternates with that of the tent. The idea of the heavenly garment is widespread in Jewish apocalyptic as well as in Gnosticism; cf. the excursus in Lietzmann, 119f., in Windisch, 164f., and cf. Jonas, *Gnosis* I, 102. Cf. especially the Asc Is 7:22; 8:26; 9:2,8f., 17,24ff.; Act Thom 111–113; Hebrew or 3 Enoch 12; 18:22 (garment of brilliance, or of life). In addition, cf. Odeberg, *3 Henoch*, Teil II, p. 32, and p. 120, and also Teil I, p. 163. The idea is especially frequent in the Mandaean writings, in close connection and mingling with the figure of the structure; cf. Vielhauer, *Oikodome*, 107ff., and Jonas, *Gnosis* I, 100-102.

The earthly body is described as ἐπίγειος. Cf. the σώματα ἐπίγεια in contrast to the σώματα ἐπουράνια in 1 Cor. 15:40. Here the οἰκοδομὴ ἐκ θεοῦ is contrasted with the ἐπίγειος οἰκία τοῦ σκήνους. ἐκ θεοῦ does not belong with ἔχομεν, but with οἰκοδομή, which ignores the thought of Genesis 2:7 that the earthly body is also created by God. And in order to put the contrast more sharply, an appositive is added — οἰκία ἀχειροποίητος, αἰώνιος, ἐν τοῖς οὐρανοῖς. ἀχειροποίητος (cf. Mark 14:58) denotes the supernatural as in Col. 2:11; cf. Heb. 9:11,24. As in 4:17, αἰώνιος is a natural attribute of "supernatural things" (Windisch, 159). ἐν τοῖς οὐρανοῖς does not belong with ἔχομεν, but is an attribute of οἰκία, sc. οὖσαν, which is ἀποκειμένην (Col. 1:15), τετηρημένην (1 Peter 1:4).

ἐὰν καταλυθῇ . . . ἔχομεν. No doubt, the καταλυθῆναι (often used of destroying and tearing down buildings) can only be understood of death's destruction of the earthly body, not of the ἀλλαγῆναι in 1 Cor. 15:51, as Mundle (FS. Jülicher, 95f.) following Bachmann would have it.

Then the question is, Does the ἐὰν καταλυθῇ denote 1) the moment of dying, that is, death prior to the parousia, which Paul would then consider likely, while ignoring the other possibility, 2) not dying before the parousia (1 Cor. 15:51f.; 1 Thess. 4:17),[116] or 3), does the καταλυθῆναι denote the

---

[115] Bornhäuser's suggestion in *Gebeine*, 37ff. is grotesque — the bones correspond to tent poles which are naked at death and must be clothed anew.

[116] If this were meant, then a καταλυθῆναι prior to that ἀλλαγῆναι would have to have been in mind.

process of dying described in 4:8-12, 16, so that death in the real sense would not be intended at all, but rather the καταλυθῆναι occurring in the present? Thus Brun, ZNW 28, 1929, 207-229.[117]

The decision is a difficult one. The second option, that is, that Paul does not have in mind a καταλυθῆναι by death but by transformation (1 Cor. 15:51) has support in the fact that καταλυθῆναι in verse 1 seems to be the normal possibility, and that Paul elsewhere reckons on experiencing the parousia as normal, while death before the parousia is the exception. Mundle and Brun correctly oppose the notion that in 2 Corinthians — and indeed on the basis of the event alluded to in 1:8ff. — Paul's view had changed, and he now reckoned on the probability or even the certainty of his death before the parousia. Brun demonstrates that 2 Corinthians reckons throughout with the expectation of the parousia and a being transformed by it (cf. as early as 1:10f.).[118]

Assuming the first option is correct, Windisch, 160 (with others) states that verse 1 and what follows express the expectation that the Christian is clothed with his heavenly body immediately after death. In this case the ἔχομεν is not a true present, but a future equal to ἕξομεν, which in itself is possible (Bl.-D. para. 323). Of course it is questionable whether we may immediately interpolate an "at once," and Lietzmann, 118, objects that in that case we would expect an ἐξ οὐρανοῦ instead of the ἐν τοῖς οὐρανοῖς. It will be better to construe the verb with Mundle who states that "the present ἔχομεν only accents the certainty of the possession, without drawing any inference respecting the moment of taking possession" (96). In fact, the ἔχομεν at least need only express the fact that there is comfort for us in face of death, that a heavenly body is prepared for us — which would altogether correspond to the apocalyptic idea (cf. pp. 130f.).

Under the first option, that the καταλυθῆναι denotes death before the parousia, Lietzmann, 118f., and others (construing the ἔχομεν as a true present) assert that an interim state is assumed between death and a being clothed with the heavenly garment, that is to say, a state of γυμνότης, to which verse 3 refers. They further state that verses 2-4 express Paul's longing to avoid death before the parousia, so as to avoid this state of γυμνότης.

It would be remarkable indeed if, after expressing in verse 1 the comforting certainty of the heavenly garment, immediately thereafter in verses 2-4 Paul should long to avoid death (Brun, 207f. and 218). The longing not to have to die is alleged "to ground or confirm" the certainty of "hope in the heavenly body in the event of death and nakedness" (Brun, 218). On the

---

[117] But this is scarcely possible from a grammatical standpoint! ἐὰν καταλυθῇ can still only mean, at the moment when corruption has occurred, that is, at death.

[118] But cf. 4:14, where Paul, just as in 1 Cor. 6:14, reckons on his ἐγερθῆναι entirely without reflection! In any case, 4:14 does not indicate that Paul has altered his view over against 1 Cor., as 1 Cor. 6:14 precisely shows.

contrary, only the longing for liberation from the earthly body (analogous to Rom. 8:22f.) can ground the certainty of hope.[119]

Reitzenstein gives another explanation in HMR, 354-357, according to which the ἔσω ἄνθρωπος of 4:16 is even now the inner covering, over which the heavenly σῶμα is then put on as an outer garment. Though in death we must lay aside the earthly σῶμα (Reitzenstein reads v. 3 thusly — εἴ γὲ καὶ ἐκδυσάμενοι), we would still not be naked, since we still have the ἔσω ἄνθρωπος as covering. But the ἔσω ἄνθρωπος cannot possibly be construed as a clothing!

If we eliminate Reitzenstein's interpretation, and do not venture with Brun to interpret the καταλυθῆναι of the present process of corruption, it is equally false to assign to Paul the notion of an interim state of γυμνότης, and to infer from verses 2-4 the longing to escape it. If we interpret the καταλυθῆναι of death, then there is absolutely no reflection upon an interim state, and verse 1 merely expresses the comfort which exists in view of death — death is not annihilation, because a heavenly garment is prepared for us.[120]

Verse 2: **καὶ γὰρ ἐν τούτῳ στενάζομεν, τὸ οἰκητήριον ἡμῶν τὸ ἐξ οὐρανοῦ ἐπενδύσασθαι ἐπιποθοῦντες.** We may scarcely add a τῷ σκήνει to the ἐν τούτῳ, though verse 4 reads, οἱ ὄντες ἐν τῷ σκήνει στενάζομεν. The clause is more probably adverbial, meaning "therefore," "for this reason," and corresponding to the ἐφ᾽ ᾧ οὐ θέλομεν ἐκδύσασθαι ἀλλ᾽ ἐπενδύσασθαι in verse 4. Only in this way does the logic in the train of thought clearly emerge — our sighing proves that a heavenly garment

---

[119] Cf. Mundle, FS. Jülicher, 99: "In the very moment the apostle mightily expresses the confidence of his hope in redemption, he would remind the Corinthians that an element of uncertainty also attaches to this hope, insofar as the thought of having to die before the parousia produces anxiety even for the Christian."

[120] Remarks on Brun, ZNW 28, 1929, 207ff.:

I. Those interpretations are incorrect according to which 1) Paul fears the interim state, or 2) awaits transformation at the moment of death. Mundle's interpretation is better, but to limit the γυμνότης in v. 3 and the ἐκδύσασθαι in v. 4 to the lost is incorrect. Further, the καταλυθῆναι in v. 1 can only denote death, not transformation at the parousia.

II. The presuppositions for exegesis are as follows: Paul expects to experience the parousia (1 Thess. 4:15; 1 Cor.), and he awaits transformation at the parousia. This expectation was not shaken by 2 Cor. 1:7f. According to 4:7-15, 16-18, the present time for Paul is a process of dying (thus also 6:4f.) which he endures in hope of the eschatological fulfillment at the resurrection. There is no reckoning here with death before the parousia, but rather the assumption that Paul will remain alive while in the process of dying.

III. The καταλυθῆναι is not to be construed as death before the parousia, but of the process of corruption within the present time, as described in vv. 8-16. In this situation Paul yearns to be clothed upon with the heavenly body (at the parousia); he does not wish to die (be unclothed), but to experience transformation at the parousia, for which God has fitted him by the gift of the Spirit. Vv. 6-8 harmonize with this thought, for the desire to ἐκδημῆσαι in v. 8 is not the desire to die before the parousia.

IV. 4:7-18 as well as 5:1-10 are very likely a polemic against Judaizers who cite Paul's sufferings against him, as well as against the Corinthian Gnostics who deny the resurrection.

awaits us, and that our present existence is temporary. The state of affairs
in verse 1 is the basis in reality for the sighing (στενάζειν), and the latter
is thus the basis for a knowledge of the state of affairs in verse 1.

The idea is the same as in Rom. 8:21-23. The sighing of the entire
creation as well as of Christians themselves is the basis for the knowledge
of imminent liberation from the δουλεία τῆς φθορᾶς for the ἐλευθερία τῆς
δόξης. It is thus relatively unimportant whether the ἐπιποθοῦντες yields
only the content of the στενάζειν ("as such who long"), or (perhaps better)
is intended as causal ("because we long").

After verse 1, verse 2 can of course only mean that we long for that
heavenly garment which lies ready for us, which awaits us after death —
without a word about the time of being clothed. We can certainly infer
a desire not to die before the parousia, if we construe the ἐπενδύσασθαι[121]
not as "being clothed with" or "putting on," but rather as "putting on
over," that is, over the present earthly body. The heavenly body would
then be "conceived as a garment of Nessus consuming the old corporeality
with its flame of life" (Bousset, *Schriften NT,* 191). But the contrast
between ἐκδύεσθαι and ἐπενδύεσθαι in verse 4 shows that ἐπενδύεσθαι
is thought of simply as equal to ἐνδύεσθαι — according to verse 1 the only
probable interpretation. The ἐπενδύεσθαι takes place at the parousia and
resurrection, and is synonymous with the ἀλλαγῆναι of 1 Cor. 15:51. It thus
applies to those who have died before the parousia, as well as to those who
live to see it.

If the intention is to express the desire not to die before the parousia,
then of course the sighing could not be the reason for the certainty of
verse 1, for it would certainly be a sighing from fear! The possibility of
experiencing the parousia is of course uncertain. Lietzmann, 118, naturally,
avoids this confusion by paraphrasing: "You can see how certain our hope
in the new body and the transcendent glory is by the fact that our longing
is continually directed toward it, and we experience horror of death for the
one reason only that it temporarily sets us in a state of nakedness before
we receive the new clothing." But that "for the one reason only" does not
at all appear in the text!

If we have properly understood verse 2, namely, that our longing indicates
that a heavenly garment awaits us, then verse 3 gives clear proof, that is,
indicates once more the basis in reality for the longing.

Verse 3: εἴ γε καὶ ἐκδυσάμενοι οὐ γυμνοὶ εὑρεθησόμεθα. The verse,
of course, has a special nuance, since the proof is described as something
which would certainly still apply, thus includes a side glance at those who
are of another opinion.

εἴ γε καί (the equivalent of εἴπερ in P[46] B D (G) and pc) means "if

---

[121] ἐπενδύσασθαι means to put on (to don the lion's skin) in Plut E Delph 7 (Paton, p. 8).

at least," as in Gal. 3:4: τοσαῦτα ἐπάθετε εἰκῆ, εἴ γε καὶ εἰκῆ. Cf. also the εἴ γε in Col. 1:23, Eph. 3:2, and 4:21, which means "insofar as (at least)," as well as the εἴπερ in Rom. 8:17: εἴπερ συμπάσχομεν ἵνα καὶ συνδοξασθῶμεν. The phrase should be paraphrased thus: "Insofar as it is actually true that. . . ." or "naturally on condition (assumed as obvious) that" (cf. Windisch, 162).[122]

Lietzmann's translation (120), "since, of course (only then), when we have put it on we will not be found naked," is impossible, because the εἴ γε καί cannot be simply causal, and the "only then" is interpolated. The translation is, "if it is true at least that after we have laid aside our (earthly) garment, we will not stand naked."

Now, of course, the readings vary. While in most instances the ἐνδυσάμενοι is transmitted, D* (G) it Mcion Tert Ambst and Chr (in his text) read ἐκδυσάμενοι. The first reading yields a trivial sense: "If at least, after we have been clothed, we would not stand naked." Mundle (101) translates: "We long to be clothed upon with a new body, since by putting on such a σῶμα we avoid the state of nakedness." But this robs the εἴ γε καί of its real force, and the sense remains trivial.

In the second reading, however, everything is clear: "If it at least is true that after we have laid aside our earthly garment we will not stand naked." This is obviously spoken with a side glance at those who assert that at death we lay aside the earthly garment and are naked. Verse 4 quite clearly shows that Paul is speaking from such an orientation. The verse asserts that our longing does not have to do with the ἐκδύσασθαι, but rather with the ἐπενδύσασθαι. Paul thus has those in mind who yearn precisely for the ἐκδύσασθαι, for the γυμνὸς εἶναι, that is, the Gnostics!

Cf. Corp Herm 1, 24-26[123] (instruction concerning the ascent of the soul): Πρῶτον μὲν ἐν τῇ ἀναλύσει τοῦ σώματος τοῦ ὑλικοῦ παραδίδως αὐτὸ τὸ σῶμα εἰς ἀλλοίωσιν, καὶ τὸ εἶδος ὃ εἶχες ἀφανὲς γίνεται. καὶ τὸ ἦθος τῷ δαίμονι ἀνενέργητον παραδίδως, καὶ αἱ αἰσθήσεις τοῦ σώματος εἰς τὰς ἑαυτῶν πηγὰς ἐπανέρχονται, μέρη γινόμεναι καὶ πάλιν συνανιστάμεναι εἰς τὰς ἐνεργείας. καὶ ὁ θυμὸς καὶ ἡ ἐπιθυμία εἰς τὴν ἄλογον φύσιν χωρεῖ. 25: καὶ οὕτως ὁρμᾷ λοιπὸν ἄνω διὰ τῆς ἁρμονίας . . . (the soul in its ascent surrenders its ἐνέργεια to the seven planetary spheres). 26: καὶ τότε γυμνωθεὶς ἀπὸ τῶν τῆς ἁρμονίας ἐνεργημάτων γίνεται ἐπὶ τὴν ὀγδοαδικὴν φύσιν, τὴν ἰδίαν δύναμιν ἔχων, καὶ ὑμνεῖ σὺν τοῖς οὖσι τὸν πατέρα . . . τοῦτό ἐστι τὸ ἀγαθὸν τέλος τοῖς γνῶσιν ἐσχηκόσι, θεωθῆναι. ("When thy material body is to be dissolved, first thou surrenderest the body by itself unto the work of change, and thus the form thou hadst doth vanish, and thou surrenderest thy way of life, void of its

---

[122] The equivalent of *siquidem*, cf. Bl.-D. para. 439, 2.
[123] Ginza 517 , 22 (the description is different in the Book of John, p. 121).

energy, unto the Daimon. The body's senses next pass back into their sources, becoming separate; and resurrect as energies; and passion and desire withdraw unto that nature which is void of reason. 25: And thus it is that man doth speed his way thereafter upwards through the Harmony. 26: And then, with all the energizings of the Harmony stript from him, clothed in his proper Power, he cometh to that Nature which belongs unto the Eighth, and there with those-that-are hymneth the Father . . . This the good end for those who have gained Gnosis — to be made one with God." Thrice-Greatest Hermes, II, 9f.)

Hierocl in Carm Aur XXVI (Mullach, p. 179) writes of the effect of Pythagorean instruction in κάθαρσις: ἵν' ὅταν ὁ τοῦ θανάτου καιρὸς ἐνστῇ, καταλιπόντες ἐπὶ γῆς τὸ θνητὸν σῶμα, καὶ τὴν τούτου φύσιν ἀποδυσάμενοι, πρὸς τὴν οὐρανίαν πορείαν ὦσιν εὔζωνοι οἱ τῶν φιλοσοφίας ἀγώνων ἀθληταί ("that when the time of death draws near, those practiced in the arguments of philosophy may be well-equipped for the heavenly journey, once they have left their mortal body on earth and put off its natural form" R.A.H.).

The sentence from Porphyry in Abst I, 31 scarcely belongs here: ἀποδυτέον ἄρα τοὺς πολλοὺς ἡμῖν χιτῶνας, τόν τε ὁρατὸν τοῦτον καὶ σάρκινον καὶ οὓς ἔσωθεν ἠμφιέσμεθα προσεχεῖς ὄντας τοῖς δερματίνοις, γυμνοὶ δὲ καὶ ἀχίτωνες ἐπὶ τὸ στάδιον ἀναβαίνωμεν τὰ τῆς ψυχῆς Ὀλύμπια ἀγωνισόμενοι ("We must therefore divest ourselves of our manifold garments, both of this visible and fleshly vestment, and of those with which we are internally clothed, and which are proximate to our cutaneous habiliments; and we must enter the stadium naked and unclothed, striving for [the most glorious of all prizes] the Olympia of the soul." *Porphyry On Abstinence From Animal Food,* p. 42.) — thus of the philosophical conduct of life which is compared to an Olympian competition. But is not the metaphor of the naked athlete evoked by the idea of the necessary nakedness of the soul?

Corp Herm 7, 2 does not expressly refer to nakedness, but to the necessity of laying the body aside (πρῶτον δὲ δεῖ σε περιρρήξασθαι ὃν φορεῖς χιτῶνα. . . . "But first thou must tear off from thee the cloak which thou dost wear. . . ." *Thrice-Greatest Hermes,* II, 77).

Here, of course, we need not consult ideas from Platonic myths of the next world (Lietzmann, 120 on v. 3, and Windisch, 164f.), in which the soul of the dead appears naked before the judge. Accordingly, cf. Lucian's Verae Historiae II, 12 regarding the disembodied souls on the island of the blest (καὶ ὅλως ἔοικε γυμνή τις ἡ ψυχὴ αὐτῶν περιπολεῖν τὴν τοῦ σώματος ὁμοιότητα περικειμένη; ". . . in short, it's as if their naked souls were walking about clad in the semblance of their bodies." *Selected Satires of Lucian,* 38).

But cf. for example Seneca's Dial VI, XXV, 1ff.:[124] Proinde non est quod ad sepulcrum fili tui curras: pessima eius et ipsi molestissima istic iacent, ossa cineresque, non magis illius partes quam vestes alique tegimenta corporum. integer ille nihilque in terris relinquens sui fugit et totus excessit; paulumque supra nos commoratus, dum expurgatur et inhaerentia vitia situmque omnem mortalis aevi excutit, deinde ad excelsa sublatus inter felices currit animas. ("There is no need, therefore, for you to hurry to the tomb of your son; what lies there is his basest part and a part that in life was the source of much trouble — bones and ashes are no more parts of him than were his clothes and the other protections of the body. He is complete — leaving nothing of himself behind, he has fled away and wholly departed from earth; for a little while he tarried above us while he was being purified and was ridding himself of all the blemishes and stain that still clung to him from his mortal existence, then soared aloft and sped away to join the souls of the blessed.")

Cf. Plotinus in Enn III 6, 6, 69ff.: καὶ γὰρ τὸ τῆς αἰσθήσεως ψυχῆς ἐστιν εὐδούσης· ὅσον γάρ ἐν σώματι ψυχῆς, τοῦτο εὕδει· ἡ δι᾽ ἀληθινὴ ἐγρήγορσις ἀληθινὴ ἀπὸ σώματος, οὐ μετὰ σώματος, ἀνάστασις. ἡ μὲν γὰρ μετὰ σώματος μετάστασίς ἐστιν ἐξ ἄλλου εἰς ἄλλον ὕπνον, οἷον ἐξ ἑτέρων δεμνίων· ἡ δ᾽ ἀληθὴς ὅλως ἀπὸ τῶν σωμάτων, ἃ τῆς φύσεως ὄντα τῆς ἐναντίας ψυχῇ τὸ ἐναντίον εἰς οὐσίαν ἔχει ("For the activity of sense-perception is that of the soul asleep; for it is that part of the soul that is in the body that sleeps; but the true wakening is a true getting up from the body, not with the body. Getting up with the body is only getting out of one sleep into another, like getting out of one bed into another; but the true rising is a rising altogether away from bodies, which are of the opposite nature to soul and opposed in respect of reality").[125]

Now, of course, Gnostic hope in nakedness as deliverance from the (earthly) σῶμα has its correlate in the hope of being clothed upon with the heavenly garment (cf. pp. 130f.), or in the hope of an ἀθάνατον σῶμα (Corp Herm 13, 3.14; cf. 10, 17, according to which the νοῦς obviously cannot exist as γυμνός, at least not in the σῶμα, for which reason it receives the ψυχή as a covering).

But it is certainly quite conceivable that Paul inferred from the statements of the Corinthian Gnostics a mere longing after ἐκδύσασθαι and hope in the γυμνότης. In any event, Paul's anxiety about an interim state of nakedness is not to be read from out of verse 3 (the Greek and Roman passages in Windisch, 163, to the effect that the deity does not desire to look upon human nakedness, contribute nothing to the discussion). Paul is not at all thinking of an interim state. If ἐκδύσασθαι occurs at death before the

---

[124] Plut Vitae, Romulus 28 (Ziegler, I 1, p. 72ff.).
[125] Cf. further the Corp Herm X, 16, and in addition Festugiere, 131, note 59.

parousia, then, since being clothed with the heavenly garment occurs only at the parousia, nakedness would have to be assumed for the interim state in the grave (the κοιμᾶσθαι in 1 Thess. 4:13f.; 1 Cor. 15:18, 20, 51, etc.). But this would be true only if there were no heavenly garment at the parousia, thus among the damned (Mundle, 101f. wants to interpret the reference only of them). But nakedness is certainly only one hypothetical possibility weighed by Paul — we would be γυμνοί if there were no heavenly garment. Verse 7 also renders it likely that Paul is referring to Gnostics who hope for γυμνότης. After all, it polemicizes against the Gnostic's assertion that besides πίστις they already enjoy sight.

Verse 4: **καὶ γὰρ οἱ ὄντες ἐν τῷ σκήνει στενάζομεν βαρούμενοι.** Verse 4 repeats the idea of verses 2f. in expressly polemical form. Again, the γάρ confirms verse 1 as a basis for knowledge. The actual reason for the στενάζειν is given: We sigh under the burden of the present time — **ἐφ' ᾧ οὐ θέλομεν ἐκδύσασθαι ἀλλ' ἐπενδύσασθαι.** The formulation is somewhat illogical, for Paul evidently wants to say, "Not because we merely (as such) want to be free of the body, but because we long for a new body." The ἵνα-clause makes clear that this is the yearning for the parousia — **ἵνα καταποθῇ τὸ θνητὸν ὑπὸ τῆς ζωῆς.** According to 1 Cor. 15:53, this swallowing up occurs at the parousia — δεῖ γὰρ τὸ φθαρτὸν τοῦτο ἐνδύσασθαι ἀφθαρσίαν καὶ τὸ θνητὸν τοῦτο ἐνδύσασθαι ἀθανασίαν. Mundle is thus correct that the ἐπενδύσασθαι is a being clothed upon with the new body at the parousia and resurrection, and that it applies not only to those who live to see the parousia, but also to those who have died before. If the latter are to an extent already ἐκδυσάμενοι (indeed not ἐκδεδυμένοι, as we should expect from v. 3, if Paul were really reflecting on them in v. 3), they are not so in the real sense, since the decisive destruction of the earthly σῶμα takes place only at the parousia. (Here, incidentally, we might consult the Jewish view accented by Bornhäuser, according to which the bones do not decay, though they belong to the earthly σῶμα; from this decay σάρξ καὶ αἷμα, which according to 1 Cor. 15:50 will not inherit the kingdom of God, are certainly not excepted). After all, Paul is obviously not thinking expressly of those who have died before the parousia, since he awaits the parousia in the near future, and regards it as normal that one will live to see it. In any event, the ἐκδύσασθαι does not denote simply "dying," but the decisive destruction of the earthly σῶμα.

Verse 5: **ὁ δὲ κατεργασάμενος ἡμᾶς εἰς αὐτὸ τοῦτο θεός, ὁ δοὺς ἡμῖν τὸν ἀρραβῶνα τοῦ πνεύματος.** θεός is a predicate as in 1:21 and 4:6. εἰς αὐτὸ τοῦτο is connected with the ἐπενδύσασθαι of verses 2 and 4. It makes no essential difference if one prefers to connect it with the ἵνα-clause of verse 4.

The clause gives the reason for the certainty expressed in verses 1-4. The hope is no fantasy, but is rather confirmed by God through the gift of the Spirit.

Further, that the πνεῦμα is the gift of the end-time is assumed and expressly stated in the clause ὁ ἀρραβὼν τοῦ πνεύματος, just as in 1:22 (cf. p. 43). The fact that we already possess the gift of the Spirit thus guarantees to us the eschatological future.

This clause also makes clear that the ἐπενδύσασθαι may not be restricted to those who live to see the parousia, that Paul therefore does not long for the ἐπενδύσασθαι in order to avoid the interim state of nakedness. Mundle, 105, correctly states that "if one limits the ἐπενδύσασθαι to experiencing the parousia, then in this passage Paul would be expressing the certainty that we will live to see the parousia, and would confirm this certainty with yet a reference to the fact of our possessing the Spirit in verse 5b! But it is precisely the certainty of living to see the parousia about which he is dubious, and it is not guaranteed him by the πνεῦμα."

If 5:1-5 is a polemical excursus intended to secure the Christian hope against Gnosticism (which Paul perhaps misunderstood in 1 Corinthians 15), then the idea is still essential to the entire context that the present transitoriness should be conceived as provisional. Sighing under the burden of the transient body is regarded as the perceptual basis for the imminence of an imperishable existence such as in Rom. 8:21-23. Cf. Geibel's poem, "Das Geheimnis der Sehnsucht:"

Du trägst, der Erde stummer Gast,
    In dir, was nur der Himmel faßt . . .
Dir selbst bewußt kaum ist dein Leid,
    Ein Heimweh nach der Ewigkeit.

Earth's mute guest, you bear
    in you what only heaven grasps . . .
To yourself your pain is scarcely known,
    A homesickness for eternity.

But for Paul that which allows this interpretation of longing (of the στενάζειν) is, according to verse 5, the ἀρραβὼν τοῦ πνεύματος. This is given in Baptism, but only the believer receives Baptism. In the last analysis, then, the solution to the riddle of longing is only given to the believer who can feel the power of faith as a gift of the Spirit.

Verses 6-10 show how this power of faith is manifest. If elsewhere Paul infers the imperative from the indicative of the possession of the Spirit (Gal. 5:25; cf. Rom. 8:12ff.), here he continues in the indicative, describing the conduct of a life in the Spirit as a life determined by the future attested to by the Spirit. If this is done first of all with reference to himself, since the θαρροῦντες of verse 6 resumes the οὐκ ἐγκακοῦμεν of 4:16, he at once includes all believers, and in this way describes the Christian life as a being determined by the future as such. In verse 10 the particular reference to his person is totally forgotten, so that 5:11 begins anew, for the purpose of describing his behavior as apostle.

140   *The Apostolic Office*

2. Walking as being determined by the future: 5:6-10

Verse 6: θαρροῦντες οὖν πάντοτε κτλ. The clause is an anacoluthon. To begin with, the finite verb, influenced by the clause in verse 7 which was first set down as a parenthesis, is lacking (it would be the εὐδοκοῦμεν of v. 8). Next, the θαρροῦντες is taken up again in verse 8 as the finite verb — θαρροῦμεν δε — because the parenthetical character of verse 7 has been forgotten.

The θαρροῦντες resumes the οὐκ ἐγκακοῦμεν of 4:16. The πάντοτε likewise resumes the ἐν παντί of 4:8 and the πάντοτε of 4:10, or the ἀεί of 4:11. Just as the μὴ ἐγκακεῖν in 4:16 followed from the hope described in 4:14f., so the θαρροῦντες from the hope developed in 5:1-5. We are therefore θαρροῦντες in our knowledge of 5:1-5 in the face of death, in view of which we do not anxiously cling to our earthly σῶμα so as to hold it fast, but gladly let it go.[126]

This very knowledge which yields the basis for θαρρεῖν is made explicit in the καὶ εἰδότες ὅτι κτλ.[127] The εἰδότες, then, is not at all in contrast to the θαρροῦντες, so that a καί should really have stood in place of the καίπερ (Windisch, 166). It is not at all a "reflection which must sound despondent," but precisely gives comfort. The θαρρεῖν is really fearlessness in face of impending death, which is πάντοτε threatening and already at work in sufferings. And this fearlessness follows precisely from the knowledge that our present existence is only temporary, that as long as it lasts — ἐνδημοῦντες ἐν τῷ σώματι (sc. τούτῳ or τῷ θνητῷ) — we are still far from our actual goal — ἐκδημοῦμεν ἀπὸ τοῦ κυρίου. So how could we be anxious for its continuance!

ἐνδημεῖν–ἐκδημεῖν means "to be at home, to be abroad."[128] Here the idea of being with the Lord (cf. 1 Thess. 4:17; Phil. 1:23) appears in place of the idea of ἐπενδύσασθαι. For obviously the ἐνδημῆσαι πρὸς τὸν κύριον in verse 8 refers to a final and not an interim state. From the formula alone, we might naturally infer a σὺν Χριστῷ εἶναι directly after death. But in the context it is certain that nothing else can be meant than the ἐπενδύσασθαι of verses 1-5. There is no thought of formal rivalry between the ἀπὸ τοῦ κυρίου or πρὸς τὸν κύριον of verse 8 and the ἐν Χριστῷ, which of course also applies to the believer's present existence.

Verse 7: The parenthesis expressly accents the anticipatoriness of present existence: διὰ πίστεως γὰρ περιπατοῦμεν, οὐ διὰ εἴδους. The περιπατεῖν is used as in 4:2, etc. (p. 97), and the διά denotes manner, as in 2:4

---

[126] θαρρεῖν is thus not vanquished anxiety over an interim state (Bousset, *Schriften* NT, 191).
[127] On εἰδότες cf. 4:14, p. 122.
[128] The figure of ἐνδημεῖν and ἐκδημεῖν may be occasioned by the Hellenistic idea of heaven as home; cf. Windisch, 166. Cf. Philo Poster C 135: τῇ δὲ (Λείᾳ) ἡ πρὸς τὸ γενητὸν ἀλλοτρίωσις πρὸς θεὸν οἰκείωσιν εἰργάσατο. ("But for Leah, estrangement on the human side brings about fellowship with God. . . .")

(p. 46).[129] The sense of the antithesis is made clear in the context: πίστις and εἶδος mutually explain each other, and πίστις here has the nuance of "only in faith," for example, as in Gal. 2:20: ὃ δὲ νῦν ζῶ ἐν σαρκί, ἐν πίστει ζῶ.

The element of ἐλπίς inherent in πίστις is therefore emphasized. Cf. Gal. 5:5: ἡμεῖς γὰρ πνεύματι ἐκ πίστεως ἐλπίδα δικαιοσύνης ἀπεκδεχόμεθα, and Rom. 6:8. In the same connection cf. Rom. 8:24f.: τῇ γὰρ ἐλπίδι ἐσώθημεν· ἐλπὶς δὲ βλεπομένη οὐκ ἔστιν ἐλπίς· ὃ γὰρ βλέπει τις, τί καὶ ἐλπίζει; εἰ δὲ ὃ οὐ βλέπομεν ἐλπίζομεν, δι' ὑπομονῆς ἀπεκδεχόμεθα.[130]

In contrast, εἶδος can scarcely be what is seen in the passive sense; it can scarcely be the shape. It is rather the seeing (the οὐ διὰ εἴδους corresponding to the οὐ βλέπομεν in Rom. 8:25). Dupont, *Gnosis,* 109, 2, is rightly of another opinion: The examples in Bauer for the active sense of εἶδος are questionable; εἶδος has an altogether passive sense (it appears only in this sense in L.S.), and thus belongs to the sphere of the visible (thus also Kittel in *TDNT* 2, 373f.).

Cf. Num. 12:8: στόμα κατὰ στόμα λαλήσω αὐτῷ, ἐν εἴδει καὶ οὐ δι' αἰνιγμάτων, καὶ τὴν δόξαν κυρίου εἶδεν. A διὰ εἴδους is thus reserved for the future; it would be equal to the πρόσωπον πρὸς πρόσωπον in 1 Cor. 13:12.

To this future the περιπατεῖν would naturally no longer apply; cf. Jonas, *Gnosis,* II, 1, 48: "Διὰ πίστεως γὰρ περιπατοῦμεν, οὐ διὰ εἴδους (2 Cor. 5:7) is an anti-Gnostic, basic Christian tenet, in which the περιπατεῖν on one side of the contrast is just as essential as πίστις on the other. In 'εἶδος,' that is, in the final γνῶσις, there is no longer any περιπατεῖν, no longer any temporality." Cf. *ibid.,* 47f. on 1 Cor. 13:9-13. In this passage, the ἐκ μέρους denotes the character of human temporality and finitude as such: "In the particularity of temporal human existence (*Dasein*), finality cannot in essence be realized, and thus [against Gnosticism!] is not to be striven after." Gnosticism, by supposing it can realize the τέλειον, aims to overleap facticity and, in its self-deception, avoid anticipatoriness. For Paul, faith, hope and love are the Christian "modes of existence as anticipatoriness defined with a view to the ἔσχατον. . . . They are distinguished from a γνῶσις sentenced to καταργηθῆναι not by the fact that they overcome the 'ἐκ μέρους' element as a structural element of temporality as such, but by the fact that they take this element up into their meaning in quite radical fashion, and thus are not contradicted but rather confirmed by the future τέλος which annuls temporality. (This is the meaning of the μένειν in v. 13) . . . They are modes of anticipatoriness in the radical sense that in the persistence of temporality they anticipate the ἔσχατον in any given

[129] The object of πίστις (and of εἶδος) is not Christ, so that πίστις would be removed by a *visio beatifica*. Rather, in the context the object of πίστις is the heavenly dwelling (Dupont, *Gnosis,* 109-111).

[130] Cf. John 20:29: μακάριοι οἱ μὴ ἰδόντες καὶ πιστεύσαντες.

moment as that which is no longer theirs, and qualify the given moment as anticipatoriness. In this way, they do not ignore or overleap the finitude of the moment, but precisely establish it with a view to the transcendence of every moment. Thus, what for γνῶσις is, according to its sense, a refutation, since it culminates in finality, is genuinely appropriate to the meaning of πίστις, ἐλπίς, and ἀγάπη — the absolute futurity and transcendence of the τέλος, a being set before transcendence in an absolutely anticipatory way, one's own 'being-ἐκ μέρους.'" Cf. also Calvin (against Servetus) Institutes II 9, 3 (the motto for Barth's *The Resurrection of the Dead*). Cf. also Barth, *Dogmatik* I, 68, on man as *viator*. After the Gnostic delusion is rejected in verse 7 by accenting the anticipatoriness of present existence, and after the ἐκδημοῦμεν ἀπὸ τοῦ κυρίου is secured, verse 8 again resumes verse 6.

Verse 8: **θαρροῦμεν δὲ καὶ εὐδοκοῦμεν μᾶλλον ἐκδημῆσαι ἐκ τοῦ σώματος καὶ ἐνδημῆσαι πρὸς τὸν κύριον.** θαρροῦμεν resumes the θαρροῦντες of verse 6, but takes on independence by its linkage with the parenthesis. The δέ (instead of the οὐ in v. 6) results from the parenthesis as contrast to the οὐ διὰ εἴδους. The εὐδοκοῦμεν μᾶλλον "we prefer," draws the consequence from the εἰδότες in verse 6. Precisely because we know that captivity to the body means being away from the Lord, we would rather "be away from the body in order to be able to be at home with the Lord."

Windisch, 167f., finds the relationship of θαρρεῖν to εὐδοκεῖν difficult, since the latter derives from a mood opposed to the former! Nonsense! The θαρρεῖν means that we confidently look death in the eye, and the εὐδοκοῦμεν μᾶλλον means that we actually greet it! Nothing better can happen to us!

Verse 9: **διὸ καὶ φιλοτιμούμεθα, εἴτε ἐνδημοῦντες εἴτε ἐκδημοῦντες, εὐάρεστοι αὐτῷ εἶναι.** διό means, "for this reason!" That is to say, we aim to please him in such θαρρεῖν and εὐδοκεῖν. Because whatever may happen to us can find no weak spot in us, we concentrate on only one thing — εὐάρεστοι αὐτῷ εἶναι. No anxiety or concern for ourselves deflects us from the μεριμνᾶν τὰ τοῦ κυρίου, πῶς ἀρέσωμεν τῷ κυρίῳ, cf. 1 Cor. 7:32ff. φιλοτιμεῖσθαι (also in Rom. 15:20; 1 Thess. 4:11) means "to seek his glory in it," or "it is our ambition" (Lietzmann, 120), a term scarcely chosen in reference to the reproach of φιλοτιμία or καύχησις, since the word does not occur elsewhere in 2 Corinthians.

εὐάρεστος αὐτῷ εἶναι. εὐάρεστος (τῷ θεῷ [κυρίῳ]) appears as an ethical term in Rom. 12:1f.; 14:18; Phil. 4:18; Col. 3:20; Eph. 5:10; Heb. 13:21; and 1 Clem. 35:5. εὐαρέστως is used in Heb. 12:28 and εὐρεστεῖν in Heb. 11:5f.; 13:16; and in 1 Clem. 62:2.

τὰ ἀρεστά occurs in John 8:29 (cf. Bultmann, *The Gospel of John*, 354, 2), and 1 John 3:22. ἀρεστὸς τῷ θεῷ (κυρίῳ) appears in the Didache 4:12 and Barnabas 19:2. ἀρέσκειν τῷ θεῷ (κυρίῳ) is used in Rom. 8:8; 1 Thess. 2:15; 4:1; and 1 Cor. 7:32 (ἀρεσκεία appears in Col. 1:10).

ἀρέσκω means to be obliging, to be of service, approximating the meaning of "to serve" (Nägeli, *Wortschatz,* 40). In Xenophon it is often used for accommodating oneself to the whole; cf. Stenzel, *Sokrates,* P.-W. III A, 830.

A zeal to serve the Lord which is free of anxiety not only knows no fear of death, but actually contains a tacit longing for death. The path from fear of death by way of a longing for death leads to indifference toward the question, When will death come, when will the ἐνδημῆσαι πρὸς τὸν κύριον, the ἐπενδύσασθαι take place? The zeal is the same — εἴτε ἐνδημοῦντες, εἴτε ἐκδημοῦντες. In saying this it is of no material consequence whether we add ἐν τῷ σώματι (or ἐκ τοῦ σώματος) or ἐν τῷ κυρίῳ (or ἀπὸ τοῦ κυρίου), though there is a probable relation to "σῶμα" in the idea of ἐνδημοῦντες. Here, then, the present tense is used instead of ἐκδημήσαντες, for the sake of a rhetorical antithesis.

On the polarity of expression whose purport is, "under all circumstances, in every situation," cf. 1 Thess. 5:10; Rom. 14:7f. and 1 Cor. 3:22; 10:31. The question how, as ἐκδημοῦντες ἐκ τοῦ σώματος, we can please the Lord (totally unanswerable, if an interim state were intended) is left undecided, for in that case, of course, there can be no more περιπατεῖν. Nevertheless, such speech expresses the idea that even in the δόξα beyond there is no *unio mystica* with Christ, but that he remains the κύριος.

In view of verse 9, the question of the future as a state of δόξα in general turns out to be irrelevant, just as in Rom. 14:7-9: ἐάν τε οὖν ζῶμεν, ἐάν τε ἀποθνήσκωμεν, τοῦ κυρίου ἐσμέν (cf. 1 Thess. 5:10). Cf. 1 Cor. 3:21f.: (πάντα γὰρ ὑμῶν ἐστιν) . . . εἴτε ζωὴ εἴτε ἐνεστῶτα εἴτε μέλλοντα. . . .[131]

Verse 10: τοὺς γὰρ πάντας ἡμᾶς φανερωθῆναι δεῖ. We have here the traditional idea of the eschatological judgment, before which all will receive their verdict, salvation or damnation according to their works, an idea of Jewish as well as Gentile eschatology (Windisch, 176; Lietzmann, 122f., excursus on 5:10). Cf. especially Lucian's Dial Mort 10, 13: πάντως δικασθῆναι δεήσει, καὶ τὰς καταδίκας φασὶν εἶναι βαρείας, τροχοὺς καὶ λίθους καὶ γῦπας· δειχθήσεται δὲ ὁ ἑκάστου βίος ἀκριβῶς. ("We shall have to be judged, and they say the sentences are heavy, wheels and stones and vultures; and the life of each of us will be revealed.")

τοὺς πάντας ἡμᾶς naturally does not mean "all we apostles," but all persons in general. In the context Christians are especially intended, as in Rom. 14:10, etc. The δεῖ is that of eschatological determination, cf. 1 Cor. 15:25, 53; Rev. 1:1; 4:1; and Mark 8:31, etc.

On φανερωθῆναι, cf. 1 Cor. 3:13 and 4:5, etc.

ἔμπροσθεν τοῦ βήματος τοῦ Χριστοῦ, cf. Rom. 14:10: πάντες γὰρ παραστησόμεθα τῷ βήματι τοῦ θεοῦ.

In Paul it is sometimes God (Rom. 14:10; 1 Thess. 3:13, etc.) and

---

[131] Cf. Käsemann, *Leib,* 124f., where 2 Cor. 5:11ff. is interpreted as a "model of the transformation of a Hellenistic-metaphysical tradition for the sake of a historical interest which is first with Paul" (125).

sometimes Christ (1 Thess. 2:19; 1 Cor. 4:5; 2 Cor. 5:10) who appears as world-judge.

ἵνα κομίσηται ἕκαστος τὰ διὰ τοῦ σώματος. κομίζεσθαι means "to receive the reward." That for which the reward is received is expressed by the accusative in Col. 3:25 and Eph. 6:8, just as in Lev. 20:17(19), and so also here: διὰ τοῦ σώματος.[132] The reward is for what was done in the (earthly) body, made explicit by the πρὸς ἃ ἔπραξεν, εἴτε ἀγαθὸν εἴτε φαῦλον — "according to what he has done, whether good or evil." One could unravel the clause thusly: ἵνα κομίσηται τὰ πρὸς ταῦτα, ἃ ἔπραξεν διὰ τοῦ σώματος. . . . Then the object of the τὰ πρὸς ταῦτα would be the reward itself. Whether διὰ τοῦ σώματος is construed instrumentally or temporally (while in bodily life) is of little material consequence; the latter construction would probably be better. But in what sense does verse 10 give the basis for verse 9? It furnishes the basis for the εὐάρεστος αὐτῷ εἶναι. For the one borne by zeal εὐάρεστος αὐτῷ εἶναι, fear of death vanishes. For this reason, a view to the judgment should keep that very zeal awake. But according to verses 6-8, fear of death vanishes in face of the certain future hope! Thus, a view to the judgment and to the grace which grounds that hope go together. For Paul it is no contradiction that the believer is now already justified (for example, Rom. 5:1), and that he awaits justification from the future (Gal. 5:6). God's forgiving grace is that of the judge, and faith, before it turns to sight, may never lose sight of God as judge, which means nothing else than that he continually stands upon grace; justification thus never becomes a quality which one possesses.

On the other hand, it is certain that just as δικαιοσύνη or ζωή, so the φανερωθῆναι ἔμπροσθεν τοῦ βήματος τοῦ Χριστοῦ (or τοῦ θεοῦ) is also a present reality; cf. verse 11: θεῷ δὲ πεφανερώμεθα; 2:17: κατέναντι θεοῦ . . . λαλοῦμεν, and 4:2: συνιστάνοντες ἑαυτοὺς πρὸς πᾶσαν συνείδησιν ἀνθρώπων ἐνώπιον τοῦ θεοῦ.

b. The revelation of ζωή in proclamation: 5:11—6:10

Therefore, knowing the fear of the Lord, we persuade men; but what we are is known to God, and I hope it is known also to your conscience. We are not commending ourselves to you again but giving you cause to be proud of us, so that you may be able to answer those who pride themselves on a man's position and not on his heart. For if we are beside ourselves, it is for God; if we are in our right mind, it is for you. For the love of Christ controls us, because we are convinced that one has died for all; therefore all have died. And he died for all, that those who live might live no longer for themselves but for him who for their sake died and was raised. From now on, therefore, we regard no one

---

[132] The διὰ τοῦ σώματος makes clear that the reward is according to what he has begun with himself or made of himself.

from a human point of view; even though we once regarded Christ from a human point of view, we regard him thus no longer. Therefore, if any one is in Christ, he is a new creation; the old has passed away behold, the new has come. All this is from God, who through Christ reconciled us to himself and gave us the ministry of reconciliation; that is, in Christ God was reconciling the world to himself, not counting their trespasses against them, and entrusting to us the message of reconciliation. So we are ambassadors for Christ, God making his appeal through us. We beseech you on behalf of Christ, be reconciled to God. For our sake he made him to be sin who knew no sin, so that in him we might become the righteousness of God. Working together with him, then, we entreat you not to accept the grace of God in vain. For he says, "At the acceptable time I have listened to you, and helped you on the day of salvation." Behold, now is the acceptable time; behold, now is the day of salvation. We put no obstacle in any one's way, so that no fault may be found with our ministry, but as servants of God we commend ourselves in every way: through great endurance, in afflictions, hardships, calamities, beatings, imprisonments, tumults, labors, watching, hunger; by purity, knowledge, forbearance, kindness, the Holy Spirit, genuine love, truthful speech, and the power of God; with the weapons of righteousness for the right hand and for the left; in honor and dishonor, in ill repute and good repute. We are treated as impostors, and yet are true; as unknown, and yet well known; as dying, and behold we live; as punished, and yet not killed; as sorrowful, yet always rejoicing; as poor, yet making many rich; as having nothing, and yet possessing everything.

In 5:11 to 6:10 Paul abides consistently by the theme of the apostolic office, with the exception of 5:14-17. His πεποίθησις (3:4) rests on the fact that he is the διάκονος τῆς καινῆς διαθήκης (3:6) as a διαθήκη τοῦ πνεύματος, τῆς δικαιοσύνης, as μένον (3:8-11), thus on the fact that he spreads the γνῶσις of God (2:14; 4:6) and with it ζωή (2:15f.; 4:12). If 4:7–5:10 had shown that ζωή is hidden beneath θάνατος, but proves itself to be operative precisely in θάνατος, then 5:11—6:10 explains that ζωή is manifest in proclamation. The sections are not sharply divided, for the fact that ζωή is manifest in θάνατος had indeed been shown in 4:1-15 with reference to the proclaiming apostle, and, just as 5:6 could be linked to 4:18 (p. 129), so 5:11 to 4:15. The opening clauses following 4:15, that is, the διὸ οὐκ ἐγκακοῦμεν in 4:16 and the θαρροῦντες οὖν πάντοτε in 5:6, both of which seem to continue the theme of the apostolic πεποίθησις (cf. 4:1: οὐκ ἐγκακοῦμεν, and 3:12: πολλῇ παρρησίᾳ χρώμεθα), do not actually pick up the theme but lead to statements concerning a universally Christian πεποίθησις in face of impending death. In 5:11, on the other hand, the theme of apostolic trust is actually resumed, indeed without express formulation, but in such a way that verses 11f. give clear expression to this trust. This trust is immediately grounded in the fact that with Christ the old has passed away and the new aeon has begun, and that this very saving event is continued in the proclamation (5:16ff.–6:2). Thus ζωή is at work in the proclamation, a ζωή effected by the apostle in the power of the eschatological event (6:3-10).

The polemical orientation to the reproach that Paul is a powerless, pitiful apostle is clear. In analogy with 4:7-12, 6:4-10 explains how, in the very humility of the proclaimer, the power of ζωή at work in the proclamation is manifest. And the introduction in 5:11-15 turns again to the reproach of καυχᾶσθαι.

Proclamation as the breaking in of the new creation: 5:11-19

1. The new criterion for judgment: 5:11-15

Verse 11: εἰδότες οὖν τὸν φόβον τοῦ κυρίου. The link with verse 10 shows that the φόβος τοῦ κυρίου (the κύριος, of course, is Christ before whose βῆμα verse 10 states we must appear) is φόβος before the judge. It is the יִרְאַת יהוה of the Old Testament, transferred to the κύριος.[133] It is naturally not the anxiety of which the believer is free according to Rom. 8:15 (cf. 1 John 4:17f.), but that fear of God which belongs to faith, since faith is the radical surrender of self-confidence; cf. Rom. 11:20f. and Phil. 2:12f. In the context, the φόβος τοῦ κυρίου is simply consciousness of responsibility.[134] Windisch, 176, is incorrect when he states that, in the interest of putting himself and the community to the practical test, Paul will not do without the motif of fear, and that he does not omit the numinous elements in the idea of God, "though they are stoutly suppressed by the enthusiasm of faith and love."

The εἰδότες,[135] of course, does not denote a theoretical knowledge, but an understanding of self in the fear of God. It is thus distinct from the εἰδότες ὅτι ὁ ἐγείρας in 4:14, and from the εἰδότες ὅτι ἐνδημοῦντες in 5:6 (cf. p. 140) insofar as it refers to a dogmatic knowledge. But just as such dogmatic knowledge is at the same time self-understanding, so also the εἰδότες of verse 11 is not without the dogmatic knowledge of verse 10.

The οὖν here corresponds to the οὖν in 3:12, 5:6, and 20, or to the διὰ τοῦτο in 4:1 and to the διό in 4:16. So there is a paradoxical correspondence between the εἰδότες οὖν τὸν φόβον τοῦ κυρίου and the ἔχοντες οὖν τοιαύτην ἐλπίδα in 3:12, or the θαρροῦντες οὖν in 5:6, or even the ἔχοντες τὴν διακονίαν ταύτην in 4:1. All this belongs together and forms a unity — confidence and consciousness of responsibility in awareness of the apostolic office.

---

[133] Cf. also [7:1].
[134] Cf. 2:17; 12:19: κατέναντι θεοῦ, and 4:2: ἐνώπιον τοῦ θεοῦ.
[135] Lietzmann, 122, translates, "in full consciousness of the fear of the Lord."

The ἀνθρώπους πείθομεν therefore corresponds to the πολλῇ παρρησίᾳ χρώμεθα in 3:12, to the οὐκ ἐγκακοῦμεν in 4:1, the θαρροῦμεν in 5:8, or the πρεσβεύομεν in 5:20. Paul's apostolic activity flows from a confident self-understanding and a consciousness of his responsibility. This is described here as an ἀνθρώπους πείθειν, which is perhaps a technical term for recruitment for a school, cf. Acts 18:4; 19:8, 26; 26:28; and 28:23. But it appears that with this term Paul is seizing upon a slogan of his opponents, who accuse him of πείθειν ἀνθρώπους as in Gal. 1:10,[136] since πείθειν does not occur elsewhere in Paul. For himself would he not rather have written παρακαλεῖν, as in 6:1? Cf. 5:20. And it is certainly clear in verse 15b and verse 16 that Paul counters these reproaches. So the "πείθομεν" is no doubt to be set in quotation marks.

Conscious of his responsibility, Paul thus "persuades" men — indeed! But precisely because he does so, it is true that **θεῷ δὲ πεφανερώμεθα.** Since he acts in consciousness of his responsibility, his work is manifest before God — clearly again an allusion to his opponents' reproach that he has something to hide (4:2).[137] His εἰδέναι, his self-understanding before the future judge, before whom we "must all appear" (v. 10), renders the future judge as it were a present reality. But his apostolic office requires that he be intelligible, "apparent" to his hearers, which he certainly strives to be throughout the entire epistle, as 1:13f. confirm. And the hope expressed in 1:13, ἐλπίζω δὲ ὅτι ἕως τέλους ἐπιγνώσεσθε is even stated here — **ἐλπίζω δὲ καὶ ἐν ταῖς συνειδήσεσιν ὑμῶν πεφανερῶσθαι.** The perfect infinitive after ἐλπίζω hardly gives it the attenuated sense of "I think" (Bl.-D. para. 350), but expresses Paul's optimism. It cannot be otherwise; the Corinthians must certainly understand him! — and of course ἐν ταῖς συνειδήσεσιν ὑμῶν. By his preaching he commends himself πρὸς πᾶσαν συνείδησιν ἀνθρώπων (4:2; p. 102), and the convincing truth of his preaching must certainly also convince his hearers of his own sincerity. Precisely in the interest of being clear or φανερός to them, he writes about himself, his service, and his trust. And it is this which makes him liable to the misunderstanding that he wishes to boast. Verse 12 counters this reproach:

Verse 12: οὐ πάλιν ἑαυτοὺς συνιστάνομεν ὑμῖν. Paul had already asserted this in 3:1, and cf. 4:2. His writing is not a συνιστάνειν ἑαυτόν in the sense in which he is reproached, but a self-revelation. He made himself clear to the community by making clear the essence of the gospel as the power of ζωή, and in doing so bore the offense which his apostolic self-consciousness created in apparent contradiction of his humility. But in light of the unity of apostle and gospel he must "boast," and thus also

---

[136] Cf. also 1 Cor. 2:4: οὐκ ἐν πειθοῖς σοφίας λόγοις.

[137] The antithesis θεῷ δὲ πεφανερώμεθα is not directed to the reproach that Paul wants to "persuade" God. What sense would that have? It is directed rather to the reproach of secrecy as in 4:2.

here he does not shun the possibility of misunderstanding — ἀλλὰ ἀφορμὴν διδόντες ὑμῖν καυχήματος ὑπὲρ ἡμῶν.[138] The community must boast of Paul! (καυχήματος is the equivalent of καυχήσεως which is identical to τοῦ καυχᾶσθαι). The decision for the gospel and for Paul is one and the same. If the Corinthians do not understand him, then they do not understand the gospel, for the misinterpretable claim which he makes against them is not that of the person but of the apostle, thus of the gospel; and his humility which allows that claim to appear ludicrous, is the necessary shape of ζωή. To understand him, of course, does not mean to inquire into his personal qualities and peculiarities, but rather to recognize and acknowledge him as apostle, and by doing so to surrender those authorities which boast of personal advantages (v. 12).

Windisch, 177, misconstrues the verse and thinks there is actually a συνιστάνειν of Paul here, so that the meaning is not, "we are not commending ourselves to you again," but rather, "this time our self-commendation does not apply to you, but to others to whom you should hand it on." But just as in 3:1, Paul totally rejects a συνιστάνειν ἑαυτόν. The point is exactly that the συνιστάνειν of Paul is merely apparent.

In order for the Corinthians to decide for Paul against those pseudo-authorities, Paul gives them (with all that he writes) an ἀφορμή, an opportunity, an occasion or inducement which they ought to seize. They ought to boast of him, that is, be proud of him. This would be a κρίνειν, as Paul himself makes in verse 14.

It is an error to expect a detailed ἀφορμὴ καυχήματος here, and which follows only in 6:3-10 (Windisch, 178). If Paul is manifest to the conscience of the community, then it also has the ἀφορμή! The meaning of this καύχημα as a decision for Paul and thus for the gospel is made clear by the ἵνα-clause — ἵνα ἔχητε πρὸς τοὺς ἐν προσώπῳ καυχωμένους καὶ μὴ ἐν καρδίᾳ. To the ἵνα ἔχητε add an ἀφορμήν or καύχημα, or better, a λέγειν τι (in the latter instance ἔχειν can be intransitive), meaning to be in a position to, cf. for example, Acts 4:14; Titus 2:8; John 8:6 [v. 1] and Acts 25:26).

It is clear that the καυχώμενοι are Paul's rivals at Corinth. The ἐν προσώπῳ and ἐν καρδίᾳ are not adverbial ("openly," "secretly"). Rather, the ἐν, as always with καυχᾶσθαι, gives the reason (cf. the LXX and 2 Cor. 10:17; 11:12; 12:9, etc.). ἐν προσώπῳ thus means, "by reason of external qualities," and as to content equals the κατὰ σάρκα of 11:18 (the antonym occurs in 11:17: κατὰ κύριον; cf. Phil. 3:3: καυχᾶσθαι ἐν Χριστῷ Ἰησοῦ), and cf. verse 16! ἐν καρδίᾳ means, "by reason of the hidden or invisible"; cf. Rom. 2:28 where the περιτομὴ καρδίας ἐν πνεύματι, οὐ γράμματι is

---

[138] The clause is an anacoluthon. The ἀλλὰ διδόντες is coordinated with the οὐ συνιστάνομεν, sc. perhaps λέγομεν or γράφομεν ταῦτα.

contrasted with the περιτομὴ ἐν τῷ φανερῷ ἐν σαρκί. Cf. 1 Kings 16:7: ἄνθρωπος ὄψεται εἰς πρόσωπον, ὁ δὲ θεὸς ὄψεται εἰς καρδίαν (cf. Gal. 2:6) and 1 Thess. 2:17: ἀπορφανισθέντες ἀφ᾿ ὑμῶν πρὸς καιρὸν ὥρας προσώπῳ οὐ καρδίᾳ.

Paul's καύχημα is thus grounded in the invisible (in precisely that hidden ζωή), while his opponents boast of their demonstrable qualities, their pneumatic demonstrations, and of which Paul speaks only when forced in 11:16ff. From this standpoint the following clause, at first unintelligible in the context, is also to be understood.

Verse 13: εἴτε γὰρ ἐξέστημεν, θεῷ· εἴτε σωφρονοῦμεν, ὑμῖν. In antithesis to σωφρονεῖν, ἐξίστασθαι can only mean a "being-outside-oneself" in pneumatic ecstasy, thus can only denote phenomena such as the ὀπτασίαι and ἀποκαλύψεις of 12:1, or the glossolalia of 1 Corinthians 14. As such, ἐξίστασθαι need only mean "being other than usual," or denote "states and affects deviating from the ordinary," "among them, of course, the pathological state of genuine ecstasy and frenzy" (Pfister, *Ekstasis, Pisciculi,* 17-191).

In the context, ἐξίστασθαι cannot simply be the equivalent of πνευματικὸς εἶναι — this is the opinion of Pfister, who wants to explain the term according to 1 Corinthians 2–3. There, according to Pfister, Paul writes that he cannot address the Corinthians as a πνευματικός, but only as a σώφρων. But Paul does not say this at all. He states rather that he neither could nor can speak to the Corinthians as πνευματικοί (3:1f.). He himself speaks as a πνευματικός throughout (1 Cor. 7:40: δοκῶ δὲ κἀγὼ πνεῦμα θεοῦ ἔχειν), and the contrast dominant in 1 Cor. 2 and 3 does not concern Paul's frame of mind, but rather the content of his speech. Nor does the ὑμῖν in 2 Cor. 5:13 mean, to you who are σαρκικοί and not πνευματικοί. For according to 2 Corinthians it is obvious that the Corinthians have the πνεῦμα (cf. 1:22; 3:7-18).

For this reason, the ἐξίστασθαι is also not identical with the ἐκδημῆσαι ἐκ τοῦ σώματος, as Pfister and Reitzenstein, HMR, 371f. suppose. For this event, of course, is about to occur only at death, or at the parousia. (Reitzenstein, 372, writes that "the ἐκστῆναι of vision [is] identified totally with the ἐκδημῆσαι at death"). It is the ἐνδημῆσαι ἐν τῷ σώματι which yields the contrast with ἐκδημῆσαι, not the σωφρονεῖν. And 5:9 accents the relative indifference of the ἐκδημῆσαι and ἐνδημῆσαι in face of the εὐάρεστος αὐτῷ εἶναι. But the ἐξίστασθαι and σωφρονεῖν cannot be a matter of indifference in face of the εὐάρεστος εἶναι. Rather, it is precisely in the σωφρονεῖν ὑμῖν (in Paul's service) that the εὐάρεστος εἶναι is actualized.

Much more — in the antithesis to σωφρονεῖν, the ἐξίστασθαι is a genuine ecstasy. If the ἐξίστασθαι applies to θεῷ (naturally, a dative of advantage, matching the ὑμῖν with σωφρονοῦμεν, and not an instrumental dative; cf. Pfister, *Ekstasis,* 186, note 24),[139] as contrasted with the σωφρονεῖν ὑμῖν which applies to the Corinthians, then the meaning is, "my ecstasies do not at all concern you!" But in what kind of contrast does Paul say this? It is not credible that Paul was reproached for his ecstasies, for using them to commend himself (Windisch, 179f.). First of all, according to 11:16f., and especially 12:11f., Paul certainly did not do so, and second, ecstasies as pneumatic phenomena are highly prized by the Corinthians, and it is just such phenomena which they miss in Paul. It is scarcely credible that he was scolded for having "conducted himself like a 'lunatic' at the conflict in Corinth" (Weiss, *Urchristentum,* 260, 1). That would not be called an ἐξίστασθαι.

Rather, Paul turns precisely to those critics among the Corinthians who find him lacking in pneumatic phenomena such as ecstasies.[140] This question is not at all the business of the Corinthians! Insofar as he experiences ecstasies, he has them for himself and God alone (1 Cor. 14:2, 18f.!). Only in this way does the clause also furnish the basis for verse 12 (γάρ) — the ἐν προσώπῳ καυχώμενοι boast of their ecstasies. Paul refuses to do so, and gives other evidences of his behavior, for the sake of which the Corinthians can boast of him (6:4ff.). The γάρ of verse 13 thus grounds the ἀφορμὴν διδόντες ὑμῖν κτλ. — by showing myself to you in my existence as apostle (in my dying which reveals the ζωὴ τοῦ Ἰησοῦ), I show you how you must boast of me against those who καυχώμενοι ἐν προσώπῳ. Whether such pneumatic phenomena can also be confirmed in me, as they boast of them, does not concern you at all! Only my σωφρονεῖν[141] concerns you, that is, the conscious conduct of my office. (Naturally, in the wider sense Paul's σωφρονεῖν has also to do with θεῷ; but θεῷ in the context means, "only for God," while the σωφρονεῖν ὑμῖν means, "aimed directly at the community.")

Verse 14: ἡ γὰρ ἀγάπη τοῦ Χριστοῦ συνέχει ἡμᾶς. In the context, the ἀγάπη τοῦ Χριστοῦ, which is described in the εἷς ὑπὲρ πάντων ἀπέθανεν, can only be the love shown by Christ. The τοῦ Χριστοῦ is thus a subjective genitive.[142] Naturally, Paul could also speak of his love for Christ (in actual fact, Paul only uses ἀγαπᾶν τὸν θεόν, cf. Rom. 8:38; 1 Cor. 2:9; and 8:3). But such love would be the result of συνέχειν, not its subject. Paul usually speaks of the love of Christ which encounters him. Rom. 8:35 reads: τίς ἡμᾶς χωρίσει ἀπὸ τῆς ἀγάπης τοῦ Χριστοῦ. Cf. Rom. 5:5: ὅτι ἡ ἀγάπη τοῦ θεοῦ ἐκκέχυται ἐν ταῖς καρδίαις ἡμῶν . . . (εἴ γε Χριστὸς . . . ὑπὲρ

---

[139] Dative of advantage in Bl.-D. para. 188, 2. Το θεῷ add ἐξέστημεν, and to ὑμῖν, σωφρονοῦμεν. On τῷ θεῷ cf. 1 Cor. 14:28.

[140] Käsemann puts it correctly in ZNW 41, 1942, 67f.

[141] The antithesis of "my ἐξιστάναι concerns only God" is not "my σωφρονεῖν concerns only you," but "only my σωφρονεῖν concerns you."

[142] Lietzmann, 124, thinks that ἀγάπη τοῦ Χριστοῦ is to be construed in what is probably also a mystical, dual sense.

2:14—7:4 151

ἀσεβῶν ἀπέθανεν). Rom. 8:39 reads: οὔτε τις κτίσις ἑτέρα δυνήσεται ἡμᾶς χωρίσαι ἀπὸ τῆς ἀγάπης τοῦ θεοῦ τῆς ἐν Χριστῷ Ἰησοῦ τῷ κυρίῳ ἡμῶν, and Gal. 2:20: ὃ δὲ νῦν ζῶ ἐν σαρκί, ἐν πίστει ζῶ τῇ τοῦ υἱοῦ τοῦ θεοῦ τοῦ ἀγαπήσαντός με καὶ παραδόντος ἑαυτὸν ὑπὲρ ἐμοῦ. Cf. 2 Cor. 13:13: ἡ χάρις τοῦ κυρίου Ἰησοῦ Χριστοῦ καὶ ἡ ἀγάπη τοῦ θεοῦ.

συνέχειν means first of all to hold together, which can signify either to keep in order or to bind, to lock. Second, it means to hold fast, to imprison, to rule (also to oppress, to attack, etc.), cf. συνοχή in 2:4. Here it means, "to rule,"[143] cf. Phil. 1:23: συνέχομαι δὲ ἐκ τῶν δύο, τὴν ἐπιθυμίαν ἔχων εἰς τὸ ἀναλῦσαι. Cf. the Hermetic fragment in Reitzenstein, *Poimandres*, 185: ἀπάλλαξον τὸν δεῖνα ἀπὸ τοῦ συνέχοντος αὐτὸν δαίμονος.

Windisch's (181) alternative of quietude (to keep within limits, to restrain), or motion (to incite) is incorrect. συνέχειν does not mean to incite. It is hard to decide whether ἡμᾶς, which according to verse 13 refers primarily to Paul, already has an extended meaning and applies (to all apostles or) to all Christians. In any event, as in 3:12ff., 4:16ff., and 5:6ff., Paul once more turns from describing apostolic existence to describing Christian existence, for the ἡμεῖς in verse 16 corresponds to the εἴ τις in verse 17, and the ἡμᾶς in verse 18 embraces all Christians, while the ἡμῖν in verse 19 may refer especially to Paul (and the apostles).

κρίναντας τοῦτο. The κρίνειν does not mean, "to begin a reflection" (Windisch, 181), but rather "to make a judgment" (which Windisch takes to be synonymous), that is, to resolve on the basis of a conscious decision, as in 2:1; 1 Cor. 2:9; and Acts 15:19. λογίζομαι is used in similar fashion, particularly in Rom. 3:28; 6:11; 8:18; and 14:14 (cf. 14:5, 13: κρίνειν).

ὅτι εἷς ὑπὲρ πάντων ἀπέθανεν. The ἄρα οἱ πάντες ἀπέθανον[144] which follows shows that the dominant idea in the ὑπέρ is not "for the sake of," but "in the place of" (= ἀντί). All are regarded as having died. ὑπέρ is used in the very same way in verse 21. Of course, in such utterances elsewhere, ὑπέρ always has the meaning of "for the sake of," cf. Rom. 5:6,8; 14:15; Gal. 1:4; 2:20; etc. (Lord's Supper texts, etc.), and this meaning emerges again in verse 15b. ἀντί appears in Mark 10:45 = Matt. 20:28; cf. ἀντίλυτρον in 1 Tim. 2:6.

This conclusion does not rest on the idea of a sacramental or mystical union at death (Windisch, 182). In that case, the ὑπὲρ πάντων would have to be omitted and an ἐν αὐτῷ added to the οἱ πάντες, cf. 1 Cor. 15:22. Rather, there is a juridical idea of substitution here (ὑπέρ means substitution for, cf. Deissmann, L.v.O., 132, 5; 285, 2). Those represented by the substitute are regarded as also having performed his deed.

With this idea of substitution Paul makes clear that Jesus' death is the saving event in which all (sc. believers) share. The idea which underlies it is

---

[143] Thus also Lietzmann, 124.
[144] ἄρα in the final clause means "consequently," Bl.-D. para. 451, 2d.

not juridical, since what the representative has done is not simply credited to those represented. They must die the death after him. The sacramental idea in Rom. 6:3ff. makes the same statement, where the ὑπέρ is characteristically lacking (sc. συνταφῆναι in Rom. 6:4 and συσταυρωθῆναι in Rom. 6:6).

The sequel we expect to the εἷς ὑπὲρ πάντων ἀπέθανεν is not, thus also all have risen with Christ (Windisch, 183, and which by itself would also be correct). Rather, in the context, as verse 15 states and verse 16f. explains, the sequel is, "thus sarkic existence is dispatched, that is, there is therefore no ἐν προσώπῳ καυχᾶσθαι any longer, but only an existence for others." In this sense verse 14 gives the basis for verse 13 (γάρ). Two things apply: Negatively, that as he is met with in the world, Paul means nothing (there is thus no καυχώμενος ἐν προσώπῳ), and positively, that what he is, he is in service for others. This is established in verses 14f. Strictly speaking, the (σωφρονεῖν) ὑμῖν of verse 13 is explained in verses 14f., in verse 14 toward the negative, and in verse 15 toward the positive side. The negative is then more precisely explained in verse 16, and the positive in verses 18f.

The reference to the πάντες in verse 14 is to be construed in the sense that all are given the possibility of making Christ's death their own, which of course is actualized only in faith, cf. 1 Cor. 15:22 and Rom. 5:18. Mundle (*Glaubensbegriff*, 147-149) incorrectly wishes to interpret the πάντες only of the baptized; on the other hand, Dahl's comment in *Volk Gottes*, 329, note 168, is correct.

Verse 15: καὶ ὑπὲρ πάντων ἀπέθανεν ἵνα οἱ ζῶντες μηκέτι ἑαυτοῖς ζῶσιν. The ὑπὲρ πάντων ἀπέθανεν of verse 14 is taken up again, in order to attach the positive conclusion. The ἵνα is of course not (such as would correspond exactly to the ἄρα of v. 14) equal to ὥστε, but is clearly meant to introduce a genuine result. The consequence of the ὑπὲρ πάντων ἀπέθανεν is an imperative — "therefore those who (now) live should live no longer for themselves." After the ἄρα οἱ πάντες of verse 14, we might expect οἱ ἀποθανόντες instead of οἱ ζῶντες, and the οἱ ζῶντες may be an abbreviation for οἱ ἀποθανόντες ὃ νῦν ζῶσιν (ἐν σαρκί; cf. Gal. 2:20), so that the οἱ ζῶντες should be understood just as in 4:11 — while in bodily life. But it is more probable (?) that οἱ ζῶντες denotes those who have attained to authentic "life." Then it is assumed as obvious that the ἀποθανόντες (by virtue of their appropriating Christ's death) are ζῶντες in the genuine sense, because as sharers of his death they also share in his resurrection (cf. 4:10f.; Rom. 6:5, 11, etc.).[145] The ἵνα οἱ ζῶντες μηκέτι ἑαυτοῖς ζῶσιν naturally denotes bodily life in its being destined for death, just as in Gal. 2:20: (ὃ δὲ νῦν ζῶ ἐν σαρκί) ἐν πίστει ζῶ τῇ τοῦ υἱοῦ τοῦ θεοῦ. The meaning then is that those who by virtue of appropriating Christ's death

---

[145] How obvious this is for Paul is shown at once by the τῷ ὑπὲρ αὐτῶν ἀποθανόντι καὶ ἐγερθέντι. Christ as the one who died is at the same time the Risen One.

have come to genuine life should now no longer live their (earthly) life for themselves; they no longer belong to themselves (cf. 1 Cor. 6:19: καὶ οὐκ ἐστὲ ἑαυτῶν).

But the negative statement is only the foil for the ἀλλὰ τῷ ὑπὲρ αὐτῶν ἀποθανόντι καὶ ἐγερθέντι. Those who have died by virtue of appropriating Christ's death belong to him.[146] Just as in 4:7-15 believing existence is characterized by the death of existence as met with in the world and by service for others, an existence in which ζωή is evident, so here it is characterized as a having died and at the same time as a life for. . . . That life is not described in this passage as service for others, but as life for Christ, is, of course, no contradiction; life for Christ is naturally a life in service for others, a life in that διακονία described in verses 18f.

The basis for the ὑμῖν in verse 13 is thus given in the τῷ ὑπὲρ αὐτῶν ἀποθανόντι καὶ ἐγερθέντι. And in verse 15 it is not a "mythical" idea which has moved over into the "ethical" (Windisch, 183). Rather, to the negative statement a positive statement is now attached, which was in mind from the very outset in verse 13. There was no reference at all to "mysticism." From the very beginning apostolic (and Christian) existence as determined by the ἀγάπη τοῦ Χριστοῦ had been viewed from its dual aspect: The apostle or the Christian is dead to existence as met with in the body, so that all καυχᾶσθαι ἐν προσώπῳ (v. 12) is at an end, and with it life is set in the service of Christ, and that means, of others.

This statement yields the criterion for judging Paul. The proclamation can be understood as the breaking in of the new creation, as verses 16-19 describe it, first by again setting forth the negative in verses 16f. — it is really all over with the old; then the positive in verses 18f. — the proclamation is grounded in the saving event which brings the old to an end. Verses 16f. draw the consequence of verse 14, and verses 18f. the consequence of verse 15.

2. The basis for the proclamation in the saving event: 5:16-19

Verse 16: ὥστε ἡμεῖς ἀπὸ τοῦ νῦν οὐδένα οἴδαμεν κατὰ σάρκα. Verse 16 is by no means "one of those characteristically Pauline transitional clauses" (Lietzmann, 125), or a "transitional thought" (Wendland, 133), but just as the ὥστε (parallel to it) in verse 17, it draws the consequence of verses 14f. (If v. 16b were attached to v. 16a by a γάρ, then we would have to construe v. 17 as drawing the conclusion from v. 16b. But v. 16b does not give the basis for v. 16a [the latter already takes its basis from v. 14]. Rather, v. 16b merely cites the extreme instance of the clause in v. 16a, in which the sense of v. 16a becomes crystal clear.)[147]

The ἡμεῖς cannot mean Paul (and the apostles) in particular, but embraces

---

[146] Cf. the [εἶναι] Χριστοῦ in 1 Cor. 3:23 and Rom. 14:8.
[147] Still, it is possible that the ὥστε in v. 17 is intended to draw the conclusion from v. 16b.

all believers who seize the possibility of verse 14. The term corresponds to the εἴ τις of verse 17. A tenet of Christian teaching is expressed in the first person plural as, for example, in Rom. 7:6; in the first person singular as in Gal. 2:19f., or in the imperative as in Rom. 6:11.

Grammatically, the κατὰ σάρκα could belong with οὐδένα, as with the Χριστός in verse 16b. What is at issue in the context is how a person should be understood and judged, that is to say, not according to appearance, according to visible qualities or weaknesses, but according to what cannot be seen of his true nature; cf. the ἐν προσώπῳ — ἐν καρδίᾳ in verse 12.

σάρξ is the sphere of the empirical, an entity. A person κατὰ σάρκα is such an entity or person with respect to what is empirically observable in him. Cf. for example, ὁ Ἰσραὴλ κατὰ σάρκα in 1 Cor. 10:18 (the antonym is ὁ Ἰσραὴλ τοῦ θεοῦ in Gal. 6:16); Ἀβραὰμ τὸν προπάτορα ἡμῶν κατὰ σάρκα in Rom. 4:1; τοῦ γενομένου ἐκ σπέρματος Δαυὶδ κατὰ σάρκα in Rom. 1:3,[148] and ἐξ ὧν ὁ Χριστὸς τὸ κατὰ σάρκα in Rom. 9:5.

In this sense κατὰ σάρκα most often appears with nouns. But with verbs it has the meaning of "according to the criterion, the norm of the empirical, of worldliness." Cf. for example, περιπατεῖν κατὰ σάρκα in 2 Cor. 10:2 and Rom. 8:4; βουλεύεσθαι κατὰ σάρκα in 2 Cor. 1:17, and καυχᾶσθαι κατὰ σάρκα in 2 Cor. 1:18. Cf. also Rom. 8:5: οἱ γὰρ κατὰ σάρκα ὄντες τὰ τῆς σαρκὸς φρονοῦσιν, οἱ δὲ κατὰ πνεῦμα τὰ τοῦ πνεύματος.

1 Cor. 1:26 makes clear the distinction: The σοφοὶ κατὰ σάρκα are not the wise with a view to their empirical character, but those who are wise after the fashion of the σάρξ.

Since to regard people with a view to their empirical character means also to regard them after the fashion of the σάρξ, the distinction in the use of κατὰ σάρκα can be a matter of indifference. That is the case here. To know people as they are met with in the world means also to know them in worldly fashion. For this reason it is a matter of indifference whether κατὰ σάρκα is linked with οὐδένα or with οἴδαμεν.

εἰδέναι, just as the γινώσκειν in verse 16b, means simply "to know," and in this passage scarcely with the nuance "to recognize," but rather "to understand" (as ἐπιγινώσκειν in 1:13f.), so that the one known is "evident" (v. 11). ἀπὸ τοῦ νῦν[149] is not the terminology of conversion (Windisch, 185), but of eschatology. Ever since the event of verse 14 the world is new (v. 17; 6:2), the old has passed away — in the objective sense, of course, and not for me as one converted, however surely it is realized for me through my conversion. But this ἀπὸ τοῦ νῦν is now to be seized by faith and actualized.

Verse 16 thus draws the consequence of verse 14. Since we have all died

---

[148] The antonym is τοῦ ὁρισθέντος υἱοῦ θεοῦ ἐν δυνάμει κατὰ πνεῦμα ἁγιωσύνης in Rom. 1:4.

[149] "νῦν is the moment of conversion"! (Lietzmann, 126).

to the sarkic existence of what can be encountered in the world, our judgment of persons may and can no longer be oriented to what can be encountered in the world.[150] Just as the ἐν προσώπῳ καυχᾶσθαι (v. 12) is at an end, so the ἐν προσώπῳ καυχώμενοι may no longer thrust themselves on the Corinthians. And the Corinthians must orient their judgment of Paul accordingly.

εἰ καὶ ἐγνώκαμεν κατὰ σάρκα Χριστόν, ἀλλὰ νῦν οὐκέτι γινώσκομεν (sc. κατὰ σάρκα).[151] The general sense of the clause is clear. The extreme (which could also have been cited as basis) is cited, in which a γινώσκειν τινὰ κατὰ σάρκα is at issue. The tenet in verse 16a is confirmed in the extreme case of verse 16b: Even with respect to Christ it is true that οὐδένα οἴδαμεν κατὰ σάρκα. The εἰ καί thus means "even if."[152]

Naturally, Χριστόν does not denote the Jewish Messiah figure or Jewish ideal of Messiah, but rather — as is obvious in the context — Christ himself, as person.[153] The Χριστὸς κατὰ σάρκα is Christ as he can be encountered in the world, before his death and resurrection. He should no longer be viewed as such (or, or one wishes to connect κατὰ σάρκα with ἐγνώκαμεν — cf. above on v. 16a — one should no longer view him after the manner of the σάρξ, which comes round to the same thing). But what would a γινώσκειν Χριστὸν κατὰ σάρκα mean? There are two possible interpretations, both of which yield sense in the context:

The first is that the phrase refers to Christ with respect to the advantages he enjoyed during his worldly existence, that he was David's son, worked miracles and the like. This figure would contrast with the Christ whom one ought to regard, the very ἐν μορφῇ δούλου γενόμενος, the ἐσταυρωμένος — of course in respect of his hidden δόξα. In this case, the clause would be polemically aimed at the καυχώμενοι ἐν προσώπῳ of verse 12.

The second is that it refers to Christ in his plainness, in his σχῆμα ὡς ἄνθρωπος, his μορφὴ δούλου (Phil. 2:7). The Χριστὸς κατὰ πνεῦμα would then be the δοξασθείς[154] in the σῶμα τῆς δόξης αὐτοῦ (Phil. 3:21), ὅς ἐστιν ἐν δεξιᾷ τοῦ θεοῦ (Rom. 8:34).[155] In that case, Paul would be stating a

---

[150] The "we" is thus not individual (I, Paul), but general — we Christians (cf. pp. 153f.). Cf. v. 17: εἴ τις.

[151] Cf. Dupont, Gnosis, 180-186. Instead of εἰ καί (in P⁴⁶ B ℵ* D* and pc) K has εἰ δέ (impossible!). C ℜ and pm read εἰ δὲ καί, and G latsyᵖ read καί εἰ.

[152] Does he reproach his opponents for knowing only the Christ κατὰ σάρκα? Or have they hurled this reproach at him (say, on the basis of 1 Cor. 2:2)? Neither! He is merely citing the extreme.

[153] The interpretation of Schlatter, Bote, 562f., Wendland, 133f. and others, to the effect that εἰ καὶ κτλ. refers to Paul's pre-Christian behavior as persecutor is impossible. It is such already because of the εἰ καί.

[154] The ὁρισθεὶς υἱὸς θεοῦ ἐν δυνάμει κατὰ πνεῦμα ἁγιωσύνης ἐξ ἀναστάσεως νεκρῶν in Rom. 1:4.

[155] Dupont, Gnosis, especially p. 186, who (without giving a reason, as though it were obvious) connects the κατὰ σάρκα with ἐγνώκαμεν, states that the counterpart of γινώσκειν κατὰ σάρκα is not a γινώσκειν κατὰ πνεῦμα, but rather the εἶναι καινὴ κτίσις. False "acquaintance" is not countered by a proper "perception," but by a new existence.

generally recognized proposition, and the application to his own person
would be quite directly intended: The apostle may not be regarded with a
view to the θάνατος at work in him, but with a view to the ζωὴ τοῦ Ἰησοῦ
at work through him (4:7-12). The second possibility is the more obvious.[156]

With the first possibility the γινώσκειν κατὰ σάρκα could denote personal
acquaintance with the earthly Jesus, of which Paul's opponents (or at least
their authorities) boasted (thus also Fridrichsen, *Miracle,* 37-39, who in other
respects correctly understands the context). But nowhere in 2 Corinthians
or elsewhere does Paul refute claims derived from personal acquaintance
with Jesus. And the formulation in no way proves Paul's own personal
acquaintance with the earthly Jesus.[157]

Grammatically, of course, the εἰ καὶ ἐγνώκαμεν is a simple condition,
but according to its sense it is a condition contrary to fact (Reitzenstein,
HMR, 374-376), or a "hypothetical, simple condition" (Lietzmann, 125)
as in Gal. 5:11: ἐγὼ δέ, ἀδελφοί, εἰ περιτομὴν ἔτι κηρύσσω, τί ἔτι
διώκομαι. Cf. the classical examples in Lietzmann, 125. The meaning is
thus, "and supposing we have known Christ according to the flesh, despite
that fact we know him thus no longer." (Or also, "agreed that . . . then
nevertheless. . . ."). The relation between the conditional and the final
clause is thus not really conditional in the sense that the εἰ-clause actually
states the condition for the final clause — "if I had known him, then
I would know him now; but I do not know him, thus did not know
him even then." Rather, the conditional particle is used in a purely
adversative sense here: Supposing that . . . then, for that reason, still not
yet (Reitzenstein, HMR, 376).[158]

On the subject matter, cf. Luther on Gal. 1:11 (Galaterbrief 1516/1517,
p. 36, 4ff.) and on Gal. 4:4f. (1531 WA 40, 1, p. 568, 9ff.). The meaning is
thus that not even Christ may be regarded as he can be met with in the
world. What was said in verse 16a, therefore, applies all the more.

Verse 17: Verse 17 unfolds the idea of the ἄρα οἱ πάντες ἀπέθανον in
verse 14, or the thought in verse 16. In contrast to the limited statement
in verse 16, that the old εἰδέναι has ceased to be, the radical assertion
now is made that everything old has ceased to be — ὥστε εἴ τις ἐν Χριστῷ,
καινὴ κτίσις· τὰ ἀρχαῖα παρῆλθεν, ἰδοὺ γέγονεν καινά.

It is thus of little import whether we construe the ὥστε as parallel to the
ὥστε in verse 16 (p. 153), or whether we read verse 17 as a new conclusion
drawn from verse 16. The εἴ τις corresponds to the ἡμεῖς of verse 16, and

---

[156] In any case, Paul argues *a majore ad minus.* The extreme case, that the Χριστὸς
κατὰ σάρκα no longer avails, is admitted. Therefore it holds that οὐδένα οἴδαμεν κατὰ
σάρκα — so also I may not be viewed κατὰ σάρκα.

[157] Quite apart from the fact that the "we" does not refer to Paul, but embraces the
entire community (cf. pp. 153f.).

[158] The proposal to read ἄλλα instead of ἀλλά is absurd: ". . . then we know nothing
else any longer" — cf. Dupont, *Gnosis,* 181, 2.

indicates once more that Paul is not speaking particularly of an apostle's but of the Christian's existence.

The meaning of ἐν Χριστῷ is clear in the context — whoever seizes the possibility named in verse 14 (or differently formulated in v. 19); therefore, whoever shares in the saving event brought about by God in Christ. That person is ἐν Χριστῷ who was received by Baptism into the community as the σῶμα Χριστοῦ — cf. Gal. 3:26-28: πάντες γὰρ υἱοὶ θεοῦ ἐστε διὰ τῆς πίστεως ἐν Χριστῷ Ἰησοῦ· ὅσοι γὰρ εἰς Χριστὸν ἐβαπτίσθητε, Χριστὸν ἐνεδύσασθε. (On εἰς Χριστόν, cf. 2 Cor. 1:21) οὐκ ἔνι Ἰουδαῖος οὐδὲ Ἕλλην . . . πάντες γὰρ ὑμεῖς εἷς ἐστε ἐν Χριστῷ Ἰησοῦ; 1 Cor. 12:13: καὶ γὰρ ἐν ἑνὶ πνεύματι ἡμεῖς πάντες εἰς ἓν σῶμα ἐβαπτίσθημεν, and Rom. 12:5: οὕτως οἱ πολλοὶ ἓν σῶμά ἐσμεν ἐν Χριστῷ.[159]

The ἐν Χριστῷ is thus not a formula of mysticism, but rather of eschatology, or it has an eschatological-ecclesiological sense.[160] But along with that the ἐν Χριστῷ marks the believers' new life as an existence which is eschatologically determined. And this eschatological existence is described as a καινὴ κτίσις.

The term corresponds to the Rabbinic בְּרִיאָה חֲדָשָׁה, cf. Dalman, *The Words of Jesus,* 178; Str.-B. II, 421ff. (on John 3:3), and III, 519 (on 2 Cor. 5:17). It is used as an eschatological term (cf. the Messianic time as new creation, Midrash Teh. 2(9.) v. 7, ed. Buber, p. 28; translation by Wünsche, p. 26), but also as a term for a new epoch in history (Noah, Abraham, Moses). Finally, it is applied to the individual in the sense of external healing or rescue, especially of the forgiveness of sins.[161] Cf. also Windisch, 189f. and Merx, *Johannes,* on John 8:1-12, p. 177f. The Stoic doctrine of world periods has nothing in common with it (Windisch, 190).

Here, as in Gal. 6:15, the term is clearly applied to the individual, and just as clearly in the eschatological sense, for the explanation is τὰ ἀρχαῖα παρῆλθεν, ἰδοὺ γέγονεν καινά. The allusion here is to Isa. 43:18f.; cf. Isa. 65:17. Just as in 6:2, so here the eschatological prophecy is regarded as fulfilled in Christ.[162] Cf. also Rev. 21:4f.[163]

Naturally, we may not assume Paul would be obliged to say εἰ ἐγνώκαμεν κατὰ πνεῦμα Χριστόν (Windisch, 189), for the εἰ-clause in verse 17 is by no means parallel to the εἰ καὶ ἐγνώκαμεν of verse 16, but is rather a genuinely conditional clause. The γινώσκειν κατὰ πνεῦμα would not at all lay the basis for the καινὴ κτίσις εἶναι but is itself contained in the καινὴ κτίσις εἶναι and established by the ἐν Χριστῷ εἶναι, or by the saving act in

[159] Bultmann, *Theology,* 310ff.
[160] Bultmann, *Theology,* 327ff.
[161] In addition, cf. Moore, *Judaism* I, 533.
[162] Cf. the reference to the new heaven and earth, and utterances of such kind in Isa. 66:22; Eth. Enoch 45:4f.; 72:1; 90:28f.; 91:16; 4 Ezra 7:75; Syr. Baruch 32:6; 44:12 and Rev. 21:1. On καινὴ κτίσις cf. Barn. 6:11, 13f.; 16:8; Ign Trall 8:1 and Just Apol 61:1.
[163] Against the overemphasis on discontinuity between the old and new, cf. Schumann, *Kirche,* 158f.

verse 14. Paul thus could say ὥστε εἴ τις ἐν Χριστῷ, κατὰ πνεῦμα Χριστὸν (or ἕκαστον) γινώσκει.

The ἀρχαῖα comprises everything under the old aeon. In the context the empirical comes under consideration as something on which a judgment κατὰ σάρκα might be based. All this has lost its value; now only a judgment in Christ is necessary and appropriate, as καινὴ κτίσις, that is, κατὰ πνεῦμα.

In light of verse 11 the conclusion now would be: Therefore you may not follow those who ἐν προσώπῳ καυχῶνται (v. 12), but must reach the proper judgment of me, not by judging me κατὰ σάρκα, but as καινὴ κτίσις must regard me also as καινὴ κτίσις. Paul leaves this conclusion to the readers. He unfolds the positive side of the idea in verses 14f. and thus in verse 15 as follows: The new eschatological existence as a life ὑπὲρ Χριστοῦ is the apostle's service. With that he returns to the theme of apostolic existence, indeed, not by speaking of himself, but by characterizing this apostolic service as grounded in the saving event (vv. 18f.), and then by actually exercising it in the appeal in 5:20—6:2.

Verse 18: The **τὰ δὲ πάντα ἐκ τοῦ θεοῦ** refers to what was said in verses 14 and 16f., not to what was said in verse 15, for this is of course resumed in verses 18f. **τοῦ καταλλάξαντος ἡμᾶς ἑαυτῷ διὰ Χριστοῦ**. With respect to its content, God's καταλλάσσειν is explained by the μὴ λογιζόμενος αὐτοῖς τὰ παραπτώματα αὐτῶν in verse 19. The assumption is that men were God's enemies (ἡμᾶς is used in the wider sense, corresponding to the πάντες in vv. 19f.) prior to the saving deed of God occurring in Christ, cf. Rom. 5:10f.: εἰ γὰρ ἐχθροὶ ὄντες κατηλλάγημεν τῷ θεῷ διὰ τοῦ θανάτου τοῦ υἱοῦ αὐτοῦ, πολλῷ μᾶλλον καταλλαγέντες σωθησόμεθα ἐν τῇ ζωῇ αὐτοῦ· οὐ μόνον δέ, ἀλλὰ καὶ καυχώμενοι ἐν τῷ θεῷ διὰ τοῦ κυρίου ἡμῶν Ἰησοῦ [Χριστοῦ], δι' οὗ νῦν τὴν καταλλαγὴν ἐλάβομεν.

The καταλλαγέντες in Rom. 5:10 corresponds to the δικαιωθέντες in 5:1 and 9. Here, too, it is clear that "reconciliation" is the purging of sins, and of course by means of the saving event. The διὰ Χριστοῦ in 2 Cor. 5:18 is equivalent to the διὰ τοῦ θανάτου τοῦ υἱοῦ αὐτοῦ in Rom. 5:10. The δικαιωθείς is the καταλλαγείς, insofar as the δικαιωθείς possesses εἰρήνη (Rom. 5:1). As the enmity between God and humankind was an objective state of affairs, so is now the reconciliation.

The fact of enmity is given with sins, with the παραπτώματα, with the life of humans "according to the flesh," cf. Rom. 8:7: διότι τὸ φρόνημα τῆς σαρκὸς ἔχθρα εἰς θεόν. But this need not imply subjective hostility.[164] And if ἐχθρός used of persons (or of the σάρξ) has the meaning of being "hostile toward," it can likewise contain the passive sense of "being hated," as the continuation in Rom. 8:8 indicates: οἱ δὲ ἐν σαρκὶ ὄντες θεῷ ἀρέσαι οὐ δύνανται. ἐχθρός is used in corresponding fashion in Rom. 5:10

---

[164] Cf. the explication τῷ γὰρ νόμῳ τοῦ θεοῦ οὐχ ὑποτάσσεται, οὐδὲ γὰρ δύναται.

and 11:28: κατὰ μὲν τὸ εὐαγγέλιον (the Jews are) ἐχθροὶ δι' ὑμᾶς. This does not express a particularly hostile disposition on God's part, but rather an objective state of affairs. It is the way in which God encounters sinful humans, just as God's ὀργή is not his wrathful passion, but rather the judgment which his activity spells for sinners, the way in which he must appear to the sinner.

Correspondingly, the καταλλαγή is not a change in subjective mood, so that we would have to ask, Whose mind has changed, God's or ours? (Windisch, 191ff.). It is clear that the καταλλαγή is not an event occurring between two persons (God and the individual), in which both surrender their mutual hostility. It is rather God's deed alone, which he carries out ἡμῶν ἔτι ἐχθρῶν ὄντων; cf. Rom. 5:10: εἰ γὰρ ἐχθροὶ ὄντες κατηλλάγημεν τῷ θεῷ. People can only share God's saving deed or shut themselves off from it; they can "receive" the καταλλαγή (Rom. 5:11: δι' οὗ νῦν τὴν καταλλαγὴν ἐλάβομεν), just as one "receives" δικαιοσύνη (Rom. 5:17: οἱ τὴν περισσείαν τῆς χάριτος καὶ τῆς δωρεᾶς τῆς δικαιοσύνης λαμβάνοντες). The λόγος καταλλαγῆς in verse 19 is not the conciliatory and reconciling word, but the message of reconciliation already occurred; and the καταλλάγητε τῷ θεῷ in verse 20 does not mean, "be reconcilable," but invites one to faith in the message that the reconciliation has been carried out. God's καταλλάσσειν is his establishing a condition of peace by not allowing his ὀργή to prevail, or it proffers the possibility that his ὀργή is not at work because he does not reckon sins.

The question, How is God reconciled? is falsely put, however correct the reference to the remoteness of the ethical notion that people do something in order to placate God. Paul does not at all reflect on the idea of God's having to be reconciled; God himself has reconciled the world to himself, but that does not mean he has set aside its anger, but rather annulled the relationship of objective hostility and established peace through the forgiveness of trespasses.[165] This is done through the death of Christ; in what way, is not said. But it is clear that Paul's meaning is not that the earlier notion of God was false, so that the καταλλαγή (insofar as it could then be spoken of at all) would be carried out through an explanation of the true concept of God.

Cf. Vischer, *Paulus,* 134: "It is part of Paul's Jewish way of thinking not merely to say that the legal structure of religion was imperfect, or to speak of a change or purification of human notions about God, but rather to allow God himself to alter his dealings with humankind and, in place of the earlier, to allow a new order to appear."

So the Christian message is not that "God (till now misjudged according

---

[165] Cf. John 3:36: ὁ δὲ ἀπειθῶν τῷ υἱῷ οὐχ ὄψεται ζωήν, ἀλλ' ἡ ὀργὴ τοῦ θεοῦ μένει ἐπ' αὐτόν.

to his nature) is gracious," but rather that "God has acted graciously, and this grace is available to the one who opens himself to it." The activity of God is not an interior influence on human disposition, however, so that καταλλαγή would take place in inward agitation and transformation, but it is a deed which has occurred apart from people, independent of their conversion; it is the surrender of Christ into death.

The difficulty lies in understanding the death of Christ as a deed of grace, that is, in understanding to what extent the μὴ λογίζεσθαι τὰ παραπτώματα is grounded in Christ's death.

Paul uses various concepts in order to render it intelligible.

First, in the context, the idea of substitution occurs in the ὑπὲρ πάντων of verse 14, and in the ὑπὲρ ἡμῶν of verse 21. It is also present in Gal. 3:13: γενόμενος ὑπὲρ ἡμῶν κατάρα, and perhaps in Rom. 8:3.

Second, death is viewed as a means of expiation. Note the ἱλαστήριον in Rom. 3:25, which is used according to a traditional formulation. Christ's blood is thereby conceived as a means of atonement; cf. Rom. 5:9: δικαιωθέντες νῦν ἐν τῷ αἵματι αὐτοῦ. And in most of the ὑπέρ-passages this idea will appear; cf. Rom. 4:25 (8:3?); 1 Cor. 11:24f. and 15:3.

The two concepts interlace as in verses 14f. and thus in Rom. 3:21ff., for if forgiveness of sins has occurred during the ἀνοχὴ τοῦ θεοῦ through the ἱλαστήριον, then Christ has certainly suffered death in place of sinners.

Third, the concept is used in the singular in 1 Cor. 5:7, where Christ is conceived as the paschal offering which averts punishment.

Fourth, the idea of ransom appears in Gal. 3:13; 4:4f.; 1 Cor. 6:20 and 7:23.

Finally, the death of Christ can be construed as a cosmic event such as in the Hellenistic mystery religions or Gnosticism: Because Christ died, all have died with him, insofar as by Baptism they share in his death (cf. Rom. 6:3-10; 2 Cor. 4:7-12; and Phil. 3:10); accordingly his resurrection draws after it the resurrection of all (cf. Rom. 5:12-21 and 1 Cor. 15:21-23, 44-49).

All these trains of thought are mythological. It is necessary to discover the basic, nonmythological idea behind them (cf. Bultmann, *Theology,* 300f.).[166]

καὶ δόντος ἡμῖν τὴν διακονίαν τῆς καταλλαγῆς. The διακονία τῆς καταλλαγῆς is precisely the διακονία τοῦ πνεύματος, or τῆς δικαιοσύνης (3:7-9), contrasted with the διακονία τοῦ θανάτου, or τῆς κατακρίσεως. It is the apostolic office which proclaims the saving event, so that in verse 19 the

[166] The solution to the difficulty derives from the insight that Jesus' death is not the fate of one individual, but a "cosmic" event in which a person shares who is "in Christ," who has died with him. Or it is an eschatological event. This means that this death is the end of the world for the one who recognizes Christ as Lord. The word offers him this possibility; that is, it states that God regards the one who acknowledges Christ as Lord as having died and risen with him. In this way, the "cosmic" event becomes an historical event; or the eschaton becomes history always by faith.

λόγος τῆς καταλλαγῆς can appear in place of the διακονία τῆς καταλλαγῆς. Institution of the proclamation thus belongs with the καταλλαγή. This is actualized, of course, by means of the preaching (v. 20); only in the preaching and in the faith which accepts it does the individual realize the καταλλαγή instituted by God prior to all human effort. Thus the preaching itself belongs to the saving event, cf. 2:14f. (p. 62).

The ἡμῖν can refer to Paul or to the apostles in general, but it more likely refers to the Christian community, for the ἐν ἡμῖν in verse 19 clearly means among people, or among the believers, in the community.

Verse 19: ὡς ὅτι θεὸς ἦν ἐν Χριστῷ κόσμον καταλλάσσων ἑαυτῷ. θεὸς ἦν is very likely to be connected with καταλλάσσων (a periphrastic subjunctive, frequent in the New Testament, though indeed not in Paul, occurring especially in the imperfect, probably under Aramaic influence; Bl.-D. para. 353). The ἐν Χριστῷ then equals διὰ Χριστοῦ in verse 18. The connection can scarcely be θεὸς ἦν ἐν Χριστῷ, so that καταλλάσσων would be attributive or in apposition, since for Paul, after all, the εἶναι of God ἐν Χριστῷ is an inconceivable idea.

It is striking that Paul does not construct the sentence as in 1:21; 4:6; or 5:5 (ὅτι θεὸς ὁ καταλλάσσων ἐν Χριστῷ), probably because he does not intend to give the reason but the content of the διαθήκη τῆς καταλλαγῆς.

Besides 2 Cor. 5:19,[167] the unclassical ὡς ὅτι (Bl.-D. para. 396) occurs three times in Paul.

The expression appears in 2 Cor. 11:21: κατὰ ἀτιμίαν λέγω, ὡς ὅτι ἡμεῖς ἠσθενήκαμεν. It appears in 2 Thess. 2:2: μήτε δι᾽ ἐπιστολῆς ὡς δι᾽ ἡμῶν, ὡς ὅτι ἐνέστηκεν ἡ ἡμέρα τοῦ κυρίου. In these two passages, the Vulgate translates with a "quasi," which Bl.-D. deem appropriate and which also suits 2 Cor. 5:19, where the Vulgate translates *quoniam quidem*.[168] The intent is clearly to explain the concept of the διακονία τῆς καταλλαγῆς. Thus as in 11:21 and 2 Thess. 2:2 ὡς ὅτι appears after a verb of speaking — "the content of which is that God has reconciled the world to himself through Christ."[169]

κόσμον denotes persons (as in Rom. 1:8 and 1 Cor. 4:9, where the angels of course are included; Rom. 5:12f., etc.), corresponding to the ἡμᾶς in verse 18, and subsequently included again in the αὐτοῖς.

μὴ λογιζόμενος αὐτοῖς τὰ παραπτώματα αὐτῶν. The μὴ λογιζόμενος is

---

[167] The simplest translation is, "namely that. . . ." On ὡς ὅτι cf. Plut Gen Socr 598e: εὐθέως δὲ οἱ μὲν (the trumpeter) ἐπὶ τῆς ἀγορᾶς ἐσήμαινον οἱ δὲ κατ᾽ ἄλλους τόπους, πανταχόθεν ἐκταράττοντες τοὺς ὑπεναντίους, ὡς πάντων ἀφεστώτων (= that all have deserted). ("They at once set to blowing their trumpets, some in the market place, others elsewhere, from all sides filling our opponents with alarm as if the whole city had risen.") Plut Is et Os 39: κραυγὴ τῶν παρόντων ὡς εὑρημένου τοῦ Ὀσίριδος. (". . . a great shout . . . from the company for joy that Osiris is found.")

[168] Bl.-D. para. 396 = ὡς θεοῦ ὄντος.

[169] Just as in the Pseudo-Clementine Homilies 14, 7, 2 (Rehm, p. 208) where εἰρηκέναι ὡς ὅτι is used in direct address.

subordinated to the ἦν καταλλάσσων, as the καὶ θέμενος κτλ. is coordinated with the μὴ λογιζόμενος, so that the μὴ λογιζόμενος . . . καὶ θέμενος explains the ἦν καταλλάσσων (καὶ θέμενος — sc. ἦν — can scarcely be coordinated with the ἦν καταλλάσσων).

The αὐτοῖς refers to the κόσμον, a *constructio ad sensum,* cf. Bl.-D. para. 282, 3.

The λογίζεσθαι τινί τι means "to apply to someone's account," and is also a Greek idiom; cf. Heidland, *Anrechnung,* 25.

παράπτωμα (current in later Greek since Polybius, and also in the papyri) denotes a false step, a transgression. In the New Testament, with the exception of Rom. 5:15, 17f., 20; 11:11f., and Galatians 6:1, it always appears in the plural. In Gal. 6:1 it seems to be used in a sense distinct from ἁμαρτία, that is, as an occasional and not severe transgression — ἐὰν καὶ προλημφθῇ ἄνθρωπος ἔν τινι παραπτώματι.

Elsewhere there is no detectable difference from ἁμαρτία (for differences which have been contrived, cf. Trench, *Synonyms* 158f.). Cf. Rom. 4:25: ὃς παρεδόθη διὰ τὰ παραπτώματα ἡμῶν, which materially corresponds with the ἀπέθανεν ὑπὲρ τῶν ἁμαρτιῶν ἡμῶν in 1 Cor. 15:3, or with the τοῦ δόντος ἑαυτὸν ὑπὲρ τῶν ἁμαρτιῶν ἡμῶν in Gal. 1:4, etc. Rom. 5:15ff. deals with Adam's παράπτωμα, while according to 5:12 δι' ἑνὸς ἀνθρώπου ἡ ἁμαρτία εἰς τὸν κόσμον εἰσῆλθεν. In Rom. 5:20 the ἵνα πλεονάσῃ τὸ παράπτωμα is resumed in the οὗ δὲ ἐπλεόνασεν ἡ ἁμαρτία. Cf. Col. 2:13: ὑμᾶς νεκροὺς ὄντας τοῖς παραπτώμασιν; Eph. 2:1: ὑμᾶς ὄντας νεκροὺς τοῖς παραπτώμασιν; and Eph. 2:5: καὶ ὄντας ἡμᾶς νεκροὺς τοῖς παραπτώμασιν. Instead of τὰ παραπτώματα, James 5:16 (thus also Mark 1:5 = Matt. 3:6) reads ἐξομολογεῖσθε τὰς ἁμαρτίας.

In its content, the μὴ λογιζόμενος αὐτοῖς τὰ παραπτώματα αὐτῶν corresponds to the ἀφιέναι τὰς ἁμαρτίας. Thus ἀφιέναι τὰ παραπτώματα appears in Mark 11:25 and Matt. 6:14f., and conversely in Rom. 4:8 λογίζεσθαι ἁμαρτίαν is parallel to ἀφιέναι ἀνομίας (according to Ps. 31:1f.). Cf. in addition 2 Tim. 4:16, which reads μὴ αὐτοῖς λογισθείη.[170]

The μὴ λογιζόμενος αὐτοῖς τὰ παραπτώματα αὐτῶν is juridical terminology. Taken in its strict sense, the μὴ λογίζεσθαι would set aside the condition of guilt and men (under the law) and then have to begin all over again. But he is a καινὴ κτίσις and that means free from the lordship of sin reigning in the old aeon. The account of guilt is not simply erased, but the possibility of a *non peccare* is created, cf. Romans 6 and Gal. 5:16ff., etc.

καὶ θέμενος ἐν ἡμῖν τὸν λόγον τῆς καταλλαγῆς. The clause is no doubt coordinated with the μὴ λογιζόμενος, cf. above. On the ἐν ἡμῖν which means, "in the community," cf. p. 161 on verse 18. On λόγος τῆς

---

[170] Cf. Aristoph, Vesp 745f.: λογίζεταί τ' ἐκεῖνα πάνθ' ἁμαρτίας, ἃ σοῦ κελεύοντος οὐκ ἐπείθετο. "He feels his former life was wrong. Perchance he'll now amend his plan."

καταλλαγῆς, cf. p. 161 on verse 18. The λόγος τῆς καταλλαγῆς is not the conciliatory word, but the preaching of reconciliation already accomplished, cf. p. 159.

God's τίθεσθαι is an erecting, an arranging, disposing, a "determining;" cf. 1 Cor. 12:18: νῦν δὲ ὁ θεὸς ἔθετο τὰ μέλη, and Acts 1:7: καιροὺς οὓς ὁ πατὴρ ἔθετο.

The practice of proclamation: 5:20—6:10

The statement in 5:11-19 is not applied by Paul's summoning the Corinthians to a proper understanding of his person or to a proper judgment about himself, but first of all by addressing them in 5:20—6:2, as proclaimer and in this way proving that he is a διάκονος τῆς καταλλαγῆς or τοῦ πνεύματος and τῆς δικαιοσύνης (3:8f.). Thus he addresses them as one who spreads the ὀσμὴ τῆς γνώσεως of God (2:14), who allows the γνῶσις τῆς δόξης τοῦ θεοῦ to shine (4:6), in whom the ζωὴ τοῦ Ἰησοῦ is therefore at work (4:10f.). Accordingly, in 6:3-10 and again in apologetic-polemic fashion, Paul describes how he commends himself, that is, by the fact that in his practice of proclamation the power of ζωή or the eschatological event is manifest.

1. Proclamation as eschatological event: 5:20—6:2

Verse 20: **ὑπὲρ Χριστοῦ οὖν πρεσβεύομεν.** πρεσβεύειν means first of all, "to be older, to rule, to prevail," then "to be an envoy," a special term for the legates of Caesar (and used with ὑπέρ). For this reason, it is a matter of little concern whether ὑπὲρ Χριστοῦ is construed as "for Christ" (thus Lietzmann, 126: "Thus we work for Christ"),[171] or "in Christ's cause," "in Christ's commission," or "in Christ's stead," since the commissioned messenger certainly speaks in place of, as representative of the one commissioning.[172]

The **ὡς τοῦ θεοῦ παρακαλοῦντος δι' ἡμῶν** gives a heightened explanation to the ὑπὲρ Χριστοῦ — "things are certainly such that,"[173] "since of course," "since, as you must know, God calls you" (on ὡς cf. Bl.-D. para. 425, 3).[174]

As Christ's messenger and representative, the apostle is also God's messenger and representative, and his labor as διάκονος τῆς καταλλαγῆς belongs to the work of atonement itself, cf. pp. 160f. Verse 20 is thus the

---

[171] "To work" is a poor translation; Bauer s.v. "to proclaim."
[172] Cf. for example Thuc VIII 45, 4: αὐτὸς (Alcibiades) ἀντιλέγων ὑπὲρ τοῦ Τισσαφέρνους = "taking it upon himself to answer on behalf of Tissaphernes." The very same usage appears in 56, 4.
[173] "It is just as. . . ."
[174] Lietzmann, 126: "while God as it were [?] preaches through us (our mouth)" ("directly" is better than "as it were").

most intense expression of Paul's παρρησία, and the οὖν corresponds exactly to the conclusions drawn in 3:12; 4:1, 16; 5:6 and 11.

δεόμεθα ὑπὲρ Χριστοῦ, καταλλάγητε τῷ θεῷ. The δεόμεθα ὑπὲρ Χριστοῦ resumes the ὑπὲρ Χριστοῦ πρεσβεύομεν, in order to attach to it the content of the message: καταλλάγητε τῷ θεῷ — corresponding to the description of the proclamation as the λόγος τῆς καταλλαγῆς — accept the tidings of reconciliation! Make the death of Christ (v. 14), the saving deed of God (vv. 18f.), your own! People must now seize the καταλλαγή which God has brought about apart from them and prior to all human action and behavior. Naturally, the καταλλάγητε does not mean, "be conciliatory minded! Let go your anger against God," as though God and humans were equal partners, but rather, "submit yourselves to the reconciling work of God," cf. p. 159. The summons is none other than that of the ὑπακοὴ πίστεως (Rom. 1:5), just as reconciliation denotes the forgiveness of sins (v. 19) or δικαιοσύνη (v. 21). The resolve of faith is thus required (cf. κρίνειν in v. 14); it is a resolve on the basis of συνείδησις (4:2; 5:11), the resolve of δέξασθαι (6:1). The acceptance is recognition, one's submission to God's grace (6:1).

Just as Windisch finds the idea of conversion in verse 16, so he thinks he sees a "missions style" (196) in verse 20, since the appeal — καταλλάγητε — can actually be directed only to the yet unconverted world, not to a community long since established, as though he were offering it forgiveness again. "What is voiced here is rather the choir of apostles which shouts the message of Christ into the world" (196).

Nonsense! Such an alternative does not exist at all for Paul. Naturally, he speaks in a "missions style." But this is always the style appropriate to eschatological preaching. For the action of δέχεσθαι is never a thing of the past, but as genuine decision must always be carried out anew. The old world which has died with Christ is never silenced once for all, but must continually be given into death. The eschatological νῦν (6:2), concretized in the preaching in any given moment of time, is beyond the course of time which is, after all, disposed of with the old aeon. The καταλλάγητε is thus altogether appropriately addressed to the Corinthian community.

Verse 21: The καταλλάγητε in verse 20 is further developed here, because Paul (though explication was certainly given in vv. 18f.) is now speaking directly as apostle and thus describing the work of atonement in a new formulation — τὸν μὴ γνόντα ἁμαρτίαν ὑπὲρ ἡμῶν ἁμαρτίαν ἐποίησεν. The τὸν μὴ γνόντα ἁμαρτίαν is Christ.

The γινώσκειν naturally refers to the practical knowledge of Rom. 3:20 and 7:7. It is the εἰδέναι of verse 11. Cf. Herm sim IX, 29, 1: ὡς νήπια βρέφη . . . (sc. οἱ) οὐδὲ [ἔγνω]σαν, τί ἐστι πονηρία, ἀλλὰ πάντοτε ἐν νηπιότητι διέμειναν; ("as innocent babes . . . nor have they known what wickedness is, but have ever remained in innocence."); mand II, 1: ὡς τὰ νήπια τὰ μὴ γινώσκοντα τὴν πονηρίαν; ("as the children who do not know the wickedness . . ."). Cf. also Aesch Eum 85f.: ἄναξ Ἄπολλον, οἶσθα μὲν τὸ μὴ ἀδικεῖν· ἐπεὶ δ᾽ ἐπίστα, καὶ τὸ μὴ ἀμελεῖν μάθε. "Lord Apollo, thou knowest not to be unrighteous; And, since thou knowest, learn also not to be unheedful." The Rabbinic expression is, "who does not know what taste of sin is" (or, "do not taste the flavor of sin," "taste no sin"), and is used thus, for example, of children, Str.-B. III, 520.

The "sinlessness" of Christ is thus maintained, not indeed up to a certain point in time at which God "made" him "to be sin" (thus Windisch, 197, who for this reason construes the clause as causal — "since he had not sinned"), whether at his incarnation or his death, but totally.[175] This is precisely the paradox, that the sinless one as such was made a sinner.

With ἁμαρτίαν ἐποίησεν the abstract is used for the concrete (= ἁμαρτωλόν), just as with δικαιοσύνη (= δίκαιοι), so as to make clear the principle meaning of the clause. Cf. Gal. 3:13: γενόμενος ὑπὲρ ἡμῶν κατάρα.

The meaning is, just as believers are "just" because God regards ("reckons") and treats them as such, though they are sinners, so Christ is regarded and treated by God as sinner (cf. Rom. 8:3: ὁ θεὸς τὸν ἑαυτοῦ υἱὸν πέμψας ἐν ὁμοιώματι σαρκὸς ἁμαρτίας) though he is sinless. Naturally, there is no reference to the earthly Jesus' having sinful qualities, at least to the extent he could be tempted (Windisch, 198, with reference to Heb. 4:15). Rather, he was absolutely sinless (cf. John 7:18; 8:46 and 1 John 3:5).

And, of course, Christ is treated as sinner by the fact that God allows him to die like a sinner on the cross (Gal. 3:13). The ὑπὲρ (ἡμῶν) thus has the same sense as in verse 14 — Christ died as our representative (without the substitutionary idea of Rom. 8:3).

ἵνα ἡμεῖς γενώμεθα δικαιοσύνη θεοῦ ἐν αὐτῷ. As elsewhere in Paul, the δικαιοσύνη θεοῦ is a righteousness given by God. So the meaning is that through Christ's death we have become righteous (that is, we have the possibility of being righteous, a possibility realized by faith), that our righteousness does not consist in a self-induced moral quality, but in God's judgment, that is, in the forgiveness of our sins (*aliena justitia*). This corresponds to the statement that whoever is ἐν Χριστῷ is a καινὴ κτίσις (v. 17). For him the old world has sunk together with its sins.

Further, it is doubtful whether the ἐν αὐτῷ is to be construed locally, as the ἐν Χριστῷ in 5:17, so that the Gnostic-cosmological idea would be linked to the idea of substitution, or whether it is intended instrumentally as in verse 19 (the equivalent of διὰ Χριστοῦ in v. 18), which would better conform to the substitutionary idea. In any event, even in a local sense, ἐν Χριστῷ does not have a "mystical" sense but rather the eschatological force of verse 17.

---

[175] Christ's sinlessness is his ὑπακοή in Rom. 5:19 (cf. 15:3: οὐχ ἑαυτῷ ἤρεσεν), and in Phil. 2:8 (cf. 2 Cor. 8:9: δι᾽ ὑμᾶς ἐπτώχευσεν πλούσιος ὤν).

166 The Apostolic Office

As a result of the correspondence of clauses in verse 21, the character of δικαιοσύνη also spells a μὴ γινώσκειν ἁμαρτίαν. And in fact for Paul the negative aspect in the μὴ λογίζεσθαι τὰ παραπτώματα cannot be separated from the positive aspect of freedom from sin (cf. p. 162), just as in verses 14f. the negative and positive form a unity. Accordingly, Rom. 8:3f. reads: καὶ περὶ ἁμαρτίας κατέκρινεν τὴν ἁμαρτίαν ἐν τῇ σαρκί, ἵνα τὸ δικαίωμα τοῦ νόμου πληρωθῇ ἐν ἡμῖν τοῖς μὴ κατὰ σάρκα περιπατοῦσιν ἀλλὰ κατὰ πνεῦμα. Here too, of course, the possibility of a new περιπατεῖν is included with the δικαιοσύνη θεοῦ (and in the context this means that the righteous do not judge according to the old criteria of the σάρξ; in the context particular moral defects are not in view).

Windisch is thus correct when he denies that Paul looses deliverance from sin from justification, but he is incorrect when he construes δικαιοσύνη as a peculiarity of our new "nature" which has actually penetrated our being: "In mystical communion with him the sinless Christ who only temporarily [!] was sin, gives us a share in his holy, sinless, righteous, God-pleasing nature"! (199). The link between justification and deliverance from sin is given rather with the character of justification as forgiveness. For forgiveness is the only means of destroying sin (insofar as it is not construed juridically, but genuinely as a forgiveness which renews the relationship between God and man), of destroying the presence of the past in the now. And since forgiveness can only be accepted in the surrender of the "I" to the forgiver, so the resolve to accept it is also the resolve to realize the possibility of the περιπατεῖν κατὰ πνεῦμα. Forgiveness grounds freedom in the negative as well as the positive sense.

Verse 1: συνεργοῦντες δὲ καὶ παρακαλοῦμεν. The παρακαλοῦμεν again takes up the πρεσβεύομεν or δεόμεθα of 5:20, and the συνεργοῦντες resumes the idea of the ὑπὲρ Χριστοῦ or ὡς τοῦ θεοῦ παρακαλοῦντος δι᾿ ἡμῶν in 5:20. A τῷ θεῷ (in any case a Χριστῷ) must of course be added to the συνεργοῦντες; cf. 1 Cor. 3:9: θεοῦ γάρ ἐσμεν συνεργοί; cf. also 1 Cor. 4:1.

To the divine commission in 5:20 nothing is added of any personal motive on Paul's part to "support" God's message (Windisch, 199). There is no reference to personal and psychological motives, but rather to material necessities. Paul "works together with," that is, the apostolic preaching belongs to the revelatory event.

μὴ εἰς κενὸν τὴν χάριν τοῦ θεοῦ δέξασθαι ὑμᾶς. The clause corresponds to the καταλλάγητε in 5:20. The δέξασθαι is thus ingressive, and means "to receive" (not "to have received"). The aorist infinitive is used following παρακαλεῖν as in 2:8; Rom. 12:1; 15:30; and Eph. 4:1.

The χάρις τοῦ θεοῦ is the very saving deed of God described in 5:18f. and 21, just as is χάρις in Gal. 2:21; 5:4; and Rom. 5:2. The μὴ εἰς κενὸν δέξασθαι is the equivalent of εἰς κενόν, and means in vain, just as in Gal. 2:2 and Phil. 2:16. It is also used in the LXX and in the Greek, cf.

Bauer, s.v. The apostolic preaching can only set the hearers before an either-or — acceptance or nonacceptance. Since acceptance takes place in obedient submission, thus in resolve, it would be futile to misconstrue it as the mere theoretical acceptance of a doctrine, as a declaration of intent to join a religious society. The resolve, the decision, is genuine only when it persists as such; if it does not, the acceptance was in vain. The warning, μὴ εἰς κενὸν δέξασθαι, thus admonishes to a true acceptance which accepts the consequences of the saving deed for the conduct of life, and that means also for judgment, for evaluations, cf. 12:21.

Verse 2: λέγει γάρ. The formula is Rabbinic, cf. Bonsirven, *Exegese,* 30f. sc. ὁ θεός or ἡ γραφή. The verb is used in the same fashion in Rom. 15:10 and Gal. 3:16; cf. φησίν in 1 Cor. 6:16 and Heb. 8:5; cf. also εἴρηκα in Heb. 4:4.

καιρῷ δεκτῷ ἐπήκουσά σου καὶ ἐν ἡμέρᾳ σωτηρίας ἐβοήθησά σοι. The phrase is a literal rendering of Isa. 49:8 according to the LXX. The Hebrew reads: בְּעֵת רָצוֹן עֲנִיתִיךָ וּבְיוֹם יְשׁוּעָה עֲזַרְתִּיךָ — "In a time of favor I answer you, And in a day of salvation I help you." As the εὐπρόσδεκτος in his exegesis indicates, Paul does not construe the δεκτός after the Hebrew term רָצוֹן which it translates as pleasure, grace, or the will of God (Rabbinic exegesis in Str.-B. III, 520f. clearly construes it in this fashion, and the Targum actually reads, "at the time when you do my will"), but rather construes it as "welcome." But Paul agrees with Rabbinic exegesis when he construes the word in harmony with the text as an eschatological prophecy of the saving deed.

ἰδοὺ νῦν καιρὸς εὐπρόσδεκτος, ἰδοὺ νῦν ἡμέρα σωτηρίας. The prophecy of the prophets is therefore now fulfilled. "Now," that is, the event in Christ is the eschatological event. Indeed, there is more. This "now" is present in the apostolic preaching at the moment the preaching encounters its hearers — even where it encounters them a second time, as it does the Corinthian community right now. The admonition, therefore, is that it receive the message μὴ εἰς κενόν by recognizing that Paul's word encounters it as Christ's and God's eschatological word, that it thus understand itself as a new creation, and with that achieve a proper understanding of the gospel and the apostle — the apostle whose activity belongs to the eschatological saving deed. And 6:3-10 makes this clear once more by repeating the paradox of 4:7-15 in new form.

2. The apostle in the power of the eschatological event: 6:3-10

These verses do not appear "altogether abruptly" (Lietzmann, 127; Wendland, 138: "With v. 3, Paul suddenly turns again to his self-defense"), but are quite organically connected with the basic idea that Paul's appearance conforms to the nature of the gospel.

According to Windisch, 202f., the text is confused, and he proposes three possibilities for its arrangement:

1. A transition passage (perhaps such as in 4:1f.) has been omitted between 6:2 and 3. (But the pertinent parallel to 4:1f. is certainly contained in 5:20);

2. The section 6:14—7:1 belongs behind 6:2. (Impossible! Because 6:2 explicates the καταλλάγητε τῷ θεῷ in 5:20, it cannot really be described as paraenesis, and it certainly does not turn into an admonition directed against the μολυσμὸς σαρκὸς καὶ πνεύματος (7:1). Nor does 6:3ff. fit behind 7:1, for 7:1 is an ethical admonition, whereas 6:3ff. deals with Paul's standing the test in past and present); and

3. 6:3-10 belong between 5:13 and 14 (but 6:11 links poorly with 6:2; the link with 6:10 is excellent).

6:3-10 is syntactically dependent on the παρακαλοῦμεν of verse 1, to which are subordinated the two participles διδόντες and συνιστάνοντες in verse 3. The predicates which follow are loosely dependent on the συνιστάνοντες ἑαυτούς, etc., but the participles in verse 9 (ὡς ἀγνοούμενοι, etc.) are actually without syntactical connection and construed as finite verbs. The division is as follows:[176]

3: μηδεμίαν ἐν μηδενὶ διδόντες προσκοπήν,
        ἵνα μὴ μωμηθῇ ἡ διακονία,
4: ἀλλ᾽ ἐν παντὶ συνιστάνοντες ἑαυτοὺς ὡς θεοῦ διάκονοι,
        ἐν ὑπομονῇ πολλῇ
    ἐν θλίψεσιν, ἐν ἀνάγκαις, ἐν στενοχωρίαις,
5:      ἐν πληγαῖς, ἐν φυλακαῖς, ἐν ἀκαταστασίαις,
        ἐν κόποις, ἐν ἀγρυπνίαις, ἐν νηστείαις,
6: ἐν ἁγνότητι, ἐν γνώσει,
        ἐν μακροθυμίᾳ, ἐν χρηστότητι,
    ἐν πνεύματι ἁγίῳ, ἐν ἀγάπῃ ἀνυποκρίτῳ,
7:      ἐν λόγῳ ἀληθείας, ἐν δυνάμει θεοῦ·
    διὰ τῶν ὅπλων τῆς δικαιοσύνης
        τῶν δεξιῶν καὶ ἀριστερῶν,
8: διὰ δόξης καὶ ἀτιμίας,
        διὰ δυσφημίας καὶ εὐφημίας·
    ὡς πλάνοι καὶ ἀληθεῖς,
9:      ὡς ἀγνοούμενοι καὶ ἐπιγινωσκόμενοι,
    ὡς ἀποθνήσκοντες καὶ ἰδοὺ ζῶμεν,
        ὡς παιδευόμενοι, καὶ μὴ θανατούμενοι,
10: ὡς λυπούμενοι ἀεὶ δὲ χαίροντες,
        ὡς πτωχοὶ πολλοὺς δὲ πλουτίζοντες,
        ὡς μηδὲν ἔχοντες καὶ πάντα πατέχοντες.

The theme appears in verses 3-4b, and its development in verses 4c-10. Verses 4c-5 continue a catalogue of peristases or crises which explains

---

[176] On the division, cf. Fridrichsen, CN 9, 1944, 27ff.

the ἐν ὑπομονῇ πολλῇ. Verses 6-7 contain a catalog of "virtues" or powers without precise differentiation between the two. The first virtues named (ἁγνότης, γνῶσις, μακροθυμία, χρηστότης) are referred back to the divine powers, to the πνεῦμα ἅγιον, the λόγος ἀληθείας, and the δύναμις θεοῦ, but recur in the ἀγάπη ἀνυπόκριτος and the ὅπλα τῆς δικαιοσύνης. The virtues thus appear under the viewpoint of the charisms. The groups in 4c-5 and 6-7 thus form an antithesis, whereas in 8-10 the individual parts comprise the antitheses. Verses 8-10 then contain a catalog of peristases, describing the paradox of the revelation in hiddenness (vv. 8-9a), and of life in death (vv. 9-10).

The entire paragraph characterizes the apostle's service in the power of the eschatological event which parallels 4:7-12, but in such a way that the meaning of life now becomes clearer. (There is a similar catalog of virtues and peristases in Slavonic Enoch 66, 6f.; cf. p. 173). So this is not a "monument" which Paul erects to himself (Bousset, *Schriften NT,* 197), though only unintentionally, and it is not a "proud song of praise" (Lietzmann, 129) or a "hymn" (Windisch, 201ff.; Wendland, 138).[177] Concerning the antithetical form of verses 8-10 cf. Bultmann, *Diatribe,* 27, 80 and Windisch, 207f.

Verse 3: μηδεμίαν ἐν μηδενὶ διδόντες προσκοπήν.[178] προσκοπή (in use since Polybius, but otherwise absent from the LXX and the New Testament, which instead use πρόσκομμα, a term frequent since Plutarch; cf. Rom. 14:13, 20 and 1 Cor. 8:9) means "offense" in terms of "an occasion for taking offense" or "taking a false step" (Bauer). Paul thus asserts that he is guilty of doing nothing which would allow the offense which might be taken at his person to throw his office in a bad light — **ἵνα μὴ μωμηθῇ ἡ διακονία,** which means, lest the service be slandered (Lietzmann, 126). (μωμᾶσθαι means to deride, jeer, criticize, ridicule; it is in use since Homer, but seldom in the LXX; it appears elsewhere in the New Testament only in 2 Cor. 8:20).

Naturally, Paul does not intend to avoid the reproach of God (Bachmann, 278), but rather that of people. Only this interpretation has sense in the context (cf. 1 Cor. 9:12: πάντα στέγομεν ἵνα μή τινα ἐγκοπὴν δῶμεν τῷ εὐαγγελίῳ τοῦ Χριστοῦ).[179] And certainly διακονία (without a μου or ἡμῶν) cannot mean "my conduct of office," but "the office, the apostolic service," in the objective sense. We must therefore add a τοῦ θεοῦ! corresponding to the ὡς θεοῦ διάκονοι in what follows.

Verse 4: ἀλλ᾽ ἐν παντὶ συνιστάνοντες ἑαυτοὺς ὡς θεοῦ διάκονοι. The

---

[177] The parallel to Dio Chrys Or VIII, 15ff. cited by Höjstad, CN 9, 1944, 22f., is only a parallel to the peristases and the attitude toward them.

[178] On the rhetorical construction of vv. 3f., cf. Windisch, 203. The antitheses are: ἐν μηδενί — ἐν παντί. Regarding the alliterations, cf. Plat Leg VII 824b: μηδεὶς μηδέποτε ἐάσῃ μηδαμοῦ θηρεῦσαι. ("No one shall ever allow to hunt anywhere.")

[179] Cf. also 1 Thess. 2:10: ὡς ὁσίως καὶ δικαίως καὶ ἀμέμπτως ὑμῖν . . . ἐγενήθημεν.

phrase does not read ὡς θεοῦ διακόνους.[180] For this reason, the translation "we (commend) ourselves as servants of God" is misleading (Lietzmann, 126ff.). The sense is, we commend (prove) ourselves in a manner as befits a servant of God ("as such who are God's servants"), that is to say, as is described in what follows. Of course, this is again spoken with reference to the reproach of συνιστάνειν ἑαυτόν, cf. 3:1; 5:12; 10:12; and 10:18. διάκονος θεοῦ is used by Paul of himself only here (in 1 Thess. 3:2 it is used of Timothy, and in Rom. 13:4 of governmental authority). Elsewhere, Paul calls himself a δοῦλος Χριστοῦ Ἰησοῦ; cf. Rom. 1:1, Gal. 1:10, and 1 Cor. 4:1: οὕτως ἡμᾶς λογιζέσθω ἄνθρωπος ὡς ὑπηρέτας Χριστοῦ καὶ οἰκονόμους μυστηρίων θεοῦ.

Cf. διάκονος Χριστοῦ in 11:13 and Col. 1:7: διάκονος τοῦ εὐαγγελίου in Col. 1:23 and Eph. 3:7; διάκονος τῆς ἐκκλησίας (τῆς ἐν Κεγχρεαῖς) in Rom. 16:1 and Col. 1:25; διάκονος καινῆς διαθήκης in 3:6 and διάκονος δικαιοσύνης in 11:15.

ἐν ὑπομονῇ πολλῇ is the equivalent of ἐν τῷ ὑπομένειν, and the meaning is, "by our preserving great patience, perseverance, steadfastness." ὑπομονή differs from the nouns which follow by the fact that it does not describe a peristasis or suffering, but rather Paul's behavior. That in which Paul maintains his ὑπομονή is stated by the catalog which follows. ὑπομονή appears in the enumeration of 12:12; cf. 1 Thess. 1:3 and Rom. 5:3f.

ἐν θλίψεσιν, ἐν ἀνάγκαις[181] are to be translated, "in tribulations, in distresses," and ἐν στενοχωρίαις means "in oppressions or afflictions." All three nouns are in essence synonymous. θλῖψις and ἀνάγκη are also linked in 1 Thess. 3:7; θλῖψις and στενοχωρία are linked in Rom. 2:9 and 8:35, and ἀνάγκη and στενοχωρία appear in the enumeration of 12:10.

Verse 5: ἐν πληγαῖς, ἐν φυλακαῖς are to be translated, "in beatings, in prison." Cf. 11:23: ἐν φυλακαῖς περισσοτέρως, ἐν πληγαῖς ὑπερβαλλόντως. On φυλακαί cf. also Heb. 11:36. In the enumeration of 1 Cor. 4:11 κολαφιζόμεθα appears in place of πληγαί. ἐν ἀκαταστασίαις means "in riots" (Lietzmann, 128). Because πληγαί is classified with φυλακαί, Windisch, 205, does not want to interpret ἀκαταστασίαι as the absence of peace or rest as such (wanderings, flight, and the like), but as disturbances in the sense of pogrom. Bousset, *Schriften NT,* 197, and Weiss, *Urchristentum,* 316, render the term as "uproar."[182] On this signification cf. Bauer, s.v. Cf. also 1 Clement 3:2: διωγμὸς καὶ ἀκαταστασία, and Luke 21:9: πολέμους καὶ ἀκαταστασίας — terms used especially in astrological enumerations of calamities.[183] But "flight" (on the way of flight) would suit well; cf.

---

[180] This is the reading in D* g vg and Ambrosiaster.

[181] Fridrichsen, *op. cit.,* 29, writes that ἀνάγκη can denote both calamity (thus here) as well as the means of coercion (chains, stocks, and the like; thus 12:10).

[182] Cf. also the catalog of vices in 12:20 where the term denotes disorder.

[183] In Herm sim VI 3, 4f. ἀκαταστασία and ἀκαταστατεῖν are used of the restlessness of life in the enumeration of the peristases (ζημίαι denotes losses, ἀσθένειαι ποικίλαι, ὑστερήσεις).

1 Cor. 4:11: ἄχρι τῆς ἄρτι ὥρας καὶ πεινῶμεν καὶ διψῶμεν, καὶ γυμνιτεύομεν καὶ κολαφιζόμεθα καὶ ἀστατοῦμεν (we are unsettled, homeless).

While troubles ensuing from persecutions were listed in verses 4c and 5a, verse 5b names distresses resulting from laboring at one's calling. ἐν κόποις such as in 11:23 and 27, is a general description of toil; ἐν ἀγρυπνίαις, ἐν νηστείαις denote special distresses, for in the context νηστείαι are naturally not a ritual or ascetic fasting, but compulsory deprivation due to lack of money or time for meals. Both terms appear also in 11:27 (cf. also 1 Thess. 2:9).

Verse 6: On the catalog of virtues cf. Gal. 5:22f.; Rom. 12:2; 14:17; Phil. 4:8 and Col. 3:12-14.[184]

ἐν ἀγνότητι. ἀγνότης denotes integrity, purity. In the New Testament it occurs only here and in 11:3, v. 1. On the other hand, the term appears in Herm vis III, 73; mand IV, 4, 4, and in an inscription (IG IV, 588, 14f.: δικαιοσύνης ἕνεκεν καὶ ἀγνότητος). ἀγνός is used more frequently in the New Testament; cf. Phil. 4:8; Titus 2:5 and James 3:17. As to the development of meanings of ἀγνός cf. Williger, *Hagios,* 37-69, who states that it is first of all a cultic term (that which awakens religious awe and is cultically pure). Next, it denotes religious purity, holiness. Finally (already early), in the ethical sense it is synonymous with δίκαιος, often used for the administration of officials (Williger, 68f.). The term appears alongside δίκαιος in Phil. 4:8.

ἐν γνώσει. γνῶσις[185] here does not, as in 2:14 and 4:6, denote Christian knowledge as such; but, as in 8:7, 1 Cor. 1:5, and 12:8, it clearly denotes a Christian charism, in which basic Christian knowledge is manifest in the individual, such as for example in 1 Cor. 7:25: γνώμην δὲ δίδωμι ὡς ἠλεημένος ὑπὸ κυρίου πιστὸς εἶναι. Cf. 11:6.

ἐν μακροθυμίᾳ denotes "long suffering," "patience," and ἐν χρηστότητι "goodness," "mildness," "friendliness." Both terms (together with ἀνοχή) are used of God in Rom. 2:4, and both appear in the catalog of virtues in Gal. 5:22 and Col. 3:12. μακροθυμεῖν appears alongside χρηστεύεσθαι in 1 Cor. 13:4. μακροθυμία appears in the catalog of virtues in Eph. 4:2; 2 Tim. 4:2, and elsewhere. μακροθυμεῖν likewise appears in 1 Thess. 5:14, and μακροθυμία and ὑπομονή are linked in Col. 1:11. Clearly, ἐν πνεύματι ἁγίῳ here does not refer to the πνεῦμα as source of all virtues (Gal. 5:22f.), but as always manifest in the concrete moment of apostolic activity, cf. 1 Cor. 2:4; 1 Thess. 1:5; and Rom. 15:19. It is thus evident in the σημεῖα, τέρατα, and δυνάμεις of 12:12.

ἐν ἀγάπῃ ἀνυποκρίτῳ. ἀγάπη appears in the catalog of virtues in

[184] The loose connection is already indicated by the fact that the virtues or charisms can no longer explain the ἐν ὑπομονῇ πολλῇ as do the peristases in vv. 4 and 5, but rather are really parallel to it.
[185] The connection of ἀγνότης and γνῶσις leads Dupont, *Gnosis,* 415f. back to their consonance. Gnosis is the capacity to teach in conformity with Jewish tradition.

Gal. 5:22. It is the crowning or summing up of all the virtues in Gal. 5:13f., Rom. 13:8-10, and Col. 3:14.[186]

The requirement that ἀγάπη be ἀνυπόκριτος is stated also in Rom. 12:9 and 1 Peter 1:22 (φιλαδελφία). It is an attribute of πίστις in 1 Tim. 1:5 and 2 Tim. 1:5, as well as an attribute of σοφία in James 3:17.

In addition to πνεῦμα, ἀγάπη does not appear as a human achievement, but as a supernatural power.[187]

Verse 7: The ἐν λόγῳ ἀληθείας can scarcely refer to a true or honorable word, but is used in the technical sense to denote the gospel, thus in Col. 1:5, Eph. 1:13, 2 Tim. 2:15, and James 1:18. At the same time, λόγος can mean the word with respect to its content. The genitive ἀληθείας would then be an explicative genitive, denoting the word which is true. But it is better to construe λόγος as an action noun referring to the preaching or sermon. ἀλήθεια would then be an objective genitive referring to the word which mediates the truth;[188] cf. the τῇ φανερώσει τῆς ἀληθείας in 4:2. The expression is certainly Old Testament-Jewish.

Ps. 118:43 reads: καὶ μὴ περιέλῃς ἐκ τοῦ στόματός μου λόγον ἀληθείας (דְּבַר־אֱמֶת [Heb. 119]).[189]

Cf. Ps. 118:89f.: εἰς τὸν αἰῶνα, κύριε, ὁ λόγος σου διαμένει ἐν τῷ οὐρανῷ εἰς γενεὰν καὶ γενεὰν ἡ ἀλήθειά σου. Ps. 118:160 reads: ἀρχὴ τῶν λόγων σου ἀλήθεια, and Eth Enoch 104:8 admonishes: "Alter not the words of uprightness, nor charge with lying the words of the Holy Great One." In James 1:18 also the expression is originally Jewish. Cf. finally the Odes of Solomon 8:8: "Hear the word of truth, And receive the knowledge of the Most High."

With respect to content, ἐν δυνάμει θεοῦ is equal to the ἐν πνεύματι ἁγίῳ in verse 6, and is thus used in the sense of 12:12, etc., cf. p. 171. Or, it is equal to the ἐν χάριτι θεοῦ of verse 1:12 (cf. p. 34 and the alternation of χάρις and δύναμις in 12:8f.). The **διὰ τῶν ὅπλων τῆς δικαιοσύνης τῶν δεξιῶν καὶ ἀριστερῶν** indicates the apostle's consciousness of himself as warrior, as in 10:4ff. (or just as the Christian in 1 Thess. 5:8, Rom. 13:12, and Eph. 6:10-17; cf. 2 Tim. 2:3). διὰ τῶν ὅπλων means "by means of" or "fitted out with," cf. 2:4; 3:11 and Bl.-D. para. 223, 3. The τῶν δεξιῶν καὶ ἀριστερῶν means to be fitted out with sword and shield.

In the context, δικαιοσύνη is not the δικαιοσύνη θεοῦ, but rather uprightness, since the genitive is scarcely objective, meaning "in the battle for, for the defense of righteousness." Rather, as in Rom. 6:13 (παραστήσατε . . . τὰ μέλη ὑμῶν ὅπλα δικαιοσύνης τῷ θεῷ) it is a genitive of quality, denoting weapons appropriate or corresponding to righteousness. Or, it is an ex-

---

[186] Cf. Dupont, *Gnosis*, 379-417, especially 393ff.

[187] The distinction between powers and virtues is relative; the virtues are charisms.

[188] Lietzmann, 128: "In the preaching of truth."

[189] Cf. the Test Gad 3:1: καὶ νῦν ἀκούσατε λόγον ἀληθείας, τοῦ ποιεῖν δικαιοσύνην.

plicative genitive denoting weapons consisting of righteousness. It may also be a subjective genitive, denoting weapons which righteousness gives.

Cf. Rom. 6:13: ὅπλα ἀδικίας — ὅπλα δικαιοσύνης; 13:12: τὰ ὅπλα τοῦ φωτός; Eph. 6:14: τὸν θώρακα τῆς δικαιοσύνης, and 2 Cor. 10:4: τὰ γὰρ ὅπλα τῆς στρατείας ἡμῶν οὐ σαρκικὰ ἀλλὰ δυνατὰ τῷ θεῷ.

Windisch on p. 207 states that "the expression presumably derives from colloquial speech, where it denotes the proper weapons used in a fair battle"? Cf. the paraenesis in Slav Enoch 66:6: "Walk, my children, in long-suffering, in meekness, honesty, in provocation, in faith and in truth, in reliance on promises, in illness, in abuse, in wounds, in temptation, in nakedness, in privation, loving one another, till you go out from this age of ills, that you become inheritors of endless time" (R. H. Charles, II, 468). Here, too, virtues and peristases are apparently mixed without clear antitheses.

Verse 8: διὰ δόξης καὶ ἀτιμίας, διὰ δυσφημίας καὶ εὐφημίας.[190] διά is used as in verse 7c of the attendant circumstance and means, "with," "amid," "in."

"In honor and shame ["honored and despised"], in slander and praise" (Lietzmann, 128), with an evil or good name, "in good and evil repute" (Windisch, 207) ["abused and praised"].

A distinction between the two antitheses is scarcely intended. Bengel, 693, writes: δόξα . . . et ἀτιμία cadit . . . in praesentes: infamia et bona fama . . . in absentes; ("δόξα . . . and ἀτιμία . . . fall upon those who are present; evil report and good report . . . fall upon the absent." Bengel, III, 387). Windisch, 207, states that δόξα is used by Paul's "friends and pupils, by the communities devoted to him" (cf. Gal. 4:14), and that εὐφημία is used also by "Gentiles who judge him kindly" — a questionable interpretation.

ὡς πλάνοι καὶ ἀληθεῖς. πλάνος is the one who strays hither and yon, the vagrant, the trickster, but also the seducer, as here. ἀληθής means "true," "honest." Here and in what follows the ὡς is related to both expressions respectively. It thus cannot be translated "apparently," but rather "as one who," so that the meaning in the thesis is, "as one whom the world regards — according to its judgment — (as πλάνος)," and in the antithesis, "and yet as one who is (true)." Cf. especially ὡς ἀποθνήσκοντες καὶ ἰδοὺ ζῶμεν. The meaning is thus not as Michaelis has it, "(on the one hand slandered) as seducers and (on the other hand extolled) as true." Actually, ὡς πλάνοι does not at all have the force of "being slandered as seducer," but of being regarded "by human judgment (that is, necessarily) as seducer." Cf. the antitheses which follow. The thesis always denotes what is for human eyes or from the human standpoint.[191] The antithesis states what is visible only to faith; it describes the hidden ζωή, just as the thesis describes the visible θάνατος.

Verse 9: ὡς ἀγνοούμενοι καὶ ἐπιγινωσκόμενοι. The ἀγνοούμενος is one "of whom none knows anything" (Lietzmann, 128), the *ignotus, obscurus*. In the antithesis the ἐπιγινωσκόμενος can hardly be the one known by God, but is rather the one known by people (Lietzmann, 128 states that the διὰ δόξης up to ἐπιγινωσκόμενοι [v. 9] describes the diversity in people's reception of Paul"). Paul wants to be recognized, understood by them, cf. 1:13f., 5:11. But perhaps we ought not to ask, understood by whom? The sense may be paradoxical — we, the *homines ignoti*, are the persons who are most accessible.

The phrase, **ὡς ἀποθνήσκοντες καὶ ἰδοὺ ζῶμεν** is used in the sense of 4:7ff. (cf. 11:23: ἐν θανάτοις πολλάκις, and Rom. 8:36 according to Ps. 43:23: ἕνεκα σοῦ θανατούμεθα ὅλην τὴν ἡμέραν). But then the ἰδοὺ ζῶμεν does not mean, "but we escape with our life" (we are saved from the worst distresses, Windisch, 208), but is rather to be construed in the sense of 4:10f. — the ζωή is what cannot be perceived. In any event, Windisch, *op. cit.* incorrectly regards the description as more of the Old Testament or Stoic sort than as specifically Christian, since there is no mention of following Christ.

ὡς παιδευόμενοι (D* G it Ambst read πειραζόμενοι) **καὶ μὴ θανατούμενοι.** The phrase is synonymous with the preceding antithesis, but with an Old Testament coloration according to Ps. 117:18: παιδεύων ἐπαίδευσέν με ὁ κύριος καὶ τῷ θανάτῳ οὐ παρέδωκέν με.

Verse 10: ὡς λυπούμενοι ἀεὶ δὲ χαίροντες. With the ὡς λυπούμενοι, the human point of view which the thesis reflects is less than with the ὡς πλάνοι and ὡς ἀγνοούμενοι, a point of view actually taken by onlookers. It is more the human point of view of the apostle himself, which he has surmounted. Admittedly, this was already true of the ὡς ἀποθνήσκοντες and ὡς παιδευόμενοι, but it is now made explicit in the ὡς λυπούμενοι. On the λύπη of the apostle cf. 2:1ff. and Phil. 2:27. On the ἀεὶ δὲ χαίροντες cf. Rom. 12:12: τῇ ἐλπίδι χαίροντες; Phil. 3:1: χαίρετε ἐν κυρίῳ and 4:4: χαίρετε ἐν κυρίῳ πάντοτε· πάλιν ἐρῶ, χαίρετε. Cf. also 2 Cor. 13:11; 1 Thess. 5:16;[192] Rom. 14:17: οὐ γάρ ἐστιν ἡ βασιλεία τοῦ θεοῦ βρῶσις καὶ πόσις, ἀλλὰ δικαιοσύνη καὶ εἰρήνη καὶ χαρὰ ἐν πνεύματι ἁγίῳ; 15:13: ὁ δὲ θεὸς τῆς ἐλπίδος πληρώσαι ὑμᾶς πάσης χαρᾶς καὶ εἰρήνης ἐν τῷ πιστεύειν, and finally Phil. 1:25: εἰς τὴν ὑμῶν προκοπὴν καὶ χαρὰν τῆς πίστεως.

In the context there is no thought of concrete joy over the community

---

[191] This need not be the view of opponents or unbelievers (thus πλάνοι and ἀγνοούμενοι), but also that of Paul himself (thus ἀποθνήσκοντες, λυπούμενοι, πτωχοί, μηδὲν ἔχοντες).

[192] Cf. the χαρά in the catalog of virtues in Gal. 5:22.

(2:3; 7:4; 13:9; 1 Thess. 2:19f.; 3:9; cf. Philemon 7), or over special events (1 Cor. 16:17; 2 Cor. 7:7ff.; Phil. 1:18; 2:17; 4:10), or even thought of a specifically human joy (Rom. 12:15; 1 Cor. 7:30).

ὡς πτωχοὶ πολλοὺς δὲ πλουτίζοντες, ὡς μηδὲν ἔχοντες καὶ πάντα κατέχοντες: Here too, of course, there is no reference to anything concrete or special, but rather to the gift and possession of the γνῶσις τῆς δόξης τοῦ θεοῦ ἐν προσώπῳ Χριστοῦ (4:6). Cf. 1 Cor. 3:21f.: πάντα . . . ὑμῶν. πλουτίζειν is also used in a figurative sense in 9:11, as is πλουτεῖν in Rom. 10:12 and 1 Cor. 4:8. Related antitheses appear in Cynic thought, cf. Windisch, 209.[193]

3. The plea for trust [6:14—7:1 is an interpolation]: 6:11—7:4

Our mouth is open to you, Corinthians; our heart is wide. You are not restricted by us, but you are restricted in your own affections. In return — I speak as to children — widen your hearts also. . . . Open your hearts to us; we have wronged no one, we have corrupted no one, we have taken advantage of no one. I do not say this to condemn you, for I said before that you are in our hearts, to die together and to live together. I have great confidence in you; I have great pride in you; I am filled with comfort. With all our affliction, I am overjoyed.

After the material statements describing Paul's apostolic office, and in such fashion that the Corinthians recognize him in his humble state as bearer of this office, there follows a personal plea for the community's trust and the confident expression that he is given it — all the more since in 5:20—6:10 he had fully exposed himself in his apostolic character.

Verse 11: τὸ στόμα ἡμῶν ἀνέῳγεν πρὸς ὑμᾶς, Κορίνθιοι. The address Κορίνθιοι marks out the section and at the same time gives the clause emphasis, cf. Gal. 3:1 and Phil. 4:15. τὸ στόμα — ἀνέῳγεν is used intransitively, in Ionic-Hellenistic fashion, Bl.-D. para. 101. By itself, ἀνοίγειν τὸ στόμα means merely "to speak," but in the context it means "to speak freely, openly." It is scarcely different from the πολλή μοι παρρησία πρὸς ὑμᾶς in 7:4.

Cf. Judg. 11:35f. Jephthah says to his daughter returning: (A) ἐγὼ δὲ ἤνοιξα τὸ στόμα μου περὶ σοῦ πρὸς κύριον . . . (B) καὶ ἐγώ εἰμι ἤνοιξα κατὰ σοῦ τὸ στόμα μου πρὸς κύριον καὶ οὐ δυνήσομαι ἐπιστρέψαι. The daughter replies: (A) εἰ ἐν ἐμοὶ ἤνοιξας . . . (B) πάτερ, ἤνοιξας τὸ στόμα σου πρὸς κύριον· ποίησόν μοι ὃν τρόπον ἐξῆλθεν ἐκ στόματός σου. Cf. Job 3:1: μετὰ τοῦτο ἤνοιξεν Ιωβ τὸ στόμα αὐτοῦ καὶ κατηράσατο τὴν ἡμέραν αὐτοῦ; Sirach 51:25: ἤνοιξα τὸ στόμα μου καὶ ἐλάλησα, and Matt. 5:1: καὶ ἀνοίξας τὸ στόμα αὐτοῦ ἐδίδασκεν αὐτούς.

---

[193] Note especially the Epistolographi Graeci, ed. Hercher, p. 209 (Cratetis Epistolae VII): καὶ ἔχοντες μηδὲν πάντ᾿ ἔχομεν.

The expression thus refers to a weighty, solemn utterance. Cf. 1 Kings 2:1: ἐπλατύνθη ἐπὶ ἐχθροὺς τὸ στόμα μου.

The clause of course refers to 6:3-10 where Paul said more than required as proclaimer, where he explicitly "commended" himself. ἡ καρδία ἡμῶν πεπλάτυνται means "my heart has become wide." In the context it cannot denote relief obtained by Paul through his own words (Luther: our heart is comforted), but is synonymous with the previous clause.[194] It denotes Paul's openness or trust which "makes no murderer's pit" of his heart. Cf. Ps. 118:32: ὁδὸν ἐντολῶν σου ἔδραμον, ὅταν ἐπλάτυνας τὴν καρδίαν μου, where the reference is of course to relief, to a joyful state of mind.

Windisch, 210, does not understand how Paul can make this statement following 6:3-10, in which he did not speak cordially and personally to the Corinthians! And yet, Windisch adds, the perfect tense of the verbs assumes that Paul is not just now beginning to speak cordially, but is in the very midst of doing so! For this reason, Windisch concludes, 6:11f. does not belong after 6:10. As though Paul did not reveal himself in 6:3-10 so as to gain the Corinthians' understanding (cf. 5:11; 1:13f.)!

Verse 12: οὐ στενοχωρεῖσθε ἐν ἡμῖν, στενοχωρεῖσθε δὲ ἐν τοῖς σπλάγχνοις ὑμῶν. The phrase means, "you are not straitened,"[195] and it is the result of the ἡ καρδία ἡμῶν πεπλάτυνται. ἐν ἡμῖν is thus equal to ἐν τῇ καρδίᾳ ἡμῶν, just as the ἐν τοῖς σπλάγχνοις, synonymous with ἐν καρδίᾳ, immediately makes its appearance in the antithesis (in Greek literature also τὰ σπλάγχνα is used for the heart, and in the LXX translates רַחֲמִים). The utterance has the same sense as in 7:3: ὅτι ἐν ταῖς καρδίαις ἡμῶν ἐστε, and together with the προείρηκα in 7:3 clearly refers to 6:11f. The meaning is therefore, "I do not keep aloof from you; my love is directed toward you."

As antithesis one might expect στενοχωροῦμαι δὲ ἐγὼ ἐν τοῖς σπλάγχνοις ὑμῶν. Paul, however, does not intend to complain, but rather to contrast the Corinthians' behavior with his own. For the figurative use of στενοχωρεῖν cf. Epict Diss I, 25, 26-29 concerning a στενοχωρία which is self-induced: (28) . . . ἑαυτοὺς θλίβομεν, ἑαυτοὺς στενοχωροῦμεν, τοῦτ' ἔστι τὰ δόγματα ἡμᾶς θλίβει καὶ στενοχωρεῖ; ("we crowd ourselves, we make close quarters for ourselves, that is to say, the decisions of our will crowd us and make us close quarters"). Thus στενοχωρεῖσθε δὲ κτλ. means, you are restricted in your own affections, which in the antithesis has this sense: "You keep aloof from me," that is, "you misunderstand my love, you give it no entry among you," and corresponds to the πλατύνθητε καὶ ὑμεῖς in verse 13. Thus the meaning is not, "you feel restricted."[196]

The figure of wideness and narrowness has a bit different use in verse 12 than in verse 11. Being wide in verse 11 denotes openness in utterance, and

---

[194] And it is in contrast to what follows — στενοχωρεῖσθαι (Luther: "to be anxious").

[195] Lietzmann, 128, translates, "you are not straitened."

[196] Luther translates, "but you are anxious out of cordial intent."

in verse 12 openness for acceptance. But in their content, the openness of self-utterance and of acceptance form a unity; the openness of utterance is that of trust which opens the heart to the other.

Verse 13: τὴν δὲ αὐτὴν ἀντιμισθίαν, ὡς τέκνοις λέγω, πλατύνθητε καὶ ὑμεῖς. The πλατύνθητε καὶ ὑμεῖς is the conclusion drawn from the words in verses 11f., "my heart is open to you." Then follows, "therefore open your heart also to me!" "give my love entry!" the equivalent of χωρήσατε ἡμᾶς in 7:2.

The τὴν δὲ αὐτὴν ἀντιμισθίαν[197] makes clear that such behavior is the response to his behavior — "give like for like!" It is all the same whether we simply add an ἀποδιδόντες (or ποιήσαντες: Windisch, 211), or whether we construe τὴν αὐτὴν ἀντιμισθίαν as the internal object of πλατύνθητε. The verse might thus have read, τὸν αὐτὸν πλατυσμὸν ὡς ἀντιμισθίαν πλατύνθητε καὶ ὑμεῖς (Lietzmann, 129, Bl.-D. para. 154), or, ὡσαύτως δὲ καὶ ὑμεῖς πλατύνθητε, ἥτις ἔσται ἡ ἐμὴ ἀντιμισθία (Rückert, 204).[198]

Further, the ὡς τέκνοις λέγω reminds the Corinthians once more of Paul's love, and appeals to their mutual love. There are similar expressions in 1 Cor. 4:14 and Gal. 4:19.

In 7:2 the χωρήσατε ἡμᾶς is linked to the πλατύνθητε καὶ ὑμεῖς and means, "you also be wide, that is, toward us; make room for us!" It is nothing else than a plea for trust.

Following the plea and supporting it is the protestation of innocence which Paul as apostle neither wanted nor indeed was obliged to utter (cf. 1:15ff., p. 39), as though he regarded the community as a forum before which he had to justify himself (cf. 1 Cor. 4:3). But this protestation of innocence belongs to that very ἀνοίγειν τὸ στόμα in 6:11, in which Paul goes beyond his proclamation. He is not speaking officially, but personally, not suing for faith in the gospel but for trust in him. Basically, then, he is not defending himself, any more than he is complaining (πρὸς κατάκρισιν).

No doubt, Paul has accusations from the community in mind. οὐδένα ἠδικήσαμεν appears to refer to a particular accusation involving an offense or insult (thus ἀδικήσαντος in v. 12).

οὐδένα ἐφθείραμεν — "we have ruined no one,"[199] but in what sense? Is a particular reproach in mind here also? Or does Paul choose such strong expression only in a moment of passion? Or again, is φθείρειν (as ἀπολλύναι in 1 Cor. 8:11 and Rom. 14:15) meant in terms of spiritual ruin or seduction? Cf. 11:3.

---

[197] Till now ἀντιμισθία has been documented only in Christian sources, though ἀντίμισθος and ἀντιμισθίον appear in pagan sources.
[198] Lietzmann, 128, translates, "now reward me with the same . . . you also be wide."
[199] "Ruined" (by πλεονεξία?).

178 The Apostolic Office

οὐδένα ἐπλεονεκτήσαμεν. This seems to be the chief rebuke, against which Paul gives detailed defense in 12:14-18.[200]

Verse 3: The πρὸς κατάκρισιν οὐ λέγω in verse 3 — "I do not say this in order to condemn you" — does not intend to remove a misunderstanding. It is only an (superfluous) expression of Paul's love, his suing for trust. That this is the motive is stated in the words which follow — προείρηκα γὰρ ὅτι ἐν ταῖς καρδίαις ἡμῶν ἐστε εἰς τὸ συναποθανεῖν καὶ συζῆν. The meaning is, "Indeed I have just told you that . . ." that is, in 6:12 or in 6:11f. The προείρηκα need not at all refer to a statement made much earlier, nor to a previous, oral utterance, nor to 4:12 (certainly, much less to 1:5ff., since 1:1—2:13 belong to a later epistle).

The ἐν ταῖς καρδίαις ἡμῶν ἐστε εἰς τὸ συναποθανεῖν καὶ συζῆν describe Paul's love in the strongest terms. In the context, we cannot add a σὺν Χριστῷ, and neither dying as putting off the old man nor resurrection life is in mind here. Rather, Paul is using an expression often met with to describe the inviolable bond between persons — "bound with us in death and life" (Lietzmann, 130).

Cf. 2 Sam. 15:21 (Ittai to David): οὗ ἐὰν ᾖ ὁ κύριός μου, καὶ ἐὰν εἰς θάνατον καὶ ἐὰν εἰς ζωήν, ὅτι ἐκεῖ ἔσται ὁ δοῦλός σου, and Euripides Or 307f. (Electra to Orestes): σὺν σοὶ καὶ θανεῖν αἱρήσομαι καὶ ζῆν; ("With thee will I make choice of death or life . . ."). Cf. also Eur Ion 852f.: καὶ τροφεῖα δεσπόταις ἀποδοὺς θανεῖν τε ζῶντα φέγγος εἰσοραν: "repaying so My lords their nurture, let me die or live!" Cf. also 857f.: κἀγώ, φίλη θέσποινα, συμφορὰν θέλω κοινουμένη τήνδ᾽ ἢ θανεῖν ἢ ζῆν καλῶς: "I too, dear mistress, I consent to share Thy fate, — or death, or honourable life." Horace in Carm III 9, 24 writes: tecum vivere amem, tecum obeam libens ("I should love to live with you; I should gladly die with you." [R.A.H.]); and Athen VI 54 (Vol. II, Kaibel, p. 56) writes: τούτους (sc. the life-guard) δ᾽ οἱ βασιλεῖς ἔχουσι συζῶντας καὶ συναποθνήσκοντας ("but the kings keep them to live or die with them." [R.A.H.]). Cf. Olivier, συναποθνήσκω, and the same term in RThPh, 17, 1929, 103-133; Hirzel, ARW 11, 1908, 79, 1.

Verse 4: πολλή μοι παρρησία πρὸς ὑμᾶς. παρρησία is not used here in quite the same sense as in 3:12 (pp. 84f.), since Paul is not speaking as apostle, but personally. The term is thus almost equal to the τὸ στόμα ἡμῶν ἀνέῳγεν in 6:11. Yet in the context (parallel to the καύχησις which follows) it does not simply denote "openness," but the confidence linked to it. It is trust, as is certainly also implied in the τὸ στόμα ἡμῶν ἀνέῳγεν.

πολλή μοι καύχησις ὑπὲρ ὑμῶν. καύχησις, parallel to παρρησία, is the self-consciousness which derives from confidence. The question, To whom is Paul boasting about the Corinthians? is out of place (cf. 1:14; 7:14; 8:24; 9:2; 1 Thess. 2:19; Phil. 2:16).

---

[200] Lietzmann, 130, translates, "to take advantage of."

According to the usual view, Paul's παρρησία and καύχησις are to be explained from news of the congregation which, according to verses 5ff., Titus brought to him. But verse 4 loses its real force and its connection with what precedes if we interpret it according to verses 5ff. (which also renders improbable the ἐπὶ πάσῃ τῇ θλίψει in v. 4b). Rather, 7:5ff. belongs after 2:13, and the redaction attaches it here merely *ad vocem* παράκλησις.

The παρρησία and καύχησις are nothing else than a trust which is certain that it must be returned. It assumes that the fellowship to which it is invited in 6:11 already exists.

πεπλήρωμαι τῇ παρακλήσει. Paul's comfort springs from the very fact that in his writing he made himself intelligible to the Corinthians as apostle and expressed his trust in them without reservation. Because the δύναμις of God must still be effective in what he said, he needs no comfort from the outside.

ὑπερπερισσεύομαι τῇ χαρᾷ ἐπὶ πάσῃ τῇ θλίψει ἡμῶν. For this very reason Paul is rich in joy (ὑπερπερισσεύομαι appears also in Rom. 5:20; περισσεύειν is a favorite with Paul; cf. 1:5, etc.). ἐπὶ πάσῃ τῇ θλίψει generalizes the clause, and we may of course construe it to mean, "in every tribulation in which we presently find ourselves" (cf. v. 5). But the better reading is, "in every tribulation which can overtake us."[201]

Verse 4 is thus an exuberant expression of trust which is certain of being returned.

On behalf of the original sequence of 7:5ff. after 7:4, Lietzmann, 131, appeals to the following correspondence:

Verse 4:	παρακλήσει	Verse 6:	παρακαλῶν, παρεκάλεσεν
		Verse 7:	παρακλήσει ἣ παρεκλήθη
Verse 4:	χαρᾷ	Verse 7:	χαρῆναι
Verse 4:	θλίψει	Verse 5:	θλιβόμενοι

This correspondence, of course, merely indicates the redaction's point of view.

Weiss, *Urchristentum,* 265, and Loisy, Rev. d'hist. et de litt. rel. 7, 1921,111, also remove 2:142—7:4 from the context, and connect it with Chapters 10–13. In the same fashion, Windisch, 223ff., wants to connect 7:5-16 with 2:13, and would even reconstruct the original order as follows:

2:1-4	Paul's failure to appear and his letter.
2:12f.	The journey to Macedonia.
7:5-10	The arrival of Titus.
2:5-11	The case of the λυπῶν.

The argument is too complicated, and the sequence of verses 2:5-11 after

---

[201] The articles with παράκλησις and χαρά certainly have this sense, "the comfort and joy which I needed but lacked when I began, I have gained while writing."

7:5-16 too improbable. There is no basis for Schnedermann's contention, 341, that Titus just arrived between 7:3 and 7:4!

Does 10:1—13:10 belong to the beginning of the epistle? Would 2:14—7:4 then have followed, then Chapter 9, and would 13:11-13 have formed the conclusion?

6:14—7:1 (An insertion)

Do not be mismated with unbelievers. For what partnership have righteousness and iniquity? Or what fellowship has light with darkness? What accord has Christ with Belial? Or what has a believer in common with an unbeliever? What agreement has the temple of God with idols? For we are the temple of the living God; as God said, "I will live in them and move among them, and I will be their God, and they shall be my people. Therefore come out from them, and be separate from them, says the Lord, and touch nothing unclean; then I will welcome you, and I will be a father to you, and you shall be my sons and daughters, says the Lord Almighty." Since we have these promises, beloved, let us cleanse ourselves from every defilement of body and spirit, and make holiness perfect in the fear of God.

The paraenesis is typically Jewish, cf. especially Test XII (Test Lev 19; Naph 3), and Philo as well. Has it been revised in Christian fashion? Was Χριστοῦ substituted for θεοῦ in verse 15?

It is possible that Paul himself cited such a piece. In that case, it is very likely a fragment from the lost first epistle. It might have preceded the admonition μὴ συναναμίγνυσθαι πόρνοις (1 Cor. 5:9-11!), since this admonition would connect well with 7:1.[202]

---

[202] On 6:15, cf. Aristoph Thes 140: τίς δαὶ κατόπτρου καὶ ξίφους κοινωνία — "how comes a sword beside a looking glass?" Cf. Eur Iph Taur 254: καὶ τίς θαλάσσης βουκόλοις κοινωνία; ("Now what have herdmen with the sea to do?"); also Epict Gnom Stob c. 36 (Schenkl, p. 471): οὔτε γὰρ κακία ἀρετῇ κοινωνεῖ οὔτε ἐλευθερία δουλεία; ("For neither evil shares with virtue, nor freedom with slavery." [R.A.H.]) and Philo Frag ex Joh Damsc Sacr Parall, Philo ed. Mangey, Vol. 2, p. 649: ἀμήχανον συνυπάρχειν τὴν πρὸς κόσμον ἀγάπην τῇ πρὸς τὸν θεὸν ἀγάπῃ, ὡς ἀμήχανον συνυπάρχειν ἀλλήλοις φῶς καὶ σκότος; ("No more can love for God live together with love for the world than light and darkness can live with each other." [R.A.H.]).

[Editor's addition: on the section 6:14—7:1, which Bultmann regards as non-Pauline, cf. the newer literature].

Chapter 3

Chapters 10–13
[Letter C]

1. Paul's ταπεινότης and πεποίθησις, or the threat of his personal appearance: 10:1-11.
   a. The plea not to provoke him: 10:1-2.
   b. Proof and purpose of the πεποίθησις: 10:3-6.
   (Under orders to take the field for the γνῶσις τοῦ θεοῦ).
   c. The threat of his personal appearance: 10:7-11.
2. Paul's τόλμα, or a comparison with his opponents: 10:12—12:18.
   a. The first introduction: The criterion for boasting: 10:12-18.
   b. The second introduction: The plea to endure his καυχᾶσθαι: 11:1-21.
   The insertion at 11:7-15: The question of Paul's sincerity.
   c. Boasting: 11:22—12:18.
   Boasting κατὰ σάρκα: 11:22-33.
   Boasting in weakness: 12:1-10.
   Conclusion to the καυχᾶσθαι: 12:11-18, including 12:13-18: Once more the question of Paul's sincerity.
3. The threat of δοκιμή at the third visit: 12:19—13:10.
   a. The threat: 12:19—13:4.
   b. Admonition: 13:5-9.
   c. Threat: 13:10.
4. Conclusion of the letter: 13:11-13.

1. Paul's ταπεινότης and πεποίθησις, or the threat of his personal appearance: 10:1-11[1]

I, Paul, myself entreat you, by the meekness and gentleness of Christ —
I who am humble when face to face with you, but bold to you when I

---

[1] Cf. Käsemann, "Legitimität," ZNW 41 (1942), 33-71.

am away! — I beg of you that when I am present I may not have to show boldness with such confidence as I count on showing against some who suspect us of acting in worldly fashion. For though we live in the world we are not carrying on a worldly war, for the weapons of our warfare are not worldly but have divine power to destroy strongholds. We destroy arguments and every proud obstacle to the knowledge of God, and take every thought captive to obey Christ, being ready to punish every disobedience, when your obedience is complete. Look at what is before your eyes. If any one is confident that he is Christ's, let him remind himself that as he is Christ's, so are we. For even if I boast a little too much of our authority, which the Lord gave for building you up and not for destroying you, I shall not be put to shame. I would not seem to be frightening you with letters. For they say, "His letters are weighty and strong, but his bodily presence is weak, and his speech of no account." Let such people understand that what we say by letter when absent, we do when present.

a. The appeal not to provoke him (his πεποίθησις): 10:1-2

Verse 1: αὐτὸς δὲ ἐγὼ Παῦλος. It seems that Paul is not contrasting himself with others from whom he remains aloof (as in 1 Thess. 2:18, by means of the ἐγὼ μὲν Παῦλος). The αὐτὸς δὲ ἐγὼ evidently intends to accent the speaker's authority, just as the αὐτὸς ἐγώ in 12:13; Rom. 9:3; 15:14 or the ἴδε ἐγὼ Παῦλος in Gal. 5:2; cf. 1 Cor. 16:21: ὁ ἀσπασμὸς τῇ ἐμῇ χειρὶ Παύλου.

παρακαλῶ ὑμᾶς διὰ τῆς πραΰτητος καὶ ἐπιεικείας τοῦ Χριστοῦ. παρακαλῶ means to admonish, as in 6:1, etc., and is used with διά which means "through the mediation of," that is, "by reference or by appeal to," cf. Romans 12:1: παρακαλῶ οὖν ὑμᾶς ἀδελφοί, διὰ τῶν οἰκτιρμῶν τοῦ θεοῦ; 15:30: παρακαλῶ δὲ ὑμᾶς, ἀδελφοί, διὰ τοῦ κυρίου ἡμῶν Ἰησοῦ Χριστοῦ καὶ διὰ τῆς ἀγάπης τοῦ πνεύματος, and 1 Cor. 1:10: παρακαλῶ δὲ ὑμᾶς, ἀδελφοί, διὰ τοῦ ὀνόματος τοῦ κυρίου ἡμῶν Ἰησοῦ Χριστοῦ. The διὰ τῆς πραΰτητος κτλ., seems to refer to the Pre-existent One, such as in 8:9, Rom 15:3, and Phil. 2:6ff. (ἐταπείνωσεν ἑαυτόν). And Paul of course refers to these attributes of Christ because he has the theme of ταπεινότης in mind (πραΰς as well as ταπεινός are the LXX translation for עָנָו). If this theme is to be treated, then Christ's πραΰτης and ἐπιείκεια must be recalled.

πραΰτης in terms of the friendliness, kindness, and condescension of Christ is used only here.[2] It is cited as a Christian virtue in 1 Cor. 4:21; Gal. 5:23; 6:1; Col. 3:12; Eph. 4:2; 1 Tim. 6:11 (πραϋπαθία); 2 Tim. 2:25; Titus 3:2; James 1:21; 3:13; and 1 Peter 3:16.

---

[2] In the Greek πραΰτης and ἐπιείκεια are readily connected, cf. Windisch, 292, and Lietzmann, 140.

πραΰς is used of Jesus in Matthew 1:29 (21:5). It is cited as a Christian virtue in Matt. 5:5 and 1 Peter 3:4. ἐπιείκεια is used of Christ only here, and denotes mildness, leniency. It appears elsewhere in Acts 24:4. ἐπιεικής is referred to as a Christian virtue in Phil. 4:5; 1 Tim. 3:3; Titus 3:2; and James 3:17; it appears elsewhere in 1 Peter 2:18.

By referring at the beginning of his polemic to Christ's πραΰτης and ἐπιείκεια in this paradoxical way, Paul is stating in no uncertain terms that it is up to you whether or not the connection between us shall be governed by πραΰτης and ἐπιείκεια. And the reason is that the content of the παρακαλῶ ὑμᾶς is resumed by the δέομαι in verse 2: "Take care that at my presence I remain ταπεινός!"

On the one hand, the intention is to exhort the Corinthians to πραΰτης; on the other, it is to urge them not to misunderstand Paul's ταπεινότης — which they will not do precisely when they themselves are ταπεινοί.

The exhortation by reference to Christ's ταπεινότης and ἐπιείκεια gives to what follows a strongly ironic tone — **ὃς κατὰ πρόσωπον μὲν ταπεινὸς ἐν ὑμῖν, ἀπὼν δὲ θαρρῶ εἰς ὑμᾶς.**[3] Naturally, the clause alludes to the reproach aimed at Paul. Cf. 10:2, 10; 13:3; and the slogan ταπεινῶν in 11:7 and 12:21. As a reproof from his opponents, θαρρῶ of course has another sense than in 7:16 (and other than in 5:6) where it denotes confidence (ἐν ὑμῖν). Here it means audacity, impudence. ταπεινός of course has a disdainful tone where Paul's opponents are concerned. It means "servile," "cowardly," and this very disdain is rendered ironic by reference to Christ's πραΰτης and ἐπιείκεια — when you despise me as ταπεινὸς κατὰ πρόσωπον, think of Christ's mildness and friendliness, and do not suppose that my ταπεινότης is a weakness! Verse 2 makes clear that it is not such.

Verse 2: δέομαι δὲ τὸ μὴ παρὼν θαρρῆσαι. δέομαι (which means "I ask," not "I pray," and which resumes the παρακαλῶ in v. 1) τὸ μὴ . . . θαρρῆσαι (just as in classical Greek after verbs of hindering) appears in place of a clause with ἵνα μή, Bl.-D. para. 399, 3. παρών is in the nominative because the subject is the same; cf. Bl.-D. para. 405, 1; Radermacher, 181. As for the **τῇ πεποιθήσει ᾗ λογίζομαι τολμῆσαι,** the definition obviously belongs to θαρρῆσαι, not to δέομαι.

The misunderstanding of Paul's ταπεινότης assumes that he also cannot be κατὰ πρόσωπον θαρρῶν. But what he lacks, he would rather not produce. One should not provoke him! His ταπεινότης could change to a θαρρεῖν which derives from his apostolic πεποίθησις (cf. 1:15; 3:4; cf. 1:9; 2:3), and of which he has every bit as much as his opponents (v. 7). On the basis of this πεποίθησις (or by means of it: ᾗ) Paul renders the decision τολμῆσαι (used absolutely it means "to appear boldly," "to venture an attack," and almost "to challenge" — was this a slogan of his opponents? cf. v. 12; 11:21).

---

[3] For κατὰ πρόσωπον cf. Gal. 2:11; Acts 3:13; and 25:16.

ἐπί τινας τοὺς λογιζομένους. Since λογίζεσθαι is repeated in 10:7, 11; 11:5; and 12:6 (cf. 3:5, pp. 75f.), it is evidently an allusion to a slogan of Paul's opponents, who presume to judge him and whose λογίζεσθαι he repudiates in verse 4 by the λογισμοὺς καθαιροῦντες, so that λογίζεσθαι almost takes on the sense of "to fancy oneself." Accordingly, λογίζομαι or "I fancy myself," would be construed as irony, thus in quotation marks.

ἡμᾶς ὡς κατὰ σάρκα περιπατοῦντας. Does the κατὰ σάρκα περιπατεῖν denote unreliability (cf. 1:12, 17)? Does it denote insincerity (cf. 1:12), particularly deceitful avarice (11:7ff.; 12:14ff.), or does it denote the reproach of the Corinthian pneumatics, that Paul acts without the πνεῦμα, without ἐξουσία (cf. vv. 7f.; 13:1ff.)? This is presumably the chief reproof to which the others may be linked. In any event, for Paul the κατὰ σάρκα has the broader meaning of selfishness. Most probably, verse 4 indicates that the κατὰ σάρκα is construed in the sense of being sickly, whereas the περιπατεῖν refers to a moral quality. But both terms must be taken as a unity.[4]

Reitzenstein, HMR, 361, states that "they turned against Paul his own proof that they are merely νήπιοι ἐν Χριστῷ: ὅπου γὰρ ἐν ὑμῖν ζῆλος καὶ ἔρις, οὐχὶ σαρκικοί ἐστε καὶ κατὰ ἄνθρωπον περιπατεῖτε; (1 Cor. 3:3). They contend that he himself brings ἔρις and ζῆλος, so that the κατὰ ἄνθρωπον περιπατεῖ is true also of him. . . . Thus he too is only an ἄνθρωπος, thus σαρκικός, his praise of self inadmissable, a παραφρονεῖν." (11:2 replies to the reproach that he is ζῆλος — ζηλῶ γὰρ ὑμᾶς θεοῦ ζήλῳ)

b. Proof and purpose of the πεποίθησος: 10:3-6

Verse 3: ἐν σαρκὶ γὰρ περιπατοῦντες οὐ κατὰ σάρκα στρατευόμεθα. In both expressions the σάρξ-concept is the same. σάρξ is the worldly and empirical (correctly defined by Schauf in *Sarx*, 127f.). Certainly! In this sphere Paul's conduct and activity are played out, and for this reason he too labors as ταπεινός without great pneumatic display — but not κατὰ σάρκα, not according to the criterion of the σάρξ. His activity is described as a στρατεύεσθαι. The figure also appears in 1 Cor. 9:7 (cf. also 2 Cor. 6:7; 11:8); 1 Tim. 1:18; 2 Tim. 2:3f.; especially in 1 Thess. 5:8; Eph. 6:11-17 and later (Windisch, 296).

Verse 3 (γάρ) gives the basis for verse 2, since a dismissive No! can be heard behind verse 2. The meaning is, "I can cope with opponents, can punish them for lies, because. . . ."

Verse 4: This verse yields the basis for the οὐ κατὰ σάρκα στρατευόμεθα by retaining the metaphor and describing Paul's weapons — τὰ γὰρ ὅπλα τῆς στρατείας ἡμῶν οὐ σαρκικά.

Obviously, as the description in verse 4 shows, Paul's στρατεία is his apostolic activity. His weapons are thus the tools of his activity. These

---

[4] Note how in Did 11 and Herm mand XI the (alleged) prophet's moral vulnerability proves that he does not have the Spirit.

weapons are not σαρκικά.⁵ If we keep in mind the opponents' reproach (v. 2), the reference is to the πανουργία and δολοῦν of 4:2. If we keep in mind the contrast ἀλλὰ δυνατά, the reference is to the weakness of the earthly. But the opponents' censure amounts to just this, that Paul is no pneumatic.

ἀλλὰ δυνατὰ τῷ θεῷ. The τῷ θεῷ means either, "in God's eyes, acknowledged by God" (cf. Acts 7:20: ἀστεῖος τῷ θεῷ, Bl.-D. para. 192, a Hebraism), or it is better construed as a dative of advantage meaning, "for God" (Bl.-D. para. 188, 2), that is, "with them God can. . . ."

The characterization is synonymous with πνευματικά, which we would have expected in antithesis to σαρκικά. Cf. also 1 Cor. 2:4: ὁ λόγος μου καὶ τὸ κήρυγμά μου οὐκ ἐν πειθοῖς σοφίας λόγοις, ἀλλ' ἐν ἀποδείξει πνεύματος καὶ δυνάμεως.

πρὸς καθαίρεσιν ὀχυρωμάτων. ὀχύρωμα denotes a firm place, fortress, stronghold, and καθαίρεσις denotes destruction. The metaphor occurs also in Prov. 21:22: πόλεις ὀχυρὰς ἐπέβη σοφὸς καὶ καθεῖλεν τὸ ὀχύρωμα, ἐφ ᾧ ἐπεποίθεισαν οἱ ἀσεβεῖς. It appears in the same fashion in Philo's Conf Ling 128ff. For a description of the wise man's battle, cf. Windisch, 297.

The participles καθαιροῦντες and αἰχμαλωτίζοντες (v. 5), and the ἐν ἑτοίμῳ ἔχοντες (v. 6) interpret the figure, first of all by using the terminology metaphorically, since καθαιροῦντες refers to the πρὸς καθαίρεσιν ὀχυρωμάτων. All three participles could be subordinated to the περιπατοῦντες of verse 3, parallel to the στρατευόμεθα. But it is better to construe them as abstract nouns, loosely joined as in 6:9f.; 9:11; 10:15; 11:6, etc.

λογισμοὺς καθαιροῦντες. This is an obvious allusion to the opponents' slogan, to their arrogant judgments concerning Paul, cf. on verse 2, p. 183.

Verse 5: καὶ πᾶν ὕψωμα ἐπαιρόμενον κατὰ τῆς γνώσεως τοῦ θεοῦ. The clause contains new metaphors. Along with Prov. 21:22 (cf. v. 4 above) is Job 19:6 of influence here? (γνῶτε οὖν ὅτι ὁ κύριός ἐστιν ὁ ταράξας, ὀχύρωμα δὲ αὐτοῦ ἐπ' ἐμὲ ὕψωσεν).

ὕψωμα denotes a rampart, very likely used as a metaphor for opposition in a quite general sense, not for pride in particular.

κατὰ τῆς γνώσεως τοῦ θεοῦ. The knowledge is that which Paul spreads in 2:14 and 4:6. The formulation is probably chosen with a view to the gnosis of which the Corinthians boast (1 Cor. 8:1ff.), and which they deny to Paul (11:6).

The **καὶ αἰχμαλωτίζοντες πᾶν νόημα εἰς τὴν ὑπακοὴν τοῦ Χριστοῦ** is a new metaphor. The figure of αἰχμαλωτίζειν is used in another sense in Rom. 7:23; 2 Tim. 3:6; Ign Eph 17:1; and Phil. 2:2. In the Odes of Solomon 10:3f. the usage is the same as in our passage: "[the Lord gave me to

---

⁵ The Old Testament contrast between weapons of war and weapons of God, Windisch, 296, is remote, since Paul of course is concerned merely with the battle metaphor.

speak . . .] to convert the lives of those who desire to come to Him, And to capture a good captivity for freedom. I took courage and became strong and captured the world . . ." (Charlesworth, 48). The Odes of Solomon 29:8f. read: "And He gave me the sceptre of His power, That I might subdue the devices of the Gentiles, And humble the power of the mighty. To make war by His Word, And to take victory by His power" (Charlesworth, 112). Cf. also the epiclesis in the Acts of Thomas 52, p. 168, 17ff.: ἡ δύναμις τῆς σωτηρίας ἡ ἀπὸ τῆς δυνάμεως ἐκείνης ἐρχομένη τῆς τὰ πάντα νικώσης καὶ ὑποτασσούσης τῷ ἰδίῳ θελήματι; (". . . the power of salvation that cometh from that power which conquers all things and subjects them to its own will . . ." Edgar Hennecke, *New Testament Apocrypha,* II, 472).

In contrast to λογισμοί, πᾶν νόημα can emphasize the element of striving or willing (cf. the reference in 2:11 to the νοήματα of Satan, his designs; cf. p. 50), but need not exclude thought (cf. 3:14, p. 86, and 4:4).

The εἰς τὴν ὑπακοὴν τοῦ Χριστοῦ is the equivalent of εἰς τὸ ὑπακούειν τῷ Χριστῷ. The ὑπακοὴ τοῦ Χριστοῦ (objective genitive) is primarily the obedience of faith, cf. 9:13; Rom. 1:5, etc., and especially verse 6 with verse 15. But verse 6 shows that it must be actualized anew moment by moment in the believer's life and preserved in a concrete ὑπακοή towards the apostle.

Paul's labor is described quite generally in verses 4f., and what is said naturally applies to his missionary activity as well. But this is not the primary thought here, and it clearly does not determine the expression. The thought is rather of opposition to a proper understanding of the gospel and to the apostle within the Christian communities, thus not of pagan resistance. The proper ὑπακοὴ τοῦ Χριστοῦ is at the same time ὑπακοή towards Paul, verse 6.

Verse 6: καὶ ἐν ἑτοίμῳ ἔχοντες ἐκδικῆσαι πᾶσαν παρακοήν. The third participle is no longer metaphorical.

ἐν ἑτοίμῳ ἔχειν is the equivalent of *in promptu habere* (it has this sense in Philo and Polybius, cf. Wettstein, N.T.G. 2, 203) or ἑτοίμως ἔχειν in 12:14, etc.

ἐκδικῆσαι πᾶσαν παρακοήν means to punish every disobedience. (Since according to 7:11 the congregation has already attended to ἐκδίκησις, Chapters 10–13 cannot belong together with 7:5-16. 7:15 makes clear that the "obedience" of the community, for the sake of which Paul had written according to 2:9, has been restored).

ὅταν πληρωθῇ ὑμῶν ἡ ὑπακοή. Now, while Paul is writing the letter, the Corinthians' obedience is not yet complete, and the clause betrays the awkwardness of his situation. He clearly hopes to win the entire community, in order, when necessary, to proceed to punish a few opponents.

Verse 6 is first of all formulated in a general sense, just as in verses 4f., but the ὅταν κτλ. indicates that Paul has in mind only the present case. The ἐν ἑτοίμῳ ἔχοντες does not denote his continual but his present readiness, and πᾶσα παρακοή is any insubordination encountering him at Corinth. Verse 6 is thus as verse 2 and verses 7-11 a threatening reference to Paul's impending visit, cf. 12:14 and 13:1.

c. The threat of his personal appearance: 10:7-11

These verses comprise a new beginning. Paul is no longer describing his apostolic task as in verses 3-6, but just as in verses 1f. he is addressing the Corinthians in a quite personal way and characterizing his personal conduct, or is stating how he will make concrete his apostolic activity described in verses 3-6.

Verse 7: **τὰ κατὰ πρόσωπον βλέπετε.** Does the τὰ κατὰ πρόσωπον mean "what is clear," so that βλέπετε would be an imperative and the clause would have the same sense as in 1 Cor. 10:15: ὡς φρονίμοις λέγω· κρίνατε ὑμεῖς ὅ φημι? Would it thus be an appeal "to sound human understanding"? Lietzmann, 141, and Windisch, 300,[6] interpret in this fashion.

It is scarcely credible that one could construe τὰ κατὰ πρόσωπον to mean what is due or what is peculiar to a person. Windisch, 300, proposes this reading by way of reference to Epictetus' Diss I, 2: πῶς ἄν τις σῴζοι τὰ κατὰ πρόσωπον ἐν παντί ("How may a man preserve his proper character [that is, that which corresponds to his role] upon every occasion?").

In the context following 5:12 (πρὸς τοὺς ἐν προσώπῳ καυχωμένους) it is probably best to read the clause as a question (or reproachful utterance): "Do you look to what can be seen outwardly?"

εἴ τις πέποιθεν ἑαυτῷ Χριστοῦ εἶναι. The πεποιθέναι ἑαυτῷ means to be certain of oneself, cf. BGU IV, 1141, 17: Πέποιθα γὰρ ἐματῶι. The ἑαυτῷ is very likely added for the sake of the contrast — if one is convinced of it for oneself (for which one bears responsibility) . . . then one must also concede it to me. Χριστοῦ εἶναι is apparently a slogan of Paul's opponents (and not of a Christ-party which is neither referred to elsewhere nor proven by 1 Cor. 1:12). Ordinary Christian existence cannot be intended (1 Cor. 3:23; 15:23; Rom. 8:9; Gal. 3:29), but rather something distinctive. And of course it cannot be the relation to the historical Jesus, for in that case Paul could not have retorted, οὕτως καὶ ἡμεῖς, but would have had to reject this remark, since he refused to appeal to the Χριστὸν κατὰ σάρκα (5:16). In addition, a specific authorization of his apostleship through Christ is hardly intended, for nowhere in Chapters 10–13 does Paul appeal to his calling through Christ (on the other hand, cf. 1 Cor. 9:1; Gal. 1:11ff.).

---

[6] In a letter, K. Grobel translates κατὰ πρόσωπον in accordance with v. 1 — "face to face," present in person. He construes τὰ κατὰ πρόσωπον adverbially or as an accusative object, meaning either, "as touching my presence in person, take care!" or "beware of eye to eye," that is, do not suppose that personal encounter will be to your advantage!

According to what follows, the issue can only be the pneumatic relation to Christ which gives the pneumatic his ἐξουσία (v. 8).

Cf. 13:3: ἐπεὶ δοκιμὴν ζητεῖτε τοῦ ἐν ἐμοὶ λαλοῦντος Χριστοῦ, and the appeal to pneumatic phenomena in 12:1ff. Cf. also 1 Cor. 7:40: δοκῶ δὲ κἀγὼ πνεῦμα θεοῦ ἔχειν.

Reitzenstein in HMR, 362 writes that Paul's opponents have appropriated the confession which Paul required of them (Χριστοῦ εἰμι, cf. 1 Cor. 3:23), and interpret it on their terms.

τοῦτο λογιζέσθω πάλιν ἐφ᾽ ἑαυτοῦ. With the λογιζέσθω Paul is clearly returning the reproach (cf. v. 2, p. 184) — his opponents' λογίζεσθαι ought to see the facts!

The ἐφ᾽ ἑαυτοῦ (P⁴⁶ B ℵ L pc d g) means, "with himself," whereas ἀφ᾽ ἑαυτοῦ (C ℜ D G pl) would mean, "from himself."

The πάλιν clearly means, "on the other hand" (scarcely "once more"), whether or not it is to be linked with λογιζέσθω or ἐφ᾽ ἑαυτοῦ. Lietzmann, 140, translates simply, "and."

ὅτι καθὼς αὐτὸς Χριστοῦ, οὕτως καὶ ἡμεῖς. To begin with, the reason why Paul does not reply, "only I belong to Christ, not you," is that in principle he can allow a Χριστοῦ εἶναι also to others. But, in addition, the καθὼς αὐτός . . . οὕτως καὶ ὑμεῖς says nothing of the objective facts in the case, but merely that Paul has the same right as the Corinthians, and that they may not deny him the Χριστοῦ εἶναι.

Whether they really have a right to their πεποιθέναι may remain open. The καθὼς αὐτὸς Χριστοῦ does not mean, καθώς . . . ἐστίν, but rather καθὼς πέποιθεν εἶναι. The translation is thus, "I have as much claim to it as he!" (In the antithesis there is no πέποιθα answering to the πέποιθεν, but simply the assertion of πεποίθησις.) Although the reference is to τίς and αὐτός (cf. the ὁ τοιοῦτος in v. 11), it does not follow that only a single opponent is involved; according to verse 12 there are τίνες.

Verse 8: The **ἐάν τε γὰρ περισσότερόν τι καυχήσωμαι περὶ τῆς ἐξουσίας ἡμῶν** (the τε is not copulative, but only strengthens the ἐάν, cf. Rom. 7:7 and Radermacher, 5. 37) means, "if I should really boast this once." The formulation is general, yet verse 9 indicates that a καυχᾶσθαι in his letters is intended. Even if there had been a περισσότερόν τι, that is, even if the objective facts in the case actually called for it or seemed to justify it, even then the **οὐκ αἰσχυνθήσομαι** applies — "I will not need to be ashamed," or "I shall not be put to shame," cf. Phil. 1:20.

The object of boasting is the ἐξουσία, Paul's apostolic authority as in 13:10, not Christian freedom as in 1 Cor. 8:9, and yet cf. 1 Cor. 9:4ff. It is given him with the distinctive Χριστοῦ εἶναι of verse 7, and in this sense verse 8 gives the basis for verse 7 — the opponent who denies the Χριστοῦ εἶναι to Paul and thus contests his ἐξουσία, will get a taste of Paul's ἐξουσία and with it his Χριστοῦ εἶναι.

The apostolic ἐξουσία is described as follows: ἧς ἔδωκεν ὁ κύριος εἰς οἰκοδομὴν καὶ οὐκ εἰς καθαίρεσιν ὑμῶν. Regarding οἰκοδομή as a "metaphor" for founding, preserving, and furthering the community, cf. Vielhauer, *Oikodome,* especially pp. 77f. With this term, the καθαίρεσις of verse 4 acquires its antonym.[7]

But the expression seems odd after the description of the apostle's activity in verses 4f. Weiss (*Aufgaben,* 31) wants to eliminate the clause as an interpolation from 13:10. That is impossible! The description of ἐξουσία, however, does not really contradict verses 4f., because verse 8 has the community (ὑμῖν!) and not hostile contrary powers in mind. And the description is conceivable as a transitional thought. It explains why till now Paul's ἐξουσία was not evident as his opponents wish or mockingly require: When hostile forces arose in the community, Paul would have had to use his ἐξουσία εἰς καθαίρεσιν, had he wanted to prove his καυχᾶσθαι. For this reason we should perhaps add, "and which for this reason I did not make use of till now."

What is misleading in Paul's situation derives from the fact that, since he regards his ἐξουσία as given εἰς οἰκοδομήν, his καυχᾶσθαι appears to be without basis. Despite this he shall not be put to shame, for given the circumstances he is able to use his ἐξουσία also εἰς καθαίρεσιν — but the Corinthians should not challenge it. The thought is exactly the same as in 13:1-10.

Verse 9: ἵνα μὴ δόξω ὡσὰν ἐκφοβεῖν ὑμᾶς διὰ τῶν ἐπιστολῶν. The ἵνα-clause is linked to the οὐκ αἰσχυνθήσομαι — "I shall not be put to shame, so that it does not turn out," or better, "so that the result is not that I terrify you only by letter," "so that I do not appear as one who. . . ." We may add, "but I will know how to use my ἐξουσία (v. 11!) in order that (or so that) it does not appear as though. . . ."

In any event, we may attach the ἵνα-clause (Lietzmann, 142, Wendland, 153) to the εἰς οἰκοδομὴν καὶ οὐκ εἰς καθαίρεσιν ὑμῶν, and in verses 8f. identify the tangling of two ideas: 1) if I boast of my authority, I am not put to shame, and 2) I possess my authority εἰς οἰκοδομήν, not εἰς καθαίρεσιν, for which reason I will be silent about it lest I come under suspicion of wanting to intimidate you by my letters. But first of all the letters (and the one in hand would then be especially meant) are no proof at all of Paul's ἐξουσία. Rather, the real question is whether he can actually exercise the ἐξουσία maintained in his letters. Paul cannot intend to say, "if I wished to speak, it would lead to καθαίρεσις." And secondly, verse 10 indicates that the διὰ τῶν ἐπιστολῶν does not refer to the present but to earlier epistles.

---

[7] The terminology is from Jer. 1:10; 24:6; 51:34 (in the Hebrew 45:4) and elsewhere. Besides Vielhauer, cf. also Dupont, *Gnosis,* 240f.

Thus no ellipse is to be assumed (as indeed ら vg al assume when they insert a δέ after the ἵνα) — "but I refrain lest it seem. . . ."

ἐκφοβεῖν with the meaning "to terrify" or "intimidate" appears only here in the New Testament. It does, however, appear in the LXX, cf. Windisch, 305.

ὡς ἄν, or ὡσάν means "as it were," and bolsters the idea of the (ἵνα μὴ) δόξω.

Verse 10: Verses 10f. give the basis for the statement in verses 8f. Paul's καυχάσθαι which his letters do indeed contain may not be despised in view of his unimposing personal appearance, for he can enforce the gravity of his letters also by deeds. The relation between verses 10 and 11 is that between "of course" and "however."

ὅτι αἱ ἐπιστολαὶ μέν, φησίν, βαρεῖαι καὶ ἰσχυραί. φησίν is the customary quotation formula, used especially of an opponent's objection, cf. Bultmann, *Diatribe,* 10. 66f.

βαρεῖαι καὶ ἰσχυραί means "weighty, heavy and forceful." Clearly, the reference is not only to a general self-consciousness as expressed in the letters, but especially to the admonitions and prescriptions. Cf. 1:24: οὐχ ὅτι κυριεύομεν ὑμῶν τῆς πίστεως.

ἡ δὲ παρουσία τοῦ σώματος ἀσθενής. The παρουσία τοῦ σώματος denotes the personal presence; cf. ἀπὼν τῷ σώματι in 1 Cor. 5:3. In the context, ἀσθενής does not mean "sick" (thus in 1 Cor. 11:30, etc.) but rather "weak," which scarcely refers to bodily appearance (cf. Act Thecl 3) or to the artisan's trade (βάναυσος), but rather to conduct, demeanor.

The **καὶ ὁ λόγος ἐξουθενημένος** does not refer to something secondary, but to the chief thing at Paul's παρουσία — the proclamation in respect of its form and its content. Rhetoric and σοφία (γνῶσις) may have been lacking, cf. 1 Cor. 2:3f., and especially 2 Cor. 11:6, where the same reproach is apparent in the rebuttal: εἰ δὲ καὶ ἰδιώτης τῷ λόγῳ, ἀλλ᾽ οὐ τῇ γνώσει. In the catenae, ἐξουθενημένος is identical to εὐκαταφρόνητος, and the verb occurs in 1 Cor. 1:28 (parallel to ἀσθενής!); 6:4; 16:11, etc.

The reproach is the same as in verse 1. The αἱ ἐπιστολαί κτλ. corresponds to the ἀπὼν δὲ θαρρῶ, just as the ἡ δὲ παρουσία τοῦ σώματος κτλ. which follows corresponds to the κατὰ πρόσωπον μὲν ταπεινός.

Cf. Reitzenstein, HMR, 362f., who writes that in the view of the Corinthian pneumatics the apostle's δύναμις must be demonstrated in impromptu speech. Cf. the false prophet in Herm mand 11, who only prophesies in solitude or before a few, but loses his power and is silent in the community.

Verse 11: In verse 11 the **τοῦτο λογιζέσθω ὁ τοιοῦτος** again corrects the λογίζεσθαι of Paul's opponents, cf. vv. 2,7. Clearly, the ὁ τοιοῦτος is not an individual as in 2:6f., but "whoever says such." Lietzmann, 142, translates, "such people" (cf. 11:13). These are the τίνες of verse 12; in any event, not a Judaizing apostle or even Peter, who certainly could not impress by rhetoric and γνῶσις.

ὅτι οἷοί ἐσμεν τῷ λόγῳ δι᾿ ἐπιστολῶν ἀπόντες, τοιοῦτοι καὶ παρόντες τῷ ἔργῳ. In the contrast between λόγος and ἔργον, λόγος has a somewhat different sense than in verse 10. It denotes the word by letter, which of course is not ἐξουθενημένος, but βαρύς and ἰσχυρός. The λόγος of verse 10 belongs precisely to the ἔργον. The meaning in verse 10 is "speech" (oral), in verse 11 "word" (for one cannot refer the καὶ ὁ λόγος κτλ. in verse 10 to the written word and construe it to mean that Paul's personal presence is weak and [therefore] his [written] word is contemptible).

Paul thus does not recognize the contradiction which his opponents certify. When present, he will prove to be the same as appears in his letters. Naturally, he does not maintain that when παρών he will comply with his opponents' demands, but that he will give proof of his ἐξουσία. He is thus confident of an impressive appearance in the power of Christ (cf. 13:3f.). He will have his way in the community and smite his opponents — when forced to it.

2. Paul's τόλμα, or a comparison with his opponents: 10:12—12:18

Evidently, the situation is that Paul must defend himself against being regarded by the community as his opponents picture him — weak and without courage because lacking in ἐξουσία. He can lay down no proof of the Christ who speaks in him (13:3). He has no pneumatic δύναμις — or he should show it! The community measures him by the portrait of his opponents who appear as pneumatics and boast of their superiority.

On the one hand, Paul must state that he is not nor will be as his opponents, and on the other that he is superior to his opponents, precisely in respect of his apostolic ἐξουσία and δύναμις. So he is forced to compare himself with his opponents, that is, forced to a καυχᾶσθαι, and thus καυχᾶσθαι is the main theme treated in 11:22—12:18.

But it is only with reluctance and after worrisome preparation that Paul seizes on the theme, first by stating in 10:12-18 that he will not compare himself with them, while at the same time he actually does so and thus develops the variant criterion for boasting. Then in 11:1-21 follows the appeal to allow his καυχᾶσθαι, and only in 11:22 does the καυχᾶσθαι itself begin.

a. The first introduction: The criterion for boasting: 10:12-18

Not that we venture to class or compare ourselves with some of those who commend themselves. But when they measure themselves by one another, and compare themselves with one another [Bultmann reads: But we measure ourselves by, and compare ourselves (only) with ourselves, and omits:] they are without understanding. But we will not boast beyond limit, but will keep to the limits God has apportioned us, to reach even to you. For we are not overextending ourselves, as though we did not reach you; we were the first to come all the way to you with the gospel of Christ. We do not boast beyond limit, in other men's labors; but our hope is that as your faith increases, our field among you may be greatly enlarged, so that we may preach the gospel in lands beyond you, without boasting of work already done in another's field. "Let him who boasts, boast of the Lord." For it is not the man who commends himself that is accepted, but the man whom the Lord commends.

Verse 12: οὐ γὰρ τολμῶμεν ἐγκρῖναι ἢ συγκρῖναι ἑαυτούς τισιν τῶν ἑαυτοὺς συνιστανόντων. Paul has been accused of a lack of τόλμα (as well as of a lack of θαρρεῖν in v. 1). Cf. 11:21: ἐν ᾧ δ' ἂν τις τολμᾷ, ἐν ἀφροσύνῃ λέγω· τολμῶ κἀγώ. The γὰρ cannot furnish the basis for verse 11 by way of the οὐ τολμῶμεν, but rather by means of the thought of verse 12 already in mind — "for indeed we do not dare . . . but we may lay claim to you." Paul, however, prepares for the main idea by distinguishing himself from his opponents in order thus indirectly to make clear the foundation for his own claim over against their unjustified claim. (Lietzmann, 143, writes that γὰρ is a "purely formal connection;" similarly Windisch, 308, states that it is "a pause in the dictation.") The fact that in verse 12 Paul does not restrict himself to a συγκρῖναι, but also writes μετροῦντες makes clear that he has verse 13 in mind.

The οὐ τολμῶμεν is ironic, as though Paul's refusal were a weakness, whereas it actually is a superiority. Paul therefore does not speak with πραΰτης and ἐπιείκεια (Windisch, 308), but with superior pride. He will not set himself on the same level with his opponents (ἐγκρῖναι means to associate oneself with them, and συγκρῖναι to compare oneself). The τισὶν τῶν κτλ. does not mean, "as though there were others with whom we would do so," but simply, "with certain people who. . . ."

While the refusal to συνιστάναι ἑαυτόν is ironically represented as weakness, in reality it is branded as unworthy, as is made explicit at the conclusion of verse 18. Paul has already repudiated such behavior in 5:12 and since the opposite of self-commendation is commendation from God (v. 18), the same people may be involved who commended themselves by letter to the community (3:1).

ἀλλὰ αὐτοὶ ἐν ἑαυτοῖς ἑαυτοὺς μετροῦντες καὶ συγκρίνοντες ἑαυτοὺς ἑαυτοῖς οὐ συνιᾶσιν. According to what precedes, the ἀλλὰ αὐτοί refers most naturally to Paul, not to his opponents. If it referred to his opponents, we would expect an αὐτοὶ δέ (or a οἱ τοιοῦτοι, or a οὗτοι δέ). The ἀλλά corresponds to the οὐ — τολμῶμεν, to which we would have to add a ἡμεῖς if the ἀλλά-clause had another subject (Kümmel, 208, incorrectly states that "αὐτοί indicates a new subject"). Only of himself can Paul say συγκρίνοντες ἑαυτοὺς ἑαυτοῖς, since he has just refused to compare himself with others. According to the text of B, etc., the αὐτοί must of course be

Paul's opponents, of whom it is said that οὐ συνιᾶσιν, that is, that they are not rational, and Paul would be contrasting himself with them by means of the ἡμεῖς δέ. But the omission of the οὐ συνιᾶσιν, ἡμεῖς δὲ in D* G pc it Ambst (in the vg only the συνιᾶσιν is lacking) must be original, since 1) criticism by way of οὐ συνιᾶσιν would be extremely feeble and say nothing in the context;[8] 2) the elimination and resultant Paulinizing of the idea would hardly be conceivable, and 3) Paul has just refused to measure himself by others, that is, will not make himself greater than he is.

The ἑαυτοῖς ἑαυτοὺς μετρεῖν cannot be the characteristic of Paul's opponents, but only his own. Nevertheless, the μετρεῖν ἑαυτοὺς ἑαυτοῖς is in contrast to the ὑπερεκτείνειν ἑαυτόν of verse 14, and compatible with the μεγαλυνθῆναι of verse 15. In what should the opponents' ἑαυτοῖς ἑαυτοὺς μετρεῖν consist? They indeed boast by comparing themselves with Paul and exhibiting themselves as superior to him. He does not boast by comparing himself with others. Moreover, for Paul, comparing himself with others belongs with encroaching on others' territory (vv. 13-16). This, of course, is the method of his opponents. To keep to his limit means at the same time to restrict himself to his field of action.

There is no contradiction (Lietzmann, 143) between Paul's measuring himself by himself and measuring himself by the criterion given by God (v. 13). It is the genuinely Pauline idea, corresponding to everything said in 2:14—7:4, according to which judgment of the apostle takes its criterion from his task, his office. Keeping to the κανών of God means that Paul will not make himself greater than he is, that is, that he measures himself by himself. God's κανών is his κανών, cf. verse 15.

In verses 13-16 this thought is developed in such fashion that Paul measures his own boasting by the criterion of actual success. From where does Paul recognize his own or the divine κανών? From what he has done, or was given him to do. In his achievement the divine δύναμις is indeed at work (1 Cor. 2:4f.; 15:10). It can be seen in the success of his work (this principle also appears in Gal. 6:4). Thus the measuring of himself becomes a measuring of his καυχᾶσθαι according to the δύναμις actually at work, and hence a boasting in the δύναμις of God (cf. 4:7). **ἡμεῖς δὲ οὐκ εἰς τὰ ἄμετρα καυχησόμεθα**, means that an εἰς τὰ ἄμετρα καυχᾶσθαι cannot occur, for which reason also there can be no encroaching on alien territory (v. 13) — as is the method of his opponents (and as can be seen in vv. 14f.).

Verse 13: Verse 13b yields the thought intended from the outset in verse 12, and which gives the basis for verse 11 — I will appear among you

---

[8] Incidentally, συνίημι never occurs in Paul except (in a quotation from Ps. 14:2) in Rom. 3:11 and (in a quotation from Isa. 52:15) in Rom. 15:21; [Eph. 5:17]. And σύνεσις (and συνετός) occurs only in 1 Cor. 1:9 in a quotation from Isa. 29:14; [Col. 1:9; 2:2; Eph. 3:4; 2 Tim. 2:7].

with power, because you are my field of labor, because you fall under my jurisdiction. Since this thought is set over against the εἰς τὰ ἄμετρα καυχᾶσθαι peculiar to his opponents, Paul's right is made doubly clear — **ἀλλὰ κατὰ τὸ μέτρον τοῦ κανόνος οὗ ἐμέρισεν ἡμῖν ὁ θεὸς μέτρου** . . . sc. καυχώμεθα. Paul's boast thus has an established limit. It is determined by the criterion given him by God. It τοῦ κανόνος is not simply a synonymic genitive, then κανών denotes a criterion which yields the μέτρον, the measure taken or to be taken.

In the οὗ ἐμέρισεν clause, the οὗ . . . μέτρου is attracted to τοῦ κανόνος, and should not be linked to κατὰ τὸ μέτρον. Paul intends to say, "according to the measure of the criterion which God has given me as measure (for the purpose of measuring off)." The meaning is, "my boasting has its limit owing to the criterion which God has apportioned to me, in order to find the limit by means of it."

Characteristically, Paul writes ἐμέρισεν, not simply ἔδωκεν, because the ἐμέρισεν contains the idea of giving the share due to one in a distribution. Paul writes in the same fashion of God's μερίζειν in 1 Cor. 7:17: εἰ μὴ ἑκάστῳ ὡς μεμέρικεν ὁ κύριος, ἕκαστον ὡς κέκληκεν ὁ θεός, and especially in Rom. 12:3: ἑκάστῳ ὡς ὁ θεὸς ἐμέρισεν μέτρον πίστεως. So the meaning of μερίζειν is something like "to mete out."

The criterion for καυχᾶσθαι is thus not self-chosen, but allotted by God who sets to each his limit. Having conceded this, Paul must still maintain his claim to the Corinthians' community — **ἐφικέσθαι ἄχρι καὶ ὑμῶν**. We would really have expected a τοῦ ἐφικέσθαι. The term is an infinitive of result,[9] and is dependent on ἐμέρισεν μέτρου, provided it is not merely an exegesis of μέτρον meaning, "that is to say, that we have reached as far as to you." The καί is emphatic so that the force of the clause is, "yes, surely, precisely you, too, fall within our jurisdiction." If the ἐφικέσθαι ἄχρι καὶ ὑμῶν interprets the μέτρον, then it is clear that Paul's καυχᾶσθαι denotes his claim to a specific area of mission, while the εἰς τὰ ἄμετρα καυχᾶσθαι denotes encroachment on alien territory (cf. v. 15). In this way Paul's introduction of the concept of μέτρον or μετρεῖν (v. 12) for the first time really becomes clear.

It is also clear that the clause applies to opponents who claim jurisdiction over the Corinthian community, and thus if not explicitly, then in actuality, dispute Paul's jurisdiction. In opposition, verses 14f. state that Paul has jurisdiction according to the κανών assigned him by God.

Verse 14: Verses 14-16 form one sentence. The ruling verb is οὐ ὑπερεκτείνομεν ἑαυτούς. First, the ὡς μὴ ἐφικνούμενοι is subordinated to it, and then (v. 15) the οὐκ . . . καυχώμενοι, since the ἄχρι-clause is to be

---

[9] On the infinitive of result cf. Bl.-D. para. 391, 4, and Radermacher, 186. It could also be an infinitive of intent, as after διδόναι, Bl.-D. para. 390, 2.

construed as a parenthesis. Likewise the antithetical ἐλπίδα δὲ ἔχοντες is subordinated to the οὐκ . . . καυχώμενοι. The infinitive μεγαλυνθῆναι is dependent upon the ἐλπίδα ἔχοντες. The εἰς τὰ ὑπερέκεινα ὑμῶν εὐαγγελίσασθαι οὐκ . . . καυχήσασθαι interprets the εἰς περισσείαν (cf. p. 196), or it is a "parallel clause in apposition" (Lietzmann, 144).

οὐ γὰρ ὡς μὴ ἐφικνούμενοι εἰς ὑμᾶς ὑπερεκτείνομεν ἑαυτούς. Since the οὐ . . . ὑπερεκτείνομεν ἑαυτούς appears in place of the οὐκ εἰς τὰ ἄμετρα καυχησόμεθα (v. 13), it is clear that in the context the καυχᾶσθαι is not simply a swaggering, but also raising a claim. For ὑπερεκτείνειν (documented only in Christian literature; cf. Luc Icaromenipp 7: ὑπερδιατείνω) which means "to stretch out beyond," cannot refer to boastful speech (Bachmann, 355: οἷον τῷ κόμπῳ τῶν λόγων), but is to be construed after the figure of the measure, and thus connotes stretching oneself beyond the limit. The meaning is, "we do not exceed the limit (the measure allotted to) set for us."

ὡς μὴ ἐφικνούμενοι εἰς ὑμᾶς obviously alters the meaning of ἐφικνεῖσθαι ("to reach") to the figurative, since it is in the present tense. It thus cannot mean, "as those who would not have reached you," and yet it can scarcely be a timeless description. Paul's intention then would have to be to refer to his opponents — "as such who do not come to you," that is, as missionaries.[10] But even in this case ἐφικνεῖσθαι would in all likelihood denote simply jurisdiction, and thus be meant figuratively — "as such who do not reach you (with their legitimate claim)." Bousett, *Schriften NT,* 208, translates: "As though you did not belong within our range." Proof of actually having reached is of course stated in the ἐφθάσαμεν of the parenthesis.

ἄχρι γὰρ καὶ ὑμῶν ἐφθάσαμεν ἐν τῷ εὐαγγελίῳ τοῦ Χριστοῦ. Proof for the assertion that Paul does not overstep his bounds when he claims jurisdiction over the Christian community is that he is the founder of the community. He came to Corinth with the εὐαγγέλιον τοῦ Χριστοῦ (an objective genitive; εὐαγγέλιον denotes the preaching as in 2:12 and 8:18). At the same time, the ἐφθάσαμεν need not mean, we came (ahead) as first, but merely (as elsewhere in later Greek) we reached, cf. 1 Thess. 2:16 and Phil. 3:16.

Verse 15: οὐκ εἰς τὰ ἄμετρα καυχώμενοι. This clause contains the second subordinate participle, provided we do not prefer to construe it as loosely attached in lieu of a finite verb.

The verse is a repetition of what was said in verses 12f., but in such fashion that by the addition of ἐν ἀλλοτρίοις κόποις the εἰς τὰ ἄμετρα καυχώμενοι is made concrete as a taking up space and laying claim to alien mission territory. It is also an indirect description of Paul's opponents who have invaded his mission field.

---

[10] Then it would actually read ὡς τινες τῶν μὴ ἐφικνούντων κτλ., cf. v. 12.

The κόποι are, of course, the work of mission or its results; cf. 1 Thess. 3:5 and especially John 4:38. The principle is enunciated as in Rom. 15:20: οὕτως δὲ φιλοτιμούμενον εὐαγγελίζεσθαι οὐχ ὅπου ὠνομάσθη Χριστός, ἵνα μὴ ἐπ᾽ ἀλλότριον θεμέλιον οἰκοδομῶ.

ἐλπίδα δὲ ἔχοντες αὐξανομένης τῆς πίστεως ὑμῶν ἐν ὑμῖν. The clause is antithetically coordinated with the οὐκ . . . καυχώμενοι. The intention is to ward off the misconception that keeping to the μέτρον spells restriction to the Corinthian community or to what has been achieved till now. Paul's motive is thus not "modesty" in the human sense. Rather, the ἐλπίδα δὲ ἔχοντες expresses his proud sense of superiority over opponents who do not capture new territory as independent missionaries.

Paul's hope is in the **μεγαλυνθῆναι** — explained in verse 16 by the εἰς τὰ ὑπερέκεινα ὑμῶν εὐαγγελίσασθαι — since ἐν ὑμῖν is not to be linked with μεγαλυνθῆναι, in which case we would expect the sequence μεγαλυνθῆναι ἐν ὑμῖν. We would also expect a καί or καὶ μετὰ ταῦτα (Lietzmann, 144) before the κατὰ τὸν κανόνα ἡμῶν, for the **κατὰ τὸν κανόνα ἡμῶν εἰς περισσείαν** certainly cannot belong with an ἐν ὑμῖν μεγαλυνθῆναι. Rather, the εἰς περισσείαν, which cannot be separated from the κατὰ τὸν κανόνα ἡμῶν, can only mean the same thing, which is then explained by the ὑπερέκεινα ὑμῶν. The ἐν ὑμῖν μεγαλυνθῆναι would mean, "to achieve greatness or esteem among you, in your estimation." But the ἐλπίδα δὲ ἔχοντες in the antithesis to verse 15a naturally expresses the hope of reaching beyond Corinth.[11]

ἐν ὑμῖν thus belongs to αὐξανομένης τῆς πίστεως, and the genitive absolute gives the condition or presupposition which must be fulfilled so that Paul may turn to new mission fields beyond the community. As to content, the clause is equivalent to the ὅταν πληρωθῇ ὑμῶν ἡ ὑπακοή in verse 6 (cf. p. 186 on v. 5: εἰς τὴν ὑπακοὴν τοῦ Χριστοῦ).

Once this presupposition is fulfilled there can actually be a μεγαλυνθῆναι, a "being enlarged," that is, through further mission, as verse 16 describes. Indeed, it is a μεγαλυνθῆναι εἰς περισσείαν, a being enlarged to excess, a "growth to the loftiest height" (Lietzmann, 142) — yet not a ὑπερεκτείνειν ἑαυτόν, as the carefully added κατὰ τὸν κανόνα ἡμῶν expressly notes — with the proviso of course that Paul can recognize the κανών first of all in his missionary successes.

Verse 16: εἰς τὰ ὑπερέκεινα ὑμῶν εὐαγγελίσασθαι. The clause is parallel and loosely joined to the μεγαλυνθῆναι. Is it "a parallel clause in apposition" (Lietzmann, 144; then it would really have to be linked by a καί!), or does it explain the εἰς περισσείαν? If so, the expression would be condensed

---

[11] Kümmel, 209, is of another opinion. He connects ἐν ὑμῖν with μεγαλυνθῆναι, and to the latter links κατὰ τὸν κανόνα ἡμῶν εἰς περισσείαν, in order then to construe the εἰς τὰ ὑπερέκεινα ὑμῶν εὐαγγελίσασθαι as a consecutive clause dependent on the ἐλπίδα ἔχοντες.

from εἰς τὸ εἰς τὰ ὑπερέκεινα εὐαγγελίσασθαι.[12] It indicates how the μεγαλυνθῆναι is to be understood, not as an attaining to greater worth, but as a mastering of greater tasks. It is possible that Paul already has the missionizing of the west in mind, cf. Rom. 15:23f.

Distance from ὑπερεκτείνειν ἑαυτόν is expressed once more by another loosely joined infinitive, which can no longer be construed independently of the ἐλπίδα ἔχοντες (the conjecture of Windisch, 314, who wishes to insert a θέλοντες, is needless) — **οὐκ ἐν ἀλλοτρίῳ κανόνι εἰς τὰ ἕτοιμα καυχήσασθαι**. As to content, the clause is identical to verse 15a.

The ἐν ἀλλοτρίῳ κανόνι means, "in the area of an alien criterion," or "in the area allotted to another by his κανών." Or, does it mean, "based on or together with it?"

The εἰς τὰ ἕτοιμα corresponds to the ἀλλότριοι κόποι of verse 15. The area already missionized is meant, and we are not at all struck by the absence of a ὑπ' ἄλλων, a ὑφ' ἑτέρων, or the like (Windisch, 314). It is not difficult to construe the καυχᾶσθαι εἰς as shaped in analogy with the εἰς τὰ ὑπερέκεινα, and as dissimilar to the ἐν ἀλλοτρίῳ κανόνι. Further, it was not difficult for Paul to write καυχᾶσθαι εἰς, since in the context[13] καυχᾶσθαι clearly means "the claim to. . . ." One need not at all refer to Aristotle's Pol V 10, p. 1311b4, where καυχᾶσθαι εἴς τι (= to boast of a matter) is used (Lietzmann, 144).

Verse 17: The ruling principle — **ὁ δὲ καυχώμενος ἐν κυρίῳ καυχάσθω** — is formulated with a scriptural word which Paul also cites in 1 Cor. 1:31. The word is from Jer. 9:22(23)f.: μὴ καυχάσθω ὁ σοφὸς ἐν τῇ σοφίᾳ αὐτοῦ, καὶ μὴ καυχάσθω ὁ ἰσχυρὸς ἐν τῇ ἰσχύι αὐτοῦ, καὶ μὴ καυχάσθω ὁ πλούσιος ἐν τῷ πλούτῳ αὐτοῦ, ἀλλ' ἢ ἐν τούτῳ καυχάσθω ὁ καυχώμενος, συνίειν καὶ γινώσκειν ὅτι ἐγώ εἰμι κύριος ποιῶν ἔλεος καὶ κρίμα καὶ δικαιοσύνην ἐπὶ τῆς γῆς.

Verse 18: From this word Paul draws his conclusion respecting opponents who, according to verse 12, commend themselves, and he does so in just as basic a formula as in verse 17 — **οὐ γὰρ ὁ ἑαυτὸν συνιστάνων, ἐκεῖνός ἐστιν δόκιμος, ἀλλὰ ὃν ὁ κύριος συνίστησιν.**

The use of δόκιμος is motivated by the intrigues at Corinth, where a δοκιμή is demanded of Paul (13:3), where the intention is to test him to see whether or not he is ἀδόκιμος (13:5).

Paul does not write that he is δόκιμος, but sets forth a principle. If only the one whom the κύριος commends is δόκιμος, then it cannot be stated unequivocally that a person is such, since the συνιστάνειν of the κύριος does not result in human words, but is manifest in the δύναμις at work in

---

[12] A conjecture: If we substituted εἰς τό for εἰς τά, then τοῦ εὐαγγελίσασθαι (purpose or result) would be the better reading.

[13] Or does Paul combine καυχήσασθαι with εἰς here because the preceding ἐν denoted the area? Kümmel, 209, translates: "In regard to what was already settled."

a person's activity. The recognition or denial of such commendations is thus always a matter of faith.

The divine κανών is just as equivocal. It, too, does not come to light in words. Rather, each must find it for himself, and each is ignorant of the extent of his capacity and thus of his task. He can only venture it when, without glancing at others, he inquires into his own κανών; when he proceeds in purely objective fashion and does not carry on his work in his own interest, but conceives it as a service; when he is not intent on his own glory, but on the glory of God or the κύριος.

From this principle practical maxims naturally result, among which is the one stated here, that one does not nest on an alien field of work, just as, under certain circumstances, one is forced to conflict and polemic for the sake of the cause.

b. The second introduction: The plea to endure his καυχᾶσθαι: 11:1-21

I wish you would bear with me in a little foolishness. Do bear with me! I feel a divine jealousy for you, for I betrothed you to Christ to present you as a pure bride to her one husband. But I am afraid that as the serpent deceived Eve by his cunning, your thoughts will be led astray from a sincere and pure devotion to Christ. For if some one comes and preaches another Jesus than the one we preached, or if you receive a different spirit from the one you received, or if you accept a different gospel from the one you accepted, you submit to it readily enough. I think that I am not in the least inferior to these superlative apostles. Even if I am unskilled in speaking, I am not in knowledge; in every way we have made this plain to you in all things. Did I commit a sin in abasing myself so that you might be exalted, because I preached God's gospel without cost to you? I robbed other churches by accepting support from them in order to serve you. And when I was with you and was in want, I did not burden any one, for my needs were supplied by the brethren who came from Macedonia. So I refrained and will refrain from burdening you in any way. As the truth of Christ is in me, this boast of mine shall not be silenced in the regions of Achaia. And why? Because I do not love you? God knows I do! And what I do I will continue to do, in order to undermine the claim of those who would like to claim that in their boasted mission they work on the same terms as we do. For such men are false apostles, deceitful workmen, disguising themselves as apostles of Christ. And no wonder, for even Satan disguises himself as an angel of light. So it is not strange if his servants also disguise themselves as servants of righteousness. Their end will correspond to their deeds. I repeat, let no one think me foolish; but even if you do, accept me as a fool, so that I too may boast a little. (What I am saying I say not with the Lord's authority but as a fool, in this boastful confidence; since many boast of worldly things, I too will boast.) For you gladly bear with fools, being wise yourselves! For you bear it if a man makes slaves of you, or preys upon you, or takes advantage of you, or puts on airs, or strikes you in the face. To my shame, I must say, we were too weak for that! But whatever any one dares to boast of — I am speaking as a fool — I also dare to boast of that.

This section, written with such passion, is borne by the ἀνέχεσθε idea — "bear it, when I boast this once!" Twice Paul begins with this plea, in verse 1 and in verse 16. In the first instance the plea extends to verse 6, and with a triple motivation: 1) in verses 2f. with Paul's zeal (ζῆλος) in view of the danger threatening the community; 2) in verse 4 with his reference to the community's readiness to ἀνέχεσθαι his opponents; and 3) in verses 5f. with his assertion that he is not inferior to his opponents, and thus is able to claim the same right.

Then follows an insertion in verses 7-15, proving Paul's equality with his opponents in face of the accusation that, by refusing support from the community, he has proved he has no title to apostleship, ending in a sharp invective against his opponents (vv. 13-15).

In verse 16 the ἀνέχεσθε is taken up again by the δέξασθέ με. On the one hand, the καυχᾶσθαι which the community ought to tolerate in Paul is described as ἀφροσύνη (vv. 16-17), and on the other the motif of verse 4 is modified to the effect that others do likewise and the community submits to it (vv. 18-21).

There is no firm connection of thought between 11:1-21 and what precedes; 11:1 is rather a new beginning. Yet, 11:1-21 is linked to what precedes by the general idea of comparison between Paul and his opponents as well as by the καυχᾶσθαι motif, since verses 16ff. indicate that the ἀφροσύνη of verse 1 consists in καυχᾶσθαι.

Verse 1: ὄφελον ἀνείχεσθέ μου μικρόν τι ἀφροσύνης. ὄφελον (G H K L 33 pm read ὤφελον; cf. Bl.-D. para. 67, 2, who state that ὄφελον is a participle originally supplemented by ἐστιν) is used instead of the classical εἴθε ὤφελον (cf. Bl.-D. para. 359, 1) to denote an unrealizable wish; the same usage occurs in 1 Cor. 4:8.

The μου is obviously not dependent on the ἀνείχεσθε (as on the ἀνέχεσθε which directly follows). If it were, the μικρόν τι ἀφροσύνης would be the second object of ἀνείχεσθε — "bear with me in a little foolishness" (Lietzmann, 144). The μου rather belongs to ἀφροσύνης.[14]

The wish denoted as unrealizable (if we do not assume that the imperfect ἀνείχεσθε is used in place of the optative, cf. Bl.-D. para. 384; Windisch, 317, 1) is viewed by way of qualification as realizable — ἀλλὰ καὶ ἀνέχεσθέ μου. The verb certainly cannot be an imperative — "yes, I even demand

---

[14] Lietzmann, 144, writes: "Aside from what follows, we would always link the μου to μικρόν τι ἀφροσύνης. No doubt Paul also intended it so, and afterward repeated the ἀνέχεσθέ μου without really sensing the μου might be construed otherwise."

(that would have had to be stated!) that you bear with me (or tolerate it in me)!" It is rather an indicative — "but you certainly also bear with me!" — which of course cannot express certain knowledge, but only hopeful expectation (Lietzmann, 144, writes: "ἀνέχεσθε cannot be an imperative, because the same idea would recur in the strongly antithetical ἀλλὰ καί, though in different form").

Verses 16ff. indicate in what the ἀφροσύνη consists. It consists in καυχᾶσθαι — not at all expressly stated here, given the liveliness of speech.

Paul is hardly picking up a slogan here (Lietzmann, 144), as though he had been accused of ἀφροσύνη. If he was thought to lack σοφία or γνῶσις (v. 6), then the positive pole would be the reproach of μωρία, which appears in 1 Cor. 1:18ff. as the antonym of σοφία. Cf. also 1 Cor. 4:10: ἡμεῖς μωροὶ διὰ Χριστόν, ὑμεῖς δὲ φρόνιμοι ἐν Χριστῷ. The antonym of ἀφροσύνη is σωφροσύνη. In addition, for Paul, ἀφροσύνη cannot appear in the same antithesis to σοφία (γνῶσις) as does μωρία. He must and will be μωρός in his opponents' eyes for the sake of the character of the gospel which is μωρία to the world (1 Cor. 1:21). As such he is precisely a σοφός *sub specie Dei.* But he is ἄφρων to the extent he boasts — not in the eyes of the world, but precisely *sub specie Dei* (v. 17).

Verse 2 (γάρ) gives the basis for the ἀνέχεσθέ μου (or for the ὄφελον ἀνείχεσθε) — "and this is proper, because. . . ." Paul bases the demand that the Corinthians bear with him in his ζῆλος — **ζηλῶ γὰρ ὑμᾶς θεοῦ ζήλῳ.** Obviously, ζῆλος does not simply mean zeal, but jealousy, for as the following indicates, Paul senses that he is in the role of father of the bride or suitor (cf. Windisch, 319f.).

(Paul does not arrive at this formulation because his opponents have hurled back at him the accusation of 1 Cor. 3:3; cf. Reitzenstein, HMR, 361.)

θεοῦ ζήλῳ means, "with divine jealousy." Cf. σπλάγχνα Χριστοῦ in Phil. 1:8 and νοῦς Χριστοῦ in 1 Cor. 2:16. The genitive is probably neither of origin nor author ("as God gives it") but of quality — "as is God's" — or better, as the equivalent of κατὰ θεόν — "as corresponds to God's will." Cf. λύπη κατὰ θεόν — λύπη τοῦ κόσμου in 7:10, and cf. 1:12: ἁγιότης καὶ εἰλικρίνεια τοῦ θεοῦ, cf. p. 33. Paul's jealousy is established in the **ἡρμοσάμην γὰρ ὑμᾶς ἑνὶ ἀνδρί** — "for I betrothed you to one single man." ἁρμόζεσθαι (the middle is used for the active voice, cf. Bl.-D. para. 316, 1) is a technical term for "to betroth."

The ἑνὶ ἀνδρί means, "to none other beside or instead of him." So the idea in mind is that defection from Paul would also be defection from the true gospel for an ἄλλος Ἰησοῦς (v. 4).

On the traditional figure of marriage to Christ, cf. Windisch, 320-322, and Schlier, *Christus,* 60ff. We must distinguish 1) the Old Testament idea of Yahweh's marriage to Israel, or the Jewish-apocalyptic idea of Messiah as bridegroom and the nation as bride, as especially appear in the Apocalypse of John, and 2) the Gnostic idea of the heavenly syzygy, as in Ephesians. There are other mythological ideas in Windisch, *op. cit.*[15]

The metaphor here refers to the relation between Christ and the individual community. Paul might have invented it at the moment of writing, but it is more probable that he is moving in traditional figurative speech.

In the παρθένον ἁγνὴν παραστῆσαι τῷ Χριστῷ, the infinitive of intent or result (Bl.-D. para. 390; Radermacher, 186) is dependent on the ἡρμοσάμην. ἁγνός is used here in the sense of "pure," chaste, as is usual in Greek.

The term παραστῆσαι means to conduct, as occurs at a wedding. Did Paul also have in mind the juridical use of παραστῆσαι (cf. on 4:14, p. 122)? In any event the παραστῆσαι occurs at Christ's parousia, at which Paul will conduct the community to Christ.

Verse 3: φοβοῦμαι δὲ μή πως . . . φθαρῇ τὰ νοήματα ὑμῶν. The phrase τὰ νοήματα ὑμῶν means, "your thought and striving," cf. 2:11, p. 50.

ἀπὸ τῆς ἁπλότητος [καὶ τῆς ἁγνότητος — a phrase omitted by various witnesses] τῆς εἰς Χριστόν. On ἁπλότης cf. 1:12, p. 33. (On ἁγνότης cf. p. 171 on 6:6.) The φθαρῆναι ἀπό is very likely used after the analogy of πλανᾶσθαι ἀπό (Lietzmann, 145), and ἀπό occurs instead of the genitive of separation, cf. Bl.-D. para. 211. (Lietzmann, 144, translates, "so also your thought is enticed [and turned] away from pure devotion to Christ.")

ὡς ὁ ὄφις ἐξηπάτησεν Εὕαν ἐν τῇ πανουργίᾳ αὐτοῦ. πανουργία denotes artifice as in 4:2, cf. p. 101. Presumably, not only Gen. 3 is in mind, but also the Rabbinic legend of the serpent's seduction of Eve (also in 1 Tim. 2:14?); cf. Lietzmann, 145_(and the supplements in Kümmel, 209f.); Windisch, 323f.; Michel, *Bibel,* 25-27; Bornkamm, *Mythos,* 25; Bousset, *Religion,* 336, 408; Dibelius, *Geisterwelt,* 50f. and cf. also Just Dial 100, 5 (MPG 6, column 709).

Verse 4: εἰ μὲν γὰρ ὁ ἐρχόμενος ἄλλον Ἰησοῦν κηρύσσει . . . καλῶς ἀνέχεσθε. This verse (γάρ) could give the reason for the φοβοῦμαι in verse 3. But since the request for ἀνέχεσθε dominates the context till verse 6, verse 1 should certainly be given a reason — "bear with me, you surely bear with others!" After all, the καλῶς ἀνέχεσθε is not to be construed as a question ("would it be easy for you to bear it?"), since Paul is clearly not setting up a hypothetical case, but referring to an actual instance, as verses 19f. indicate. The καλῶς (used ironically) corresponds to the ἡδέως of verse 19.[16]

---

[15] Cf. Philo Fug 114: "A maiden of the hallowed people" is wedded to the λόγος, that is, a virgin καθαρὰ καὶ ἀμίαντος καὶ ἀδιάφθορος εἰς ἀεὶ γνώμη.

[16] The interpretation once offered by Hausrath, *Paulus,* 423, and Schlatter, *Bote,* 635, is impossible. They construe ὁ ἐρχόμενος ("one who should come") to mean an arbitrator awaited from Jerusalem — Peter, for example. The meaning then would be: "You readily submit to opponents, if someone coming could preach another Jesus, etc., but that is impossible." Cf. Käsemann to the contrary, who states that nowhere else in Chapters 10–13 is there reference to an arbitrator, ZNW 41 (1942), 38. Further, Paul does not speak of κηρύσσειν

Instead of ἀνέχεσθε (P⁴⁶ B D* 33 pc sa syᵖ) א 𝔐 G pm and vg read ἀνείχεσθε. The verb would be either a true imperfect ("when another Christ is preached, you bore it — till now, or always — well enough"), which is most improbable, or an imperfect in a conditional clause ("would you bear it readily then?"), but the present tense of the protasis need not without reason be construed as conditional! (5:16 gives no analogy, since an actual condition is involved, cf. pp. 154f.).

It is also unnecessary to read καλῶς ἂν εἴχεσθε, in which case εἴχεσθε would be the equivalent of εἴχετε — "which is of course not documented but possible" (Lietzmann, 145) — and would mean, "then you would be all for it!" or in question form, "would it then really matter to you?" (Reitzenstein, HMR, 366). Then, of course, verse 6 would be smoothly connected. (The transitional thought would be, you would do well by me alone.) But the connection with verses 1-3 would be lost, and it is from this that the γάρ in verse 5 must be understood, cf. below. Then, too, what appears in verses 19f. as real would be set up as contrary to fact.

Thus the situation at Corinth is that another mission has penetrated it, which of course is also clear from 10:12-18. At the same time, ὁ ἐρχόμενος need not be an individual any more than the ὁ τοιοῦτος in 10:11, the ὁ ταράσσων in Gal. 5:10, or the ὁ συλαγωγῶν in Col. 2:8. The article can be general and is such according to verse 5 — τῶν ὑπερλίαν ἀποστόλων — and verse 13. **ἄλλον . . . Ἰησοῦν κηρύσσει ὃν οὐκ ἐκηρύξαμεν, ἢ πνεῦμα ἕτερον λαμβάνετε ὃ οὐκ ἐλάβετε, ἢ εὐαγγέλιον ἕτερον, ὃ οὐκ ἐδέξασθε.** The rival mission is thus in opposition to the mission of Paul. In this context, there is of course no difference between ἄλλος and ἕτερος. Cf. for example, Acts 4:12: καὶ οὐκ ἔστιν ἐν ἄλλῳ οὐδενὶ ἡ σωτηρία· οὐδὲ γάρ ὄνομά ἐστιν ἕτερον ὑπὸ τὸν οὐρανὸν τὸ δεδομένον ἐν ἀνθρώποις, and also Windisch, 327.

Paul naturally assumes that there is actually no other gospel, etc., than he proclaims, cf. Gal. 1:6f.: ὅτι οὕτως ταχέως μετατίθεσθε . . . εἰς ἕτερον εὐαγγέλιον, ὃ οὐκ ἔστιν ἄλλο.

What kind of proclamation is meant (cf. Käsemann, ZNW 41, 1942, 39f.)? It cannot be the Judaizing gospel of the Galatian agitators, since in that case the antithesis in verse 6 would not be intelligible, since the Judaizers could not appear with the slogans of λόγος and γνῶσις, and further, since the debate over the law plays no role in Chapters 10-13 (or in 2 Corinthians as a whole). The Ἰησοῦν (instead of Χριστόν) is no proof to the contrary, since Paul can use Ἰησοῦς and Χριστός without differentiation. Cf. 10:7 and 11:23, where the Χριστοῦ εἶναι, or διάκονοι Χριστοῦ is the title of his opponents; cf. 4:10f., where Paul writes Ἰησοῦς where we would expect Χριστός; and cf. 4:4-6 where Χριστός, Χριστός Ἰησοῦς, Ἰησοῦς and again Χριστός alternate without any difference in meaning. Further, such a differentiation would have to be in force in 5:16, if Paul drew a fundamental distinction between Jesus and Christ.

The formula in no way requires a reference to specific, dogmatic, Christological doctrines, and Paul of course conducts no polemic at all against such. For him, the denial of his apostleship and the arrogance of a false apostolate (vv. 13-15) already spells a falsification of the gospel. Above all, it is clear that Paul's opponents are Gnostic pneumatics, and the very exercise of their ἐξουσία, their καυχᾶσθαι and their behavior toward such questions as are discussed in 1 Corinthians 5–14 indicate that they proclaim another Jesus, another Spirit, and bring another gospel. For example, they preach a Christ who ἑαυτῷ ἤρεσεν (Rom. 15:3), a Christ κατὰ σάρκα (5:16), that is, they bring a proclamation which allows for ἐν προσώπῳ καυχᾶσθαι, and which does not understand the old nature's being given unto death. Of course, dogmatic teachings may also be involved, such as the doctrine of the resurrection from the dead in 1 Corinthians 15, or of the heavenly garment in 2 Cor. 5:1ff., cf. p. 130.

Verse 5: λογίζομαι γὰρ μηδὲν ὑστερηκέναι τῶν ὑπερλίαν ἀποστόλων. The λογίζομαι is no doubt chosen with reference to the opponents' λογίζεσθαι, cf. 10:2, p. 184 — "I allow myself to judge."

ὑστερηκέναι is not used instead of the aorist (I was inferior then in my missionary preaching, cf. 12:11: οὐδὲν γὰρ ὑστέρησα τῶν ὑπερλίαν ἀποστόλων) but is rather a present perfect ("I am not inferior," Bl.-D. para. 341; Radermacher, 152f.).

The ὑπερλίαν ἀπόστολοι, who according to verse 6 boast of their λόγος and γνῶσις, can certainly be only the Gnostic pneumatics opposed in the context, and who confuse the community. They cannot be the original apostles. Toward the latter Paul would certainly have had to make his authority explicit by an appeal to his calling, just as he does in Galatians. In addition, he could not describe them as ψευδαπόστολοι (v. 13), and could hardly maintain that he is more a διάκονος Χριστοῦ (v. 23) than they.[17]

Just as verse 4, so now verse 5 (γάρ) establishes the basic idea — "bear with me, just as you bear with them!" Cf. p. 200. The train of thought is exactly the same as in verse 21.

Hagge's proposal (JpTh, 2, 1876, 481-531) to insert 1 Corinthians 15 between verses 4 and 5 is absurd!

Verse 6: εἰ δὲ καὶ ἰδιώτης τῷ λόγῳ, ἀλλ᾿ οὐ τῇ γνώσει. ἰδιώτης denotes a lay person; cf. 1 Cor. 14:16. The datives in τῷ λόγῳ καὶ τῇ γνώσει are datives of relation, cf. Bl.-D. para. 197.

When Paul calls himself an ἰδιώτης τῷ λόγῳ, he hardly has a specific rhetorical education in mind — an education which certainly is not charac-

---

ἄλλον Χριστόν as a possibility, but as actually occurring at Corinth, 11:13-15. In that case, the clause would certainly have to be a condition contrary to fact.

[17] Schlatter, *Bote*, 636ff., and Käsemann, ZNW 41 (1942) 41ff. interpret this phrase of the original apostles; on the other hand, Kümmel, 210, writes: ". . . besides, the connection between 11:4 and 5 indicates that the ὁ ἐρχόμενος and the οἱ ὑπερλίαν ἀπόστολοι denote the same people who are active at Corinth."

teristic of Gnostic pneumatics — but either a scientific education or such spontaneous and imposing pneumatic speech as the pneumatics missed in Paul. Cf. 10:10; 1 Cor. 2:4; Reitzenstein, HMR, 362f.; thus also Käsemann, ZNW 41, 1942, 35. On the other hand, cf. Kümmel, 210 ("but Paul would not have described himself as an ἰδιώτης in this sense, and the parallel in 1 Cor. 2:4 clearly argues for λόγος in terms of 'schooled speech.'"). Very likely, the former is meant. The λόγος would then consist of Gnostic speculations (πειθοῖς σοφίας λόγοις, 1 Cor. 2:4), which, if the opponents were "Hebrews"(v. 22), were conveyed by way of Alexandrian allegory, say, after the style of Apollos. Cf. 1 Cor. 1:11ff. and Acts 18:24.

Naturally, Paul himself took up the difference between λόγος and γνῶσις, and when he writes ἀλλ᾽ οὐ τῇ γνώσει he may be thinking either of the σοφία which he has for the τέλειοι according to 1 Cor. 2:6, or of the γνῶσις mediated by the gospel as such (cf. 2:14; 4:6), actualized in the individual (6:6), and for which he struggles as apostle (10:5). The latter is the more probable according to 10:5. Paul then would simply oppose the preaching of the true gospel to the γνῶσις of the Gnostics.

ἀλλ᾽ ἐν παντὶ φανερώσαντες ἐν πᾶσιν εἰς ὑμᾶς. The phrase is scarcely intelligible, but in any case αὐτήν (τὴν γνῶσιν) must be added to φανερώσαντες, though the resultant expression is harsh. For this reason the following variants appear: 1) ℵ * B (G) pc read: ἐν παντὶ φανερώσαντες ἐν πᾶσιν εἰς ὑμᾶς; 1a) G reads the same, but without the ἐν πᾶσιν; 2) M min read: ἐν παντὶ φανερώσαντες + ἑαυτοὺς ἐν πᾶσιν εἰς ὑμᾶς; 3) bo sa read: ἐν παντὶ φανερώσαντες + ἑαυτοὺς ἐν πᾶσιν —. 4) K L P go Chr read: ἐν παντὶ φανερωθέντες ἐν πᾶσιν εἰς ὑμᾶς; 5) pe read: ἐν παντὶ φανερωθέντες — εἰς ὑμᾶς; 6) D* Ambst read: ἐν παντὶ φανερωθεὶς ἐν πᾶσιν εἰς ὑμᾶς, and 7) (vg) latt read: in omnibus autem manifestus sum vobis.

The entire clause ἀλλ᾽ . . . ὑμᾶς is lacking in P⁴⁶. Variants 2 through 7 are obviously corrections. Variant 2, as well as 6 and 7 would of course suit 5:11, but the idea that Paul is plainly intelligible to the community has no support in the context, and is not suitable as the antithesis to verse 6a. Reitzenstein's (HMR, 367) addition of φανερώσαντες (ἀμέμπτους ἡμᾶς) would of course fit well with what follows, but not with verse 6a. We would have to assume a change in thought, and in fact a new idea does emerge in verse 7.

Lietzmann, 147, proposes a φανερώσαντες (τὸ μυστήριον τῆς γνώσεως or τῆς πίστεως), which from the standpoint of content is, in any event, as appropriate as (αὐτήν) or (τὴν γνῶσιν). Cf. 2:14: θεῷ . . . τῷ . . . τὴν ὀσμὴν τῆς γνώσεως αὐτοῦ φανεροῦντι δι᾽ ἡμῶν ἐν παντὶ τόπῳ. Cf. also 4:2: μηδὲ δολοῦντες τὸν λόγον τοῦ θεοῦ, ἀλλὰ τῇ φανερώσει τῆς ἀληθείας συνιστάνοντες ἑαυτοὺς πρὸς πᾶσαν συνείδησιν. Even Schlatter, *Bote*, 642 writes that "we can hardly believe this little clause is not damaged."

The ἐν παντί (in every respect) and ἐν πᾶσιν (among all) fits well. Paul has offered γνῶσις neither partially nor only to a favored few. Thus he can certainly expect that they "bear with" him, that is, give him a hearing now. But before Paul really makes use of his right to a hearing (v. 16), he refers in verses 7-15 to the slander of opponents that he himself did not dare to appear in Corinth as a true apostle, since he did not maintain the right of an apostle to support by the community. This must certainly be the reproach of his opponents, and not an assertion that he scorned the community's aid out of pride. Is this true later on, in verse 11 and 12:15?

This polemic is linked to what precedes by the idea that any ὑστερηκέναι is out of the question, though Paul's waiver of the rights of an apostle gives this appearance.

The insertion at 11:7-15: The question of Paul's sincerity

Verse 7: ἢ ἁμαρτίαν ἐποίησα ἐμαυτὸν ταπεινῶν ἵνα ὑμεῖς ὑψωθῆτε. Is the ἢ equal to the Latin *an* ("or") or does it simply introduce a question? Cf. Bl.-D. para. 440, 1. Does the ἁμαρτίαν ἐποίησα simply mean, "did I commit a sin?" or is it to be taken in the full sense of ἁμαρτία — "was it a sin that I. . . ?" But at this point his opponents surely cannot have spoken of a ἁμαρτία of Paul. Cf. 12:13: χαρίσασθέ μοι τὴν ἀδικίαν ταύτην — "this wrong" (which is none at all).

ἐμαυτὸν ταπεινῶν. What Paul's abasement and the community's exaltation consist of is made clear only in what follows.

ὅτι δωρεὰν τὸ τοῦ θεοῦ εὐαγγέλιον εὐηγγελισάμην ὑμῖν. The ὅτι is not causal but explicates the ἁμαρτίαν ἐποίησα; cf. Lietzmann, 146, who translates "seeing that."

Paul has therefore not allowed himself to be paid support by the community, support to which he would have been entitled according to 1 Cor. 9:4ff. The δωρεάν corresponds to the ἀδάπανον of 1 Cor. 9:18. The "abasement" thus consisted in enduring privation and labor. Cf. 1 Cor. 4:12 where the ἡμεῖς μωροί, ἀσθενεῖς and ἄτιμοι of 4:10 is interpreted by the κοπιῶμεν ἐργαζόμενοι ταῖς ἰδίαις χερσίν. At the same time Paul's "abasement" is his waiver of the apostolic ἐξουσία. Just as the ταπεινῶν consists in a refusal of support, so the ὑψωθῆτε is explained by the ἀβαρῆ in verse 9. The meaning is hardly, "that you might attain the δόξα Χριστοῦ" (Lietzmann, 147).

Verse 8: ἄλλας ἐκκλησίας ἐσύλησα λαβὼν ὀψώνιον πρὸς τὴν ὑμῶν διακονίαν. The exaggerated ἐσύλησα as well as the ὀψώνιον are again military figures, cf. 10:4. The διακονία is the apostolic service, but as the ὑμῶν which is linked to it indicates, it is not used as a technical term as in 3:7ff., etc. The ἄλλαι ἐκκλησίαι are the Macedonian communities of verse 9. Is the meaning that Paul allowed himself to be fitted out by other communities (in Macedonia) for his missionary journey to Corinth? After all, the παρών in verse 9 stands out from verse 8.

Verse 9: καὶ παρὼν πρὸς ὑμᾶς καὶ ὑστερηθεὶς οὐ κατενάρκησα οὐθενός. Does the καὶ παρών contain this idea: "After provisions for the journey were used up"?

The ὑστερηθείς ("when I was in want") conceals the fact, surely not falsely, that Paul was able to support himself from his earnings (1 Cor. 4:12; cf. 1 Thess. 2:9). Rather, he had to go to work as a ὑστερηθείς. Of course, there is no reference to that here, but only to the fact that he received support from the outside — τὸ γὰρ ὑστέρημά μου προσανεπλήρωσαν οἱ ἀδελφοὶ ἐλθόντες ἀπὸ Μακεδονίας. It is a matter only of simple contrast — "I have not been a burden to you; others have borne the burden." This of course implies that Paul can make use of his apostolic right. His labor was a bitter necessity, and perhaps the earnings were not sufficient.

The brothers from Macedonia may have been emissaries of the community (especially from Philippi, cf. Phil. 4:15f.), or also Silas and Timothy, cf. Acts 18:5.

οὐ κατενάρκησα οὐθενός (the genitive is used due to the κατά, Bl.-D. para. 181). Elsewhere κατεναρκάω is documented only as a medical term meaning, "to anesthetize." It was taken by the Latin and Syrian versions as well as by Chrysostom and Theodoret to mean simply *onerosus esse, gravare*. Was it usual in this sense, so that it meant merely an ἀβαρῆ ἐμαυτὸν ἐτήρησα? Or does it conceal a repudiation of the other accusation (cf. 12:16f.) that he wanted to line his own pocket secretly?

καὶ ἐν παντὶ ἀβαρῆ ἐμαυτὸν ὑμῖν ἐτήρησα καὶ τηρήσω. Cf. 1 Thess. 2:9: πρὸς τὸ μὴ ἐπιβαρῆσαί τινα ὑμῶν, and 12:16: ἔστω δέ, ἐγὼ οὐ κατεβάρησα ὑμᾶς. Even if Paul at the time of writing had already enjoyed occasional hospitality at Corinth, as he did later according to Rom. 16:23, this clause would be no contradiction, for in the long run such would have been an exception.

How little such behavior spells renunciation of Paul's apostolic claim, and how little one may infer from this the avowal that he is no true apostle is stated in the καὶ τηρήσω.

Verse 10: Quite to the contrary! states verse 10. It is precisely in such behavior that Paul's καύχησις consists — ἔστιν ἀλήθεια Χριστοῦ ἐν ἐμοί (an oath formula, cf. Rom. 9:1: ἀλήθειαν λέγω ἐν Χριστῷ; other formulae appear in 1:18, etc., cf. p. 39). The genitive Χριστοῦ is a subjective genitive or genitive of origin, cf. 13:3: τοῦ ἐν ἐμοὶ λαλοῦντος Χριστοῦ. Cf. 1 Cor. 2:16 and 7:40: Christ, or God's Spirit is in Paul.

ὅτι ἡ καύχησις αὕτη οὐ φραγήσεται εἰς ἐμὲ ἐν τοῖς κλίμασιν τῆς Ἀχαΐας. The ὅτι follows the oath formula, Bl.-D. para. 397, 3. φράσσω means "to lock, to obstruct." Is this the meaning, "my boast (my καύχημα, cf. 1:12, 14, p. 33) shall not be limited, lessened, neutralized," or, "my boast shall not be obstructed, silenced"? Cf. 1 Cor. 9:15: τὸ καύχημά μου οὐδεὶς κενώσει.

According to 1 Cor. 9:15-18 as well, it is Paul's boast that he proclaims the gospel free of charge. At the same time other motifs are at work — πρὸς τὸ μὴ ἐπιβαρῆσαί τινα ὑμῶν in 1 Thess. 2:9; cf. also love for the community in verse 11 and 12:4f., and the avoidance of evil gossip in 1 Cor. 9:12; cf. also verse 12 (2 Thess. 3:6ff. gives examples for the sluggish).

Verse 11: Here the motif of καύχησις is explicitly traced to something still deeper — **διὰ τί; ὅτι οὐκ ἀγαπῶ ὑμᾶς; ὁ θεὸς οἶδεν.**

Paul's opponents scarcely traced his behavior to a lack of love, cf. p. 204 on verse 6. But, of course, they may have said that he does not love the community, if Paul himself does not sense that the reproach could arise from the community in view of the fact stated in verse 9 that he received support from Macedonia. The question is repulsed by the formula-like ὁ θεὸς οἶδεν (cf. 12:2f. and Wettstein, *N.T.G.* II, 207). The answer is almost like that of 12:15.

Verse 12: The **ὁ δὲ ποιῶ, καὶ ποιήσω** — "what I do I will also continue to do" — corresponds to the καὶ τηρήσω in verse 9, but with a new statement of motive. Bachmann, 371, and Windisch, 339, are not willing to construe καὶ ποιήσω as a final clause. According to them, what is stated is not that Paul will also do in the future what he did till now (this already occurred in the τηρήσω of v. 9), but rather the purpose of his present and future activity. They conclude that a γίνεται or διὰ τοῦτο should be added as a final clause — "what I am doing and what I will do I do in order to rob them of the occasion. . . ."

ἵνα ἐκκόψω τὴν ἀφορμὴν τῶν θελόντων ἀφορμήν, ἵνα ἐν ᾧ καυχῶνται εὑρεθῶσιν καθὼς καὶ ἡμεῖς. ἀφορμή denotes occasion, pretext, opportunity, and ἐκκόπτειν means to cut off, to root out, to exterminate, to cut away. The second ἵνα-clause cannot give Paul's motive in tandem with the first, but can only be dependent on the second ἀφορμήν and give the motive of his opponents. To be more logical the clause would have to read, ἵνα ἐν ᾧ καυχῶνται αὐτοί, κἀγὼ εὑρεθῶ. Since his opponents presume that Paul does not dare assert his apostolic ἐξουσία, they clearly aim at inducing him to surrender the δωρεάν-principle in order to snatch from him any advantage he might have in the community's eyes. Their motive is therefore jealousy. But precisely for their sake Paul does not allow himself to be dissuaded from his principle — the community shall see the difference! This will give it the possibility of recognizing his rivals as ψευδαπόστολοι (cf. γάρ in v. 13).[18]

---

[18] Kümmel, 210f., is of another opinion: "Rather, Paul is explaining that his opponents wish to boast of their apostolic office just as he does (by the very fact that they allow themselves to be supported by the community; ἐν ᾧ καυχῶνται thus refers to the apostolic claim!). Since Paul, who is an apostle, does not allow himself from now on to be supported by the community, he robs his opponents of the occasion to boast of their apostolic office based on their being supported by the community (thus Bachmann, Windisch)." The situation is rather the reverse — Paul would rob them of this ἀφορμή if he allowed himself to be supported, for then they could not oppose their practice to his as the apostolic ἐξουσία.

Verse 13: After verses 7-12 have compared Paul with his opponents, a furious attack against these people follows in verses 13-15, until verse 16 begins again with the plea to bear with him.

The οἱ γὰρ τοιοῦτοι means, "for these persons of such a type" (Windisch, 341), or perhaps it would be better to take the clause in a more general sense — "this kind of people" (Lietzmann, 148), cf. 10:11, p. 190.

The term ψευδαπόστολοι is of course a predicate, not a subject (sc. εἰσίν).[19] It may describe their subjective behavior (they act as if they were apostles; they are hypocrites) as well as the objective fact (though they regard themselves as true apostles, they are not, since they bring an εὐαγγέλιον ἕτερον, cf. v. 4, and correspondingly behave as described in v. 12). Obviously the latter is intended.

ἐργάται δόλιοι denotes deceitful, crafty workers. ἐργάτης is used of the missionary in Matt. 9:37 and its parallel in Luke 10:2; in Luke 10:7 and its quotation in 1 Tim. 5:18, and in each case is used figuratively. The term is refined in 2 Tim. 2:15. Cf. the use of ἔργον for missionary work in 1 Cor. 3:13-15, and 9:1. The term is of course used differently in Phil. 3:2: βλέπετε τοὺς κακοὺς ἐργάτας. On δόλιος (used only here in the New Testament), cf. 4:2: μηδὲ δολοῦντες τὸν λόγον τοῦ θεοῦ, and 1 Thess. 2:3: ἡ γὰρ παράκλησις ἡμῶν οὐκ ἐκ πλάνης οὐδὲ ἐξ ἀκαθαρσίας, οὐδὲ ἐν δόλῳ. Cf. 12:16.

The ἐργάται δόλιοι clearly denote the opponents' subjective character, their lack of integrity, in consequence of which they really are false apostles.

μετασχηματιζόμενοι εἰς ἀποστόλους Χριστοῦ. Paul's opponents disguise themselves as apostles of Christ (ἀπόστολος is used in the broader sense of missionary, cf. 1 Cor. 9:5, etc.). This certainly need not describe their subjective intent, as though these persons really did not desire to work for Christ at all; it is merely stated that they actually do not do so. Verse 13 gives the reason (γάρ) for verse 12 — "I do not allow myself to be influenced by these people" — or for the general idea dominant in verses 7ff. — "I put up with nothing from these people."

The opponents, of course, cannot be the first apostles, whom Paul could not have described as ψευδαπόστολοι, etc. They are the same opponents as are everywhere attacked in 2 Corinthians 10–13 (versus Reitzenstein, HMR, 367, who wishes to interpret the ὑπερλίαν ἀπόστολοι in 11:5 and 12:11, as well as the Ἑβραῖοι in 11:22 of the first apostles). Those named in 11:13 are the very same intended in 7-12, and to which verses 4f. already referred (cf. v. 5, p. 203). In addition, verse 20 again takes up verse 4, so that verses 22ff. have the same opponents in mind. 12:11 likewise resumes the statement in 11:6.

---

[19]By way of reference to Rengstorf, *TDNT* I, 445f., Kümmel, 211, writes: "ψευδαπόστολος is of course a word shaped by Paul, denoting persons who wish to be authorized by Christ but are not."

Verse 14. Verse 14 gives the reason for the harsh characterization in verse 13 — καὶ οὐ θαῦμα (a diatribe formula, cf. Windisch, 341f.) — "how can one wonder about that!"

αὐτὸς γὰρ ὁ σατανᾶς μετασχηματίζεται εἰς ἄγγελον φωτός.[20] Paul assumes such mythological stories are well known. In Vit Ad 9, etc., when the devil tempts Eve for the second time, he appears as an angel of light, cf. Windisch, 342, and Dibelius, *Geisterwelt,* 48-50. Was this legend perhaps connected with that of Eve's temptation by Satan (v. 3)?

Verse 15: οὐ μέγα οὖν κτλ. The clause is a conclusion *a minori ad maius* (cf. the קַל וַחוֹמֶר in Str.-B. III, 223ff.), but in Greek form, cf. Diog. L VI 44. Diogenes speaks: Περδίκκου ἀπειλήσαντος, εἰ μὴ ἔλθοι πρὸς αὐτόν, ἀποκτενεῖν, ἔφη "οὐδὲν μέγα· καὶ γὰρ κάνθαρος καὶ φαλάγγιον (a spider) τοῦτ᾽ ἂν πράξοιεν." ("Perdiccas having threatened to put him to death unless he came to him, 'That's nothing wonderful,' quoth he, 'for a beetle or a tarantula would do the same.'") Cf. μέγα εἰ in 1 Cor. 9:11; Gen. 45:28 and in Plato, Menex 235d.

εἰ καὶ οἱ διάκονοι αὐτοῦ μετασχηματίζονται. The statement, of course, is not intended mythologically, so that particular angels of Satan are disguised as particular apostles, any more than in Mark 8:33 Peter is Satan disguised. What is meant rather is that Satan is operative in the false apostles, that he has made them his servants.[21]

ὡς διάκονοι δικαιοσύνης. This is naturally not a description of these people as preachers of the law, for aside from the fact that then τῆς ἐκ τοῦ νόμου or the like would have to be added, in the context διάκονοι δικαιοσύνης must correspond to the ἄγγελος φωτός and denote the mask of the true servant of Christ. The ψευδαπόστολοι can certainly not be preachers of the law. According to 3:9, the apostolic office is the διακονία τῆς δικαιοσύνης. (Is this an indication of the intimate connection between Chapters 10–13 and 2:14—7:4?)

ὧν τὸ τέλος ἔσται κατὰ τὰ ἔργα αὐτῶν. The meaning is that God will judge them. τέλος is used here as in Rom. 6:21f. and Phil. 3:19 (ὧν τὸ τέλος ἀπώλεια).

The proviso appears just as in Rom. 3:8: ὧν τὸ κρίμα ἔνδικόν ἐστιν; cf. Phil. 3:19 (it is not a relative clause in 1 Thess. 2:16). Cf. Muson VII (Hense, p. 30, 5f.): ὧν τὸ σφάλμα θάνατός ἐστιν, and Philo Virt 182: ὧν τὰ τέλη βαρύταται ζημίαι σώματός τε καὶ ψυχῆς εἰσι.

b. **The second introduction: the plea to endure his καυχᾶσθαι: 11:16-21 (a continuation)**

---

[20] Demons deceive men by assuming the appearance of gods, Porphyr Abst II 40, 42; cf. ps.-Clementine Homilies 9, 13 (ed. Rehm, p. 136f.).

[21] On μετασχηματίζεσθαι as a tactic of the devil, cf. Bachmann, 373.

Verse 16: In verse 16 the ἀνέχεσθε of verse 1 is resumed in the δέξασθέ με (cf. pp. 199f.), as is expressly stated in the πάλιν λέγω. It appears, of course, in a new formulation — **μή τίς με δόξῃ ἄφρονα εἶναι**. The μή τίς με δόξῃ is ingressive — "do not let it come to mind!" — but corresponds again with verse 1 when it continues, **εἰ δὲ μή γε, κἂν ὡς ἄφρονα δέξασθέ με**. Just as in classical Greek, the εἰ δὲ μή γε means "otherwise," Bl.-D. para. 439, 1; 480, 6, and κἂν means "at least," "though only," Bl.-D. para. 18, 374.

The μή τίς με δόξῃ ἄφρονα εἶναι merely appears to contradict the ὄφελον ἀνείχεσθέ μου μικρόν τι ἀφροσύνης of verse 1, when in that passage Paul exhorts his readers to bear with his ἀφροσύνη, but here warns against taking him for an ἄφρων. In verse 1 it was quite clear that Paul's ἀφροσύνη is only an assumed disguise, and the μή τίς με δόξῃ in this verse warns against misconstruing his role. But even at the risk of being misunderstood, he intends on playing out his role (εἰ δὲ μή γε κτλ.) — naturally, not in order to remain misunderstood, but gradually to make the Corinthians conscious of how the question of deciding between him and his rivals takes shape for them.[22]

Lastly, the **ἵνα κἀγὼ μικρόν τι καυχήσωμαι** indicates that the role of ἄφρων consists in καυχᾶσθαι.

Hence for the apostle καυχᾶσθαι in itself is inappropriate and an error. This judgment agrees with that of Greek philosophy (cf. Windisch, 345) to the extent that it rejects boasting and self-praise (especially Plutarch, περὶ τοῦ ἑαυτὸν ἐπαινεῖν ἀνεπιφθόνως). But it is not true that Paul thoroughly shares the Greek view (Windisch, *loc. cit.*). For the Greeks, boasting is an offense against αἰδώς ("nobility," "noble restraint," "reserve"), and thus a sign of ἀνελεύθερος which damages dignity and brings one into servile dependence on others. At best, the original Greek view according to which αἰδώς is opposed to ὕβρις, and καυχᾶσθαι is a ὕβρις, is comparable to Paul. For Paul, καυχᾶσθαι is prohibited because it takes from God what belongs to God (cf. 10:17), and forgets that people are set entirely on God's grace (cf. 12:9; 4:7; 1 Cor. 15:10, etc.). But there is a difference also at this point, since the Greek does not submit to the divine grace, but fears its φθόνος.

Verse 17: This verse emphasizes once more that the issue is of an assumed role, and thus explains the μή τίς με δόξῃ of verse 16.

ὁ λαλῶ, οὐ κατὰ κύριον λαλῶ. The κατὰ κύριον is analogous to the κατὰ σάρκα (v. 18) and means, not according to the intention of the κύριος. This has less the example of Christ in mind (cf. for example, Rom. 15:3;

---

[22] Alcibiades' behavior in Plato, Symp 212dff. is acutally comparable to the irony here (Windisch, 345).

Phil. 2:6) than the fact that for the one who is in the Lord, that is, who has died with Christ, there can no longer be any boasting. Cf. 5:12ff. and Phil. 3:7ff.

The ἀλλ᾽ ὡς ἐν ἀφροσύνῃ softens the ὡς and means, "in the role of ἄφρων."

ἐν ταύτῃ τῇ ὑποστάσει τῆς καυχήσεως may scarcely be translated, "in this confidence of being able to boast" (Lietzmann, 148). If so, why would Paul not have written ἐν ταύτῃ τῇ πεποιθήσει (cf. 10:2; 1:15; 3:4)? Then, too, the appeal to his confidence would have no meaning here. The translation is rather, "in this matter," that is, "on this theme" (cf. 9:4?), equivalent in content to "in this role," "with this plan" or "intention" (L.-S.). Its sense then is "because you have forced me to it" (12:11, cf. the δεῖ in 12:1), "because you have set the topic for discussion" (Chrysostom: κατὰ τοῦτο τὸ μέρος). Or, cf. Schlatter, *Glaube,* 617, who states that ὑπόστασις τῆς καυχήσεως is equivalent to ὑποστῆναι καύχησιν (or καυχήσασθαι) and of Paul writes that he "dares" to boast. The meaning is thus, "with this presumption." Other possibilities are given in Windisch, 346.

Verse 18: This verse refers back beyond verse 17, and gives the reason for the δέξασθέ με in verse 16 — **ἐπεὶ πολλοὶ καυχῶνται κατὰ [τὴν] σάρκα, κἀγὼ καυχήσομαι.**

In antithesis to the κατὰ κύριον of verse 17, κατὰ σάρκα means, "in a fleshly manner," "corresponding to the intention of the σάρξ" (as in 10:3, etc.). But this cannot be detached from the meaning, "on the basis of fleshly advantages," such as are enumerated in verses 22f.; cf. καυχᾶσθαι ἐν προσώπῳ in 5:12, and πεποιθέναι ἐν σαρκί in Phil. 3:3f.

Verse 19: Verse 19 gives a further, this time ironic, motivation to the δέξασθέ με, corresponding to the καλῶς ἀνέχεσθε in verse 4 — **ἡδέως γὰρ ἀνέχεσθε τῶν ἀφρόνων φρόνιμοι ὄντες.**

The φρόνιμοι ὄντες of course does not mean "although you. . ." but is used ironically, "since you are sensible people." The reason given in verse 20 indicates that the reference is not to a display of tolerance on the Corinthians' part. Rather, they are called φρόνιμοι because they endure patiently when addressed by fools. At the same time, Paul's opponents are characterized as ἄφρονες, for they boast κατὰ σάρκα, a role, of course, which they do not concede.

Verse 20: In verse 20 just as in verse 4 the Corinthians' capacity for ἀνέχεσθαι is given as the reason.

ἀνέχεσθε γὰρ εἴ τις ὑμᾶς καταδουλοῖ. What is in mind, of course, is not a καταδουλοῦν under the law (Gal. 2:4), but rather the presumptuous behavior of Paul's opponents who insinuate themselves as masters, cf. 1:24.

The **εἴ τις κατεσθίει** clearly refers to the exercise of apostolic right, cf. verse 12 (also Gal. 5:15; Prov. 24:37).

The εἴ τις λαμβάνει (sc. ὑμᾶς) means, 'when someone traps you," takes you captive, takes possession of you in order to exploit you."[23]

εἴ τις ἐπαίρεται means, "when someone assumes superiority over you, deals with you haughtily, insolently."

The εἴ τις εἰς πρόσωπον ὑμᾶς δέρει is the strongest expression for indicating that for such people the Corinthians are only an object of exploitation, of presumption. The phrase may be proverbial; cf. Philostr Vit Ap VII, 23 (Vol. I, Kayser, p. 278), where it is also used figuratively — μόνον οὐκ ἐπὶ κόρης παίει, which means "what is lacking is only that he slap him in the face."

We shall not inquire to what extent the description is correct. No doubt, Paul also intends to strike at the subjective attitude of his opponents. But the chief thing is the objective situation in which the Corinthians find themselves by their dependence on his rivals. "Don't you see at all, that for these people you are only a means to an end?" Naturally, the Corinthians' ἀνέχεσθαι is not an attitude actually required of Christians. What is at issue is not a patient enduring of an injustice done and which is perceived as such (cf. 1 Cor. 4:12: διωκόμενοι ἀνεχόμεθα). Rather, the Corinthians are proud of their new authorities, and their ἀνέχεσθαι can only be dubbed ἀνέχεσθαι in irony.

Verse 21: κατὰ ἀτιμίαν λέγω. If an ὑμῶν were to be added ("I say it to your shame," cf. 1 Cor. 6:5: πρὸς ἐντροπὴν ὑμῖν λέγω; 15:34: πρὸς ἐντροπὴν ὑμῖν λαλῶ; cf. also 1 Cor. 4:14 and 2 Cor. 8:8), then Paul would drop the irony, but the ὡς ὅτι κτλ. indicates that he retains it. A ἡμῶν should thus be added — "I say it to my shame."

The ὡς ὅτι ἡμεῖς ἠσθενήκαμεν may be translated, "that we were too weak for that," in which the ὡς ὅτι is construed as dependent on the λέγω and as interpreting it; on 5:19 cf. p. 161. It is also possible to construe the ὡς ὅτι as the equivalent of *quasi,* thus identical to ὡς ἡμῶν ἀσθενησάντων — "as if we were too weak for that." Then the λέγω would have to be construed absolutely (sc. "it"). Lietzmann, 148, translates, "for we were (for you, of course, too) weak." The "for you, of course" and the "weak" are hardly correct. Windisch, 348, likewise translates, "since we, of course, allegedly [!] proved ourselves as weaklings." Kümmel, 211, is correct when he states that Lietzmann's interpretation requires the addition of ὑμῖν behind κατὰ ἀτιμίαν λέγω, and a λέγουσιν behind the ὡς, which is not possible at all. The ἠσθενήκαμεν is an ironic allusion to the accusation in 10:10.

Verse 21b finally begins with the boast, and is the introduction to 11:22—12:18. Paul as it were rouses himself from his "weakness" — ἐν ᾧ δ'

---

[23] Lattey, JThSt 44 (1942) 148 translates, "to seize by force in order to drag off," consistent with LXX parallels (Kümmel, 211). At best, that could mean here to estrange from Paul, but this does not fit in the context.

ἄν τις τολμᾷ, ἐν ἀφροσύνῃ λέγω, τολμῶ κἀγώ. But he still retains the posture of the ἄφρων. His τολμᾶν is thus not the θαρρεῖν of 10:2 (and 11), but a τολμᾶν which can only appear in the Corinthians' eyes as strength. It consists in καυχᾶσθαι, and so he writes ἐν ἀφροσύνῃ λέγω. It is already clear from verses 23ff. that Paul is speaking precisely as φρόνιμος since he begins only with such advantages of which his opponents boast, while his boast becomes a boast in his ἀσθένεια (v. 30), a condition in which his opponents would never take pride.

c. Boasting: 11:22 — 12:18

Are they Hebrews? So am I. Are they Israelites? So am I. Are they descendants of Abraham? So am I. Are they servants of Christ? I am a better one — I am talking like a madman — with far greater labors, far more imprisonments, with countless beatings, and often near death. Five times I have received at the hands of the Jews the forty lashes less one. Three times I have been beaten with rods; once I was stoned. Three times I have been shipwrecked; a night and a day I have been adrift at sea; on frequent journeys, in danger from rivers, danger from robbers, danger from my own people, danger from Gentiles, danger in the city, danger in the wilderness, danger at sea, danger from false brethren; in toil and hardship, through many a sleepless night, in hunger and thirst, often without food, in cold and exposure. And, apart from other things, there is the daily pressure upon me of my anxiety for all the churches. Who is weak, and I am not weak? Who is made to fall, and I am not indignant? If I must boast, I will boast of the things that show my weakness. The God and Father of the Lord Jesus, he who is blessed for ever, knows that I do not lie. At Damascus, the governor under King Aretas guarded the city of Damascus in order to seize me, but I was let down in a basket through a window in the wall, and escaped his hands. I must boast; there is nothing to be gained by it, but I will go on to visions and revelations of the Lord. I know a man in Christ who fourteen years ago was caught up to the third heaven — whether in the body or out of the body I do not know, God knows. And I know that this man was caught up into Paradise — whether in the body or out of the body I do not know, God knows — and he heard things that cannot be told, which man may not utter. On behalf of this man I will boast, but on my own behalf I will not boast, except of my weaknesses. Though if I wish to boast, I shall not be a fool, for I shall be speaking the truth. But I refrain from it, so that no one may think more of me than he sees in me or hears from me. And to keep me from being too elated by the abundance of revelations, a thorn was given me in the flesh, a messenger of Satan, to harass me, to keep me from being too elated. Three times I besought the Lord about this, that it should leave me; but he said to me, "My grace is sufficient for you, for my power is made perfect in weakness." I will all the more gladly boast of my weaknesses, that the power of Christ may rest upon me. For the sake of Christ, then, I am content with weaknesses, insults, hardships, persecutions, and calamities; for when I am weak, then I am strong. I have been a fool! You forced me to it, for I ought to have been commended by you. For I was not at all inferior to these superlative apostles, even though I am nothing. The signs of a true apostle were performed among you in all patience, with signs and wonders and mighty works. For in what were you less favored than the rest of the churches, except that I myself did not burden you? Forgive me this wrong! Here for the third time I am ready to come to you. And I will not be a burden, for I seek not what is yours but you; for children ought not to lay up for their parents, but parents for their children. I will most gladly spend and be spent for your souls. If I love you the more, am I to be loved the less? But granting that I myself did not burden you, I was crafty, you say, and got the better of you by guile. Did I take advantage of you through any of those whom I sent to you? I urged Titus to go, and sent the brother with him. Did Titus take advantage of you? Did we not act in the same spirit? Did we not take the same steps?

Boasting κατὰ σάρκα: 11:22-33

Verse 22: Ἑβραῖοί εἰσιν; κἀγώ. Ἰσραηλῖταί εἰσιν; κἀγώ. σπέρμα Ἀβραάμ εἰσιν; κἀγώ. The three titles are titles of honor for Palestinian Jews and describe the nation as a natural community as well as the people of salvation history with its promises. Any differentiation is scarcely intended.

Ἑβραῖος does not denote the Jew who still speaks Hebrew (thus Windisch, 350; on the other hand, cf. Lietzmann, 150), but indeed the Jew who still originated from Palestine, or whose family has emigrated from Palestine. In this sense Paul in Phil. 3:5 calls himself a Ἑβραῖος ἐξ Ἑβραίων. In Acts 6:1, the Ἑβραῖοι are very likely Jews born in Palestine, in contrast to Ἑλληνισταί. (Ἑβραῖος, of course, was also used to designate the language and literature.) In any event, in Paul's time Ἑβραῖος was the archaic term or title of respect for a nation.

Ἰσραήλ, originally a sacral concept, denotes membership in a people and religion, and is used in self-designation, while the originally political concept Ἰουδαῖος is the name of a people over against and in the mouth of other peoples. Of course, among Hellenistic Jews, Ἰουδαῖος is also a self-designation, and so it is with Paul. But here Ἰσραήλ is used in liturgical speech and is a title of honor for the people of God; thus also in Romans 9–11. For this reason also the concept Ἰσραὴλ κατὰ σάρκα is formed in 1 Cor. 10:18, and Ἰσραὴλ τοῦ θεοῦ in Gal. 6:16. Cf. the *TDNT* 3, 359 ff. on Ἰσραήλ, etc. σπέρμα Ἀβραάμ denotes the people of salvation history and promise such as in Rom. 9:7; 11:1; John 8:33, 37; Heb. 2:16, etc.

With these titles Paul maintains equality with his opponents, but they are titles used in boasting; they are enumerated ἐν ἀφροσύνῃ, because Paul does not set his confidence in them (Phil. 3:5: ἐκ γένους Ἰσραήλ, φυλῆς Βενιαμίν, Ἑβραῖος ἐξ Ἑβραίων. . . .).

The opponents who claim these titles can only be those attacked from 10:1 onward, and who are also in mind in verses 18-21 — not, say, their supporters, the first apostles (cf. p. 208 on v. 13). It is out of the question that these opponents are Judaizers, since νόμος and circumcision are nowhere at issue. They are rather gnosticizing pneumatics. What is involved therefore is a syncretistic movement. Cf. the false teachers of Colossians and the Pastorals; cf. also Philo (and Jewish magic). Kümmel, 211, writes that the Ἑβραῖοι are Palestinian Jewish Christians who reproach Paul for lack of personal knowledge of Jesus, and thus are Judaizers. At Corinth they have linked themselves with the pneumatics, so that Paul must fight on a dual front. But where does Paul fight against Judaism? If they boasted in the law, Paul would have to speak as he does in Phil. 3:5f.!

Verse 23: διάκονοι Χριστοῦ εἰσιν; παραφρονῶν λαλῶ, ὑπὲρ ἐγώ. The διάκονοι Χριστοῦ are the apostles, cf. p. 76 on 3:6, and cf. verses 13 and 15. Does the opponents' usage explain why Paul does not write ἀπόστολοι? So Knox assumes in *St. Paul*, 129, 4.[24]

It is naturally no contradiction when Paul calls his opponents ψευδαπόστολοι in verse 13, for only their title and claim is involved here ("they call themselves servants of Christ," and are such in their own eyes). Their right to them is left undecided.

The παραφρονῶν λαλῶ is a heightening of the ἀφροσύνη — "in madness" — since Paul is not only asserting his equality here but his superiority. The ὑπὲρ ἐγώ (ὑπέρ is used adverbially as in Philemon 16; cf. Bl.-D. para. 230) means, "I all the more!" With this phrase Paul's comparison with his opponents really changes into a comparison of another sort, to the extent the ὑπὲρ ἐγώ is interpreted by the enumeration of crises which follows. These crises which prove Paul's superiority are of course not such advantages of which his opponents boast, but are in essence the ἀσθένεια of verse 30, thus the paradoxical proof of the δύναμις of 4:7ff. The paradox is therefore essentially twofold, insofar as this δύναμις is made the object of a καυχᾶσθαι κατὰ σάρκα. The paradoxical character of the καυχᾶσθαι is especially clear, if Paul is consciously borrowing the style of the memorial chronicle of the *res gestai* (for example, of the Monumentum Ancyranum); Fridrichsen, SO VII, 1928, 25-29; VIII, 1928, 78-82. There is no reference to miracles or the like as in the apocryphal acts of the apostles! Only 12:12 refers to such things!

ἐν κόποις περισσοτέρως, ἐν φυλακαῖς περισσοτέρως, ἐν πληγαῖς ὑπερβαλλόντως, ἐν θανάτοις πολλάκις. Since, in the enumeration of verse 26, the instrumental dative appears in place of ἐν, we must add not

---

[24] Cf. the reference to the parallel term "minister Augusti" (an official of the Caesar cult?) in Deissmann, L.v.O., 322.

merely an ἐγενόμην, but διάκονος Χριστοῦ ἐγενόμην in continuation of the ὑπὲρ ἐγώ.

περισσοτέρως and ὑπερβαλλόντως (from the adverbial participle; favored in the Koine, not unclassical in usage, cf. Bl.-D. para. 102, 6) are comparative concepts. πολλάκις is simply used positively. From the juxtaposition of comparatives emerges a simple enumeration, and "the more (ὑπέρ) automatically results from the stifling profusion of περιστάσεις" (cf. Fridrichsen, SO VII, 26, who indicates that πολλάκις is characteristic of the memorial chronicle in inscriptions). On κόποι, cf. 6:5; 1 Thess. 2:9, and verse 27. Cf. also 1 Cor. 15:10. On πληγαί, cf. 6:5. On θάνατος — mortal dangers, mortal perils — cf. 1:10. The term thus denotes separate events, not the continual εἰς θάνατον παραδίδοσθαι of 4:11 (Windisch, 354), or the ἀποθνήσκειν and θανατοῦσθαι of 6:9.

Verse 24: ὑπὸ Ἰουδαίων πεντάκις τεσσεράκοντα παρὰ μίαν ἔλαβον. (παρά here means less, cf. Bl.-D. para. 236, 4). The absolute τεσσεράκοντα (without πληγάς) corresponds to the absolute אַרְבָּעִים less the מַכּוֹת among the Rabbis, cf. Str.-B. III, 527. Concerning the synagogue punishment of scourging, cf. *op. cit.* 527-530, and Windisch, 355f. According to Deut. 25:2f., forty lashes are the maximum number; instead of these Paul received thirty-nine.

Verse 25: The τρὶς ἐρραβδίσθην of verse 25 comprise the punishment (*virgis caedere*) imposed by the Roman authorities, and which Paul received at Philippi according to Acts 16:22f., while the scourging of verse 24 is not recorded in Acts.

Punishment of Roman citizens with the rod was forbidden; but there were breaches (cf. Windisch, 356). It is possible that in a given instance Paul made no use of his civic rights.

The ἅπαξ ἐλιθάσθην is recorded in Acts 14:19 (at Lystra). Acts reports nothing of the τρὶς ἐναυάγησα.

νυχθήμερον ἐν τῷ βυθῷ πεποίηκα. νυχθήμερον denotes one day and one night or 24 hours. βυθός denotes the depth of the sea, as in the LXX and in Greek literature. ποιεῖν means to spend (with the accusative of time; used in Greek literature, and frequent in the papyri) as in Acts 15:33; 18:23; and James 4:13. The perfect πεποίηκα appears between the aorists for no perceptible reason, cf. Bl.-D. para. 343, 2.

The precise enumeration πεντάκις (v. 24), τρίς, ἅπαξ, τρίς (v. 25) corresponds to the style of the memorial chronicle (cf. Fridrichsen, SO VIII, 1929, 81f.).

Verse 26: ὁδοιπορίαις πολλάκις, κινδύνοις ποταμῶν, κινδύνοις λῃστῶν, κινδύνοις ἐκ γένους, κινδύνοις ἐξ ἐθνῶν, κινδύνοις ἐν πόλει, κινδύνοις ἐν ἐρημίᾳ, κινδύνοις ἐν θαλάσσῃ, κινδύνοις ἐν ψευδαδέλφοις. The dative is instrumental, and the διάκονος Χριστοῦ ἐγενόμην is always in view. The genitives ποταμῶν and λῃστῶν are used in terms of specifications which follow — ἐκ γένους, ἐξ ἐθνῶν — dangers caused by rivers and by robbers, cf. Bl.-D. para. 166. ἐκ γένους means, from one's own kinfolk, and ἐξ ἐθνῶν from the Gentiles. Articles may be lacking with nouns such as γένος and θάλασσα, cf. Bl.-D. para. 253 (ἥλιος, γῆ, etc. use the article), and with personal names such as θεός, κύριος, νεκροί and ἔθνη, cf. Bl.-D. para. 254. ἐν ψευδαδέλφοις refers, of course, not only to such in the Corinthian community.

Verse 27: κόπῳ καὶ μόχθῳ mean, in toil and hardship, and are also combined in 1 Thess. 2:9 and 2 Thess. 3:8.

In the phrase ἐν ἀγρυπνίαις πολλάκις, ἀγρυπνία is used just as in 6:5.

λιμός in the phrase ἐν λιμῷ καὶ δίψει appears in Rom. 8:35; Rev. 6:8; 18:8; and δίψος is used only here in the New Testament; cf. 1 Cor. 4:11 — πεινῶμεν καὶ διψῶμεν.

The phrase ἐν νηστείαις πολλάκις is used just as in 6:5.

In the phrase ἐν ψύχει καὶ γυμνότητι, ψῦχος is used only here in the New Testament. Cf. the καὶ γυμνιτεύομεν in the enumeration of 1 Cor. 4:11 (cf. above), and the γυμνότης in Rom. 8:35 (in addition to λιμός, cf. above).

Verse 28: χωρὶς τῶν παρεκτός ἡ ἐπίστασίς μοι ἡ καθ' ἡμέραν. Add a γινομένων to the τῶν παρεκτός, and translate, "apart from what I leave unmentioned," "apart from all the rest."

The term ἐπίστασις very likely does not denote attention directed toward something (as often in Polybius) but rather pressure. Cf. Acts 24:12: ἐπίστασιν ποιοῦντα ὄχλου, and also 2 Macc. 6:3. The μοι (𝔐 D pl μου) is dependent on the verb implicit in ἐπίστασις, Bl.-D. para. 202.

The ἡ μέριμνα πασῶν τῶν ἐκκλησιῶν naturally refers to Paul's concern for his own communities.

Verse 29: In verse 28, the μέριμνα especially is illustrated by the rhetorical questions in which "the oriental hymnic style (breaks) through" (Fridrichsen, SO VIII, 1929, 82) — τίς ἀσθενεῖ, καὶ οὐκ ἀσθενῶ. The phrase is clearly used in the figurative sense of 1 Cor. 8:7ff.; 9:22; and Rom. 14:1f. But of course the καὶ οὐκ ἀσθενῶ does not denote accommodation to the standpoint of the "weak," but rather a shared concern.

In the clause τίς σκανδαλίζεται, καὶ οὐκ ἐγὼ πυροῦμαι, the term σκανδαλίζεσθαι is used just as in 1 Cor. 8:13 and means to be enticed to evil or what is false. πυροῦσθαι is used in the figurative sense, and means to be excited (stirred up, restless, to tremble) as in 1 Cor. 7:9; 2 Macc. 10:35; 3 Macc. 4:2, etc., and also in Greek literature.

Verse 30: εἰ καυχᾶσθαι δεῖ, τὰ τῆς ἀσθενείας μου καυχήσομαι. In the εἰ καυχᾶσθαι δεῖ the point of view expressed in verses 22ff. surfaces once more, obviously in a concluding survey. The τὰ τῆς ἀσθενείας naturally does not refer to the ἀσθενεῖν of verse 29, but now sets everything said in verses 23-29 under the viewpoint of ἀσθένεια, in ironic reference to the accusation in 10:1, 10; cf. verse 21, p. 212. This viewpoint is then further developed in 12:5-10.

Verse 31: ὁ θεὸς καὶ πατὴρ τοῦ κυρίου Ἰησοῦ οἶδεν, ὁ ὢν εὐλογητὸς εἰς τοὺς αἰῶνας, ὅτι οὐ ψεύδομαι. The phrase is a solemn oath formula — cf. verse 10; Gal. 1:20, etc. — used together with a Jewish doxology: ὁ ὢν εὐλογητὸς εἰς τοὺς αἰῶνας. Cf. 1:3 (p. 20); Rom. 1:25; 9:5, etc. Cf. also Str.-B. III, 64, 530.

Verse 31 can scarcely be linked to verses 32f., since the latter simply report in chronicle fashion, not in any apologetic-polemic tone. And verse 32 is hardly intended to confirm the truth of verse 30, that Paul will only boast of his "weakness." It rather confirms the truth of the data enumerated in verses 23-29.

Verses 32f.: ἐν Δαμασκῷ ὁ ἐθνάρχης Ἀρέτα τοῦ βασιλέως ἐφρούρει τὴν πόλιν Δαμασκηνῶν πιάσαι με, καὶ διὰ θυρίδος ἐν σαργάνῃ ἐχαλάσθην διὰ τοῦ τείχους καὶ ἐξέφυγον τὰς χεῖρας αὐτοῦ. The incident is somewhat differently reported in Acts 9:23-25, and is lodged chronologically between Paul's sojourn in Damascus after his conversion and the journey to Jerusalem. Is the chronological arrangement in Acts correct?

In Acts the flight is traced to an attempt by the Jews on Paul's life, a tendentious alteration.

The Nabataean prince Aretas could have occupied Damascus after Tiberias (A.D. 14-37) and before Nero (A.D. 54-68; from A.D. 34 onward Roman coins are missing from Damascus); cf. Schürer I, 736ff.; II, 108, 153f. Or, did Aretas let men lie in wait for Paul by the gates? Or again, was he in charge of the Arabic population at Damascus answerable to the Romans? Cf. Schwartz, NGG, 1906, 367f.

πιάζω means to arrest, as in Acts 12:4; John 7:30, etc.

A θυρίς is a window.

A σαργάνη is a basket.

Why is the event narrated here? Since the report is entirely free of tendentiousness, it appears that Paul's flight from Damascus was not exploited against him by his opponents. Is it then a simple addition to verses 23-29? We see no reason for it. Or is it an interpolation? According to Windisch, 364, it is from Paul's amanuensis to whom he told it while dictating.

Boasting in weakness: 12:1-10

Paul now drops the motif of comparison, and the καυχᾶσθαι ἐν ταῖς ἀσθενείαις motif becomes the theme. With this feature the ἀφροσύνη is actually abandoned, since the καυχᾶσθαι is no longer κατὰ σάρκα (v. 18). Still, Paul retains the role of the ἄφρων (12:11ff.), and retains it also in 12:1ff., first of all insofar as he boasts of ὀπτασίαι and ἀποκαλύψεις. But this boast is only a foil for the καυχᾶσθαι ἐν ταῖς ἀσθενείαις, not merely because it is broken off at verse 6, but chiefly because it is shifted in verse 5. Since Paul is totally beside himself in ecstasy, he cannot really boast of it. It is sheer grace, and consequently falls under the viewpoint of καυχᾶσθαι ἐν ταῖς ἀσθενείαις, for it is this which boasts of the divine χάρις.

Verse 1: Paul writes **καυχᾶσθαι δεῖ** — once the theme (the ὑπόστασις in 11:7) has been set for discussion. Cf. verse 11 — ὑμεῖς με ἠναγκάσατε. The **οὐ συμφέρον μέν** is reminiscent of the reservation in 11:17 — οὐ κατὰ κύριον λαλῶ.

In the phrase **ἐλεύσομαι δὲ** (a Greek transitional expression; cf. Windisch, 369; cf. also a similar expression in Luc Prom 18) **εἰς ὀπτασίας καὶ ἀποκαλύψεις κυρίου**, ὀπτασίαι denotes "appearances," "sights," "visions" as in Mal. 3:2; Sirach 43:16; Luke 1:22 and Acts 26:19 (the vision of Paul's calling). Special apocalyptic visions are recorded in Dan. 9:23 and 10:1,7 (Theodotion's version).

The term ἀποκαλύψεις here is not used as in Rom. 2:5; 8:19; etc., of the occurrence of eschatological events, but as in Gal. 1:19; 2:2; cf. Acts 16:9f.; etc., of pneumatic revelations.

Is the κυρίου an objective or subjective genitive? And with ὀπτασίας? In any event, there is no reference in verse 4 to a sight of the κύριος. For this reason κυρίου can scarcely be an objective genitive. The two concepts are not sharply distinguished. Clearly, those events are intended which Paul experiences as a pneumatic, and of which verses 2-5 give an example. The plural is used less to indicate that Paul is thinking of various experiences than to mark the theme of visions and revelations. What is the reason for naming ὀπτασίαι and ἀποκαλύψεις? In any case, Paul intends to say that he is the equal of his opponents and, if he wishes, he may also boast of such pneumatic experiences as they brag of — after stating in 5:13 that his pneumatic experiences, after all, have nothing to do with the community (cf. pp. 149f). Naturally, he cannot intend to say that his opponents may not speak of such things, but "only I" (Windisch, 369).

Verse 2: **οἶδα ἄνθρωπον ἐν Χριστῷ πρὸ ἐτῶν δεκατεσσάρων.** Nowhere else does Paul speak of himself in the third person. This is hardly "modesty style" (Windisch, 370). The expression derives from the idea in verse 5 that Paul's responsible "I" did not participate, that something occurred to him of which he was, as it were, an observer, or which in retrospect happened to him as to an alien ("to distance oneself from the event reported," Käsemann, ZNW 41, 1942, 64). This gives expression to the unusual phenomenon, also described in the εἴτε ἐν σώματι . . . εἴτε ἐκτὸς τοῦ σώματος.

(On the subject as a whole, cf. Käsemann, ZNW 41, 1942, 66.) The ἐν Χριστῷ belongs with ἄνθρωπος, not with ἁρπαγέντα. It does not describe the person simply as Christian, but as intimately joined to Christ. What Paul tells is possible only for a person ἐν Χριστῷ, since the person as such is nothing.

We need scarcely recall the Jewish habit of speaking of the "I" (or the you) in the third person ("this or that man," "this or that woman;" cf. Str.-B. III, 530f., and also Fiebig, *Wundergeschichten*, 10:3; 27:4). In Jewish examples, the third person appears without the introduction which differentiates the contrasted "he" from the speaking "I," such as the οἶδα ἄνθρωπον of Paul. (For example, "this man [I] does not ask after his children;" "this man [you] rises to greatness;" "that woman [I] has ten sons," or "woe to this man" [to you].)

In any event, this style of speech does not originate in the dual consciousness of the pneumatic, aware of himself as mortal and as divine (Reitzenstein, HMR, 85), as though the ἄνθρωπος known to Paul were this divine person, or actually the ἔσω ἄνθρωπος of 4:16. It is this person who is joined to the σῶμα which bears the νέκρωσις τοῦ Ἰησοῦ. It is not something present at hand, but rather the authentic self seized by faith.

There may be a comparable expression in Soph Oed Tyr 813ff., where Oedipus recites in the first person how he slew Laius: εἰ δὲ τῷ ξένῳ τούτῳ προσήκει Λαΐῳ τι συγγενές, τίς τοῦδ' ἀνδρὸς νῦν ἔστ' ἀθλιώτερος — "But if Betwixt this stranger there was ought in common With Laius, who more miserable than I (this man)?" Cf. 828f.: ἆρ' οὐκ ἀπ' ὠμοῦ ταῦτα δαίμονός τις ἂν κρίνων ἐπ' ἀνδρὶ τῷδ' ἂν ὀρθοίη λόγον — "If one should say, this is the handiwork Of some inhuman power (this is inflicted on this man), who could blame His judgment?" Cf. 1462ff., where Oedipus says to Creon: τοῖν δ' ἀθλίαιν οἰκτραῖν τε παρθένοιν ἐμαῖν, αἷν οὔποθ' ἡμὴ χωρὶς ἐστάθη βορᾶς τράπεζ' ἄνευ τοῦδ' ἀνδρός — "But for my daughters twain, poor innocent maids, Who ever sat beside me (this man) at the board Sharing my viands . . . For them, I pray thee, care. . . ." In Oed Col. 353ff., Oedipus says to Ismene: σὺ δ', ὦ τέκνον, πρόσθεν μὲν ἐξίκου πατρὶ μαντεῖ' ἄγουσα πάντα, Καδμείων λάθρα, ἃ τοῦδ' ἐχρήσθη σώματος — "Eluding the Cadmeions' vigilance, To bring thy father all the oracles Concerning Oedipus (this body)." In 450, Oedipus says of his sons: ἀλλ' οὔ τι μὴ λάχωσι τοῦδε συμμάχου — "No! me (this one) they ne'er shall win for an ally." In 649, Theseus says to Oedipus: θάρσει τὸ τοῦδέ γ' ἀνδρός· οὔ σε μὴ προδῶ — "Fear not for me (this man); I shall not play thee false." In 1472f., Oedipus says: ὦ παῖδες, ἥκει τῷδ' ἐπ' ἀνδρὶ θέσφατος βίου τελευτή — "Daughters, upon me (this man) the predestined end Has come," and in 1544ff.: ἀλλ' ἐᾶτέ με αὐτὸν τὸν ἱερὸν τύμβον ἐξευρεῖν, ἵνα μοῖρ' ἀνδρὶ τῷδε τῇδε κρυφθῆναι χθονί — "But let me all alone Find out the sepulchre that destiny Appoints me (this man) in this land." Finally, in 1617f., Oedipus says to his daughters: τὸ γὰρ φιλεῖν οὐκ ἔστιν ἐξ ὅτου πλέον ἢ τοῦδε τἀνδρὸς ἔσχεθ' — And love from me (this man) ye had — from no man more."

The expression πρὸ ἐτῶν δεκατεσσάρων — 14 years ago — is Hellenistic in style, cf. Bl.-D. para. 213. Grammatically, it is joined to ἁρπαγέντα or to the ἡρπάγη in verse 4. As to the time when, dare we recall the dating of the prophetic visions (Isa. 61:1; Jer. 1:1ff.; 26:1; Ezek. 1:1; 3:16; 8:1; Amos 1:1; Hos. 1:1; Zech. 1:1; 7:1, etc.)? Hardly! Cf. Windisch, 373, concerning attempts to date the event chronologically.

εἴτε ἐν σώματι οὐκ οἶδα, εἴτε ἐκτὸς τοῦ σώματος οὐκ οἶδα, ὁ θεὸς οἶδεν. The parenthesis is intended to describe the strangeness of the event, for which not Paul but God alone is answerable. The terminology used to describe the ecstasy may not be harmonized with Paul's usual anthropological terminology. We might perhaps add τῆς σαρκός to the ἐν σώματι and the ἐκτὸς τοῦ σώματος. Paul knows nothing of an absolutely non-somatic existence!

Cf. Plot Enn V 5, 7 on the vision of the φῶς by the νοῦς — ὥστε ἀπορεῖν ὅθεν ἐφάνη, ἔξωθεν ἢ ἔνδον, καὶ ἀπελθόντος εἰπεῖν "ἔνδον ἄρα ἦν καὶ οὐκ ἔνδον αὖ" — "so that he does not know whence it appears, from without or within, and when it is gone says: 'so it was within and yet again not within.' "

ἁρπαγέντα τὸν τοιοῦτον ἕως τρίτου οὐρανοῦ. On the heavenly journey of the soul in ecstasy, cf. Lietzmann, 153f., and the article on ἔκστασις (Oepke) in TDNT II, 449-458. ἁρπάζεσθαι denotes miraculous rapture also in 1 Thess. 4:17, Acts 8:39, Revelation 12:5, and elsewhere; cf. Reitzenstein, HMR, 415, 1. The third heaven is conceived as highest, and containing Paradise (v. 4). In Judaism, at least from the second half of the second century (but probably even earlier), seven heavens were often listed. The idea of three heavens is older. Paradise is located in the third (or beyond it?), though seven heavens were listed. The locating of Paradise in the highest heaven is not documented (Dupont, *Gnosis,* 189, 1). Cf. Str.-B. III, 531-533, and Windisch, 371-373. Cf. also Windisch, 374-376, on the various forms of rapture-visions.

Verse 3: καὶ οἶδα τὸν τοιοῦτον ἄνθρωπον — εἴτε ἐν σώματι εἴτε χωρὶς τοῦ σώματος [οὐκ οἶδα], ὁ θεὸς οἶδεν. Verses 3f. are parallel to verse 2, though they read ὅτι ἡρπάγη instead of ἁρπαγέντα, εἰς τὸν παράδεισον (on this phrase, cf. on v. 2) instead of ἕως τρίτου οὐρανοῦ, and at the conclusion are expanded by the καὶ ἤκουσεν κτλ.

The experience of verses 3f. is naturally identical with that of verse 2. Clearly, verses 3f. are set off from verse 2 because in verse 2 only the fact of the rapture is indicated (the ἕως τρίτου οὐρανοῦ is a datum of place and belongs to the rapture as such), while in verse 3f. there is some intimation of the content of the experience and its glory.

Verse 4: ὅτι ἡρπάγη εἰς τὸν παράδεισον. Cf. Käsemann, ZNW 41, 1942, 65. On the location of Paradise, cf. on verse 2. The Rabbis distinguish 1) the Paradise of Adam, hidden after the Fall; 2) the heavenly Paradise, where the souls of the righteous linger between death and resurrection, and 3) the Paradise appearing at the end-time, identified throughout with the Paradise of Adam; cf. Str.-B. III, 533f.

καὶ ἤκουσεν ἄρρητα ῥήματα can mean both "words which cannot

be uttered" and "words which may not be uttered." In the second sense it would be used technically for formulae and teachings of the mysteries, as well as of apocalyptic (which of course recites such teaching, though the apocalypses are secret writings). Cf. the examples in Lietzmann, 154, and Windisch, 377f. The term is used here in the second sense, as is expressly stated — ἃ οὐκ ἐξὸν ἀνθρώπῳ λαλῆσαι.

According to Dupont, *Gnosis,* 189, 1, 190, the ἄρρητα ῥήματα correspond to 1 Cor. 2:9 (ἃ ὀφθαλμὸς οὐκ εἶδεν κτλ.), and do not refer to things which by nature are inexpressible, but to mysteries of the saving economy. Paul has thus seen the eschatological blessings of salvation, of which 1 Cor. 2:9 speaks(?).

Reitzenstein, HMR, 369, believes that ἀνθρώπῳ denotes more than τινί. Whoever is merely human, is not yet τέλειος, may not hear the words. The Corinthians are excluded. But in the context ἄνθρωπος hardly contains this antithesis (then of course it could not be the subject, but the addressee of λαλῆσαι). It certainly expresses more than a τίς, but the contrast is simply between the earthly and the heavenly, the human and the divine sphere.

By this definition the experience is clearly shown to be ecstatic-mystical, and as such is fundamentally different from the visions of Old Testament prophets or of the vision of Paul's call. These take their character from the commission to speak or proclaim what is seen and heard. What is at issue, then, is a mystical experience whose meaning is its *fruitio*. Peterson's statement in ZZ 3, 1925, 288 and 290 (versus Althaus, ZSTh 2, 1924, 281ff.) is thus correct, to the extent that Paul is speaking of the third heaven, not of Christ, to whom he first refers in verses 8-10. For Paul, Christ certainly does not denote the object of a *fruitio*, but rather the δύναμις of activity.

For just such an experience the use of the third person is characteristic. It is a mere happening toward which Paul need take no position, from which no consequences follow for his activity. The converse is true of the vision of his conversion which was also a vision of his call. It encountered him as persecutor, demanded recognition of Christ as his Lord, and gave him a commission. The one event involved an obligation to service, the other an added something, a heavenly delight. To this verse 5 corresponds.

Verse 5: ὑπὲρ τοῦ τοιούτου καυχήσομαι, ὑπὲρ δὲ ἐμαυτοῦ οὐ καυχήσομαι εἰ μὴ ἐν ταῖς ἀσθενείαις. The ὑπὲρ τοῦ τοιούτου is not neuter but masculine, harking back to the τοῦ τοιούτου in verses 2f., and again distancing Paul from his experience. The καυχᾶσθαι ὑπὲρ is equivalent to περί, cf. Bl.-D. para. 196, and (καυχᾶσθαι) ἐν denotes the object of boasting, as always in Paul.

Precisely because the experience is a mere happening for which Paul is not responsible, he may boast of it — which according to verse 6 would not be ἀφροσύνη, but rather ἀλήθεια. And thus he may do so because there is really no mention at all of him, but of the one who enraptured him. Insofar as he boasts with reference to himself, he may only boast of his weakness — which again takes us to the thought in 11:30 (Windisch gives the parallels in Plutarch, 381).

Verse 6: Before further confirmation is given the καυχήσομαι ἐν ταῖς ἀσθενείαις (vv. 7-10), Paul states that he of course would also have a right to boast. Thus he need not boast of his weakness because he would have no other choice — **ἐὰν γὰρ θελήσω καυχήσομαι, οὐκ ἔσομαι ἄφρων, ἀλήθειαν γὰρ ἐρῶ.** In contrast to verse 5, only ὑπὲρ ἐμαυτοῦ, ἐν ταῖς ὀπτασίαις καὶ ἀποκαλύψεσιν or the like may be added to καυχήσασθαι, and perhaps the καὶ τῇ ὑπερβολῇ τῶν ἀποκαλύψεων at the beginning of verse 7 is misplaced and belongs here after καυχήσασθαι.

In what sense can Paul say that if he were to boast of his pneumatic experiences he would still not be ἄφρων? Would ἀφροσύνη in that case be excluded by the fact that he would be speaking the truth and not lying? Must his opponents then be lying when they boast of their pneumatic experiences, and is a κατὰ σάρκα καυχᾶσθαι eliminated when one speaks the truth?! Paul too would be boasting κατὰ σάρκα, thus as ἄφρων, if he were to brag about his pneumatic experiences. Certainly! But at the moment Paul is not reflecting on them! Here, however, that he could boast of them without being ἄφρων can only mean that he would be speaking the truth. This is, of course, confirmed by the ἀλήθειαν γὰρ ἐρῶ. The sense then is, I could list still more experiences like that in verses 2-5; I have really had them.

The **φείδομαι δέ, μή τις εἰς ἐμὲ λογίσηται ὑπὲρ ὃ βλέπει με ἢ ἀκούει ἐξ ἐμοῦ** explains why Paul does not list more experiences. We need scarcely add a ὑμῶν to the φείδομαι, for a "sparing" such as in 1:23 and 13:2 is not at all the issue here, since further listing of pneumatic experiences cannot be described as a severe treatment of the community. Hence, as is often the case, φείδομαι is used without a qualifier — "I do without it, I forego it." λογίζεσθαι εἴς τινα is a commercial term, and means "to pen to someone's account, to credit."

The meaning cannot be that Paul wants to forestall all malicious distortion of his revelations, but merely that he will not impress the Corinthians with advantages which could bribe them. They should see him exactly as one who is ταπεινός and ἀσθενής, and recognize him as such; only in this way can they truly perceive the character of ζωή hidden beneath the mask of death (4:7ff.). His pneumatic experiences do not concern them at all (5:13; cf. p. 150), any more than does his speaking in tongues (1 Cor. 14:19). In these experiences he is not the apostle acting responsibly. He may encounter others only as apostle, thus in ἀσθένεια. Only in this fashion do his apostleship and message escape misunderstanding. (Käsemann, ZNW 41, 1942, 69 states that 12:6 reflects the fact that "he wants to be understood merely from the viewpoint of his διακονία"). For this reason,

Paul might also have written φείδομαι δέ, μή τις δόξῃ με καυχᾶσθαι κατὰ σάρκα, since in the Corinthians' eyes further listing of pneumatic experiences would appear to be a καυχᾶσθαι κατὰ σάρκα.

Verse 7: καὶ τῇ ὑπερβολῇ τῶν ἀποκαλύψεων. διὸ ἵνα μὴ ὑπεραίρωμαι, ἐδόθη μοι σκόλοψ τῇ σαρκί. Due to the διό which follows, the καὶ τῇ ὑπερβολῇ τῶν ἀποκαλύψεων should be linked to what precedes, which, however, is a grammatical impossibility. The attempts to link it to what precedes include: 1) construing the clause as a dative of relation with φείδομαι — "and I refrain from other divine revelations;" 2) construing it as dative, dependent on a τοῦ καυχᾶσθαι added to the φείδομαι; 3) construing the καὶ τῇ ὑπερβολῇ τῶν ἀποκαλύψεων as a distant object of καυχήσασθαι, so that what precedes from ἀλήθειαν γὰρ ἐρῶ onward (or from φείδομαι up to ἐμοῦ) would be a parenthesis, and 4) construing the καὶ τῇ ὑπερβολῇ τῶν ἀποκαλύψεων as a continuation of the ἐν ταῖς ἀσθενείαις in verse 5, so that all of verse 6 would be a parenthesis, which would alter the meaning to its opposite.[25]

If καὶ τῇ ὑπερβολῇ τῶν ἀποκαλύψεων belongs to what follows, then the διό must be omitted (thus as in P⁴⁶ ℵ D pl latsy Ir Or, versus ℵ A B bo G). Then the construction is smooth and the meaning clear. But can the secondary interpolation of διό be explained? Is there a greater corruption of the text here? Does the καὶ τῇ ὑπερβολῇ τῶν ἀποκαλύψεων belong behind the ἐὰν γὰρ θελήσω καυχήσασθαι, or behind the ἵνα μὴ ὑπεραίρωμαι at the end of verse 7?

At any rate, verses 7-9 yield the basis for Paul's point of view — for the καυχήσασθαι ἐν ταῖς ἀσθενείαις — by showing that even Paul had to learn that he was himself thrust into an ἀσθένεια whose meaning was later disclosed to him. As in Heb. 13:12 διό is an unemphatic anticipation of ἵνα (Molland, Serta Rudbergiana 49f.).

ἐδόθη μοι σκόλοψ τῇ σαρκί. The τῇ σαρκί gives the definition of place to ἐδόθη. The σκόλοψ is not an epexegetical comment on μοι (cf. Rom. 7:18), for the effect of suffering does not merely extend to the area of the σάρξ (cf. Radermacher, who writes that the μοι reinforces the verbal aspect).

σκόλοψ[26] (stake, splinter, thorn) is used figuratively of a bodily malady which persists despite repeated prayer (v. 8), thus obviously a chronic malady. As a counterforce opposing Paul, this suffering is described as an ἄγγελος σατανᾶ, thus as an expression of the antigodly cosmos which also threatens and entices the believer. (In Rabbinic usage, "thorn" is used for what causes pain, and not especially for sickness, Str.-B. III, 534); as early as in the LXX, שֵׂכִּים is translated σκόλοπες in Numbers 33:55).

---

[25] Should we read κατά instead of καί? (cf. Schmithals, *Gnosis*, 213f.).
[26] Cf. Kierkegaard, "The Thorn in the Flesh," passim, and *Concluding Unscientific Postscript*, 406f., where in connection with 2 Cor. 12:7 suffering is characterized as a mark of blessedness.

Of course, the ἵνα μὴ . . . ἐδόθη μοι already states that the suffering, and thus Satan, is in the service of the κύριος or of God. Finally, then, it is God himself who is encountered in the counterforce — a tenet which of course cannot be known and applied as a general truth, but only discovered in the struggle with suffering or with oneself. This struggle, as verses 8f. show, is played out in prayer. On the angel of Satan, cf. Damask 16:4f., and Reicke, SyBU 6, 1946, 18.

The ἵνα με κολαφίζῃ seems to indicate that the suffering was painful. For the rest, it is not to be diagnosed (cf. the attempts by Lietzmann, 156f. and Windisch, 385-388, who suggest hysteria [including diseases of the eye, cf. Gal. 4:15], epilepsy, headache and migraine, malaria, sciatica or intense rheumatism; cf. Preuschen, ZNW 2, 1901, 193-195, and Eisler, Ἰησοῦς Βασιλεύς II, 426-429, who suspect leprosy; cf. also the literature in Bauer under the term σκόλοψ). The diagnosis is irrelevant to the context, for the reason that the sickness in verse 10 appears on the same footing as the ὕβρεις, ἀνάγκαι, διωγμοί and στενοχωρίαι. The subsequent ἵνα μὴ ὑπεραίρωμαι is lacking in ℵ* A D G pc lat Ir and Chr. Is the omission a stylistic correction (Lietzmann, 155)? Regarding the onslaught of evil spirits as causing sickness, cf. Weinreich, *Heilungswunder,* 59f.

Verse 8: ὑπὲρ τούτου τρὶς τὸν κύριον παρεκάλεσα, ἵνα ἀποστῇ ἀπ᾽ ἐμοῦ. The ὑπὲρ τούτου is very likely masculine, since the subject of ἀποστῇ is the ἄγγελος τοῦ σατανᾶ. The κύριος is no doubt Jesus, cf. verse 9 — ἡ δύναμις τοῦ Χριστοῦ.

παρακαλεῖν means to call on; cf. Schlatter, *Josephus,* 74f. There are pagan examples in Deissmann, L.v.O. 121, 11; 261; and in Harder, *Gebet,* passim. τρίς denotes the thrice repeated prayer (such as Jesus' prayer in Gethsemane), frequently attested to in the Old Testament, in Judaism, as well in Greek literature, cf. Windisch, 389f., and Harder, 18.

Verse 9: καὶ εἴρηκέν μοι· ἀρκεῖ σοι ἡ χάρις μου. Clearly, this word of the Lord is not to be construed as something heard in an ecstatic experience. Verse 9 certainly does not belong with the ὀπτασίαι καὶ ἀποκαλύψεις, and the ἀρκεῖ σοι κτλ. is not an ἄρρητον ῥῆμα.

The ἀρκεῖ σοι is first of all a retort — "you will not get more," "you must make do with this." But because of the reason given — ἡ γὰρ δύναμις ἐν ἀσθενείᾳ τελεῖται — it takes on the meaning, "you can make do with this," "more is not needed," in fact, "this is all." To content oneself means really to have enough. So there is no resignation here as in Deut. 3:23ff., where to Moses' plea, "let me go over . . . and see the good land" God answers, "let it suffice you (רַב לָךְ; in the LXX, ἱκανούσθω σοι); speak no more to me of this matter!" The intention is exactly the same in Sifre Deuteronomy 3:26, cf. Windisch, 390f., and Fuchs, *Hermeneutik,* 236. The Stoic parallels, however, are not appropriate (cf. especially Epict Diss I, 1, 7-13; IV, 10, 14-16, and Windish, 390). Indeed, Epictetus' attitude is not that of resignation, content with a minimum which is conceded. What "suffices" for him is what is κράτιστον and κυριεῦον, the power of the spirit. Further, pride in this possession and in the inner freedom and dignity won through it is not a καυχᾶσθαι κατὰ σάρκα or ἐν προσώπῳ. The spirit, not subjectivity, is God's gift. Vanity or a view which compares oneself with others is alien to Epictetus.

The difference, however, lies in the differing conception of human ἀσθένεια and the divine δύναμις. While for Paul they are both experiences, for the Stoic they are conditions or qualities. For Paul ἀσθένεια is a human nothingness brought to consciousness in experiences, not a lack impairing one's essential nature. The δύναμις is not the spirit in a person's possession, but the transcendent divine power undergone or effective in the experience. In the Stoa the spirit or δύναμις marks the person's endowment with a portion of the divine essence attaching to him by nature; ἀσθένεια denotes a lack in the person's natural equipment (the term is undialectic, and does not denote the person in his nothingness). The Stoa thus assesses ἀσθένεια in purely negative fashion as a person's encumbrance with bodily existence, and the captivity to fate mediated through it. Since this sphere cannot be viewed as ἐφ' ἡμῖν, it should also not be viewed as πρὸς ἡμᾶς. That is, the meaning of history (as a giving and taking) is eliminated. Fate has nothing to do with the person. This retreat to the inner life corresponds to the notion that the inner life is really ἐφ' ἡμῖν, that is, that the divine graciousness is at a person's disposal or risk, and is not encountered as experience. For Paul, however, it is not true that whatever is not ἐφ' ἡμῖν is also not πρὸς ἡμᾶς. Rather, what is οὐκ ἐφ' ἡμῖν is precisely of import πρὸς ἡμᾶς (— assuming that it is grasped by faith. No, not only then!).

Here, χάρις and δύναμις are in essence synonymous, just as in verse 9 the δύναμις τοῦ Χριστοῦ appears in place of the χάρις of the κύριος; cf. on 1:12, p. 34. The Hellenistic idea of χάρις is thus present here, which indeed for Paul never loses its significance as the gracious intent and activity of God. The χάρις with which Paul must be content is the power for action given him as apostle. Cf. Gal. 2:9: γνόντες τὴν χάριν τὴν δοθεῖσάν μοι . . . (Gal. 1:15: ὁ . . . καλέσας διὰ τῆς χάριτος αὐτοῦ).

The Hellenistic concept of χάρις serves to interpret the gracious act of Paul's calling as a force marking his entire life. Schlatter, *Glaube*, 285, 1, is of a somewhat different opinion: "Note 2 Cor. 12:9. What Paul gains and shares with the community from his ecstatic communion with Christ [but may v. 9 be taken as a reply heard in ecstatic communion with Christ?] is the word which points him to the grace of Christ; it is the confirmation of that state of faith which he derived from knowledge of the crucified and risen Lord." Then χάρις is not understood as the grace of the apostolic office, but as saving grace given the believer, an improbable but possible interpretation. In that case, it is also true that the Hellenistic concept of χάρις serves to interpret the saving grace as the power determining one's entire life.

χάρις is not tranquil possession, but must be understood and seized anew in every present moment. This is precisely what the ἀρκεῖ σοι ἡ χάρις μου teaches, and above all the ἡ γὰρ δύναμις ἐν ἀσθενείᾳ τελεῖται, which intimates that the one shown grace in struggle with ἀσθένεια must make sure of χάρις, must stand the test moment by moment in order to experience χάρις as δύναμις. ἀσθένεια is the situation in which — or the experience by which — the fact of one's being nothing is brought painfully to consciousness. At the same time it is this nothingness itself from out of which the person lays hold on grace, or seizes the grace which seizes him (Phil. 3:12; thus the reference to one's nothingness is dialectical). The alternation of singular (11:30; 12:9a) and plural (12:5, 9b) indicates that the individual ἀσθένειαι yield proof of the underlying ἀσθένεια. The test consists in whether one learns to understand human nothingness in the individual ἀσθένεια, whether with that one abandons the illusion of being able to be something from out of oneself. If one stands the test, then it is true that ἡ δύναμις . . . τελεῖται, which means that it achieves fulfillment— realized, of course, only in the given moment that possibility becomes reality. In this fashion ἀσθένεια is the condition for realization of the δύναμις, just as death is the condition for the φανερωθῆναι of the ζωὴ τοῦ Ἰησοῦ in 4:10f. Cf. 4:16 and 4:7: ἔχομεν δὲ τὸν θησαυρὸν τοῦτον ἐν ὀστρακίνοις σκεύεσιν, ἵνα ἡ ὑπερβολὴ τῆς δυνάμεως ᾖ τοῦ θεοῦ καὶ μὴ ἐξ ἡμῶν. τελεῖν here does fashion ἀσθένεια is the condition for realization of the δύναμις, just as death is the condition for the φανερωθῆναι of the ζωὴ τοῦ Ἰησοῦ in 4:10f. Cf. 4:16 and 4:7: ἔχομεν δὲ τὸν θησαυρὸν τοῦτον ἐν ὀστρακίνοις σκεύεσιν, ἵνα ἡ ὑπερβολὴ τῆς δυνάμεως ᾖ τοῦ θεοῦ καὶ μὴ ἐξ ἡμῶν. τελεῖν here does not mean to bring what is begun to an end, as does ἐπιτελεῖν in Phil. 1:6 (the antonym is ἐνάρχεσθαι), in Gal. 3:3 (likewise), or as τελεῖν in 2 Tim. 4:7; Matt. 7:28; 10:23; 11:1, etc., and especially in the Apocalypse. Rather, it means "to bring to realization." It is used of the fulfilling of the law in Rom. 2:27; Luke 2:39 and James 2:8; of the ἐπιθυμία σαρκός in Gal. 5:16; of the fulfillment of promise in Luke 12:50; 18:31; 22:37; and Acts 13:29 (John 19:28, 30), and of the payment of taxes in Rom. 13:6 and Matt. 17:24.

From the answer of the κύριος Paul draws the consequence — **ἥδιστα οὖν μᾶλλον καυχήσομαι ἐν ταῖς ἀσθενείαις**.

The ἥδιστα and μᾶλλον do not belong together but should read, "happily (a fixed elative in the superlative) will I rather. . . ." Cf. Bl.-D. para. 246. καυχᾶσθαι ἐν is used just as in verse 5 — "of my weaknesses."

Thus, from the fact that δύναμις is realized in ἀσθένεια results a paradoxical καυχᾶσθαι which is not a καυχᾶσθαι κατὰ σάρκα, but has radically surrendered it. In this way, what is stated in 11:30 and 12:5 is established. The admission of one's own nothingness leads one to look to the divine χάρις or δύναμις — **ἵνα ἐπισκηνώσῃ ἐπ' ἐμὲ ἡ δύναμις τοῦ Χριστοῦ**.

This makes clear that the χάρις or δύναμις actualizes itself moment by moment, that it is experienced moment by moment as given anew. (Does the ἐπισκηνώσῃ hide an allusion to the שְׁכִינָא? Cf. John 1:14 in Leisegang, *Pneuma*, 31,1.)

Verse 10: This verse shows that in essence this paradoxical καυχᾶσθαι does not occur in a boasting with words toward others, but in the joyful shouldering of suffering — **διὸ εὐδοκῶ ἐν ἀσθενείαις, ἐν ὕβρεσιν, ἐν ἀνάγκαις, ἐν διωγμοῖς καὶ στενοχωρίαις, ὑπὲρ Χριστοῦ.**

The term εὐδοκεῖν is the equivalent of the Hebrew חָפֵץ בְּ (appearing, for example, in Isa. 62:4; cf. Bl.-D. para. 196; 206, 2). It not only means, "to take pleasure," but also "to consent to," "to approve of," "to say 'Yes' to."

The ὑπὲρ Χριστοῦ belongs to εὐδοκῶ and not to the list of crises. At issue in the context cannot be the ready assumption of suffering for Christ's sake, but rather readiness for ἀσθένεια as such, and which is affirmed for Christ's sake, that is, precisely ἵνα ἐπισκηνώσῃ κτλ. (v. 9). This is clear also from the reason given in the phrase **ὅταν γὰρ ἀσθενῶ, τότε δυνατός εἰμι,** which expresses once more in paradoxical form the truth of verse 9a — ἡ γὰρ δύναμις ἐν ἀσθενείᾳ τελεῖται. Is this true only of the apostle, or of every believer? Is the χάρις in verse 8 only the grace of office given the apostle? Hardly! And it is scarcely the grace of salvation rather than the indirect gift of δύναμις. Just as 4:7ff. begin with the apostle, and at 4:16ff. alter to a description of believers (cf. 5:1-11), so also here.

After the ἐν ἀσθενείαις a catalogue of crises — which either continues the ἐν ἀσθενείαις or explains it in appositional fashion, in any case illustrates the concept of ἀσθένεια — lists the kind of situations in which a καυχᾶσθαι ἐν ἀσθενείαις occurs.

ἀνάγκαι and στενοχωρίαι are also combined in the list of trials in 6:4. ἀνάγκη and θλῖψις occur in 1 Thess. 3:7 (θλίψεις also appears with ἀνάγκη and στενοχωρία in 6:4).

στενοχωρία is combined with θλῖψις in Rom. (2:9) 8:35 in the list of crises along with διωγμός, etc. (Cf. the ἐν παντὶ θλιβόμενοι ἀλλ' οὐ στενοχωρούμενοι in the list of trials of 4:8).

In the list of trials in Rom. 8:35, διωγμοί is in the singular (cf. above). Cf. διωκόμενοι in the list of 4:9 and of 1 Corinthians 4:12. ὕβρεις appears in the list (and in Paul) only here, but cf. the προπαθόντες καὶ ὑβρισθέντες . . .ἐν Φιλίπποις in 1 Thess. 2:2. The καυχᾶσθαι ἐν ταῖς ἀσθενείαις, which is described and given its basis here, is strangely different from the καυχᾶσθαι ἐν ταῖς θλίψεσιν in Rom. 5:3. While in 2 Cor. 12 the reason for καυχᾶσθαι lies in the present experience of the δύναμις τοῦ Χριστοῦ, in Romans 5 it lies in the hope growing out of θλῖψις by way of ὑπομονή and δοκιμή. Naturally, the reason given in 2 Corinthians 12 does not exclude that given in Romans 5. Cf. 4:7-18, where the ζωή at work in θάνατος is, of course, a present reality, though with a view to the future, as 5:1-10 expressly states. Conversely, the reason given in Romans 5 does not exclude that in 2 Corinthians 12. But it is characteristic that Paul can convey that thought by itself without the other.

The experience that the struggle with suffering, that the overcoming of weakness increases power, is universally human and is clearly expressed, for example, in the Stoa. Cf. Epict Diss I, 6, 37-43, and Philo, Vit Mos I, 67-69, where Philo explains the burning bush as a parable τοῦ μὴ πρὸς τῶν ἐπιτιθεμένων φθαρήσεσθαι τοὺς ἀδικουμένους (67): "That the sufferers would not be destroyed by their aggressors." The parable summons the sufferers (τοῖς ἐν συμφοραῖς) as it were μὴ ἀναπίπτετε (do not lose heart), τὸ ἀσθενὲς ὑμῶν δύναμίς ἐστιν . . . ἀλλ᾽ ὅταν μάλιστα πορθεῖν νομίσῃ τις ὑμᾶς, τότε μάλιστα πρὸς εὔκλειαν ἐκλάμψετε ("Your weakness is your strength. . . . Nay, just when the enemy is surest of ravaging you, your fame will shine forth most gloriously." Cf. Windisch, 394). For Philo, of course, no reason is given for it, and the inner connection between ἀσθένεια and δύναμις is not made clear. There is simply reference to the πρόνοια of God who changes evil into good.

In the Stoa (and thus, for example, in the conclusion to Spitteler's *Olympische Frühling*[2]), on the other hand, the inner connection between suffering and power is manifest in the sense that the struggle with suffering is the necessary ἄσκησις by which power is awakened and shaped. But the power is that of the νοῦς, the λογικόν which learns in suffering to effect the difference between ἐφ᾽ ἡμῖν and οὐκ ἐφ᾽ ἡμῖν (things which thus are οὐ πρὸς ἡμᾶς, ἀπροαιρετικά, ἀλλότρια). It is in this action that power grows; its growth is the work of self-education.

The difference from Paul is twofold: First, in the Stoa sufferings or ἀσθένεια are understood as something which simply cannot affect man's true existence. They are not πρὸς ἡμᾶς, because our outward conditions of life, our destiny is not ἐφ᾽ ἡμῖν. And in this knowledge consists the very conquest of sufferings. For Paul ἀσθένεια characterizes the actual existence of humans as human, and of course it is not a natural quality, deriving perhaps from the imperfection of one's σῶμα, but it is the ἀσθένεια of the "I" brought to consciousness in the given historical situation. In recognition of it lies the possibility of its conquest through δύναμις. But — and herein lies the second difference — the δύναμις does not belong to one's natural equipment. It is not the power of his λογικόν as in the Stoa, but is at the same time χάρις, a gift of divine grace. Cf. Epict Diss I, 6, 37: ἀπόβλεψον εἰς τὰς δυνάμεις ἃς ἔχεις καὶ ἀπιδὼν εἰπέ· "Φέρε νῦν, ὦ Ζεῦ, ἣν θέλεις περίστασιν· ἔχω γὰρ παρασκευὴν ἐκ σοῦ μοι δεδομένην καὶ ἀφορμὰς πρὸς τὸ κοσμῆσαι διὰ τῶν ἀποβαινόντων ἐμαυτόν; ("contemplate the faculties which you have, and, after contemplating, say: 'Bring now, O Zeus, what difficulty Thou wilt; for I have an equipment given to me by Thee, and resources wherewith to distinguish myself by making use of the things that come to pass.'"). Cf. 6:40: God gave not only these δυνάμεις, but also full freedom for their use. Cf. also Sen Ep 41, 5, in which a man unbowed by misfortune awakens this impression: vis isto divina descendit ("'A divine power has descended upon that man.'"). An *animus* which remains untouched by all evil and good fate, evokes this judgment: Non potest res tanta sine adminiculo numinis stare; itaque maiore sui parte illic est unde descendit ("A thing like this cannot stand upright unless it be propped by the divine. Therefore, a greater part of it abides in that place from whence it came down to earth."). As sunbeams touch the earth, but as it were originate from it, sic animus magnus ac sacer et in hoc demissus, ut proprius [quidem] divina nossemus, conversatur quidem nobiscum sed haeret origini suae ("even so the great and hallowed soul, which has come down in order that we may have a nearer knowledge of divinity, does indeed associate with us, but still cleaves to its origin."). Despite the relationship in terminology, man's "spirit" here is conceived as a possession at his disposal. Hence, in the Stoa there is that idea of education (self-education) which is lacking in Paul. In Paul, on the other hand, there is the idea of gift. This does not serve the formation of the "I," it does not serve καρτερία in a closing oneself off from encounters or from fate, but serves mastery of the given situation in ὑπομονή or in the obedience of service. For Paul, therefore, the divine δύναμις need not be visible as σωφροσύνη, σοφία, καρτερία and the like, though it can manifest itself in relationship, in that which the one means for the other. Cf. 4:12; 13:3f. Naturally, σωφροσύνη, etc. can also be effective in service to others.

Conclusion to the καυχᾶσθαι: 12:11-18

12:11-12 takes up the conclusion of the καυχᾶσθαι theme. To an extent, Paul looks back upon the role of the ἄφρων which he had played out to the end. But if in verse 11 he appears alongside himself, as it were, interpreting his performance in the role, in verses 12f. he continues his καυχᾶσθαι, and of course comparing himself with the ὑπερλίαν ἀπόστολοι as he had done in 11:5, and over against them describing his equality in the sense of 11:22ff. But in doing so he immediately returns in verse 13 to the theme of an apostle's rights, corresponding to 11:7. And just as 11:7-15 was an insertion (cf. p. 205), here again an excursus on the same theme is added in verses 13-18, which is not occasioned by the context, but motivated by the reproaches and incitements of his opponents.

Verse 11. The phrase γέγονα ἄφρων is either a pause in reference to 11:1, or harks back to 11:16. ὑμεῖς με ἠναγκάσατε means, therefore, "you bear the responsibility for it!" How the Corinthians have forced him to it is stated in what follows — ἐγὼ γὰρ ὤφειλον ὑφ' ὑμῶν συνίστασθαι, "for I ought to have been commended by you" (as in classical Greek, the imperfect is used without the ἄν to denote necessity, cf. Bl.-D. para. 358, 1). Why would it have been their duty? Paul certainly needs no commendation! Cf. 3:1. What the community would require for its own sake is expressed as the Corinthians' duty, that is, that they recognize the superiority of Paul and his gospel over his rivals. This recognition would have been concretely expressed in their commending or boasting of him. Cf.1:14 (p. 36) and 5:12 (p. 147). Naturally, for his own sake, Paul does not need their commendation.

οὐδὲν γὰρ ὑστέρησα τῶν ὑπερλίαν ἀποστόλων. This clause gives the reason for the ἐγὼ γὰρ ὤφειλον κτλ. by repeating the clause in 11:5 with the modification that a specific οὐδὲν ὑστέρησα now appears in place of the λογίζομαι γὰρ μηδὲν ὑστερηκέναι, and that as a result of the aorist ὑστέρησα the clause does not remain a general assertion, but is spoken with reference to the activity at Corinth, as the κατειργάσθη ἐν ὑμῖν in verse 12 confirms. Above all, the clause is strangely highlighted by the addition of εἰ καὶ οὐδέν εἰμι. Is it sharpest irony — "though I am nothing in your eyes"? Or, is it the highest pathos of seriousness in the sense of 12:5-10 (cf. 1 Cor. 15:9f.) — "though I credit myself with none of it, because the divine δύναμις accomplished it all"? In any case it is an aside, since verse 12 gives the reason for the οὐδὲν ὑστέρησα.

Verse 12: τὰ μὲν σημεῖα τοῦ ἀποστόλου κατειργάσθη ἐν ὑμῖν. The τὰ σημεῖα τοῦ ἀποστόλου was evidently a fixed term or slogan. Miracles of all kinds, denoted by **σημείοις τε καὶ τέρασιν καὶ δυνάμεσιν**, are taken for such σημεῖα, without any sharp demarcation of the three concepts (the instrumental dative). There was no mention of this in 11:12ff., since Paul's opponents could also have boasted of it, and it would not have given the reason for the ὑπὲρ ἐγώ (11:23).

σημεῖον was a common label for miracle (also in Hellenistic Greek). τέρας (differently than with τὰ σημεῖα!) is the arresting-startling phenomenon caused by the deity. In the New Testament it denotes simply miracle, but is used in combination with σημεῖον and in the plural (except in Acts 2:19 according to Joel 2:30, or in the LXX 3:3). σημεῖα καὶ τέρατα, or τέρατα καὶ σημεῖα appear in Rom. 15:19; 2 Thess. 2:9; Mark 13:22; Matt. 24:24; John 4:48; Acts 2:43; and often. In this context, δύναμις really denotes the power to do miracles, as is often the case in the magical papyri (cf. Rom. 15:19: ἐν δυνάμει σημείων καὶ τεράτων), and then the miraculous deed itself (also in Hellenistic Greek) as in Gal. 3:5; 1 Cor. 12:28f.; Mark 6:2-5, etc. As here, it is combined with σημεῖα and τέρατα in Heb. 2:4 and Acts 2:22. Cf. 2 Thess. 2:9: ἐν πάσῃ δυνάμει καὶ σημείοις καὶ τέρασιν ψεύδους. It is used only with σημεῖα in Acts 8:13. Cf. the Old Testament combination of אֹתֹת וּמֹפְתִים in Exod. 7:3; Deut. 4:34; 6:22; Isa. 8:18 (the LXX has σημεῖα καὶ τέρατα throughout), etc. The same combination appears in Josephus, cf. Schlatter, *Josephus,* 52, and Asc. of Isa. 3, 20.

The fact that such miracles prove the apostle's identity is shown also in 6:6f. (cf. p. 172); 1 Cor. 2:4f.; Rom. 15:19; 1 Thess. 1:5; Heb. 2:4; and Mark 16:17-20. What Paul elsewhere regards as proof — the success of his mission (3:2; 1 Cor. 9:2) — is not named here, not even the sight of the resurrected One (1 Cor. 9:1 and Acts 1:21f.). If the second proof is omitted here, then it is clear that the opponents at Corinth cannot be Judaizers (or even the original apostles). And the first is lacking because at issue here is the use of such titles as the opponents can also exhibit. In the use of such, Paul is not inferior to them.

The miracles may have been healings of the sick, pneumatic events such as glossolalia, and very likely "conversions with special accompanying circumstances" (Windisch, 397).

The passive κατειργάσθη is characteristic, and indicates that Paul is not conscious of himself as θεῖος ἀνήρ. Cf. Rom. 15:18f.: οὐ γὰρ τολμήσω τι λαλεῖν ὧν οὐ κατειργάσατο Χριστὸς δι᾽ ἐμοῦ εἰς ὑπακοὴν ἐθνῶν, λόγῳ καὶ ἔργῳ, ἐν δυνάμει σημείων καὶ τεράτων, ἐν δυνάμει πνεύματος.

Characteristic also is the **ἐν πάσῃ ὑπομονῇ** prefixed to the σημείοις τε καὶ τέρασιν, which describes the κατειργάσθη, and which of course implies "under difficult circumstances" (Lietzmann, 158), but above all expressly states "I have not grown weary by it," "I have done my part." Cf. the emphasis on ὑπομονή in 6:4.

Paul reminds the Corinthians of things which they know, which they must concede. For this reason they cannot deny the οὐδὲν γὰρ ὑστέρησα in verse 11.

But how is the μέν to be construed? Did Paul originally intend to enumerate still further reasons for the οὐδὲν ὑστέρησα by a subsequent δέ (Windisch, 396)? Hardly! A transitional thought should be added which then gives the reason for verse 13 — "but you are still not content? You certainly can lack nothing!"

Verse 13: τί γάρ ἐστιν ὃ **ἡσσώθητε ὑπὲρ τὰς λοιπὰς ἐκκλησίας.** ἡσσώθητε is used instead of the Attic ἡττώθητε, cf. Bl.-D. para. 34, 1, and means "to succumb, to be at a disadvantage, to be inferior to." ὑπέρ is used instead of the classical genitive, occasioned by the comparative implied in the verb.

Evidently, Paul's opponents represented him as having preferred other communities to the Corinthian community, if they did not actually state that, when compared to others, the Pauline communities were not at all truly apostolic. In any case, as the εἰ μὴ κτλ. indicates, they used Paul's waiver of apostolic rights to persuade the Corinthians that he did not act toward them as a genuine apostle. How effective this strategy was is shown by the fact that following 11:7-11 Paul returns to it again, and dwells on it in verses 14-18 (cf. p. 204).

εἰ μὴ ὅτι αὐτὸς ἐγὼ οὐ κατενάρκησα ὑμῶν. The formulation is similar to that in 11:9, cf. p. 206. Paul must allow this reproach to stand, but he does so with the same irony as in 11:7, this time by begging pardon for it — χαρίσασθέ μοι τὴν ἀδικίαν ταύτην. In this sense the ἀδικία corresponds to the ἁμαρτία of 11:7; cf. p. 205.

With the αὐτὸς ἐγώ Paul sets himself off from his rivals — "for myself, I" ("even I," Lietzmann, 158) — and at the same time aims a blow at his opponents who exploit the community (v. 20), since the αὐτὸς ἐγώ is scarcely in contrast to Paul's envoys in verses 17f.

With this theme the role of the ἄφρων is abandoned. Just as the comparison with his opponents in verse 13, so also the apology in verses 14-18 is made without ἀφροσύνη.

Verse 14: ἰδοὺ τρίτον τοῦτο ἑτοίμως ἔχω ἐλθεῖν πρὸς ὑμᾶς. The τρίτον τοῦτο ("now for the third time") does not belong with ἑτοίμως ἔχω, but rather with ἐλθεῖν, since what is "thrice" resolved has no significance for the context. The chief thing is that at his third visit Paul will not behave differently than earlier. (For the different visits cf. 13:1f.; 1:15; and 2:1.) The notice of the third visit here is not as in 13:1 an end in itself, but is subordinated to the theme. Verse 14 does not begin a new section. Rather, it further explains the καταναρκᾶν of verse 13, and the accent is on the καὶ οὐ καταναρκήσω. The meaning is thus, "now when I come to you for the third time, I will. . . ."

καὶ οὐ καταναρκήσω. The affirmation is the same as in 11:12 — Paul will keep to his previous behavior. The motivation of course is different than in 11:12 — οὐ γὰρ ζητῶ τὰ ὑμῶν ἀλλὰ ὑμᾶς. His motive is to win the community's love, and is thus his love for the community, as 11:11 implied and as verse 15 states. On the formulation cf. 8:5: καὶ οὐ καθὼς ἠλπίσαμεν, ἀλλὰ ἑαυτοὺς ἔδωκαν. Cf. Cic Fin II, 26, 85: me igitur ipsum ames oportet non mea, si veri amici futuri sumus. Cf. also Phil. 4:17: οὐχ ὅτι ἐπιζητῶ τὸ δόμα, ἀλλὰ ἐπιζητῶ τὸν καρπὸν τὸν πλεονάζοντα εἰς λόγον ὑμῶν. It may be that, as in verse 16, the clause harks back to the reproach that Paul intends, by cunning, to enrich himself at the community's expense, but in any case it is spoken with a view to his opponents who enrich themselves from the community and are totally ignorant of the true relation between an apostle and the community. It is this very relationship which is accented by the figure in the following clause: οὐ γὰρ ὀφείλει τὰ τέκνα τοῖς γονεῦσιν θησαυρίζειν, ἀλλὰ οἱ γονεῖς τοῖς τέκνοις. The οὐ γὰρ ὀφείλει marks the clause as a νόμος φύσεως (Chrysostom), cf. 1 Cor. 11:14.

In the figure, θησαυρίζειν denotes the acquiring of capital for an inheritance, cf. Philo Vit Mos II, 245: νόμος φύσεώς ἐστι κληρονομεῖσθαι γονεῖς ὑπὸ παίδων ἀλλὰ μὴ τούτους κληρονομεῖν ("that the sons are the heirs of their fathers and not fathers of their sons").

The fact that this νόμος φύσεως contradicts the dominical saying in 1 Cor. 9:14 is not considered, nor is the fact that in other situations Paul could accept money from his communities. The reasons for this are: 1) like an adage, the clause yields a general truth which has its application in the given instance and thus in the present case, but not as a binding law for every instance (for example, parents not capable of earning their living must be provided for by their sons, Windisch, 399f.); 2) Paul speaks under the assumption that his relationship to the community is not a legal one (to which 1 Cor. 9:3ff. would apply), but a relationship of love, that of father to his children. In that case, then, the νόμος φύσεως holds true. But precisely in that case the possibility is not excluded that under other circumstances Paul may receive a contribution from communities such as Philippi. Thus as its application we must add to the simile, "I am your father;" "after all, we are (or should be) related as father to child."

Verse 15: ἐγὼ δὲ ἥδιστα δαπανήσω καὶ ἐκδαπανηθήσομαι ὑπὲρ τῶν ψυχῶν ὑμῶν. The simile is applied to the concrete case. The formulation is rhetorical, cf. 1 Cor. 6:12: πάντα μοι ἔξεστιν, ἀλλ᾽ οὐκ ἐγὼ ἐξουσιασθήσομαι ὑπό τινος. Cf. especially Sen Dial I, V, 4: boni viri . . . impendunt, impenduntur et volentes quidem. ("Good men . . . spend, and are spent, and withal willingly.")

The ἥδιστα is a fixed elative in the superlative form (cf. v. 9) and means, "gladly," "with joy."

The δαπανήσω, to which also the ὑπὲρ τῶν ψυχῶν ὑμῶν (for your life, for you) belongs, naturally does not mean that Paul is spending money on behalf of the Corinthian community, but that he spares it such expense by providing for his own stay. The ἐκδαπανηθήσομαι makes clear that Paul is sacrificing himself totally, is consumed in service to the community, as for example 11:28f describe. Cf. Phil. 2:17.

The motive for Paul's waiver of rights (cf. 11:10) in his καύχησις is not under consideration here. It is naturally not excluded by the motive of ἀγάπη, or vice versa. Both motives may be connected — this is his καύχησις, that he acts only out of ἀγάπη. His behavior appears under the aspect of καύχησις where his relation to his opponents is concerned.

If the rhetorical question in 12:13 is in reality already answered by verses 14 and 15a, then the rhetorical question which follows in verse 15b answers it once more, and at the same time describes Paul's love for the community as quite special: εἰ περισσοτέρως ὑμᾶς ἀγαπῶ, ἧσσον ἀγαπῶμαι? Does the περισσοτέρως mean, more than others do? No, for in that case an ἐγώ (αὐτός) would have to appear. Or does it mean, more than my other communities, or, more than is required? Or is it to be construed in correlation with ἧσσον — "the more I love you, the less should I be loved by you?"

If we read εἰ καὶ (ℜ pl vg) περισσοτέρως ὑμᾶς ἀγαπῶν (P⁴⁶ B ℜ D G pl latt) ἧσσον ἀγαπῶμαι, then the clause would have to be linked to what precedes — "even if I, though I love you more, am loved the less." But the rhetorical question, which is more forceful in the context and more characteristic of Paul, is still the more probable reading. ἀγαπῶν is thus an old scribal error (Lietzmann, 158).

In any event, Paul wishes to make the community aware of how ungrateful it is when it listens to slander.

Verse 16: ἔστω δὲ, ἐγὼ οὐ κατεβάρησα ὑμᾶς· ἀλλὰ ὑπάρχων πανοῦργος δόλῳ ὑμᾶς ἔλαβον. On κατεβάρησα cf. 11:9, etc. (p. 206), and on πανοῦργος and δόλος cf. 4:2 (p. 101). ἔλαβον is used as in 11:20 (p. 212) and means to catch. ἔστω δὲ κτλ. means, "though you must admit that I have taken no money from you, still I could be reproached for indirectly exploiting you!" Does Paul merely intend to weigh and reject every possibility? Or was this accusation actually made? The fact that verses 17f. take up the subject renders it likely. The accusation might have been attached to the raising of the collection (cf. v. 18). Of course this reproach contradicts the other (if it was made, cf. p. 207 on 11:11), that for lack of love Paul accepts nothing from the Corinthians, but different accusations might have been made by different parties.

Verse 17: μή τινα ὧν ἀπέσταλκα πρὸς ὑμᾶς, δι᾽ αὐτοῦ ἐπλεονέκτησα ὑμᾶς. τινά precedes without syntactical connection and is taken up again by the δι᾽ αὐτοῦ, cf. Bl.-D. para. 466, 1.

The ὧν is the equivalent of τούτων οὕς.

ἀπέσταλκα is in the perfect instead of the aorist tense, and as in 11:25 is without motivation, cf. Bl.-D. para. 343, 2. On ἐπλεονέκτησα cf. 7:2 (p. 178). It appears that Paul has been suspected of embezzling money from the Corinthians through his envoys. Verse 18 repeats the rhetorical question in more specific form.

Verse 18: παρεκάλεσα Τίτον καὶ συναπέστειλα τὸν ἀδελφόν. παρεκάλεσα, that is to say, ἵνα ἔρχηται πρὸς ὑμᾶς or the like (Windisch, 403). As to the τὸν ἀδελφόν, was the person originally named? Cf. 8:18, 22. The sending of Titus to Corinth must have taken place earlier.[27] But it cannot be the sending of Titus in the matter of the collection referred to in 8:6, 16-24, for Chapter 8 must have been written after Chapter 9, and is best joined to 7:16, thus belonging to D, Paul's fourth letter to the Corinthians.

Now according to 8:10, the collection at Corinth had been taken as early as ἀπὸ πέρυσι, and 12:18 clearly refers back to it. The time is naturally that between B (1 Corinthians) and C (the interim epistle), to which Chapters 10–13 belong.

The brother sent along with Titus can only have been a subordinate assistant. μήτι ἐπλεονέκτησεν ὑμᾶς Τίτος; οὐ τῷ αὐτῷ πνεύματι περιεπατήσαμεν; οὐ τοῖς αὐτοῖς ἴχνεσιν. It is assumed that the Corinthians must answer "No!" (Then it is not clear whether the sending of Titus concerned the collection, for the Corinthians certainly could not control the use of the money gathered by Titus.) "So you could accuse neither my envoys nor myself of cunning exploitation!"

The charge that the proof of Paul's unimpeachability is circular, since he seeks to prove his innocence by appeal to Titus, and seeks to prove

---

[27] In his *Introduction*, IV, 2, 67, Goguel naturally wants to interpret 12:18 on the basis of 8:6.

Titus' unimpeachability by virtue of sharing common cause with himself, can nevertheless not be maintained (Windisch, 404). As far as Titus is concerned, a simple inspection should be convincing enough.

Should the τῷ αὐτῷ πνεύματι be supplemented with a τοῦ Χριστοῦ, and the τοῖς αὐτοῖς ἴχνεσιν with an ἐν Χριστῷ? Or do the clauses simply mean, "in the same spirit, in the same steps as I?" The latter!

3. The threat of δοκιμή at the third visit: 12:19–13:10

Have you been thinking all along that we have been defending ourselves before you? It is in the sight of God that we have been speaking in Christ, and all for your upbuilding, beloved. For I fear that perhaps I may come and find you not what I wish, and that you may find me not what you wish; that perhaps there may be quarreling, jealousy, anger, selfishness, slander, gossip, conceit, and disorder. I fear that when I come again my God may humble me before you, and I may have to mourn over many of those who sinned before and have not repented of the impurity, immorality, and licentiousness which they have practiced. This is the third time I am coming to you. Any charge must be sustained by the evidence of two or three witnesses. I warned those who sinned before and all the others, and I warn them now while absent, as I did when present on my second visit, that if I come again I will not spare them — since you desire proof that Christ is speaking in me. He is not weak in dealing with you, but is powerful in you. For he was crucified in weakness, but lives by the power of God. For we are weak in him, but in dealing with you we shall live with him by the power of God. Examine yourselves, to see whether you are holding to your faith. Test yourselves. Do you not realize that Jesus Christ is in you? — unless indeed you fail to meet the test! I hope you will find out that we have not failed. But we pray God that you may not do wrong — not that we may appear to have met the test, but that you may do what is right, though we may seem to have failed. For we cannot do anything against the truth, but only for the truth. For we are glad when we are weak and you are strong. What we pray for is your improvement. I write this while I am away from you, in order that when I come I may not have to be severe in my use of the authority which the Lord has given me for building up and not for tearing down.

After settling with his opponents Paul returns to 10:1-11, especially to 10:7-11, and threatens to make formal appearance at his impending visit. Basically, everything said in 10:12–12:18 is an excursus.

a. The threat: 12:19–13:4

Verse 19: πάλαι δοκεῖτε ὅτι ὑμῖν ἀπολογούμεθα. 10:12—12:18, and particularly 12:11-18, could be misconstrued as Paul's defense before the forum of the community, but should not be understood in this way. Paul cannot recognize the community as a judicial body, and his words are not a justification in face of it. Both the ὑμῖν as well as the ἀπολογούμεθα are accented, and the following clauses relate to both: 1) The κατέναντι θεοῦ ἐν Χριστῷ λαλοῦμεν corresponds to the ὑμῖν. The court to which Paul knows he is answerable is God (cf. 1 Cor. 4:3-5, and on 1:15ff. cf. pp. 37). The formulation is exactly as in 2:17; cf. ἐνώπιον τοῦ θεοῦ in 4:2. 2) τὰ δὲ πάντα, ἀγαπητοί, ὑπὲρ τῆς ὑμῶν οἰκοδομῆς corresponds to the ἀπολογούμεθα. The motive behind Paul's statement is not self-defense but the edification or furtherance of the community. According to 10:8 and 13:10, it is for its sake that he possesses his ἐξουσία (cf. p. 249). But he takes care for the community's edification when he makes himself understood, so that it recognizes the authority of his apostleship, and he must not extract that recognition by harsh demeanor, by καθαίρεσις.

Verse 20: φοβοῦμαι γὰρ μή πως ἐλθὼν οὐχ οἵους θέλω εὕρω ὑμᾶς, κἀγὼ εὑρεθῶ ὑμῖν οἷον οὐ θέλετε. The negatives οὐχ and οὐ are used in the clauses expressing apprehension (μή πως) because the verb itself is negated (Bl.-D. para. 428, 6). According to the sense, the οὐχ belongs with οἵους, and the οὐ with θέλετε. The οὐχ οἵους θέλω εὕρω ὑμᾶς is explained by the μή πως clause which follows, and the εὑρεθῶ ὑμῖν οἷον οὐ θέλετε is to be construed according to 10:2, 11 and 13:1-10. The entire verse corresponds to the ἵνα μὴ ἐλθὼν λύπην σχῶ ἀφ' ὧν ἔδει με χαίρειν in 2:3, which refers precisely to 12:20, or it corresponds with the ἔκρινα δὲ ἐμαυτῷ τοῦτο, τὸ μὴ πάλιν ἐν λύπῃ πρὸς ὑμᾶς ἐλθεῖν in 2:1.

The situation is such that severe treatment would be required at Paul's next visit. This is the reason (γάρ) why Paul wrote the apparent apology. He would prefer to work for the community's οἰκοδομή, not its καθαίρεσις (10:8; 13:10). The γάρ thus means, "I wrote in this fashion for your οἰκοδομή, for I feared a καθαίρεσις might otherwise result."

Now the οὐχ οἵους θέλω εὕρω ὑμᾶς is explained — μή πως ἔρις, ζῆλος, θυμοί, ἐριθεῖαι, καταλαλιαί, ψιθυρισμοί, φυσιώσεις, ἀκαταστασίαι (sc. γένωνται).

The catalog of vices is surprising if we expect Paul to have written, "that I find you rebellious and disobedient towards me." But the "towards me" is not stated. Yet the vices listed are all of such kind that they characterize the condition of a community stirred up by party divisions, rivalries, scandals, and the like, just as according to 1 Cor. 3:13 ζῆλος and ἔρις also tore the community in shreds. The personal is set aside. Paul sees that if his apostolic authority falls, the moral life of the community also falls to pieces. Perhaps it is also a result of the spirituality which he has in mind that moral flaws in the community are ignored. In any case, the catalog of vices makes clear that the Corinthians (in Paul's mind) are not pneumatics, cf. 1 Cor. 3:1-3.

ἔρις and ζῆλος denote strife and jealousy, and are also combined in the catalog of vices in Gal. 5:20 and Rom. 13:13. They are differently combined in 1 Cor. 3:3. In addition, ἔρις appears in the catalogue in Rom. 1:29 and 1 Tim. 6:4. ζῆλος appears in James 3:14, 16 combined with ἐριθεία.

θυμοί signifies anger, enmity. It also appears in a catalog in Gal. 5:20, Col. 3:8, and Eph. 4:31.

ἐριθεῖαι actually denotes a suing for the favor of parties. In Paul, it is combined with ἔρις and construed as quarrelsomeness ("strife"?) or as intriguing, perhaps as "machinations." It also appears in the catalog in Gal. 5:20, and elsewhere as a vice in Rom. 2:8; Phil. 1:17; 2:3; in James 3:14, 16 it is combined with ζῆλος.

καταλαλιαί denote slanders and also appear in the catalog of vices in 1 Peter 2:1, as does κατάλαλος in Rom. 1:30. James 4:11 contains a warning against καταλαλεῖν.

ψιθυρισμοί denotes gossip, malignity. The term appears only here in the New Testament (for the rest, cf. Windisch, 408f.). ψιθυριστής appears in the catalog in Rom. 1:29.

φυσιώσεις signifies conceit, arrogance (used only here; cf. the verb in 1 Cor. 4:18f.; 5:2).

ἀκαταστασίαι denotes disorder, and is used differently here than in 6:5 (p. 170) where it probably means tumult. It also occurs in the catalog in James 3:16.

Verse 21: μὴ πάλιν ἐλθόντος μου ταπεινώσῃ με ὁ θεός μου πρὸς ὑμᾶς. The clause is dependent on the φοβοῦμαι of verse 20, so that the μὴ ταπεινώσῃ and the καὶ πενθήσω must have a sense parallel to the μή πως ἐλθὼν οὐχ οἵους θέλω εὕρω ὑμᾶς.

On the ἐλθόντος μου . . . με as a genitive absolute with the following accusative, cf. Bl.-D. para. 423, 2. On ταπεινώσῃ . . . καὶ πενθήσω (provided πενθήσω is not an aorist subjunctive but a future indicative) cf. Bl.-D. para. 369, 3, and Radermacher, 216. The πρὸς ὑμᾶς means "with you," "toward you," "before you."

The πάλιν may belong to the ἐλθόντος μου. Then the meaning would simply be, "when I come to you again (not: for the second time!)," just as the εἰς τὸ πάλιν in 13:2. But it may also belong to ταπεινώσῃ με. In that case, Paul awaits a second humiliation. The first would then have been the visit ἐν λύπῃ (2:1, 5).

Due to the continuation (καὶ πενθήσω κτλ.) as well as to the parallelism with verse 20, the humiliation feared must consist in Paul's not finding the Corinthians οἵους θέλω, but rather immersed in fierce party strife and moral vice. But in what way is this a humiliation? To the extent he must witness the futility of his apostolic activity? Or more particularly (if πάλιν belongs to ταπεινώσῃ με), to the extent his visit will again be ἐν λύπῃ, that is, will not result in an understanding but in a (in that case final) breaking off of relations?[28]

This interpretation, however, does not suit the context. The φοβοῦμαι of verse 20 not only expressed the anxiety μή πως . . . οὐχ οἵους θέλω εὕρω ὑμᾶς, but also (μή πως) κἀγὼ εὑρεθῶ ὑμῖν οἷον οὐ θέλετε. This, of course, can only mean that Paul feared he would have to carry out a judicial sentence at Corinth (cf. p. 237), an interpretation also confirmed in 13:2ff. The complaint μὴ . . . πενθήσω can thus only mean, "I fear I will then be forced to strict measures." In that case, the μὴ . . . ταπεινώσῃ με ὁ θεός must mean the same thing — the humiliation would consist in the apostle's having to use his ἐξουσία, given him for οἰκοδομή, for καθαίρεσις. It cannot consist in his having to depart this time again without success, for he traces the fruitlessness of his previous visit to his sparing the Corinthians then, which he will not do again (13:2).

It is remarkable, indeed, that for Paul the likelihood of carrying out a judicial sentence at Corinth should be in the nature of a humiliation by God before the Corinthians, especially since this judgment is supposed to be a δοκιμή of the Christ who speaks in him, and who will prove mighty toward the Corinthians (13:3). Then it is probable that an οὐ has been omitted between μου and ταπεινώσῃ. Paul fears that God will not humble him (again). That he fears and does not hope for it indicates that for him everything depends on the community's οἰκοδομή.

This harmonizes with Paul's description of himself as κατὰ πρόσωπον ταπεινὸς ἐν ὑμῖν in reference to his earlier appearance at Corinth. Such will not be the case again at his impending visit.

It thus proves to be a matter of indifference whether πάλιν is linked to ἐλθόντος μου or to ταπεινώσῃ. Even in the first instance the clause naturally refers to the ταπείνωσις of Paul's previous visit.

καὶ πενθήσω, that is, because the condition of the community would force him to stern measures, cf. above.

πολλοὺς τῶν προημαρτηκότων καὶ μὴ μετανοησάντων. The genitive participle makes no sense, since Paul cannot intend to say that he will proceed only against a few sinners and not against all. Paul clearly intends to say πολλοὺς ὑμῶν τοὺς προημαρτηκότας (cf. 13:2). The interpretation that through the effect of this letter some would be converted even before his arrival (or even at his arrival) is forced.

ἐπὶ τῇ ἀκαθαρσίᾳ καὶ πορνείᾳ καὶ ἀσελγείᾳ ᾗ ἔπραξαν. ἀκαθαρσία (immorality, especially sexual) and πορνεία (unchastity) are also combined in the catalog of vices in Gal. 5:19, Col. 3:5, and Eph. 5:3 (cf. Rev. 17:4:

---

[28] Lietzmann, 159, writes that "the ταπείνωσις no doubt consists in the expression of sorrow over the failure of his work." On the other hand, Kümmel, 213, states that "Paul's experience at finding the community in a wretched condition would in itself be sufficient humiliation for him in the Corinthians' eyes" (?).

τὰ ἀκάθαρτα τῆς πορνείας αὐτῆς). Elsewhere ἀκαθαρσία is used in Rom. 1:24; 6:19; Eph. 4:19; and 1 Thess. 4:7 (differently in 1 Thess. 2:3). πορνεία is used elsewhere in 1 Thess. 4:3, Mark 7:21, etc. πόρνος is used in the catalog of vices in 1 Cor. 6:9, Eph. 5:5, and 1 Tim. 1:10. Cf. its use elsewhere in 1 Cor. 6:12ff.; 10:8; Heb. 12:16; 13:4; etc.

ἀσέλγεια (licentiousness, luxury, revelry, excess) appears in the catalogues in Gal. 5:19, Rom. 13:13, 1 Peter 4:3, and Mark 7:22. It is used elsewhere in Eph. 4:19; Jude 4; 2 Peter 2:2, 7, and 18.

On μετανοεῖν ἐπί cf. Bl.-D. para. 235, 2. ἐπί with verbs denoting affective states is also used in the Greek in addition to περί with the accusative, dative, and the participle.

The προημαρτηκότες are scarcely those who sinned prior to Paul's second visit. In that case, special offenses against Paul would have to be intended, not the sexual vices enumerated. That precisely such as these are named indicates that the προημαρτηκότων refers to sins prior to Baptism in the pagan period. This is indicated also by the μὴ μετανοησάντων, since μετανοεῖν is the term for repentance preceding Baptism as its condition; cf. Acts 2:38, etc. Elsewhere in Paul the verb never occurs. The noun μετάνοια in this sense appears only in Rom. 2:4, and is used of the remorse of Christians in 7:9 (p. 55). The sexual vices listed are regarded as particularly pagan, and hardly have any special connection with the spirituality in Corinth. Otherwise, Paul would have attacked his opponents' teaching much earlier and in quite different fashion. He thus intends to say, "I fear I must take action against many who are still stuck fast in heathenism (not, say, who are still committing those sins! since they are, after all, the προημαρτηκότες; cf. also ἣ ἔπραξαν) and against whom I must take strong measures (by excommunication?)." The μὴ μετανοησάντων indicates that μετάνοια is linked to entrance into the community, and that this μετάνοια must determine the Christian's entire life, so that if one's life still proves one is a sinner, the μετάνοια must be regarded as not yet complete.[29]

Verse 21 thus explains only the μή πως ἐλθὼν οὐχ οἵους θέλω εὕρω ὑμᾶς in verse 20, and not the κἀγὼ εὑρεθῶ ὑμῖν οἷον οὐ θέλετε. But both clauses must obviously be heard together.

Verse 1: τρίτον τοῦτο ἔρχομαι πρὸς ὑμᾶς. The τρίτον τοῦτο is used here as in 12:14 (p. 233).

ἐπὶ στόματος δύο μαρτύρων καὶ τριῶν σταθήσεται πᾶν ῥῆμα. The clause is constructed according to Deut. 19:15 where it reads simply καὶ ἐπὶ στόματος τριῶν μαρτύρων. ῥῆμα (רָבָר) is understood as "thing;" cf. Acts 5:32, etc.

---

[29] Note how in 1 Cor. 3:1-3 Paul really denies that the Corinthians are already Christians. Though as baptized they must certainly have the πνεῦμα, they are not πνευματικοί, merely ἄνθρωποι.

Verse 2 states what thing is to be sustained. It is clearly the οὐ φείσομαι — the Corinthians should not be deceived about that!

But who are the two or three witnesses? The τριῶν μαρτύρων following the τρίτον τοῦτο lead Lietzmann, 160, and Windisch, 413, etc. to construe the witnesses as Paul's three visits to Corinth. But neither the first visit, which established the community, can testify that at his third visit Paul will not spare the community (there was certainly no occasion for such threats then), not can the third visit now be called to testify that at his third visit Paul will do what he threatens. The witnesses can only be those which attest Paul will make concrete his οὐ φείσομαι, and these witnesses are clearly the utterances named in verse 2.

The clause cannot refer to a judicial "proceeding" (Allo, 335; Schlatter, *Bote,* 675) which Paul will take up at Corinth and for which he will hear witnesses. "It is clearly not a matter of discovering secret sinners, but of moving evident sinners to repentance, for which witnesses help nothing" (Lietzmann, 160). Windisch, 413, comments: "Just as at a trial the (second or) third witness decides the issue and furnishes the basis for the judge's sentence, so Paul's third visit to Corinth ought to decide the issue, settle all strife, muffle all contradiction and all criticism." That μαρτύριον may also mean "accusation," or that μάρτυρες may thus confirm the indictment, will scarcely be in mind!

Verse 2: **προείρηκα καὶ προλέγω . . . ὅτι ἐὰν ἔλθω εἰς τὸ πάλιν οὐ φείσομαι.** The εἰς τὸ πάλιν is equivalent to πάλιν (Schmid, *Attizismus,* passim; cf. Lietzmann, 161). By this time Paul has twice told the community that he will not spare it, first in the προείρηκα — clearly during his second visit, as the παρὼν τὸ δεύτερον at once makes clear, and secondly in the προλέγω — now in reference to his impending third visit in this letter while ἀπών. These two statements are the two witnesses on which the Corinthians may rely that οὐ φείσομαι. (1:23 in letter D harks back to this thought — ὅτι φειδόμενος ὑμῶν οὐκέτι ἦλθον).

The **ὡς παρὼν τὰ δεύτερον καὶ ἀπὼν νῦν** explains the προείρηκα καὶ προλέγω. Grammatically, it cannot mean, "as if I were present a second time, though I am absent now," which would at least require a καίπερ. In that case also the τὸ δεύτερον would be meaningless. The παρὼν τὸ δεύτερον is to be supplemented with a προείρηκα, and the ἀπὼν νῦν with a προλέγω (Lietzmann, 160).

Now only the ὡς seems odd, which is not followed by a οὕτως. We would expect "as at my second appearance, so now in my absence," and the καί very likely does duty for a οὕτως καί. Or, the ὡς παρών means, "as present for the second time and (as) absent now." (ὡς with the participle is the equivalent of "as one who," cf. 1 Cor. 7:25; Bl.-D. para. 425, 3).

τοῖς προημαρτηκόσιν καὶ τοῖς λοιποῖς πᾶσιν. The προημαρτηκότες are those named in 12:21. The warning applies especially to them, but also to the entire community.

242   *2 Corinthians 10–13*

Verse 3: ἐπεὶ δοκιμὴν ζητεῖτε τοῦ ἐν ἐμοὶ λαλοῦντος Χριστοῦ. This clause gives the reason for the οὐ φείσομαι — "really, you yourselves have provoked it!" — and is formulated in obvious allusion to the accusations and challenges aimed at Paul. Verse 5 as well shows that a δοκιμή is required of him — ἑαυτοὺς πειράζετε . . . ἑαυτοὺς δοκιμάζετε. This clause clearly hurls the challenge back at the Corinthians; cf. 10:18: οὐ γὰρ ὁ ἑαυτὸν συνιστάνων, ἐκεῖνός ἐστιν δόκιμος (cf. p. 197).

The requirement that the δοκιμή be τοῦ ἐν ἐμοὶ λαλοῦντος Χριστοῦ clearly shows that proof of Paul's spirituality is demanded. One missed this proof in Paul, taking him for ταπεινός and ἀσθενής (10:1, 10), denying to him the Χριστοῦ εἶναι (10:7f., p. 187).

For the Corinthians, spirituality is clearly evidenced in external, perceptible signs of inspiration. For Paul, the λαλεῖν of Christ in him means something else. It is proved — in any case primarily — in the word which serves the community's οἰκοδομή. In this sense he interprets the χαρίσματα or πνευματικά of 1 Corinthians 12–14. He is conscious of having the νοῦς Χριστοῦ (1 Cor. 2:16) in order to search out the βάθη τοῦ θεοῦ, but above all, of having the πνεῦμα θεοῦ (1 Cor. 7:40) in order to make a proper decision in matters of Christian life, or to effect the ἐλέγχειν of his hearers in prophetic speech (1 Cor. 14:24f.). In any case, Paul is certain of finding the right word for the situation. The word of the Christ who speaks in him is thus not characterized by its demonstrative form, but by its material content. It is not a performance to astound but an accosting word. And he is certain that such a word is bound to have its effect — ὃς εἰς ὑμᾶς οὐκ ἀσθενεῖ ἀλλὰ δυνατεῖ ἐν ὑμῖν.

The οὐκ ἀσθενεῖ naturally answers to the reproach that in the community Paul is ἀσθενής (10:10; 11:21), that his λόγος is ἐξουθενημένος (10:10). The word of the Christ who speaks in Paul will not prove to be weak εἰς ὑμᾶς — toward you. He will, as punishment, apply to the Corinthians the δύναμις which dwells in him.

In the antithesis the ἐν ὑμῖν is surprising. Did it happen to be miscopied from ἐν ἡμῖν? Cf. 10:4; 12:9f. If it is original, then the δυνατεῖ ἐν ὑμῖν can have no other sense than the οὐκ ἀσθενεῖ εἰς ὑμᾶς, and we have here merely a rhetorical alternation of prepositions dear to Paul. Or, the meaning is that Christ is mighty among you as critical power, corresponding to the question in verse 5: ἢ οὐκ ἐπιγινώσκετε ἑαυτοὺς ὅτι Ἰησοῦς Χριστὸς ἐν ὑμῖν. It is not unlikely that the formulation is occasioned by the assertion that Χριστὸς δυνατεῖ ἐν ἡμῖν, ἀσθενεῖ δὲ ἐν σοί (Windisch, 418) — "but he is mighty among you, as you contend." But this shows exactly how the ἐν ὑμῖν takes on another sense for Paul than the ἐν ἡμῖν of the Corinthians. For if by this clause they meant Christ's indwelling individual pneumatics, Paul understands it to mean, "among you, the community, and precisely as critical power." The δυνατεῖ ἐν ὑμῖν will prove to be different than you think!

It is difficult to say in what way Paul conceives of his appearance and what he expects from it. In any event, he is certain of his cause and will rely on that ἐλέγχειν of 1 Cor. 14:24f. He knows that he will find the right word. This will either effect the repentance of his hearers and lead to the excommunication of persons who may prove impenitent, or, if the community remains obdurate, will hand it over to the judgment of God.

Verse 4 gives the basis for this confidence. The reason why the δύναμις of Christ will be effective in Paul, who is abused as ἀσθενής and actually living in ἀσθένεια, is that with Christ himself ἀσθένεια and δύναμις are joined.

καὶ γὰρ ἐσταυρώθη ἐξ ἀσθενείας, ἀλλὰ ζῇ ἐκ δυνάμεως θεοῦ. καὶ γὰρ appears in ℵ* B* F al; καὶ γὰρ εἰ in A 𝕽 pm, and εἰ γὰρ καί in Origen (in which case the ἀλλά introduces the following clause — "thus certainly. . . ." cf. 11:6).

The ἐξ ἀσθενείας is scarcely meant in a causal sense — "as a result of his weakness" — that is, since he could be crucified as ἐν ὁμοιώματι ἀνθρώπων γενόμενος (Phil. 2:7), for the crucifixion is after all the high point of the ἀσθένεια (γενόμενος ὑπήκοος μέχρι θανάτου, Phil. 2:8). It means merely "as one who is weak," and the ἐκ is chosen merely for the sake of its rhetorical correspondence with ἐκ δυνάμεως θεοῦ.

The ζῇ ἐκ δυνάμεως θεοῦ denotes the resurrection life. On ἐκ δυνάμεως θεοῦ cf. 1 Cor. 6:14: ὁ δὲ θεὸς καὶ τὸν κύριον ἤγειρεν καὶ ὑμᾶς ἐξεγερεῖ διὰ τῆς δυνάμεως αὐτοῦ (Rom. 6:4 reads: ὥσπερ ἠγέρθη Χριστὸς ἐκ νεκρῶν διὰ τῆς δόξης τοῦ πατρός).

The crucified and the risen Christ are contrasted. The crucified is a manifestation of ἀσθένεια, the risen One of δύναμις. The causal connection between death and resurrection is not expressed, but for Paul it is self-evident (cf. Phil. 2:6ff.). Above all, it is obvious to Paul that Christ's death and resurrection form a unity, that is, that Christ's death is not a past event followed by his resurrection, but that Christ's cross is a continually present event, that the risen One remains the crucified One, just as the crucified is the risen One. Christ's resurrection life is not conceived merely as a condition, but as a mode of operation. It is the life by virtue of which it can be said, δυνατεῖ. Paul proclaims the crucified in 1 Cor. 1:24, namely as the θεοῦ δύναμιν (καὶ θεοῦ σοφίαν). Thus it holds that whoever will share Jesus' resurrection must also share in his suffering and death, Phil. 3:10f.; cf. the comments on 4:10, p. 115. In Christ, and this is thus the meaning of the sentence, the unity of ἀσθένεια and δύναμις is manifest.

καὶ γὰρ ἡμεῖς ἀσθενοῦμεν ἐν αὐτῷ, ἀλλὰ ζήσομεν σὺν αὐτῷ ἐκ δυνάμεως θεοῦ εἰς ὑμᾶς. We would really expect a ὥστε καὶ ἡμεῖς (cf. Rom. 6:4: ἵνα ὥσπερ ἠγέρθη Χριστὸς . . . οὕτως καὶ ἡμεῖς . . .). The γάρ which is used instead could be intended to facilitate understanding — "so it must be, for also we. . . ." But no doubt it is to be construed as giving the reason for verse 3, parallel to the καὶ γὰρ ἐσταυρώθη κτλ.

The fact that the clause ἡμεῖς ἀσθενοῦμεν . . . ἀλλὰ ζήσομεν . . . has its objective basis in the ἐσταυρώθη . . . ἀλλὰ ζῇ, that the δύναμις thus corresponds to our ἀσθένεια since with Christ death and resurrection life form a unity, is expressed merely by the ἐν αὐτῷ which means, as such who are "in him" (= ἐν αὐτῷ ὄντες). The ζήσομεν thus applies insofar as our ἀσθενεῖν is a participation in the παθήματα Χριστοῦ, a taking up of the cross. To the extent this is the case, the ἀσθενής is certain of δύναμις (cf. 12:9f.). The ζωὴ τοῦ Ἰησοῦ (4:7ff.) is manifest in θάνατος.

In the context, the ζήσομεν cannot refer to the resurrection life as in Rom. 6:4f., or may do so only to the extent that it is shown to be at work already in the present. The εἰς ὑμᾶς, which corresponds to the εἰς ὑμᾶς and the ἐν ὑμῖν in verse 6, indicates that what is intended is a present effect.[30]

Grundmann, *Kraft,* 188f., note 14, wants to make the εἰς ὑμᾶς dependent on the ἐκ δυνάμεως θεοῦ, since the ζήσομεν σὺν αὐτῷ refers to the resurrection. But this construction is grammatically harsh, and it is impossible as regards content, since Paul will certainly not be raised by the power of God at work against (or in) the Corinthians! The σὺν αὐτῷ in no way indicates that the ζήσομεν refers to the resurrection life, but merely emphasizes once again that the ἀσθενεῖν and the ζήν have their basis in union with Christ.[31]

The future ζήσομεν is chosen rather than the present due to the demonstration of the power of life about to occur at Corinth. It cannot be a gnomic future. In this way, unintentional expression is given the fact that the ζωή springing from ἀσθένεια is manifest in Paul's activity (cf. 4:12), that thus what God does through him is made visible. And the ἐκ δυνάμεως θεοῦ implies that Paul himself is not involved; cf. 4:7.

b. Admonition: 13:5-9

Verse 5: ἑαυτοὺς πειράζετε εἰ ἐστὲ ἐν τῇ πίστει, ἑαυτοὺς δοκιμάζετε. The ἑαστοὺς δοκιμάζετε is Paul's answer to the challenge to prove his δοκιμή. It is explained in the prefixed ἑαυτοὺς πειράζετε κτλ. The ἑαυτοὺς δοκιμάζετε has the sense of challenging to self-examination, thus sparing Paul the proof of his δοκιμή which would spell judgment for the Corinthians. Naturally then, the δοκιμή which he on his part requires of the Corinthians is not a legitimizing demonstration of pneumatic power, but their Christian profession, precisely as the πειράζετε κτλ. states. In the context, πίστις (on the εἶναι ἐν τῇ πίστει cf. the ἑστάναι (ἐν) τῇ πίστει in 1:24 and 1 Cor. 16:13) cannot be the "mood of the new pneumatic life" (Lietzmann, 161). πίστις does not mean this at all, but rather only the obedience of faith

---

[30] The εἰς ὑμᾶς is erroneously omitted in B D³ r arm Chr (vg pc go appear to have read ἐν ὑμῖν).

[31] On σὺν Ἰησοῦ cf. 4:14, p. 122.

actualized in the περιπατεῖν κατὰ πνεῦμα (Rom. 8:4, 12f.; Gal. 5:16, 25). Cf. the αὐξανομένης τῆς πίστεως ὑμῶν in 10:15 with the ὅταν πληρωθῇ ὑμῶν ἡ ὑπακοή in 10:6, corresponding to 2:9 — εἰς τοῦτο γὰρ καὶ ἔγραψα, ἵνα γνῶ τὴν δοκιμὴν ὑμῶν, εἰ εἰς πάντα ὑπήκοοί ἐστε. Kümmel, 213f. correctly refers to στήκειν (ἐν) τῇ πίστει in 1 Cor. 16:13 and 2 Cor. 1:24, as well as to the ἐπιμένειν τῇ πίστει in Col. 1:23.

The Corinthians who boast of their spirituality are referred to πίστις, without which everything is sin (Rom. 14:23). Their possession of the πνεῦμα need not be documented in extraordinary phenomena, but in their περιπατεῖν, in the nonrecurrence of such vices as are named in 12:20f.

When Paul hurls back the Corinthians' challenge in this way instead of summoning them to a real test of his apostolic status, he assumes that when they measure themselves by the proper measure they will also apply the appropriate measure to him and recognize his δοκιμή. As verse 6 shows, self-criticism is the presupposition for the criticism of others or of him.

It is also clear that Paul is already giving active proof here of the δοκιμή which the Corinthians demanded and which he held in prospect as judgment. For when the Corinthians conduct their self-examination they will abandon the demand for δοκιμή and see that in his appeal — ἑαυτοὺς πειράζετε . . . ἑαυτοὺς δοκιμάζετε — Paul has already given concrete proof of the required δοκιμή.

The criterion for the needed self-criticism is made clear by the ἢ οὐκ ἐπιγινώσκετε ἑαυτοὺς ὅτι Ἰησοῦς Χριστὸς ἐν ὑμῖν. This is exactly what the Corinthians assert, but they do not know what it means. The meaning therefore is, "or do you not know what it means that Christ is in or among you?" It is thus a question as in 1 Cor. 3:16: οὐκ οἴδατε ὅτι ναὸς θεοῦ ἐστε καὶ τὸ πνεῦμα τοῦ θεοῦ ἐν ὑμῖν οἰκεῖ (cf. 1 Cor. 6:19 and Rom. 8:9ff. — the Christian indicative is an imperative). If they know that Christ is in them, then they must know that as Lord he is present in them as a demanding and critical power (cf. v. 3, p. 242), that he requires this very πειράζειν, εἰ ἐστὲ ἐν τῇ πίστει, that thus when Paul requires it, it is a δοκιμή τοῦ ἐν αὐτῷ λαλοῦντος Χριστοῦ.

The seemingly superfluous ἑαυτούς makes clear that knowledge of the Christ "in us" is at the same time knowledge of ourselves, that Christ in us is not a possession which is present at hand or haughtily to be enjoyed, and which one may pit against others, but precisely that he is a critical power.

The ἐν ἡμῖν, which reflects a Corinthian assertion just as the δυνατεῖ ἐν ὑμῖν in verse 3, is to be construed in the same fashion as verse 3 (p. 242). That is, Paul displaces bragging of the individual possession of the Spirit with a reference to the Christ at work in the community. In truth, the πνεῦμα of the individual belongs to the community and should serve its edification, cf. 1 Cor. 14:3-5, 12, 26. God, Christ, and the πνεῦμα are truly one, 1 Cor. 12:4-7.

So the intent of the question is not at all "to express the expectation that when it proceeds to self-examination — which it cannot help but do — the community will find that its Christianity is genuine" (Windisch, 420). Rather, the critical question is whether the Corinthians are conscious that Christ is alive in the community as a critical power.

For this reason the εἰ μήτι ἀδόκιμοί ἐστε applies. If the Corinthians do not carry out a critical self-examination, if they do not perceive that Christ is in them — which they are able to do only when they understand him as a critical power — then they are ἀδόκιμοι (unconfirmed, unfit, rejected, cf. Rom. 1:28, 1 Cor. 9:27, 2 Tim. 3:8, Titus 1:16, and Heb. 6:8).

Naturally, the meaning is not, "when their self-examination discloses that Christ is not in them." This result is not to be reckoned with at all — either from the standpoint of the Corinthian pneumatics who can never admit to it, or from the standpoint of Paul, since it is precisely in their self-examination that Christ proves he is at work in them. Christ is not in them and they are ἀδόκιμοι only when they do not examine themselves, or when in pretended self-examination they do not perceive Christ as critical power.

Verse 6: ἐλπίζω δὲ ὅτι γνώσεσθε ὅτι ἡμεῖς οὐκ ἐσμὲν ἀδόκιμοι. Surprisingly enough, Paul does not say ὅτι οὐκ ἀδόκιμοί ἐστε (or ὅτι δόκιμοί ἐστε). This indicates that both perceptions coincide. The Corinthians' δοκιμή must show itself precisely in their acknowledgement of Paul's δοκιμή. If they conduct their self-criticism, they will gain a proper view of Paul and abandon the summons to δοκιμή, since such has already been proved in his summons to them.

Of course, the ὅτι ἡμεῖς also means, "that you be not ἀδόκιμοι." Paul, however, does not say this, because the determination of the Corinthians' δόκιμος εἶναι is really not the result of their self-examination, but occurs in the very act of self-examination itself. This will have as its result the admission, "we are ἀδόκιμοι." It will lead to that λύπη and μετάνοια which Paul in 7:7-11 can then confirm in the Corinthians, just as according to 2:9 he wrote this epistle ἵνα γνῶ τὴν δοκιμὴν ὑμῶν. And it is this very μετάνοια as a μετάνοια κατὰ θεόν which proves that the Corinthians are δόκιμοι. But they cannot establish their result on their own; it is rather Paul who establishes it. They must recognize that Paul is δόκιμος.

Naturally, the γνώσεσθε does not mean that the Corinthians will recognize Paul's δοκιμή at his second visit, as if he hopes by his judgment to force them to recognition. The ἐλπίζω does not apply to this, but rather the φοβοῦμαι in 12:20f. On the contrary, the γνώσεσθε denotes knowledge won from self-examination, which Paul awaits as the result of this letter, and, as letter D indicates, justly awaits.

Verse 7: εὐχόμεθα δὲ πρὸς τὸν θεὸν μὴ ποιῆσαι ὑμᾶς κακὸν μηδέν, οὐχ ἵνα ἡμεῖς δόκιμοι φανῶμεν. Verse 7 makes clear that Paul does not await the acknowledgement that he is δόκιμος in his own interest. Rather, he awaits it because it contains the proof that the Corinthians are δόκιμοι.

The sense of the prayer μὴ ποιῆσαι ὑμᾶς κακὸν μηδέν is hardly that God may do no evil to the Corinthians, that is, mete out no judgment (through Paul) on them (Lietzmann, 161), which of course would suit the context (though κακὸν ποιῆσαι would be a strange expression for it), but which would lose the correspondence obviously intended with the following ἵνα ὑμεῖς τὸ καλὸν ποιῆτε. For this reason, Paul himself cannot be the subject of the μὴ ποιῆσαι κτλ. ("that I need do nothing evil to you"), but rather the Corinthians, "that you do nothing evil." The general formulation (instead of, perhaps, πληρωθῆναι or αὐξηθῆναι ὑμῶν τὴν ὑπακοήν, cf. 10:6, 15) is thus to be understood in such fashion that for Paul the Corinthians' obedience harmonizes with their moral behavior, cf. 12:20f.

Can ποιεῖν with the accusative ever mean "to do something to someone"? In any case, ποιεῖν κακόν may not have a second object in the accusative (Kümmel, 214), though of course it may have in the dative, cf. Matthew 20:32; 21:40; and Acts 9:13.

ποιεῖν with κακόν or ἀγαθόν as object always means to do evil or good; on the other hand, cf. καλῶς ποιεῖν τινι in Luke 6:27, etc. In the New Testament κακόν relatively seldom means "evil" (Kümmel, 214).

The prayer is thus equivalent in content with ὑμᾶς εἶναι δοκίμους, or with the prayer for the Corinthians' κατάρτισις (v. 9). This is stated in the οὐχ ἵνα ἡμεῖς δόκιμοι φανῶμεν, a clause expressly intended to avert misunderstanding. So the prayer is not for Paul's sake, but for theirs — **ἀλλ' ἵνα ὑμεῖς τὸ καλὸν ποιῆτε** — and that means at the same time that they prove themselves δόκιμοι, not he. This is stated in the **ἡμεῖς δὲ ὡς ἀδόκιμοι ὦμεν** which follows. Of course, when they prove to be δόκιμοι, he himself will also emerge as δόκιμος, but this is not the purpose of his action or the goal of his prayer. But it is naturally also not his intention that he should emerge as ἀδόκιμος. Of course, the ἡμεῖς δέ coordinated with the first ἵνα-clause means, "though in that case I may also appear ἀδόκιμος." But Paul can speak thus because if the Corinthians prove to be δόκιμοι, the necessity for establishing his identity by a δοκιμή at his visit is removed, and to that extent he will appear as ἀδόκιμος. The ἀδόκιμος is therefore spoken from the present perspective of the Corinthians who demand a δοκιμή from him. They should know that it is of no matter to him — on the contrary! The ὡς indicates that the ἀδόκιμος as uttered from the Corinthians' viewpoint is not a real ἀδόκιμος.

Verse 8: **οὐ γὰρ δυνάμεθά τι κατὰ τῆς ἀληθείας, ἀλλὰ ὑπὲρ τῆς ἀληθείας.** (On δύνασθαι with the preposition, cf. Windisch, 424, and Bauer). The clause sounds like a sentence — was it perhaps originally? But in what sense does it function in the context as furnishing a reason? The ἀλήθεια cannot be truth in the most universal sense (reality as such disclosed to knowledge), which would have no sense in the context. But it also cannot refer to conditions at Corinth, so as to make Paul say, "in my behavior toward you I let myself be guided only by the real facts of the case, and thus need not intervene to punish when you 'do the good,' in which case I must then appear ἀδόκιμος." Quite apart from the fact that elsewhere in Paul ἀλήθεια never has this formal sense, it would be inconceivable in the context why Paul should assert that he cannot act against the obvious state of affairs (and what would the ὑπέρ mean?), and that this assertion should give the reason for the statement in verse 7 that he is prepared to appear as ἀδόκιμος.

Rather, just as verse 9 gives clear reason for verse 7, that is, that Paul does not act in his own interest, but in that of the Corinthians, so verse 8 must have the same sense.

For this reason, ἀλήθεια also cannot denote the genuineness of the Corinthians' Christianity, so that the verse would admonish, test yourselves and put away sham Christianity! In that case it would have to appear after verse 5.

ἀλήθεια might sooner equal δικαιοσύνη, that is, τὸ καλὸν ποιεῖν (it very likely has this meaning in Rom. 2:8 and 1 Cor. 13:6; its antonym is ἀδικία, cf. John 3:21, etc. and Sir. 4:28: ἕως θανάτου ἀγωνίσαι περὶ τῆς ἀληθείας, which is the equivalent of אֶל הַצְדָק). The clause, "I need take no action against you if you do the good," would suit as the reason for verse 7.

It is better, however, to construe ἀλήθεια as it is used in 4:2 and 6:7, as the truth which God allows to be perceived, that is, as the gospel in contrast to a ἕτερον εὐαγγέλιον (11:4); cf. Gal. 5:7: ἀληθείᾳ μὴ πείθεσθαι. In that case Paul intends to say that his person is not the issue, since the gospel is not the only criterion of his action. He is in the service of an overpowering ἀλήθεια. His mode of existence as δόκιμος while ἀδόκιμος, as δυνατός while ἀσθενής, is rooted in the gospel, and in such fashion that the very δύναμις of others answers to his ἀσθένεια; cf. 4:12: ὥστε ὁ θάνατος ἐν ἡμῖν ἐνεργεῖται, ἡ δὲ ζωὴ ἐν ὑμῖν.

Verse 9: χαίρομεν γὰρ ὅταν ἡμεῖς ἀσθενῶμεν, ὑμεῖς δὲ δυνατοὶ ἦτε. This clause does not give the basis for verse 8 (v. 9 would have had to be linked to v. 8 by a ὥστε), but for verse 7. It is that paradoxical ἡμεῖς δὲ ὡς ἀδόκιμοι ὦμεν which is given its basis here. But in the wake of verse 8 the χαίρομεν expresses more than Paul's personal joy. It rather describes the joy which derives from the nature of the gospel. Further, for one last time now Paul is using slogans of the Corinthians who regard him as ἀσθενής (cf. 10:10; 11:21, 30; 12:5-10; 13:3f.) and boast of their δύναμις (cf. 10:4; 12:9f.; 13:3f.). If they understand him, then they see that while ἀδόκιμος and ἀσθενής he is δόκιμος and δυνατός, and that there is no longer need of a δοκιμή on his part. But he is not the issue — τοῦτο καὶ εὐχόμεθα, τὴν ὑμῶν κατάρτισιν.

The εὐχόμεθα has the same force as in verse 7, and thus describes not only a wish, but a prayer.

κατάρτισις (cf. καταρτίζειν in v. 11) denotes a putting to rights, a coming to order, a perfecting (Lietzmann, 162, renders the term somewhat weakly as "betterment"), and is used only here in the New Testament; cf. καταρτισμός in Eph. 4:12.

c. The threat: 13:10

Verse 10: διὰ τοῦτο ταῦτα ἀπὼν γράφω, ἵνα παρὼν μὴ ἀποτόμως χρήσωμαι κατὰ τὴν ἐξουσίαν. In spite of hope(v. 6) and prayer (vv. 7, 9), the Corinthians' behavior is still open to question, and in closing Paul must reconsider the possibility of an unfavorable outcome and thus return to his warning in 12:19—13:4, or 10:1-11. Now, however, it is clear that the warning serves the interest of the community.

The διὰ τοῦτο is related to the ἵνα following just as the διό in 12:7, and the ταῦτα refers to what precedes.

ἀποτόμως means strong, and is used frequently in the Greek, cf. Nägeli, *Wortschatz,* 25.

χρῆσθαι (sc. ὑμῖν) means to act, just as in the Greek and the LXX.

The ἐξουσία is described just as in 10:8 (p. 188), and in such fashion as to emphasize again in conclusion that Paul will use it for the community's benefit — ἣν ὁ κύριος ἔδωκέν μοι εἰς οἰκοδομὴν καὶ οὐκ εἰς καθαίρεσιν.

The letter is intended to forestall Paul's use of his authority εἰς καθαίρεσιν.

4. Conclusion of the letter (does it belong to C or to D?): 13:11-14

Finally, brethren, farewell. Mend your ways, heed my appeal, agree with one another, live in peace, and the God of love and peace will be with you. Greet one another with a holy kiss. All the saints greet you. The grace of the Lord Jesus Christ and the love of God and the fellowship of the Holy Spirit be with you all.

Verse 11: The epistle's conclusion is attached by means of the transitional expression λοιπόν (cf. 1 Thess. 4:1 and Ign Eph 11:1; or, τὸ λοιπόν in Phil. 3:1; 4:8; 2 Thess. 3:1; and Eph. 6:10). In addition, the conclusion is marked by the address ἀδελφοί (this term does not appear elsewhere in letter C, but occurs in 1:8 and 8:1; cf. ἀγαπητοί in 12:19).

χαίρετε, which besides other imperatives is not the equivalent of *valete* but of *gaudete* (cf. Phil. 3:1; 4:4; 1 Thess. 5:16; Rom. 12:12), would fit better after D — 1:1—2:13 and 7:5-16 (+ Chapter 8) — than after Chapters 10–13. For this reason the conclusion to the epistle may not belong to C. Only if 13:11-13 belongs to C does the καταρτίζεσθε contain an allusion to verse 9. The meaning of καταρτίζεσθε is, "better yourselves" (cf. v. 10). καταρτίζειν occurs in admonitions in 1 Cor. 1:10 and Gal. 6:1. In concluding expressions καταρτίσαι is used of God in 1 Thess. 3:10; 1 Peter 5:10; and Hebrews 13:21.

παρακαλεῖσθε means "reprove yourselves"[32] (cf. on 10:1, p. 182). It is used in the concluding admonition also in 1 Thess. 4:18 and 5:11 (παρακαλεῖτε ἀλλήλους). Just as καταρτίζειν and παρακαλεῖν are closely linked, so also are **τὸ αὐτὸ φρονεῖτε** and **εἰρηνεύετε**.

τὸ αὐτὸ φρονεῖν is used in paraenesis also in Rom. 15:5; Phil. 2:2; and 4:2. εἰρηνεύειν is also used in paraenesis in 1 Thess. 5:13, Rom. 12:18, and Mark 9:50.

A promise (future indicative) follows the imperative, but in the same liturgical language in which a wish (aorist subjunctive) most often follows — **καὶ ὁ θεὸς τῆς ἀγάπης καὶ εἰρήνης ἔσται μεθ' ὑμῶν**. Cf. Rom. 15:5: ὁ δὲ θεὸς τῆς ὑπομονῆς καὶ τῆς παρακλήσεως δῴη ὑμῖν; Rom. 15:33: ὁ δὲ θεὸς τῆς εἰρήνης μετὰ πάντων ὑμῶν (sc. εἴη); (1 Thess. 3:11: αὐτὸς δὲ ὁ θεὸς καὶ πατὴρ ἡμῶν καὶ ὁ κύριος ἡμῶν Ἰησοῦς κατευθύναι); 1 Thess. 5:23: αὐτὸς δὲ ὁ θεὸς τῆς εἰρήνης ἁγιάσαι ὑμᾶς . . . (here also immediately after the paraenetic imperatives); 2 Thess. 3:16: αὐτὸς δὲ ὁ κύριος τῆς εἰρήνης δῴη ὑμῖν, and Hebrews 13:20: ὁ δὲ θεὸς τῆς εἰρήνης . . . καταρτίσαι ὑμᾶς.

On the other hand, cf. the future indicative (a promise) in Rom. 16:20: ὁ δὲ θεὸς τῆς εἰρήνης συντρίψει τὸν σατανᾶν, and Phil. 4:19: ὁ δὲ θεός μου πληρώσει (v. l. πληρώσαι) πᾶσαν χρείαν ὑμῶν. The promise of or wish for εἰρήνη thus appears to be traditional at this spot, and need not have been chosen here with a view to the preceding εἰρηνεύετε. But since τῆς εἰρήνης is augmented by the prefixed τῆς ἀγάπης, the link with εἰρηνεύετε ought not be ignored. The καί (= and then) used instead of the usual δέ also makes this clear (εἰρήνη is thus understood as peace). For this reason the promise is neither Jewish nor Pelagian (Windisch, 426). The idea that God as the God of love and peace tarries only with those who practice love and peace need not include the idea of deserving.

On the liturgical style (assigning predicates to God in the genitive), cf. on 1:3, p. 20).

Verse 12: According to the usual style, greetings follow — **ἀσπάσασθε ἀλλήλους ἐν ἁγίῳ φιλήματι**. Is the ἐν instrumental (Bl.-D. para. 219), or an ἐν of accompaniment (Bl.-D. para. 198, 1, 2)?

The custom of the kiss of peace presumably stems from liturgical usage and had its place after the sermon (cf. Lietzmann, 162, and Windisch, 427). It is hence assumed that Paul's letter will be read in the congregational assembly. The same assumption underlies 1 Thess. 5:26; 1 Cor. 16:20; Rom. 16:16; and 1 Peter 5:14. In Judaism, the kiss is well known as a token of reconciliation, but not the liturgical rite (cf. Windisch, 427). This is attested to in Just Apol I, 65, 2, cf. Hofmann, *Philema*. Cf. the kiss of peace

---

[32] According to Windisch, 426, παρακαλεῖν may not have the sense of παρακαλεῖτε ἀλλήλους (1 Thess. 4:18), but rather of ἀνέχεσθε τὸν λόγον τῆς παρακλήσεως in Heb. 13:22 — "be warned!"

(of reconciliation) in Philo Quaest in Ex II 78, 118 (in Windisch). It is questionable whether it was also a synagogue rite. With reference to the ἀσπάζονται ὑμᾶς οἱ ἅγιοι πάντες, greetings from others besides the writer also appear in 1 Cor. 16:19f.; Phil. 4:21f.; Philemon 23; Rom. 16:16ff.; Col. 4:10ff.; 2 Tim. 4:21; Titus 3:15; 1 Peter 5:13; Heb. 13:24; 2 John 13; and 3 John 15.

The ἅγιοι are obviously Christians surrounding Paul.

Verse 13: ἡ χάρις τοῦ κυρίου Ἰησοῦ Χριστοῦ καὶ ἡ ἀγάπη τοῦ θεοῦ καὶ ἡ κοινωνία τοῦ ἁγίου πνεύματος μετὰ πάντων ὑμῶν. The blessing as conclusion also corresponds to the usage of Paul, and of course also to liturgical custom, but it is triadic only here. Elsewhere it is most always only a request for the χάρις of the κύριος, as in 1 Thess. 5:28; Gal. 6:18 (here with a μετὰ τοῦ πνεύματος ὑμῶν); 1 Cor. 16:23 (here followed by v. 24: ἡ ἀγάπη μου μετὰ πάντων ὑμῶν ἐν Χριστῷ Ἰησοῦ); Rom. 16:20; Phil. 4:23 (here also with a μετὰ τοῦ πνεύματος ὑμῶν) and Philemon 25 (likewise). Only in Rom. 15:33 do we read ὁ δὲ θεὸς τῆς εἰρήνης μετὰ πάντων ὑμῶν.

Just as in the introductory greeting in 1:2, etc. χάρις is the gift of salvation which bestows not only justification, but every blessing rooted in Christ.

The ἀγάπη of God is not used elsewhere in blessing (Rom. 15:33; see below), but it belongs to salvation, cf. Rom. 5:5 and 8:39 (2 Thess. 3:5). Naturally, the τοῦ θεοῦ is subjective genitive, just as the τοῦ κυρίου with χάρις.

The ἡ κοινωνία τοῦ ἁγίου πνεύματος certainly does not denote mutual fellowship worked by the Spirit (τοῦ ἁγίου πνεύματος would then be a genitive of author). In that case, coordination with the χάρις of the κύριος and the ἀγάπη of God would be too harsh. In addition, the μετὰ πάντων ὑμῶν would not suit. The reference is rather to fellowship with the Spirit, that is, participation in the Spirit (objective genitive). Thus Lietzmann, 162, with reference to 1 Cor. 10:16 (κοινωνία τοῦ αἵματος, or τοῦ σώματος τοῦ Χριστοῦ) and Phil. 3:10 (κοινωνία παθημάτων αὐτοῦ) writes: "In all these instances κοινωνία is established by the reception or enjoyment of what is named."[33] Cf. also 1 Cor. 1:9: εἰς κοινωνίαν τοῦ υἱοῦ αὐτοῦ Ἰησοῦ Χριστοῦ.

But just as the τοῦ κυρίου Ἰησοῦ Χριστοῦ and τοῦ θεοῦ are subjective genitives, so also the τοῦ ἁγίου πνεύματος must be, that is, the ἅγιον πνεῦμα must demonstrate the κοινωνία.[34] Then, as often in the Greek sense, κοινωνία is construed as ὁμιλία or φιλία, or more concretely as help, such as in 2 Cor. 9:13; Rom. 15:26; and Heb. 13:16.[35]

---

[33] Cf. Seesemann, ΚΟΙΝΩΝΙΑ, 56ff. and also Kümmel, 214.

[34] G. V. Jourdan's statement in JBL 67 (1948), 116ff. is thus correct.

[35] Cf. especially Corp Herm 13, 9, in which κοινωνία is the δύναμις which banishes πλεονεξία.

On the triadic formula, cf. Windisch, 429-431. It obviously did not emerge from mythological triads, for in that case the θεὸς πατήρ would precede. For this reason there is also no influence of Gnostic tradition as with Philo, for whom God, Sophia, and Logos form a trinity, for in that case Father and Spirit would have to precede. There are no parallels in genuine Judaism (such as God, Messiah, and Torah or community). No doubt derived from a stylistic-liturgical motif, the phrase was expanded from the binitarian formulae frequent in Paul (θεὸς πατήρ and κύριος in the introductory greetings, cf. also 1 Cor. 6:11; 8:6; and elsewhere). The triad also appears in 1 Cor. 12:4-6, where the reference to the πνεῦμα is occasioned by the theme, and the path from Spirit to God leads by way of the κύριος. There are later triads in Eph. 4:4-6 and 1 Peter 1:2 (Matt. 28:19 is quite secondary in light of 1 Cor. 1:12ff.; Acts 8:16; 19:5; etc.).

1 Cor. 12:4-6 and 2 Cor. 13:13 scarcely assume a liturgical use of the trinitarian formula. (The subordination of Christ to God is evident, cf. the formulas of greeting and, for example, Phil. 2:11; likewise the subordination of the Spirit, cf. 2 Cor. 3:18; Rom. 8:9, 11, etc.) The ancient church doctrine of the Trinity is un-Pauline, since it is based on an ontology alien to Paul. If one of the later Trinitarian doctrines may be regarded as Pauline, then it is the doctrine of the economic Trinity.

Chapter 4

Chapters 8 and 9
(Brief Exposition)

Chapters 8 and 9 may not be interpreted from a humanistic ideal of character (nobility), but rather from Paul's view of the collection as a χάρις in which he and the communities may cooperate. The motive, that comity between the Hellenistic communities and Jerusalem is a material necessity, is not expressed but nonetheless operative, just as is Paul's attempt to keep the promise of Gal. 2:10. In any case, ambition is not Paul's motive.

The gift as χάρις: 8:1-7

We want you to know, brethren, about the grace of God which has been shown in the churches of Macedonia, for in a severe test of affliction, their abundance of joy and their extreme poverty have overflowed in a wealth of liberality on their part. For they gave according to their means, as I can testify, and beyond their means, of their own free will, begging us earnestly for the favor of taking part in the relief of the saints — and this, not as we expected, but first they gave themselves to the Lord and to us by the will of God. Accordingly we have urged Titus that as he had already made a beginning, he should also complete among you this gracious work. Now as you excel in everything — in faith, in utterance, in knowledge, in all earnestness, and in your love for us — see that you excel in this gracious work also.

First of all, verse 7 is a direct petition, but does not begin a new section. It is rather the appropriate conclusion to verses 1-6. Verses 1-6 indicate by the example of the Macedonian communities that charitable giving is a grace of God, precisely when it proceeds from one's own distress and poverty, and is voluntary. Next, it assumes or brings to light (v. 5) that one has first given oneself to the Lord. Generosity is thus not a simple and

253

easy affair. It is a great thing, but precisely as such it is a grace which the donor has experienced, and Paul desires that the Corinthians may also experience such grace. Because grace itself must be affirmed by the will, the positive assertion contained in the περισσεύετε and the imperative are not in contradiction, as Windisch, 250, supposes, who would prefer to read εἰ rather than ὥσπερ in verse 7.

Verse 6: The ἵνα καθὼς προενήρξατο need not mean that Titus already labored for the collection when present earlier. (This reading is also possible: as Titus began in Macedonia, he should finish now in Corinth — εἰς ὑμᾶς.) This is the natural sense, however, and is in place if Chapter 9 belongs to the interim epistle (together with 2:14–7:4, and Chapters 10–13).[1]

Verse 7. The ἀλλ᾽ need not be motivated by Paul's concern that the Corinthians surrender their lukewarmness and resistance, but rather by the transitional thought, "but I have no need to admonish you; rather, as you are altogether rich in χάρις, prove it now as well."

The consequence: The voluntary nature of the gift: 8:8-12

I say this not as a command, but to prove by the earnestness of others that your love also is genuine. For you know the grace of our Lord Jesus Christ, that though he was rich, yet for your sake he became poor, so that by his poverty you might become rich. And in this matter I give my advice: it is best for you now to complete what a year ago you began not only to do but to desire, so that your readiness in desiring it may be matched by your completing it out of what you have. For if the readiness is there, it is acceptable according to what a man has, not according to what he has not.

Paul's petition may thus not be construed as a command. It is a matter of the Corinthians' volunteering, otherwise it would certainly not be understood as χάρις. The voluntary nature of the gift (from the genuineness of ἀγάπη, which cannot be roused through command, but through suggestion) proves the genuineness of the reception of grace (γάρ, v. 9!). On the other hand, the προθυμία of the gift is genuine only when θέλειν (which is the first and most important, v. 10) is also followed by ποιεῖν (v. 11).

On verse 8: Christ is prototype only insofar as he is also understood as χάρις and among the δι᾽ ὑμᾶς. He is not prototype insofar as he has somehow made someone rich by his sacrifice. Rather, those are addressed who themselves have been made rich through his sacrifice.

On verse 10: οὐ μόνον τὸ ποιῆσαι ἀλλὰ καὶ τὸ θέλειν. These words are not an error (Lietzmann, 135). Rather, the θέλειν is the chief thing (cf. αὐθαίρετοι in v. 3, προθυμία in vv. 11f., and ἀγάπη in v. 8). But now

---

[1] Does the εἰς ὑμᾶς belong only with ἐπιτελέσῃ, not with προενήρξατο? Was it Timothy, and not Titus, who began at Corinth? Cf. 12:18!

the Corinthians must prove (v. 11) that their θέλειν was genuine by its leading them to ποιῆσαι, and the ἐκ τοῦ ἔχειν in turn describes this as genuine, as having its source in θέλειν.

(In this case, the μόνον is odd indeed, and Lietzmann, 135, perhaps correctly asks, "but did he not intend to say 'not so much the doing as rather the willing'?" But this reading too is possible, "not only the doing, but, what is more, the willing." Then the accent lies on the ἐπιτελέσατε in verse 11 — now bring the doing to completion!)

In the context, verse 12 certainly does not state that the gift is measured by what one can do, and the criterion is not a wealth which the giver does not possess (Mark 12:43f.). Rather, no more is required of the giver than what one has.

Is προθυμία the subject of ἔχῃ and ἔχει? Or is τις to be added, as with a few Koine witnesses?

The gift as a concretizing of fellowship: 8:13-15

I do not mean that others should be eased and you burdened, but that as a matter of equality your abundance at the present time should supply their want, so that their abundance may supply your want, that there may be equality. As it is written, "He who gathered much had nothing over, and he who gathered little had no lack."

The gift should establish equality. It is not an ascetic performance, but serves the principle of brotherliness (as God required it in the Old Testament; v. 15). One should help the other as constant change in circumstances will require. The helper then gives aid while trusting that the other will in turn give help. But this is not intended as clever calculation, and the plea to give is certainly not motivated by it. Rather, the misunderstanding that one must give beyond one's means is averted! For this reason the idea of being obliged to each other, in which one helps the other and trusts the other, dominates the admonition. Each must know when it is one's turn to help.

Formal correctness in giving the gift: 8:16-24

But thanks be to God who puts the same earnest care for you into the heart of Titus. For he not only accepted our appeal, but being himself very earnest he is going to you of his own accord. With him we are sending the brother who is famous among all the churches for his preaching of the gospel; and not only that, but he has been appointed by the churches to travel with us in this gracious work which we are carrying on, for the glory of the Lord and to show our good will. We intend that no one should blame us about this liberal gift which we are administering, for we aim at what is honorable not only in the Lord's sight but also in the sight of men. And with them we are sending our brother whom we have often tested and found earnest in many matters, but who is now more earnest than ever because of his great confidence in you. As for Titus, he is my partner and fellow worker in your service; and as for our brethren, they are messengers of the churches, the glory of Christ. So give proof, before the churches, of your love and of our boasting about you to these men.

Just as Paul protects himself in the undertaking by formal correctness, so also the Corinthians should take care for their reputation among the communities. The gift of love should be given in a proper manner (cf. Cic Off II, 21, 75: caput autem est in omni procuratione negotii et muneris publici, ut avaritiae pellatur etiam minima suspicio; "but the chief thing in all public administration and public service is to avoid even the slightest suspicion of self-seeking").

A good reputation and mutual regard are necessary for accomplishing fellowship. Naturally, they are not the final court of appeal (cf. 6:8: διὰ δυσφημίας καὶ εὐφημίας), for striving after a good name ought not, of course, produce δοῦλοι ἀνθρώπων (1 Cor. 7:24).

2 Corinthians 9 cannot possibly follow Chapter 8, and for the following reasons: 1) The introduction, περὶ μὲν γὰρ τῆς διακονίας, clearly assumes that this theme is just now being stated, cf. 1 Cor. 16:1. 2) The description of the collection as τῆς διακονίας τῆς εἰς τοὺς ἁγίους is very odd following Chapter 8. The readers must long have known what sort of διακονία was involved, since in Chapter 8 an exact description does not appear again after 8:4. 3) The περισσόν μοί ἐστιν τὸ γράφειν ὑμῖν is unexpected after Chapter 8 (at least an ἄλλοτι or πλείονα or something of the sort should appear) and sounds as though a new theme were struck, cf. 1 Thess. 4:9; 5:1. 4) By itself the οἶδα γὰρ τὴν προθυμίαν ὑμῶν could conceivably follow Chapter 8, but when Paul goes on to state ἣν ὑπὲρ ὑμῶν καυχῶμαι Μακεδόσιν, then it is assumed that the προθυμία is much greater than Chapter 8 suggested. In Chapter 8 the Μακεδόνες were the model for Achaia, and now Achaia is the model for Macedonia. This makes sense only if Chapter 9 was written earlier than Chapter 8, and if the report Paul once gave the Macedonians of Achaia's προθυμία (the προθυμία may be the θέλειν of 8:10f.) evoked that very zeal in 8:2-5 which now can serve the Corinthians as example. Chapter 8 is best joined to letter D. 5) The discrepancy between verses 3-5 and 8:20 in stating the purpose for sending the ἀπόστολοι — in 8:20 for the sake of Paul's reputation, in verses 3-5 for the practical purpose of gathering the collection — could, if need be, be reconciled.

Exhortation to complete the promised ingathering: 9:1-5

Now it is superfluous for me to write to you about the offering for the saints, for I know your readiness, of which I boast about you to the people of Macedonia, saying that Achaia has been ready since last year; and your zeal has stirred up most of them. But I am sending the brethren so that our boasting about you may not prove vain in this case, so that you may be ready, as I said you would be; lest if some Macedonians come with me and find that you are not ready, we be humiliated — to say nothing of you — for being so confident. So I thought it necessary to urge the brethren to go on to you before me, and arrange in advance for this gift you have promised, so that it may be ready not as an exaction but as a willing gift.

The motive is the honor of Paul and the community. The fact that Paul held up the Corinthians as model was evidence of trust which they dare not disgrace. Such a petition is itself a proof of trust.

Trust in God as presupposition for the gift: 9:6-10

The point is this: he who sows sparingly will also reap sparingly, and he who sows bountifully will also reap bountifully. Each one must do as he has made up his mind, not reluctantly or under compulsion, for God loves a cheerful giver. And God is able to provide you with every blessing in abundance, so that you may always have enough of everything and may provide in abundance for every good work. As it is written, "He scatters abroad, he gives to the poor; his righteousness endures for ever." He who supplies seed to the sower and bread for food will supply and multiply your resources and increase the harvest of your righteousness.

Verse 6: Whoever gives anxiously, robs himself of blessing. Only freedom from anxiety (v. 7) renders the gift genuine. But what frees from anxiety is a sight of the power of God who as giver of all gifts (cf., for example, those named in 8:7), also enables one to give further. Eudaimonism is removed from this view of God by the fact that God's reward is not conceived from the viewpoint of enjoyment but rather of grace which enables one to give in return. (According to v. 11, the reward lurking in the material blessing of vv. 9f. is a wealth εἰς πᾶσαν ἁπλότητα.) Verses 9f. are an expression of this trust. The δικαιοσύνη in the quotation of verse 9 is to be construed as generosity, as alms whose μένειν consists in the fact that God continually makes it possible.

On verse 7, cf. the classical parallels in Windisch, 277. For believing existence, natural human nobility is not abolished. But it appears in light of the demand — such noble generosity is required by God — and at the same time in the light of grace (cf. vv. 8, 14) — fulfillment of the demand is grace.

On verse 8, cf. αὐτάρκεια in Jonas, *Augustin,* 25ff. In the Stoa, αὐτάρκεια denotes 1) the external situation (objective independence and frugality); 2) an inner attitude (an inner aloofness from things which makes possible a subjective frugality and independence).

Verse 9 contains a literal quotation from Ps. 11:9 according to the LXX.

In **verse 10** the sense of the **χορηγήσει καὶ πληθυνεῖ τὸν σπόρον** must be gleaned from the previous ὁ δὲ ἐπιχορηγῶν κτλ. Corresponding to the paradoxical fact that the very σπείρων who scatters the σπέρμα receives σπέρμα, the Corinthians, when they sow, that is, donate for Jerusalem, will richly receive σπόρος (thus earthly blessing). The γενήματα τῆς δικαιοσύνης are identical with the σπόρος. The result is a synonymous parallelism of members.

Praise of God as the meaning of the gift: 9:11-15

You will be enriched in every way for great generosity, which through us will produce thanksgiving to God; for the rendering of this service not only supplies the wants of the saints but also overflows in many thanksgivings to God. Under the test of this service, you will glorify God by your obedience in acknowledging the gospel of Christ, and by the generosity of your contribution for them and for all others; while they long for you and pray for you, because of the surpassing grace of God in you. Thanks be to God for his inexpressible gift!

Just as in 1:11 and 4:15, the ultimate meaning of human activity is the praise of God. This praise will be the result of the collection, and in it Paul joins by way of anticipation in verse 15. The collection leads to the praise of God because it results in the thanks of the recipients and in the union of recipients with donors before God. The recipients of course understand the gift as a sign of the donors' faith. They do not really give thanks for the gift but rather for the faith and goodness of the givers. They conceive the givers as recipients of χάρις, and are thus united with them in prayer and yearning, cf. Phil. 4:17 or 4:1-20.

The peculiarities of Chapters 8 and 9:

Favorite terms — περισσεύειν in 8:2, 7, 14; 9:8, 12; καυχᾶσθαι in 8:24; 9:2f.; prepositional expressions in 8:3, 7, 24; characteristic expressions in 8:8 (cf. 1 Cor. 7:6); 8:23; the juxtaposition of κύριος and ἡμεῖς in 8:5, 19.

Theology — the view of thanksgiving as χάρις in 9:13; the view of the gift as χάρις in 9:13f.; Christology in 8:9; ὑποταγή in 9:13, and προσαναπληροῦσα τὰ ὑστερήματα in 9:12 (cf. 1 Cor. 16:17, and Phil. 2:30).

Abbreviations

(To the extent they deviate from RGG³)

Bauer	Bauer, *A Greek-English Lexicon of the New Testament*
Bl.D.	Blass-Debrunner
BGU	Ägyptische Urkunden aus den Museen zu Berlin: Griechische Urkunden
Cat.	*Catenae Graecorum Patrum in Novum Testamentum*
Deissmann, B.S.	Deissmann, *Bibelstudien*
Deissmann, N.B.	Deissmann, *Neue Bibelstudien*
Deissmann, L.v.O	Deissmann, *Licht vom Osten*
DittOr	W. Dittenberger, *Orientis Graeci Inscriptiones Selectae*
FS.	Festschrift
IG	*Inscriptiones Graecae*
L.-S.	Liddell-Scott, *A Greek-English Lexicon*
Reitzenstein, Hist. Mon.	Reitzenstein, *Historia Monachorum und Historia Lausiaca*
Reitzenstein, HMR.	Reitzenstein, *Die hellenistischen Mysterienreligionen*
Str.-B.	Strack-Billerbeck
TDNT	Kittel, *Theological Dictionary of the New Testament*
Wettstein, N.T.G.	Wettstein, *Novum Testamentum Graecum*

List of Sources

Acta Apostolorum Apocrypha, ed. R. A. Lipsius-M. Bonnet, 3 vols. 1891-1903 (1959).

Aeschylus, with an English translation by Herbert Weir Smith, *The Loeb Classical Library*, Vol. II, 1963.

Ägyptische Urkunden aus den Königlichen Museen zu Berlin, Griechische Urkunden, Vol. II, 1898; Vol. IV, 1912.

Appiani Historia Romana, ed. L. Mendelsohn, 2 vols. 1879-1905.

The Apocrypha and Pseudepigrapha of the Old Testament, ed. R. H. Charles, 2 vols., Oxford, 1913 (1963-1964).

Die Apokryphen und Pseudepigraphen des Alten Testaments, ed. E. Kautzsch, 2 vols., 1900 (1962²).

New Testament Apocrypha, ed. E. Hennecke-W. Schneemelcher, English translation by R. McL. Wilson, Philadelphia, 2 vols., 1965.

The Apostolic Fathers, with an English translation by Kirsopp Lake, *The Loeb Classical Library*, Cambridge, 2 vols., 1970.

Aristophanes, with an English translation by Benjamin Buckley Rogers, *The Loeb Classical Library*, Vol. I (1967), Vol. III (1924).

Aristotelis Opera, ed. Academia Regia Borussica, Vol. II, 1. Bekker, Berlin, 1831.

Athenaei Naucratitae Dipnosophistarum libri XV, ed. G. Kaibel, 3 vols., 1887-1890.

Catenae Graecorum Patrum in Novum Testamentum (Vol. V), ed. J. A. Cramer, Oxford, 1844.

Cicero, De Finibus Bonorum et Malorum, with an English translation by H. Rackham, *The Loeb Classical Library*, Cambridge, 1961.

Cicero, De Officiis, with an English translation by Walter Miller, *The Loeb Classical Library*, Cambridge, 1921.

Clemens Alexandrinus, Stromata, Book I-VI, ed. O. Stählin, 1906, GCS 15.

The Excerpta Ex Theodoto of Clement of Alexandria, edited with a translation, introduction and notes by Robert Pierce Casey, London, 1934.

Thrice-Greatest Hermes, Studies in Hellenistic Theosophy and Gnosis, translated by G. R. S. Mead, 3 vols., London, 1964.

Damascii successoris dubitationes et solutiones de primis principiis, in *Platonis Parmenidem*, ed. C. A. Ruelle, 2 vols., Amsterdam, 1966.

Diogenes Laertius, with an English translation by R. D. Hicks, *The Loeb Classical Library*, Vol. II, 1965.

Dio Chrysostom, with an English translation by J. W. Cohoon, *The Loeb Classical Library*, Vol. II, 1961.

Epictetus, with an English translation by W. A. Oldfather, *The Loeb Classical Library*, Vol. I, 1967; Vol. II, 1966.

Epictète Entretiens, ed. J. Soyilhé, 4 vols., Paris, 1943-1965.

Epistolographi Graeci, ed. R. Hercher, Paris, 1873.
Euripides, with an English translation by Arthur S. Way, *The Loeb Classical Library,* Vol. II, 1965; Vol. IV, 1964.
Ginza, ed. M. Lidzbarski, 1925.
3 Henoch, ed. H. Odeberg, Cambridge, 1928.
Hieroclis in Aureum Pythagoreorum Carmen commentarius, ed. F. G. A. Mullach, 1853 (1971).
Hippolytus, The Refutation of All Heresies, The Ante-Nicene Fathers, ed. Alexander Roberts and James Donaldson, Vol. V, New York, 1899.
Homer, The Iliad, with an English translation by A. T. Murray, *The Loeb Classical Library,* Vol. I, 1978.
Q. Horati Flacci Opera, ed. E. C. Wickham-H. W. Garrod, 1901 (1906²).
Iamblichi Protrepticus, ed. H. Pistelli, 1888.
Inscriptiones Graecae, Vol. IV, *Inscriptiones Argolidis,* ed. M. Fraenkel, 1902.
Orientis Graeci Inscriptiones Selectae, ed. W. Dittenberger, Vol. II, 1905.
Ioannis Lydi De Magistratibus Populi Romani Libri Tres, ed. R. Wünsch, 1903.
Das Johannesbuch der Mandäer, ed. M. Lidzbarski, 1915.
Josephus, Jewish Antiquities, with an English translation by Ralph M. Marcus, *The Loeb Classical Library,* Vol. VI, 1966.
Josephus, The Jewish War, with an English translation by H. St. J. Thackeray, *The Loeb Classical Library,* Vol. III, 1961.
Irenaeus Against Heresies, The Ante-Nicene Fathers, ed. Alexander Roberts and James Donaldson, Vol. I, New York, 1899.
Isocrate, Discours, Vol. III, ed. G. Mathieu, Paris, 1942.
S.P.N. Iustini Philosophi et Martyris Opera quae extant omnia, MPG 6, Paris, 1857.
*Die Apologien Justins des M*ärtyrers, ed. G. Krüger, 1904³.
Selected Satires Of Lucian, edited and translated by Lionel Corson, Chicago, 1962.
Lucian, with an English translation by M. D. McLeod, *The Loeb Classical Library,* Vol. VII, 1969.
Mandäische Liturgien, ed. M. Lidzbarski, AGG phil.-hist. Kl. NF. XVII, I, 1920.
Midrasch Tehillim I, ed. A. Wünsche, 1892 (1967).
The New Oxford Annotated Bible With The Apocrypha, ed. Herbert G. May and Bruce M. Metzger, 1973.
The Odes Of Solomon, ed. James H. Charlesworth, *Texts and Translations 13, Pseudepigrapha Series 7, 1977.*
Papyri Graecae Magicae, ed. K. Preisendanz, 2 vols. 1928-1931.
Philonis Alexandrinii opera quae supersunt, ed. L. Cohn-P. Wendland, 6 vols. and 2 index vols., 1896-1930 (1962-1963).
Philo, with an English translation by F. H. Colson, G. H. Whitaker et al., *The Loeb Classical Library,* Vol. I, (1949); Vol. II (1929); Vol. IV (1932); Vol. V (1968); Vol. VI (1959); Vol. VII (1950).
Philonis Judaei Opera, Vol. II, ed. Th. Mangey, London, 1742.
Philo, Quaestiones in Exodum, ed. in the *Bibliotheca Sacra Patrum Ecclesiae Graecorum* II; *Philonis Judaei Opera Omnia,* Vol. VII, 1830.
Flavii Philostrati Opera, ed. C. L. Kayser, 2 vols., 1870-1871.
Platonis Opera, 5 vols., ed. J. Burnet, Oxford, 1900-1907.
Plato, with an English translation by R. G. Bury, Harold North Fowler, *The Loeb Classical Library,* Vol. I, 1960; Vol. II, 1961.
Plotini Opera, ed. P. Henry-H. R. Schwyzer, 3 vols., Paris-Brussels, 1951-1973.
Plotinus, with an English translation by A. H. Armstrong, *The Loeb Classical Library,* Vol. III, 1967.

Plutarchi Chaeronensis Moralia, Vols. I and VI, ed. G. N. Bernardakis, 1888 and 1895.

Plutarque, Le démon de Socrate, ed. A. Corlu, Paris, 1970.

Plutarchi Pythici dialogi tres, ed. W. R. Paton, 1893.

Plutarch's Moralia, with an English translation by Frank Cole Babbit, Phillip H. De Lacey et al., *The Loeb Classical Library*, Vol. II, 1971; Vol. V, 1962; Vol. VII, 1968.

Plutarchus, Vitae parallelae, Vol. I, 1, ed. K. Ziegler, 1960.

Polybii Historiae, Vol. II, ed. Th. Büttner-Wobst, 1889.

Porphyrii Philosophi Platonici opuscula selecta, ed. A. Nauck, 1886.

Porphyrios ΠΡΟΣ ΜΑΡΚΕΛΛΑΝ, ed. W. Pötscher, Leiden, 1969.

Porphyry the Philosopher to His Wife Marcella, translated by Alice Zimmern, London: George Redway, 1896.

Porphyry on Abstinence from Animal Food, translated by Thomas Taylor, New York: Barnes and Noble, 1965.

Die Pseudoklementinen I, Homilien, ed. B. Rehm, 1953, GCS 42.

Die Texte aus Qumran, ed. E. Lohse, 1971².

Seneca, Ad Lucilium Epistulae Morales, with an English translation by Richard M. Gummere, *The Loeb Classical Library*, Vol. I, 1967; Vol. II, 1962; Vol. III. 1962.

Seneca, Moral Essays, with an English translation by John W. Basore, *The Loeb Classical Library*, Vol. I, 1963; Vol. II, 1965; Vol. III, 1964.

Septuaginta, ed. by the Göttingen Akademie der Wissenschaften, Vol. 1ff., 1931ff.

Sifre ad Deuteronomium, ed. H. S. Horowitz-L. Finkelstein, 1939 (*Sifre on Deuteronomy*, New York, 1969).

Sophocles, with an English translation by F. Storr, *The Loeb Classical Library*, Vol. I, 1968.

Stoicorum Veterum Fragmenta, ed. J. v. Arnim, 3 vols., 1903-1905.

Synesii opera quae extant omnia, MPG 66, Paris, 1864.

Thucydides, with an English translation by Charles Foster Smith, *The Loeb Classical Library*, Vol. I, 1962; Vol. IV, 1965.

Die Fragmente der Vorsokratiker, Vol. I, ed. H. Diels-W. Kranz, 1951⁶.

Bibliography

Allo, E.-B. *Saint Paul, Seconde Epitre aux Corinthiens*, Paris, 1936 (1956²).

Althaus, P., "Theologie des Glaubens," *ZSTh* 2 (1924), 281-344.

Bachmann, Ph., *Der zweite Brief des Paulus an die Korinther*, 1909.

Barth, K., *The Resurrection of the Dead*, translated by H. J. Stenning, New York: Revell, 1933.

————, *Christliche Dogmatik im Entwurf*, 1, *Die Lehre vom Worte Gottes*, 1927.

————, Thurneysen, E., *Come, Holy Spirit*, translated by George W. Richards et al., New York: Roundtable, 1933.

————, "Evangelium und Gesetz," *ThEx 32, 1935 (N.F. 50, 1956)*.

Bauer, W., *A Greek-English Lexicon of the New Testament and Other Early Christian Literature*, translated by Wm. F. Arndt and F. Wilbur Gingrich, 2nd edition revised and augmented by F. Wilbur Gingrich and Frederick W. Danker, Chicago: University of Chicago Press, 1979.

Behm, J., "καινός κτλ.," *TDNT* 3, 1965, 447-454.

Bengel, J. A., *Gnomon of the New Testament*, translated by James Bryce, Edinburgh: T. & T. Clark, 1863, Vol. III.

Blass, F.-Debrunner, A., *A Greek Grammar of the New Testament and Other Early Christian Literature*, translation and revision of the 9th-10th German editions by Robert W. Funk, Chicago: University of Chicago Press, 1961.

Bonsirven, J., *Exegese rabbinique et exegese paulinienne*, Paris, 1939.

Boobyer, B. "Thanksgiving and the Glory of God in Paul," Diss. Heidelberg, 1929.

Bornhäuser, K., *Die Gebeine der Toten*, 1921.

Bornkamm, G., *Mythos und Legende in den apokryphen Thomas-Akten*, 1933.

Bousset, W., *Kyrios Christos*, translated by John E. Steely, Nashville, 1970.

————, Gressmann, H., *Die Religion des Judentums im späthellenistischen Zeitalter*, 1926³, 1966⁴.

Brandis, *Asia 3* (Die römische Provinz Asia), *PW* II, 2, 1538-1562.

Brun, L., "Zur Auslegung von II Cor. 5:1-10," *ZNW* 28 (1929), 207-229.

Bultmann, R., *Der Stil der paulinischen Predigt und die kynisch-stoische Diatribe*, 1910.

————, "Das religiöse Element in der ethischen Unterweisung des Epiktet und das NT," *ZNW* 13 (1912), 97-110, 177-191.

————, "ἔλεος κτλ.," *TDNT* 2, 1964, 477-485.

————, "καυχάομαι κτλ.," *TDNT* 3, 1965, 646-654.

Bultmann, R., *The Gospel of John*, translated by G. R. Beasley-Murray, Oxford, 1971.

————, "νεκρός κτλ.," *TDNT* 4, 1967, 892-894.

————, *Exegetische Probleme des zweiten Korintherbriefes*, *SyBu* 9, Uppsala, 1947 (in *Exegetica*, ed. E. Dinkler, 1967, 298-322).

263

————, *Theology of the New Testament*, translated by Kendrick Grobel, Vol. I, London, 1952.

Corssen, P., "Paulus und Porphyrios, zur Erklärung von 2 Kor 3, 18," *ZNW* 19 (1919/20), 2-10.

Dahl, N. A., *Das Volk Gottes*, Oslo, 1941.

Dalman, G., *The Words of Jesus*, translated by D. M. Kay, Edinburgh, 1909.

Deissmann, A., *Die neutestamentliche Formel "in Christo Jesu,"* 1892.

————, *Bibelstudien*, 1895.

————, *Neue Bibelstudien*, 1897.

————, *Licht vom Osten*, 1923⁴.

Dibelius, M., *Die Geisterwelt im Glauben des Paulus*, 1909.

————, "Christologie: I. Chr. des Urchristentums," *RGG*² I, 1927, 1592-1607.

————, *Paulus und die Mystik*, 1941.

Dupont, J., *Gnosis*, Louvain-Paris, 1949.

————, "Le chrétien, miroir de la gloire divine d'après II Cor. III, 18," *RB* 56 (1949), 392-411.

Eisler, R., ΙΗΣΟΥΣ ΒΑΣΙΛΕΥΣ ΟΥ ΒΑΣΙΛΕΥΣΑΣ, 2, 1930.

Festugiere, A.-J., *La révélation d'Hermès Trismégiste*, 1, Paris, 1950.

Fiebig, P., *Jüdische Wundergeschichten des neutestamentlichen Zeitalters*, 1933².

Frank, E., *Philosophical Understanding and Religious Truth*, New York, 1959.

Fridrichsen, A., *The Problem Of Miracle In Primitive Christianity*, translated by Roy A. Harrisville and John Hanson, Minneapolis, 1972.

————, "Zum Stil des paulinischen Peristasenkatalogs 2 Cor. 11, 23ff.," *SO* 7, 1928, 25-29.

————, "Peristasenkatalog und res gestae," *SO* 8, 1928, 78-82.

————, "Nochmals Röm 3:7-8," *ZNW* 34 (1935), 306-308.

————, "Zum Theme 'Paulus und die Stoa,'" *CN* 9, 1944, 27-32.

————, "The Apostle and his Message," *UUA* 1947, 3, Uppsala-Leipzig, 1947.

Fuchs, E., *Christus und der Geist bei Paulus*, 1932.

————, *Hermeneutik*, 1970⁴.

v. Gall, A., *Die Herrlichkeit Gottes*, 1900.

Goettsberger, J., "Die Hülle des Moses nach Ex 34 und 2 Kor. 3," *BZ* 16 (1922), 1-17.

Gogarten, F., *Die Verkündigung Jesu Christi*, 1948 (1965²).

Goguel, M., *Introduction au Nouveau Testament*, 4, 2, Paris, 1926.

————, "Rez. zu R. Reitzenstein, *Die Vorgeschichte der christlichen Taufe*," *RHPhR* 10 (1930), 194-199.

Grundmann, W., *Der Begriff der Kraft*, 1932.

Guignebert, Ch., "Contribution a l'etude de l'experience chez Paul," *RHPhR* 7 (1927), 253-264.

Gulin, E. G., *Die Freude im Neuen Testament*, 2 vols., Helsinki, 1932-1936.

Gunkel, H., *Die Psalmen*, 1926.

————, *Einleitung in die Psalmen*, zu Ende gef. v. J. Begrich, 1966².

Gutbrod, W., "Ἰουδαῖος κτλ.," *TDNT* 3, 1965, 369-391.

Hagge, H., "Die beiden Überlieferten Sendschreiben des Apostels Paulus an die Gemeinde zu Korinth," *ZpTh* 2 (1876), 481-531.

Harder, G., *Paulus und das Gebet*, 1936.

v. Harnack, A., *Das Alte Testament in den Paulinischen Briefen und in den Paulinischen Gemeinden*, *SAB phil. hist Kl.*, 1928, 12.

Hausrath, A., *Der Vier-Capitelbrief des Paulus an die Korinther*, 1870.

————, *Der Apostel Paulus*, 1872.

Heidland, H. W., *Die Anrechnung des Glaubens als Gerechtigkeit*, 1936.

Heinrici, C. F. G., *Der zweite Brief an die Korinther*, 1900³.

Heitmüller, W., ΣΦΡΑΓΙΣ, *Neutestamentliche Studien f;ur Georg Heinrici,* 1914, 40-59.
Hirzel, R., Ἄγραφος Νόμος, *AAL phil.-hist. Kl.* 20, 1, 1900.
————, "Der Selbstmord" (1), *ARW* 11 (1907), 75-104.
Höistad, R., "Eine hellenistische Parallels zu 2. Kor. 6, 3ff.," *CN* 9, 1944, 22-27.
Hofmann, K.-M., *Philema hagion,* 1938.
Jonas, H., *Gnosis und spätantiker Geist,* 1, 1964³; 2, 1, 1954.
————, *Augustin und das paulinische Freiheitsproblem,* 1965².
Kierkegaard, S., *Edifying Discourses,* translated by David F. and Lillian Marvin Swenson, Vol. IV, Minneapolis, 1946.
Kierkegaard, S., *Concluding Unscientific Postscript,* translated by David F. Swenson, with introduction and notes by Walter Lowrie, Princeton, 1941.
Kittel, G., "εἶδος κτλ.," *TDNT* 2, 1964, 373-375.
Jittel, H., *Die Herrlichkeit Gottes,* 1934.
Kleinknecht, H., "εἰκών" (Der griechische Sprachgebrauch), *TDNT* 2, 1964, 388f.
Knopf, R., *Die Briefe Petri und Judä,* 1912.
————, *Die Apostolischen Väter*1. *Die Lehre der Zwölf Apostel. Die zwei Clemens-briefe,* 1920 (*HNT* Ergbd. 1).
Knox, W. L., *St. Paul and the Church of the Gentiles,* Cambridge, 1939 (1961).
Kroll, J., *Die Lehren des Hermes Trismegistos,* 1914.
Kümmel, W. G., *Kirchenbegriff und Geschichtsbewusstsein in der Urgemeinde und bei Jesus,* SyBu 1, Zürich-Uppsala, 1943.
Kuhn, K. G., "Ἰσραήλ κτλ.," *TDNT* 3, 1965, 356-369.
Langerbeck, H., *Aufsätze zur Gnosis, AAG phil.-hist. Kl.,* 3. Folge 69, 1967.
Lattey, C., "λαμβάνειν in 2 Cor. XI.20," *JThS* 44 (1943), 148.
Leisegang, H., *Der heilige Geist,* 1, 1919.
————, *Pneuma Hagion,* 1922.
Liddell, H. G.-Scott, R. (Stuart Jones, H.-McKenzie, R.), *A Greek-English Lexicon,* Oxford, 1973.
Liechtenhan, R., *Die urchristliche Mission,* Zürich, 1946.
Lietzmann, H.-Kümmel, W. G., *An die Korinther I.II,* 1969⁵.
Ljungvik, H., "Zum Römerbrief 3:7-8," *ZNW* 32 (1933), 207-210.
Lohmeyer, E., *Vom göttlichen Wohlgeruch, SAH phil.-hist. Kl.,* 1919, 9.
————, *Die Briefe an die Philipper, an die Kolosser und and Philemon,* 1930⁸.
Loisy, A., "Les épîtres de S. Paul," *Rev. d'hist. et de litt. rel.* 7 (1921), 76-125, 213-250.
Luther, M., *Lectures on Romans,* translated and edited by Wilhelm Pauck, *The Library of Christian Classics,* Vol. XV, Philadelphia, 1961.
————, *Luthers Vorlesung über den Galaterbrief 1516/17,* ed. H. v. Schubert, *SAH phil.-hist. Kl.,* 1918, 5.
————, *Werke, Kritische Gesamtausgabe (WA)* 10, 1, 2, 1925; 40, 1, 1911; 57, 1939.
Luther, M., *Luther's Works,* ed. by Jaroslav Pelikan and Walter A. Hansen, Vol. 29, 1968.
Marmorstein, A., *The Old Rabbinic Doctrine of God,* 1, London, 1927.
Merx, A., *Die vier kanonischen Evangelien,* 2, 2, *Das Evangelium des Johannes,* 1911.
Michel, O., *Paulus und seine Bibel,* 1929.
Molland, E., ΔΙΟ, *Serta Rudbergiana,* Oslo, 1931, 43-52.
Moore, G. F., *Judaism in the First Centuries of the Christian Era,* 3 vols., Cambridge, 1927-1930.
Mundle, W., "Das Problem des Zwischenzustandes in dem Abschnitt 2 Kor. 5,

1-10," *Festgabe für A. Jülicher*, 1927, 93-109.

————, *Der Glaubensbegriff des Paulus*, 1932.

Nägeli, Th., *Der Wortschatz des Apostels Paulus*, 1905.

Nissen, Th., "Philologisches zum Text des Hebräer- und 2. Korintherbriefes," *Philologus* 92 (1937), 247f.

Norden, E., *Agnostos Theos*, 1974[6].

Peterson, E., "Über die Forderung einer Theologie des Glaubens," *ZZ* 3 (1925), 281-302.

————, "Zur Bedeutungsgeschichte von παρρησία," *R. Seeberg-Festschrift*, 1929, 283-297.

Pfister, F., "Ekstasis," *Pisciculi*, Festschrift für F. U. Dölger zum 60. Geburtstage, 1939, 178-191.

Preisigke, F., *Die Gotteskraft in der früchristlichen Zeit*, 1922 (Papyrusinstitut Heildelberg 6).

Preuschen, E., "Paulus als Antichrist," *ZNW* 2 (1901), 169-201.

Odeberg, H., *3 Henoch*, Cambridge, 1928.

Oepke, A., "ἔκστασις," *TDNT* 2, 1964, 449-458.

————, "καλύπτω κτλ.," *TDNT* 3, 1965, 556-592.

Olivier, F., "ΣΥΝΑΠΟΘΝΗΣΚΩ," *RThPh* 17 (1929), 103-133.

————, συναποθνήσκω, Lausanne, 1929.

Radermacher, L., *Neutestamentliche Grammatik*, 1925[2].

Reicke, B., *The Jewish "Damascus Documents" and the New Testament*, *SyBU* 6, 1946, 3-24.

Reitzentstein, R., *Poimandres*, 1904 (1966).

————, "Himmelswanderung und Drachenkampf in der alchemistischen und frühchristlichen Literatur," *Festschrift F. C. Andreas*, 1916, 33-50.

————, *Historia Monachorum und Historia Lausiaca*, 1916.

Reitzenstein, R., *Die hellenistischen Mysterienreligionen nach ihren Grundgedanken und Wirkungen*, 1927[3] (1973).

————, *Die Vorgeschichte der christlichen Taufe*, 1929 (1967).

Rengstorff, K. H., "ψευδαπόστολος," *TDNT* 1, 1964, 445f.

Rudberg, G., "Einige Platon-Parallelen zu neutestamentlichen Stellen," *ThStKr* 94 (1922), 179-184.

Rückert, L. J., *Der zweite Brief Pauli an die Korinther*, 1837.

Schauf, W., *Sarx*, 1924.

Schlatter, A., "Wie sprach Josephus von Gott?," *BFChTh* 14, 1, 1910 *(Kleinere Schriften zu Flavius Josephus*, ed. K. H. Rengstorff, 1970, 65-142).

————, *Der Glaube im NT*, 1927[4] (1963).

————, *Paulus der Bote Jesu*, 1956[2].

Schlier, H. *Religionsgeschichtliche Untersuchungen zu den Ignatius briefen*, 1929, *BZNW* 8.

————, *Christus und die Kirche im Epheserbrief*, 1930.

————, "βέβαιος κτλ.," *TDNT* 1, 1964, 600-603.

————, "ἐλεύθερος κτλ.," *TDNT* 2, 1964, 487-502.

Schmauch, W., *In Christus*, 1935.

Schmid, W., *Der Attizismus*, 4 vols. 1887-1897.

Schmiedel, P. W., *Die Briefe an die Thessalonicher und an die Korinther*, 1892[2].

Schmithals, W., *Gnosis in Corinth*, translated by John E. Steely, Nashville, 1971.

Schnedermann, G., *Die Briefe an die Thessalonicher, Galater, Korinther und Römer*, 1894[2].

Schneider, J., *Doxa*, 1936.

Schrenk, G., "γϱάφω κτλ..," *TDNT* 1, 1964, 742-773.

Schumann, F. K., *Um Kirche und Lehre*, 1936.

Schubert, P., *Form and Function of the Pauline Thanksgiving*, 1939.

Schürer, *Geschichte des Jüdischen Volkes im Zeitalter Jesu Christi*, 3 vols., 1901-1909⁴ (1964).

Schwartz, E., *Die Aeren von Caesarea und Eleutheropolis*, NGG phil.-hist. Kl., 1906, 340-395.

Schweitzer, A., *The Mysticism of Paul the Apostle*, translated by William Montgomery, New York, 1968.

Seesemann, H. *Der Begriff* KOINΩNIA *im Neuen Testament*, 1933.

Spitta, A., *Zur Geschichte und Litteratur des Urchristentums*, 2, 1896.

Staerck, W., *Die Erlösererwartungen in den östlichen Religionen, Soter II*, 1938.

Stenzel, J., *Sokrates*, PW 2.Reihe, 3, 1929, 811-890.

Strack, H. L.-Billerbeck, P., *Kommentar zum Neuen Testament aus Talmud und Midrasch*, 4 vols., 1922-1928.

Stübe, R., *Der Himmelsbrief*, 1918.

Trench, R. Ch., *Synonyms of the New Testament*, Grand Rapids, 1947.

Vielhauer, Ph., *Oikodome*, 1940.

Vischer, E., *Der Apostel Paulus und sein Werk*, 1921².

Weinreich, O., *Antike Heilungswunder*, 1909.

Weiss, J., *Die Aufgaben der Neutestamentlichen Wissenschaft in der Gegenwart*, 1908.

_____, *Das Urchristentum*, 1, 1914.

_____, Bousset, W., Heitmüller, W., *Die Schriften des Neuen Testaments*, 2, 1917³.

Weizsäcker, C., translation, *Das Neue Testament*, 1875.

Wendland, H.-D., *Die Briefe an die Korinther*, 1967¹².

Wetter, G. P., *Charis*, 1913.

_____, "Die Damaskusvision und das paulinische Evangelium," *Festgabe f. A. Jülicher*, 1927, 80-92.

Wettstein, J., *Novum Testamentum Graecum*, 2 vols., 1751-1752 (Graz, 1962).

Williger, E., *Hagios*, 1922.

Windisch, H., *Der zweite Korintherbrief*, 1924⁹ (newly edited by G. Strecker, 1970).

Indexes

1. Greek terms

ἀγανάκτησις, 57
ἀγάπη, 150, 171-172, 234, 251
ἅγιος, 19, 251
ἁγιότης, 33-34
ἀγνοεῖν, 174
ἁγνός, 171, 201
ἁγνότης, 171
ἀδικεῖν, 58
ἀδόκιμος, 246
αἰσχύνη, 100-101
αἰχμαλωτίζειν, 185-186
αἰώνιος, 131
ἀκαθαρσία, 239-240
ἀκαταστασία, 170, 238
ἀλήθεια, 102, 247-248
ἀλλά, 57, 86
ἁμαρτία, 165, 205
ἀνάγκη, 170
ἀνακαινοῦν, 126
ἀναπαύειν, 60
ἀναστρέφειν, 33
ἀνέχεσθαι, 199-200, 201-202, 210
ἄνθρωπος, 219-220, 222
ἀνυπόκριτος, 171-172
ἀπειπεῖν, 100
ἄπιστος, 105
ἁπλότης, 33
ἀποκάλυψις, 219
ἀπολλύναι, 103
ἀπολογία, 57
ἀπόστολος, 203, 208
ἀποτόμως, 249
ἀρέσκειν, 143
ἀρκεῖν, 225
ἁρμόζειν, 200
ἁρπάζεσθαι, 221
ἀρραβών, 43, 138-139
ἀρχαῖος, 158
ἀσέλγεια, 240
ἀσθένεια, 225-229, 243-244

ἀσθενής, 190
ἀσπάζεσθαι, 250-251
αὐγάζειν, 105-106
αὐτάρκεια, 257
ἀφορμή, 148, 207
ἀφροσύνη, ἄφρων, 199-200, 223
ἀχειροποίητος, 130

βάρος, 128-129
βεβαιοῦν, 41

γινώσκειν, 156, 164-165
γνῶσις, 63-64, 108, 171, 185, 203-205
γράμμα, 76-78
γυμνός, 137-138
γυμνότης, 132-133, 137-138

δαπανᾶν, 234
δεκτός, 167
δία, 29-30, 46, 83, 173, 182
διαθήκη, 74-76, 86-87
διακονεῖν, 71-72
διακονία, 79-80, 160-161, 169-170, 205
διάκονος, 169-170, 209, 215
δικαιοσύνη, 82-83, 165-166
διό, 224
δίψος, 217
δοκιμή, 49, 244-247
δόλος, δολοῦν, 101
δόξα, 81-83, 84-85, 87, 105-106, 108-109, 173
δύναμις, 112-113, 124, 172, 191, 193, 225-231, 243-244

Ἑβραῖος, 214-215
ἐγκακεῖν, 99, 124, 129
ἐγκαταλείπειν, 113-114
εἰδέναι, 154
εἶδος, 140-141
εἰκών, 95, 106
εἰλικρίνεια, 33-34, 69-70, 101
εἰρήνη, 250

268

ἐκδαπανᾶν, 234
ἐκδημεῖν, 140, 149
ἐκδίκησις, 57
ἐκδύεσθαι, 138
ἐκκλησία, 19
ἔκστασις, 221
ἐκφοβεῖν, 189
ἐλεεῖν, 99
ἔλεος, 99
ἐλευθερία, 89-90, 97-98
ἐλπίς, 84
ἐνδημεῖν, 140, 149
ἐξιστάναι, 149-150
ἐξουσία, 188-189, 191, 249
ἐπαίρεσθαι, 212
ἐπενδύεσθαι, 133-137, 138
ἐπί, 59
ἐπιβαρεῖν, 48
ἐπίγειος, 131
ἐπιγινώσκειν, 36, 174
ἐπιείκεια, ἐπιεικής, 182-183
ἐπιπόθησις, 54, 57
ἐπίστασις, 217
ἐπιστολή, 70-72
ἐπιτιμία, 48-49
ἐργάτης, 208
ἔργον, 208
ἐριθεία, 238
ἔρις, 238
ἑστάναι, 45
εὐαγγέλιον, 51, 102-103, 106-107, 195
εὐάρεστος, 142
εὐδοκεῖν, 228
εὐλογητός, 21
εὐχαριστεῖν, 30
εὔχεσθαι, 249
εὐωδία, 66-67
ἐφικνεῖσθαι, 145

ζῆλος, 54, 57, 200, 238
ζημιοῦν, 55-56
ζῆν, 152, 174, 243-244
ζωή, 111, 118-129, 145-146, 174

θάνατος, 56, 215-216
θαρρεῖν, 140, 142, 183
θεός, 33-34, 55, 70, 72, 103-104, 185, 200
θησαυρίζειν, 233
θησαυρός, 111
θλίβεσθαι, 24-25
θλίψις, 27, 46, 170
θριαμβεύειν, 62-63
θυμός, 238

ἰδιώτης, 203-204
Ἰησοῦς, 202
ἱκανότης, 70, 75-76

ἵνα, 28-29, 39, 56, 152, 189
Ἰσραήλ, 214

καί, 76
καινός, 126-127, 156-158
κανών, 193-194
καπηλεύειν, 69
καταισχύνεσθαι, 60
κατάκρισις, 83
καταλαλία, 238
καταλλαγεῖν, καταλλαγή, 158-164
καταλύειν, 131-132
καταναρκᾶν, 233
καταπίνειν, 49
καταρτίζειν, 249-250
κατάρτισις, 249
κατοπτρίζειν, 90-95
καυχᾶσθαι, 191, 193-195, 210, 215,
      228-230, 258
καύχημα, 36, 148
καύχησις, 33, 35, 178-179, 206, 234
κοινωνία, 251
κομίζεσθαι, 144
κόπος, 171, 196
κόσμος, 56, 161
κρίνειν, 48, 151
κυριεύειν, 44
κύριος, 89, 96-98, 106-107, 146,
      210-211, 251
κυροῦν, 49

λαμβάνειν, 212
λάμπειν, 107-108
λογίζεσθαι, 75, 161-162, 184, 203
λόγος, 69, 162-163, 172, 191, 203-204
λύπη, 47-50, 55-58

μακροθυμία, 171
μᾶλλον, 54, 59
μάχη, 52
μερίζειν, 194
μεταμορφοῦν, 95
μετάνοια, 77, 240
μετρεῖν, μέτρον, 193-194
μορφή, 95
μωμᾶθαι, 169

νέκρωσις, 115-117
νηστεία, 171
νόημα, 50, 86, 186
νόμος, 87-88
νῦν, 164

ὀδυρμός, 54
οἰκοδομή, 130-131, 189
ὀπτασία, 219
ὀσμή, 63-66, 67

ὅτι, 36, 87, 205
οὐχ ὅτι, 43-44
ὀχύρωμα, 185

πάθημα, 23-24
πάλιν, 188
πανουργία, 101, 201
παρακαλεῖν, 25, 225, 250
παράκλησις, 23-25, 26
παράπτωμα, 162
παριστάναι, 122, 201
παρουσία, 190
παρρησία, 84-85, 90, 178
πᾶς, 21-22
πείθειν, 147
πεποίθησις, 75, 145-146
περιπατεῖν, 101, 140, 184
περισσεύειν, 23-24, 179, 258
περισσοτέρως, 47, 59, 215-216
πίστις, 140-141, 244-245
πλάνος, 173-174
πλεονεκτεῖν, 50
πληγή, 170
πνεῦμα, 43, 51-52, 60, 72, 77, 89-90, 96-98,
     121, 138-139, 171, 245, 251-252
ποιεῖν, 216, 246-247
πορνεία, 239-240
πραΰς, πραΰτης, 182-183
πρεσβεύειν, 163
προσκοπή, 169
πρόσωπον, 29, 50, 187
πυροῦσθαι, 217
πώρωσις, 86

σαρκικός, 33-35
σάρξ, 39, 52, 153-155, 184, 211
σημεῖον, 231-232
σκανδαλίζειν, 217
σκηνή, 130-131
σκόλοψ, 224
σκοπεῖν, 129
σαφία, 34-35
σπλάγχνα, 60, 176
σπόρος, 258
σπουδή, 57-58
στενοχωρεῖν, 176
στενοχωρία, 170
στρατεία, 184-185
συνείδησις, 102
συνέχειν, 151
συνιστάνειν, 70, 192
συνοχή, 46
σφραγίζειν, σφραγίς, 42
σῶμα, 117-120
σωτηρία, 78

τέρας, 231

τολμᾶν, 192, 212-213

ὑπακοή, 60, 186
ὑπέρ, 24-25, 30, 151, 163
ὑπερβάλλειν, 83, 112
ὑπερβολή, 112, 128
ὑπερεκτείνειν, 195
ὑπερπερισσεύειν, 179
ὑπομονή, 170
ὕψωμα, 185

φανεροῦν, 63
φανέρωσις, 110-111, 119-120
φείδεσθαι, 223
φθείρειν, 177
φιλοτιμᾶσθαι, 142
φόβος, 52, 57
φράσσειν, 206
φυλακή, 170
φυσίωσις, 238
φωτισμός, 105-106, 108

χαίρειν, 174, 249
χαρά, 44
χαρίζεσθαι, 49
χάρις, 34-35, 38, 124, 166-167, 226-228,
     241, 253-254, 258
χάρισμα, 30
χρῆσθαι, 39, 85, 249
χρίειν, 42
Χριστός, 63, 70, 155-158, 165, 187-188, 202

ψευδαπόστολος, 203, 207-209, 215
ψιθυρισμός, 238
ψῦχος, 217

ὥς ἄν, 190
ὡς ὅτι, 161, 212

2. Literary and historical-critical concepts and questions

anacolouthon, 107, 140
antithesis, 34-35, 56-57, 72-74, 107, 113-115,
     119, 140-141, 143, 149-150, 169, 173-175,
     176, 188, 194-196, 200, 211, 242
apologetic, 16, 163, 236-237
aposiopesis, 85
asyndeton, 55

blessing, 251

catalog of vices, 237-238, 240
catalog of virtues, 169, 171-173
characterizations of God in the genitive,
     21-22, 250

conclusion a minori ad maius, 79, 209
Corinthian correspondence, 16-18, 46-47,
52, 54-55, 179-180, 209, 235, 249, 256

diatribe, 113, 169, 190, 209
doxology, 20-21, 218

epistle of tears, 17
excursus (in the text of Paul's epistle),
70, 79, 130, 139, 145, 230, 236

formula of protestation, 43 190
formula-quotation, 121, 190

hapax legomenon, 54, 190, 249
Hebraism, 124, 185
hendiadys, 33
hymn-style, 217

interim epistle, 16-17, 38, 46, 58, 254
irony, 48, 183, 192, 201, 212, 217-218,
231, 232

Jewish formula, 21, 28, 72, 218
juridical terminology, 41, 57-58, 121, 151,
163

liturgical style, 20-22, 62, 66, 214, 250-252

memorial chronicles, 197-198
military figures, 185-186, 205
missions-style, 164

oath formula, 39, 206, 218
opponents of Paul in Corinth, 40, 69-71,
75, 89-90, 101, 102-103, 107, 111, 130,
134-139, 147, 148-150, 156, 177, 183-186,
187, 190-192, 193, 195-198, 200, 202-215,
218-219, 223, 230-231, 235-237, 240,
in Galatia, 202
oxymoron, 56

paradox, 75, 111-112, 114, 119-120, 124,
129, 165, 183, 215, 227-228, 248, 258
parallelismus membrorum, 258
parenthesis, 48, 54-55, 89, 140-142,
194-195, 221, 224
paronomasia, 113
participial-style, 22, 42, 53, 84
partition problems in 2 Corinthians, 17-18,
52, 179-180, 235, 249, 254, 256
Paul's visits, 37-39, 43, 51-52, 233, 241
peristasis-catalog, 113, 168-171, 216, 228
plerophoria, 105
polemic, 16, 69, 138, 139, 146, 163, 183,
203, 205
prepositions, 67, 128, 242

proemium, 27, 30-31

Rabbinic speech, 51, 68, 112, 126-127,
131, 157, 165, 167, 216, 220, 224
redactor, 52, 62, 179-180
rhetorical questions, 39, 70, 81, 217, 234

Septuagint phrases, 60, 72-73, 76, 172, 231

3. Theological themes

apostle, 16, 24, 26, 36, 44-45, 48-51, 60,
66-67, 69-70, 101-102, 107, 111-112, 116,
129, 145-148, 163, 223
apostolate, 16, 19, 78-79, 98-99, 101-102,
153, 158, 160, 166, 169, 184, 188-189,
236-237
atonement, 159-160

baptism, 24, 42-43, 68-69, 117, 160, 240

Christian existence, 16, 24, 57, 116-119,
123, 126, 140-142, 152-153, 156-157,
226-228
Christology, 23-24, 40-41, 96-98, 106-107,
108-109, 117-120, 151-152, 155-156, 160,
164-165, 200-201, 210-211, 243, 245-246,
254

dying-death, 27-28, 82, 115-117, 119-120,
131-134, 143,
eschatology, 19, 42, 56, 63, 67, 81-82, 97,
119, 123-124, 126-127, 143, 154, 157, 164,
167, 169
ethics, 50-51, 74

faith, 28, 112, 114-115, 117, 120-121, 245

glory, 30, 81-84, 85-87, 108-109, 129
God, 20-23, 28, 35, 112-113, 117-118,
143-144, 158-159, 225, 258; thanks to
God, 21-22 29-30, 37
gospel, 68, 103, 106-107
grace, 34-35, 124, 253-254

indicative-imperative, 26, 139, 245
intermediate state, 133-139

joy, 44-46, 174-175

law, 72, 77-78, 87-88
life, 28, 82, 111, 115-127, 152-153, 243-244

man, 114-115, 124-126

New Testament, 78, 88

Old Testament, 87-88

prayer, 29-31, 41, 225, 247
present-future, 126, 141-142, 147
proclamation preaching, 16, 63, 66-69, 89,
    102, 106-107, 111, 121, 124, 147, 160-161,
    166, 242

resurrection, 134, 138, 243-244
righteousness, 82-83, 166

Spirit, 43, 77-78, 82, 96-98, 121, 138-139,
    245
suffering, 23-27, 115-117, 224-225

4. History of religions concepts
    and references

aeon, 23, 103-104

dwelling in tents, 130-131

ecstasy, 97, 149-150, 218-223, 225, 227

gnosis, 23, 65-66, 97-98, 104, 117, 124-125,
    127-128, 130-131, 135-139, 141, 160, 165,
    201, 203-204, 215
Greek ethic, 35, 55, 84, 101
Greek philosophy, 64, 112-113, 124-125, 136

Hellenistic cultus, 30, 97-98
Hellenistic mysteries, 42, 95-97, 171, 221-222
Hellenistic belief in immortality, 127
Hellenistic ideas, 35, 81, 129, 143, 226-227
heavenly garment, 131-133

Jewish apocalyptic, 97, 131-132, 221-222
Jewish circumcision, 42
Jewish Hellenism, 55, 84-85, 97
Jewish paraenesis, 180
Jewish self-designations, 214-215
Jewish theologoumena, 76, 109, 126-127,
    129, 138, 143, 159, 221

Mandaeans, 128, 130-131
miracles, 231-232
mythological ideas, 71-72, 82, 97, 126, 209

Rabbinic exegesis, 80-81, 167
Rabbinic legend, 201, 209

the Stoa, 44, 57, 97, 114, 124-125, 157,
    225-226, 229-230, 257